John Keats

Ode to a Nightingale
(Complete Edition)

e-artnow 2018

Reading suggestions (available from e-artnow as Print & eBook)

Henry James
The Portrait of a Lady (The Unabridged Edition)

Samuel Taylor Coleridge
The Complete Works of Samuel Taylor Coleridge: Poetry, Plays, Literary Essays, Lectures, Autobiography and Letters (Classic Illustrated Edition)

Zane Grey
The Ohio River Trilogy + The Purple Sage Saga + The Lone Star Ranger + The Border Legion (7 Western Classics in One Volume)

Robert Browning
The Complete Poetry

John Keats
Ode on a Grecian Urn (Complete Edition)

John Keats
John Keats: Ode to a Nightingale (Unabridged)

John Keats
Lamia (Complete Edition)

Samuel Taylor Coleridge
Christabel & Kubla Khan: A Vision in a Dream (Unabridged)

Robert Browning
My Last Duchess (Unabridged)

Samuel Taylor Coleridge
The Complete Poetry (The Classic Illustrated Edition)

John Keats

Ode to a Nightingale (Complete Edition)

e-artnow, 2018
Contact: info@e-artnow.org
ISBN 978-80-268-9145-1

Contents

Life of John Keats by Sidney Colvin	11
Preface	12
Chapter I	14
Chapter II	26
Chapter III	43
Chapter IV	55
Chapter V	80
Chapter VI	98
Chapter VII	119
Chapter VIII	140
Chapter IX	156
Chapter X	168
Chapter XI	179
Chapter XII	197
Chapter XIII	210
Chapter XIV	229
Chapter XV	246
Chapter XVI	260
Chapter XVII	274
Appendix	291
Ode to a Nightingale	297

Life of John Keats by Sidney Colvin

Preface

To the name and work of Keats our best critics and scholars have in recent years paid ever closer attention and warmer homage. But their studies have for the most part been specialized and scattered, and there does not yet exist any one book giving a full and connected account of his life and poetry together in the light of our present knowledge and with help of all the available material. Ever since it was my part, some thirty years ago, to contribute the volume on Keats to the series of short studies edited by Lord Morley, (the *English Men of Letters* series), I have hoped one day to return to the subject and do my best to supply this want. Once released from official duties, I began to prepare for the task, and through the last soul-shaking years, being over age for any effectual war-service, have found solace and occupation in carrying it through.

The following pages, timed to appear in the hundredth year after the publication of Keats' first volume, are the result. I have sought in them to combine two aims not always easy to be reconciled, those of holding the interest of the general reader and at the same time of satisfying, and perhaps on some points even informing, the special student. I have tried to set forth consecutively and fully the history of a life outwardly remarkable for nothing but its tragic brevity, but inwardly as crowded with imaginative and emotional experience as any on record, and moreover, owing to the openheartedness of the man and to the preservation and unreserved publication of his letters, lying bare almost more than any other to our knowledge. Further, considering for how much friendship counted in Keats' life, I have tried to call up the group of his friends about him in their human lineaments and relations, so far as these can be recovered, more fully than has been attempted before. I believe also that I have been able to trace more closely than has yet been done some of the chief sources, both in literature and in works of art, of his inspiration. I have endeavoured at the same time to make felt the critical and poetical atmosphere, with its various and strongly conflicting currents, amid which he lived, and to show how his genius, almost ignored in its own day beyond the circle of his private friends, was a focus in which many vital streams of poetic tendency from the past centred and from which many radiated into the future. To illustrate this last point it has been necessary, by way of epilogue, to sketch, however briefly, the story of his posthumous fame, his after life in the minds and hearts of English writers and readers until to-day. By English I mean all those whose mother language is English. To follow the extension of Keats' fame to the Continent is outside my aim. He has not yet, by means of translation and comment in foreign languages, become in any full sense a world-poet. But during the last thirty years the process has begun, and there would be a good deal to say, did my scheme admit it, of work upon Keats done abroad, especially in France, where our literature has during the last generation been studied with such admirable intelligence and care.

In an attempt of this scope, I have necessarily had to repeat matters of common knowledge and to say again things that others have said well and sufficiently already. But working from materials hitherto in part untouched, and taking notice of such new lights as have appeared while my task was in progress, I have drawn from them some conclusions, both biographical and critical, which I believe to be my own and which I hope may stand. I have not shrunk from quoting in full poems and portions of poems which everybody knows, in cases where I wanted the reader to have their text not merely in memory but actually before him, for re-studying with a fresh comment or in some new connexion. I have also quoted very largely from the poet's letters, even now not nearly as much read as things so full of genius should be, both in order that some of his story may be told in his own words and for the sake of that part of his mind — a great and most interesting part — which is expressed in them but has not found its way into his poems. It must be added that when I found things in my former small book which I did not see my way to better and which seemed to fit into the expanded scale of this one, I have not hesitated sometimes to incorporate them — to the amount perhaps of forty or fifty pages in all.

I wish I could hope that my work will be found such as to justify the amount and variety of friendly help I have had in its preparation. Thanks for such help are due in more quarters than I can well call to mind. First and foremost, to Lord Crewe for letting me have free and constant access to his unrivalled collection of original documents connected with the subject, both those inherited from his father (referred to in the notes as 'Houghton MSS.') and those acquired in recent years by himself (referred to as 'Crewe MSS.'). Speaking generally, it may be assumed that new matter for which no authority is quoted is taken from these sources. To Miss Henrietta Woodhouse of Weston Lea, Albury, I am indebted for valuable documentary and other information concerning her uncle Richard Woodhouse. Next in importance among collections of Keats documents to that of Lord Crewe is that of Mr J. P. Morgan in New York, the chief contents of which have by his leave been transcribed for me with the kindliest diligence by his librarian Miss Greene. For other illustrative documents existing in America, I believe of value, I should like to be able to thank their owners, Mr Day and Mr Louis Holman of Boston: but these gentlemen made a condition of their help the issue of a limited edition *de luxe* of the book specially illustrated from their material, a condition the publishers judged it impossible to carry out, at any rate in war-time.

Foremost among my scholarly helpers at home has been my friend Professor W. P. Ker. For information and suggestions in answer to enquiries of one kind or another I am indebted to Professor Israel Gollancz and Mr Henry Bradley; to Professor Ernest Weekley, the best living authority on surnames; to Mr A. H. Bullen; to Mr Falconer Madan and Mr J. W. Mackail; to Mr Thomas J. Wise; to Mr H. C. Shelley; to Mr J. D. Milner, Director of the National Portrait Gallery; and to my former colleague Mr A. H. Smith, Keeper of Greek and Roman Antiquities at the British Museum. Mr George Whale supplied me with full copies of and comments on the entries concerning Keats in the books of Guy's Hospital. Dr Hambley Rowe of Bradford put at my disposal the results, unfortunately not yet conclusive, of the researches made by him as a zealous Cornishman on Keats' possible Cornish descent. I must not omit thanks to Mr Emery Walker for his skill and pains in preparing the illustrations for my book. With reference to these, I may note that the head from the portrait painted by Severn in 1859 and now in Lord Crewe's possession was chosen for colour reproduction as frontispiece because it is the fullest in colouring and, though done from memory so long after the poet's death, to my mind the most satisfying and convincing in general air of any of the extant portraits. Of the miniature done by Severn from life in 1818, copied and recopied by himself, Charles Brown and others, and made familiar by numberless reproductions in black and white, the original, now deposited by the Dilke Trustees in the National Portrait Gallery, has the character of a monochrome touched with sharp notes or suggestions of colour in the hair, lips, hands, book, *etc.* I have preferred not to repeat either this or the equally well known — nay, hackneyed — and very distressing deathbed drawing made by Severn at Rome. The profile from Haydon's life-mask of the poet is taken, not, like most versions of the same mask, from the plaster, but from an electrotype made many years ago when the cast was fresh and showing the structure and modellings of the head more subtly, in my judgment, than the original cast itself in its present state. Both cast and electrotype are in the National Portrait Gallery. So is the oil-painting of Keats seated reading, begun by Severn soon after the poet's death and finished apparently two years later, which I have reproduced, well known though it is, partly for its appositeness to a phrase in one of his letters to his sister. Besides the portraits of Keats, I have added from characteristic sources those of the two men who most influenced him at the outset of his career, Leigh Hunt and Haydon. A new feature in my book is provided by the reproductions of certain works of art, both pictures and antiques, which can be proved or surmised to have struck and stimulated his imagination. The reproductions of autographs, one of his own and one of Haydon's, speak for themselves.

Chapter I

1795-1815: BIRTH AND PARENTAGE: SCHOOLDAYS AND APPRENTICESHIP

For all the study and research, that have lately been spent on the life and work of Keats, there is one point as to which we remain as much in the dark as ever, and that is his family history. He was born at an hour when the gradually re-awakened genius of poetry in our race, I mean of impassioned and imaginative poetry, was ready to offer new forms of spiritual sustenance, and a range of emotions both widened and deepened, to a generation as yet only half prepared to receive them. If we consider the other chief poets who bore their part in that great revival, we can commonly recognize either some strain of power in their blood or some strong inspiring quality in the scenery and traditions of their home, or both together. Granting that the scenic and legendary romance of the Scottish border wilds were to be made live anew for the delight of the latter-day world, we seem to see in Walter Scott a man predestined for the task alike by origin, association, and opportunity. Had the indwelling spirit of the Cumbrian lakes and mountains, and their power upon the souls and lives of those living among them, to be newly revealed and interpreted to the general mind of man, where should we look for its spokesman but in one of Wordsworth's birth and training? What, then, it may be asked, of Byron and Shelley, the two great contrasted poets of revolution, or rather of revolt against the counter-revolution, in the younger generation, — the one worldly, mocking, half theatrically rebellious and Satanic, the other unworldly even to unearthliness, a loving alien among men, more than half truly angelic? These we are perhaps rightly used to count as offspring of their age, with its forces and ferments, its violent actions and reactions, rather than of their ancestry or upbringing. And yet, if we will, we may fancy Byron inspired in literature by demons of the same froward brood that had urged others of his lineage on lives of adventure or of crime, and may conceive that Shelley drew some of his instincts for headlong, peremptory self-guidance, though in directions most opposite to the traditional, from the stubborn and wayward stock of colonial and county aristocracy whence he sprang.

Keats, more purely and exclusively a poet than any of these, and responding more intuitively than any to the spell alike of ancient Greece, of mediæval romance, and of the English woods and fields, was born in a dull and middling walk of London city life, and 'if by traduction came his mind', — to quote Dryden with a difference, — it was through channels hidden from our search. From his case less even than from Shakespeare's can we draw any argument as to the influence of heredity or environment on the birth and growth of genius. His origin, in spite of much diligent inquiry, has not been traced beyond one generation on the father's side and two on the mother's. His father, Thomas Keats, was a west-country lad who came young to London, and while still under twenty held the place of head ostler in a livery-stable kept by a Mr John Jennings in Finsbury. Seven or eight years later, about the beginning of 1795, he married his employer's daughter, Frances Jennings, then in her twentieth year. Mr Jennings, who had carried on a large business in north-eastern London and the neighbouring suburbs, and was a man of substance, retired about the same time to live in the country, at Ponder's End near Edmonton, leaving the management of the business in the hands of his son-in-law. At first the young couple lived at the stable, at the sign of the Swan and Hoop, Finsbury Pavement, facing the then open space of Lower Moorfields. Here their eldest child, the poet John Keats, was born prematurely on either the 29th or 31st of October, 1795. A second son, named George, followed on February 28, 1797; a third, Tom, on November 18, 1799; a fourth, Edward, who died in infancy, on April 28, 1801; and on the 3rd of June, 1803, a daughter, Frances Mary. In the meantime the family had moved from the stable to a house in Craven Street, City Road, half a mile farther north.

The Keats brothers as they grew up were remarked for their intense fraternal feeling and strong vein of family pride. But it was a pride that looked forward and not back: they were bent on raising the family name and credit, but seem to have taken no interest at all in its history, and have left no record or tradition concerning their forbears. Some of their friends believed their father to have been a Devonshire man: their sister, who long survived them, said she remembered hearing as a child that he came from Cornwall, near the Land's End.

There is no positive evidence enabling us to decide the question. The derivation of English surnames is apt to be complicated and obscure, and 'Keats' is no exception to the rule. It is a name widely distributed in various counties of England, though not very frequent in any. It may in some cases be a possessive form derived from the female Christian name Kate, on the analogy of Jeans from Jane, or Maggs from Margaret: but the source accepted as generally probable for it and its several variants is the Middle-English adjective 'kete', a word of Scandinavian origin meaning bold, gallant. In the form 'Keyte' the name prevails principally in Warwickshire: in the variants Keat (or Keate) and Keats (or Keates) it occurs in many of the midland, home, and southern, especially the south-western, counties.

Mr Thomas Hardy tells me of a Keats family sprung from a horsedealer of Broadmayne, Dorsetshire, members of which lived within his own memory as farmers and publicans in and near Dorchester, one or two of them bearing, as he thought, a striking likeness to the portrait of the poet. One Keats family of good standing was established by the mid-eighteenth century in Devon, in the person of a well-known headmaster of Blundell's school, Tiverton, afterwards rector of Bideford. His son was one of Nelson's bravest and most famous captains, Sir Richard Godwin Keats of the 'Superb', and from the same stock sprang in our own day the lady whose tales of tragic and comic west-country life, published under the pseudonym 'Zack', gave promise of a literary career which has been unhappily cut short. But with this Bideford stock the Keats brothers can have claimed no connexion, or as schoolboys they would assuredly have made the prowess of their namesake of the 'Superb' their pride and boast, whereas in fact their ideal naval hero was a much less famous person, their mother's brother Midgley John Jennings, a tall lieutenant of marines who served with some credit on Duncan's flagship at Camperdown and by reason of his stature was said to have been a special mark for the enemy's musketry. In the form Keat or Keate the name is common enough both in Devon, particularly near Tiverton, and in Cornwall, especially in the parishes of St Teath and Lanteglos, — that is round about Camelford, — and also as far eastward as Callington and westward as St Columb Major: the last named parish having been the seat of a family of the name entitled to bear arms and said to have come originally from Berkshire.

But neither the records of the Dorsetshire family, nor search in the parish registers of Devon and Cornwall, have as yet yielded the name of any Thomas Keat or Keats as born in 1768, the birth-year of our poet's father according to our information. A 'Thomas Keast', however, is registered as having been born in that year in the parish of St Agnes, between New Quay and Redruth. Now Keast is a purely Cornish name, limited to those parts, and it is quite possible that, borne by a Cornishman coming to London, it would get changed into the far commoner Keats (a somewhat similar phonetic change is that of Crisp into Cripps). So the identification of this Thomas Keast of St Agnes as the father of our Keats is not to be excluded. The Jennings connexion is of itself a circumstance which may be held to add to the likelihood of a Cornish origin for the poet, Jennings being a name frequent in the Falmouth district and occurring as far westward as Lelant. Children are registered as born in and after 1770 of the marriage of a John Jennings to a Catherine Keate at Penryn; and it is a plausible conjecture (always remembering it to be a conjecture and no more) that the prosperous London stable-keeper Jonn Jennings was himself of Cornish origin, and that between him and the lad Thomas Keats, whom he took so young first as head stableman and then as son-in-law, there existed some previous family connexion or acquaintance. These, however, are matters purely conjectural, and all we really know about the poet's parents are the dates above mentioned, and the fact that they were certainly people somewhat out of the ordinary. Thomas Keats was noticed in his lifetime as a man of sense, spirit, and conduct: 'of so remarkably fine a commonsense and native respectability,' writes Cowden Clarke, in whose father's school the poet and his brother were brought up, 'that I perfectly remember the warm terms in which his demeanour used to be canvassed by my parents after he had been to visit his boys.' And again: — 'I have a clear recollection of his lively and energetic countenance, particularly when seated on his gig and preparing to drive his wife home after visiting his sons at school. In feature, stature, and manner John resembled his father.' Of Frances Keats, the poet's mother, we learn more vaguely that she was 'tall, of good figure, with large oval face, and sensible deportment': and again that she was a lively, clever, impulsive woman, passionately fond of amusement, and supposed to have hastened the birth of her eldest child by some imprudence. Her second son, George, wrote in after life of her and of her family as follows: — 'my grandfather Mr Jennings was very well off, as his will shows, and but that he was extremely generous and gullible would have been affluent. I have heard my grandmother speak with enthusiasm of his excellencies, and Mr Abbey used to say that he never saw a woman of the talents and sense of my grandmother, except my mother.'

As to the grandmother and her estimable qualities all accounts are agreed, but of the mother the witness quoted himself tells a very different tale. This Mr Richard Abbey was a wholesale tea-dealer in Saint Pancras Lane and a trusted friend of Mr and Mrs Jennings. In a memorandum written long after their death he declares that both as girl and woman their daughter, the poet's mother, was a person of unbridled temperament, and that in her later years she fell into loose ways and was no credit to her family. Whatever truth there may be in these charges, it is certain that she lived to the end under her mother's roof and was in no way cut off from her children. The eldest boy John in particular she is said to have held in passionate affection, by him passionately returned. Once as a young child, when she was ordered to be left quiet during an illness, he is said to have insisted on keeping watch at her door with an old sword, and allowing no one to go in. Haydon, an artist who loved to lay his colours thick, gives this anecdote of the sword a different turn: — 'He was when an infant a most violent and ungovernable child. At five years of age or thereabouts, he once got hold of a naked sword and shutting the door swore nobody should go out. His mother wanted to do so, but he threatened her so furiously she began to cry, and was obliged to wait till somebody through the window saw her position and came to the rescue.' Another trait of the poet's childhood, mentioned also by Haydon, on the authority of a gammer who had known him from his birth, is that when he was first learning to speak, instead of answering sensibly, he had a trick of making a rime to the last word people said and then laughing.

The parents were ambitious for their boys, and would have liked to send them to Harrow, but thinking this beyond their means, chose the school kept by a Mr John Clarke at Enfield. The brothers of Mrs Keats, including the boys' admired uncle, the lieutenant of marines, had been educated here, and the school was one of good repute, and of exceptionally pleasant aspect and surroundings. The schoolhouse had been originally built for a rich West India merchant, in the finest style of early Georgian classic architecture, and stood in a spacious garden at the lower end of the town. When years afterwards the site was used for a railway station, the old house was for some time allowed to stand: but later it was taken down, and the central part of the façade, with its fine proportions and rich ornaments in moulded brick, was transported to the South Kensington (now Victoria and Albert) Museum, and is still preserved there as a choice example of the style. It is evident that Mr Clarke was a kind and excellent schoolmaster, much above the standards of his time, and that lads with any bent for literature or scholarship had their full chance under him. Still more was this the case when his son Charles Cowden Clarke, a genial youth with an ardent and trained love of books and music, grew old enough to help him as usher in the school-work. The brothers John and George Keats were mere children when they were put under Mr Clarke's care, John not much over and George a good deal under eight years old, both still dressed, we are told, in the childish frilled suits which give such a grace to groups of young boys in the drawings of Stothard and his contemporaries.

Not long after Keats had been put to school he lost his father, whose horse fell and threw him in the City Road as he rode home late one night after dining at Southgate, perhaps on his way home from the Enfield School. His skull was fractured: he was picked up unconscious about one o'clock and died at eight in the morning. This was on the 16th of April, 1804. Within twelve months his widow had taken a second husband — one William Rawlings, described as 'of Moorgate in the city of London, stable-keeper,' presumably therefore the successor of her first husband in the management of her father's business. (It may be noted incidentally that Rawlings, like Jennings, is a name common in Cornwall, especially in and about the parish of Madron). This marriage must have turned out unhappily, for it was soon followed by a separation, under what circumstances or through whose fault we are not told. In the correspondence of the Keats brothers after they were grown up no mention is ever made of their stepfather, of whom the family seem soon to have lost all knowledge. Mrs Rawlings went with her children to live at Edmonton, in the house of her mother, Mrs Jennings, who was just about this time left a widow. The family was well enough provided for, Mr Jennings (who died March 8, 1805) having left a fortune of over £13,000, of which, in addition to other legacies, he bequeathed a capital yielding £200 a year to his widow absolutely; one yielding £50 a year to his daughter Frances Rawlings, with reversion to her Keats children after her death; and £1000 to be separately held in trust for the said children and divided among them on the coming of age of the youngest.

Between the home, then, in Church Street, Edmonton, and the neighbouring Enfield school, where the two elder brothers were in due time joined by the youngest, the next five years of Keats' boyhood (1806-1811) were passed in sufficient comfort and pleasantness. He did not live to attain the years, or the success, of men who write their reminiscences; and almost the only recollections he has left of his own early days refer to holiday times in his grandmother's house at Edmonton. They are conveyed in some rimes which he wrote years afterwards by way of foolishness to amuse his young sister, and testify to a partiality, common also to little boys not of genius, for dabbling by the brookside and keeping small fishes in tubs, —

There was a naughty boy
   Tittlebat
   And a naughty boy was he
   Not over fat,
   He kept little fishes
   Minnow small
   In washing tubs three
   As the stal
   In spite
   Of a glove
   Of the might
   Not above
   Of the Maid,
   The size
   Nor afraid
   Of a nice
   Of his Granny-good
   Little Baby's
   He often would
   Little finger —
   Hurly burly
   O he made
   Get up early
   'Twas his trade
   And go
   Of Fish a pretty kettle
   By hook or crook
   A kettle —

> To the brook
> A kettle —
> And bring home
> Of Fish a pretty kettle
> Miller's thumb,
> A kettle!

In a later letter to his sister he makes much the same confession in a different key, when he bids her ask him for any kind of present she fancies, only not for live stock to be kept in captivity, 'though I will not now be very severe on it, remembering how fond I used to be of Goldfinches, Tomtits, Minnows, Mice, Ticklebacks, Dace, Cock salmons and all the whole tribe of the Bushes and the Brooks.' Despite the changes which have overbuilt and squalidly or sprucely suburbanized all those parts of Middlesex, the Pymmes brook still holds its course across half the county, is still bridged by the main street of Edmonton, and runs countrywise, clear and open, for some distance along a side street on its way to join the Lea. Other memories of it, and of his childish playings and musings beside it, find expression in Keats' poetry where he makes the shepherd-prince Endymion tell his sister Peona how one of his lovesick vagaries has been to sit on a stone and bubble up the water through a reed, —

> So reaching back to boyhood: make me ships
> Of moulted feathers, touchwood, alder chips,
> With leaves stuck in them; and the Neptune be
> Of their petty ocean.

If we learn little of Keats' early days from his own lips, we have sufficient testimony as to the impression which he made on his school companions; which was that of a fiery, generous little fellow, handsome and passionate, vehement both in tears and laughter, and as placable and loveable as he was pugnacious. But beneath this bright and mettlesome outside there lay deep in his nature, even from the first, a strain of painful sensibility making him subject to moods of unreasonable suspicion and self-tormenting melancholy. These he was accustomed to conceal from all except his brothers, to whom he was attached by the very closest of fraternal ties. George, the second brother, had all John's spirit of manliness and honour, with a less impulsive disposition and a cooler blood. From a boy he was the bigger and stronger of the two: and at school found himself continually involved in fights for, and not unfrequently with, his small, indomitably fiery senior. Tom, the youngest, was always delicate, and an object of protecting care as well as the warmest affection to the other two.

Here are some of George Keats' recollections, written after the death of his elder brother, and referring partly to their school days and partly to John's character after he was grown up:

I loved him from boyhood even when he wronged me, for the goodness of his heart and the nobleness of his spirit, before we left school we quarrelled often and fought fiercely, and I can safely say and my schoolfellows will bear witness that John's temper was the cause of all, still we were more attached than brothers ever are.

From the time we were boys at school, where we loved, jangled, and fought alternately, until we separated in 1818, I in a great measure relieved him by continual sympathy, explanation, and inexhaustible spirits and good humour, from many a bitter fit of hypochondriasm. He avoided teazing any one with his miseries but Tom and myself, and often asked our forgiveness; venting and discussing them gave him relief.

Let us turn now from these honest and warm brotherly reminiscences to their confirmation in the words of two of Keats' school friends; and first in those of his junior Edward Holmes, afterwards a musical critic of note and author of a well-known *Life of Mozart* : —

Keats was in childhood not attached to books. His *penchant* was for fighting. He would fight any one — morning, noon, and night, his brother among the rest. It was meat and drink to him. Jennings their sailor relation was always in the thoughts of the brothers, and they determined to keep up the family reputation for courage; George in a passive manner; John and Tom more fiercely. The favourites of John were few; after they were known to fight readily he seemed to prefer them for a sort of grotesque and buffoon humour. I recollect at this moment his delight at the extraordinary gesticulations and pranks of a boy named Wade who was celebrated for this.... He was a boy whom any one from his extraordinary vivacity and personal beauty might easily fancy would become great — but rather in some military capacity than in literature. You will remark that this taste came out rather suddenly and unexpectedly. Some books of his I remember reading were *Robinson Crusoe* and something about Montezuma and the Incas of Peru. He must have read Shakespeare as he thought that 'no one would care to read *Macbeth* alone in a house at two o'clock in the morning.' This seems to me a boyish trait of the poet. His sensibility was as remarkable as his indifference to be thought well of by the master as a 'good boy' and to his tasks in general.... He was in every way the creature of passion.... The point to be chiefly insisted on is that he was *not literary — his love of books and poetry manifested itself chiefly about a year before he left school*. In all active exercises he excelled. The generosity and daring of his character with the extreme beauty and animation of his face made I remember an impression on me — and being some years his junior I was obliged to woo his friendship — in which I succeeded, but not till I had fought several battles. This violence and vehemence — this pugnacity and generosity of disposition — in passions of tears or outrageous fits of laughter — always in extremes — will help to paint Keats in his boyhood. Associated as they were with an extraordinary beauty of person and expression, these qualities captivated the boys, and no one was more popular.

Entirely to the same effect is the account of Keats given by a school friend seven or eight years older than himself, to whose appreciation and encouragement the world most likely owes it that he first became aware of his own vocation for poetry. This was the aforementioned Charles Cowden Clarke, the son of the head master, who towards the close of a long life, during which he had deserved well of literature and of his generation in more ways than one, wrote retrospectively of Keats: —

He was a favourite with all. Not the less beloved was he for having a highly pugnacious spirit, which when roused was one of the most picturesque exhibitions — off the stage — I ever saw. One of the transports of that marvellous actor, Edmund Kean — whom, by the way, he idolized — was its nearest resemblance; and the two were not very dissimilar in face and figure. Upon one occasion when an usher, on account of some impertinent behaviour, had boxed his brother Tom's ears, John rushed up, put himself into the received posture of offence, and, it was said, struck the usher — who could, so to say, have put him in his pocket. His passion at times was almost ungovernable; and his brother George, being considerably the taller and stronger, used frequently to hold him down by main force, laughing when John was 'in one of his moods,' and was endeavouring to beat him. It was all, however, a wisp-of-straw conflagration; for he had an intensely tender affection for his brothers, and proved it upon the most trying occasions. He was not merely the favourite of all, like a pet prize-fighter, for his terrier courage; but his highmindedness, his utter unconsciousness of a mean motive, his placability, his generosity, wrought so general a feeling in his behalf, that I never heard a word of disapproval from any one, superior or equal, who had known him.

The same excellent witness records in agreement with the last that in his earlier school days Keats showed no particular signs of an intellectual bent, though always orderly and methodical in what he did. But during his last few terms, that is in his fifteenth and sixteenth years, he suddenly became a passionate student and a very glutton of books. Let us turn again to Cowden Clarke's words: —

My father was in the habit, at each half-year's vacation, of bestowing prizes upon those pupils who had performed the greatest quantity of voluntary work; and such was Keats' indefatigable energy for the last two or three successive half-years of his remaining at school, that, upon each occasion, he took the first prize by a considerable distance. He was at work before the first school-hour began, and that was at seven o'clock; almost all the intervening times of recreation were so devoted; and during the afternoon holidays, when all were at play, he would be in the school — almost the only one — at his Latin or French translation; and so unconscious and regardless was he of the consequences of so close and persevering an application, that he never would have taken the necessary exercise had he not been sometimes driven out for the purpose by one of the masters....

One of the silver medals awarded to Keats as a school prize in these days exists in confirmation of this account and was lately in the market. Cowden Clarke continues: —

In the latter part of the time — perhaps eighteen months — that he remained at school, he occupied the hours during meals in reading. Thus, his *whole* time was engrossed. He had a tolerably retentive memory, and the quantity that he read was surprising. He must in those last months have exhausted the school library, which consisted principally of abridgements of all the voyages and travels of any note; Mavor's collection, also his *Universal History* ; Robertson's histories of Scotland, America, and Charles the Fifth; all Miss Edgeworth's productions, together with many other books equally well calculated for youth. The books, however, that were his constantly recurrent sources of attraction were Tooke's *Pantheon* , Lemprière's *Classical Dictionary* , which he appeared to *learn* , and Spence's *Polymetis* . This was the store whence he acquired his intimacy with the Greek mythology; here was he 'suckled in that creed outworn;' for his amount of classical attainment extended no farther than the *Æneid* , with which epic, indeed, he was so fascinated that before leaving school he had *voluntarily* translated in writing a considerable portion....

He must have gone through all the better publications in the school library, for he asked me to lend him some of my own books; and, in my 'mind's eye,' I now see him at supper (we had our meals in the schoolroom), sitting back on the form, from the table, holding the folio volume of Burnet's *History of his Own Time* between himself and the table, eating his meal from beyond it. This work, and Leigh Hunt's *Examiner* — which my father took in, and I used to lend to Keats — no doubt laid the foundation of his love of civil and religious liberty.

In the midst of these ardent studies of Keats' latter school days befell the death of his mother, who had been for some time in failing health. First she was disabled by chronic rheumatism, and at last fell into a rapid consumption, which carried her off at the age of thirty-five in February 1810. We are told with what devotion her eldest boy attended her sickbed, — 'he sat up whole nights with her in a great chair, would suffer nobody to give her medicine, or even cook her food, but himself, and read novels to her in her intervals of ease,' — and how bitterly he mourned for her when she was gone, — 'he gave way to such impassioned and prolonged grief (hiding himself in a nook under the master's desk) as awakened the liveliest pity and sympathy in all who saw him.'

From her, no doubt, came that predisposition to consumption which showed itself in her youngest son from adolescence and carried him off at nineteen, and with the help of ill luck, over-exertion, and distress of mind, wrecked also before twenty-five the robust-seeming frame and constitution of her eldest, the poet. Were the accounts of her character less ambiguous, or were the strands of human heredity less inveterately entangled than they are, it would be tempting, when we consider the deep duality of Keats' nature, the trenchant contrast between the two selves that were in him, to trace to the mother the seeds of one of those selves, the feverishly over-sensitive and morbidly passionate one, and to his father the seeds of the other, the self that was all manly good sense and good feeling and undisturbed clear vision and judgment. In the sequel we shall see this fine virile self in Keats continually and consciously battling against the other, trying to hold it down, and succeeding almost always in keeping control over his ways and dealings with his fellow-men, though not over the inward frettings of his spirit.

In the July following her daughter's death, Mrs Jennings, being desirous to make the best provision she could for her orphan grandchildren, 'in consideration of the natural love and affection which she had for them,' executed a deed putting them under the care of two guardians, to whom she made over, to be held in trust for their benefit from the date of the instrument, the chief part of the property which she derived from her late husband under his will. The guardians were Mr Rowland Sandell, merchant, who presently renounced the trust, and the aforesaid Mr Richard Abbey, tea-dealer. Mrs Jennings survived the execution of this deed more than four years, but Mr Abbey seems at once to have taken up all the responsibilities of the trust. Under his authority John Keats was withdrawn from school at the end of the summer term, 1811, when he was some months short of sixteen, and made to put on harness for the practical work of life. With no opposition, so far as we learn, on his own part, he was bound apprentice to a Mr Thomas Hammond, a surgeon and apothecary of good repute at Edmonton, for the customary term of five years.

The years between the sixteenth and twentieth of his age are the most critical of a young man's life, and in these years, during which our other chief London-born poets, Spenser, Milton, Gray, were profiting by the discipline of Cambridge and the Muses, Keats had no better or more helpful regular training than that of an ordinary apprentice, apparently one of several, in a suburban surgery. But he had the one advantage, to him inestimable, of proximity to his old school, which meant free access to the school library and continued encouragement and advice in reading from his affectionate senior, the head master's son. The fact that it was only two miles' walk from Edmonton to Enfield helped much, says Cowden Clarke, to reconcile him to his new way of life, and his duties at the surgery were not onerous. As laid down in the ordinary indentures of apprenticeship in those times, they were indeed chiefly negative, the apprentice binding himself 'not to haunt taverns or playhouses, not to play at dice or cards, nor absent himself from his said master's service day or night unlawfully, but in all things as a faithful apprentice he shall behave himself towards the said master and all his during the said term.'

Keats himself, it is recorded, did not love talking of his apprentice days, and has left no single written reference to them except the much-quoted phrase in a letter of 1819, in which, speaking of the continual processes of change in the human tissues, he says, 'this is not the same hand which seven years ago clenched itself at Hammond.' It was natural that the same fiery temper which made him as a small boy square up against an usher on behalf of his brother, — an offence which the headmaster, according to his son Cowden Clarke, 'felt he could not severely punish,' — it was natural that this same temper should on occasion flame out against his employer the surgeon. If Keats' words are to be taken literally, this happened in the second year of his apprenticeship. Probably it was but the affair of a moment: there is no evidence of any habitual disagreement or final breach between them, and Keats was able to put in the necessary testimonial from Mr Hammond when he presented himself in due course for examination before the Court of Apothecaries. A fellow-apprentice in after years remembered him as 'an idle loafing fellow, always writing poetry.' This, seeing that he did not begin to write till he was near eighteen, must refer to the last two years of his apprenticeship and probably represents an unlettered view of his way of employing his leisure, rather (judging by his general character) than any slackness in the performance of actual duty. One of the very few glimpses we have of him from outside is from Robert Hengist Horne ('Orion' Horne), another alumnus of the Enfield school who lived to make his mark in literature. Horne remembered Mr Hammond driving on a professional visit to the school one winter day and leaving Keats to take care of the gig. While Keats sat in a brown study holding the reins, young Horne, remembering his school reputation as a boxer, in bravado threw a snowball at him and hit, but made off into safety before Keats could get at him to inflict punishment. The story suggests a picture to the eye but tells nothing to the mind.

Our only real witness for this time of Keats' life is Cowden Clarke. He tells us how the lad's newly awakened passion for the pleasures of literature and the imagination was not to be stifled, and how at Edmonton he plunged back into his school occupations of reading and translating whenever he could spare the time. He finished at this time his prose version of the *Aeneid*, and on free afternoons and evenings, five or six times a month or oftener, was in the habit of walking over to Enfield, — by that field path where Lamb found the stiles so many and so hard to tackle, — to see his friend Cowden Clarke and bring away or return borrowed books. Young Clarke was an ardent liberal and disciple of Leigh Hunt both in political opinions and literary taste. In summer weather he and Keats would sit in a shady arbour in the old school garden, the elder reading poetry to the younger, and enjoying his looks and exclamations of delight. From the nature of Keats' imitative first flights in verse, it is clear that though he hated the whole 'Augustan' and post-Augustan tribe of social and moral essayists in verse, and Pope, their illustrious master, most of all, yet his mind and ear had become familiar, in the course of his school and after-school reading, with Thomson, Collins, Gray, and all the more romantically minded poets of the middle and later eighteenth century. But the essential service Clarke did him was in pressing upon his attention the poetry of the great Elizabethan and Jacobean age, from *The Shepheard's Calendar* down to *Comus* and *Lycidas*, — 'our older and nobler poetry,' as a few had always held it to be even through the Age of Reason and the reign of Pope and his followers, and as it was now loudly proclaimed to be by all the innovating critics, with Leigh Hunt and Hazlitt among the foremost.

On a momentous day for Keats, Cowden Clarke introduced him for the first time to Spenser, reading him the *Epithalamion* in the afternoon and at his own eager request lending him the *Faerie Queene* to take away the same evening. With Spenser's later imitators, playful or serious, as Shenstone and Thomson, Beattie and the more recent Mrs Tighe, Keats, we know, was already familiar; indeed he owned later to a passing phase of boyish delight in Beattie's *Minstrel* and Tighe's languorously romantic *Psyche*. But now he found himself taken to the fountain head, and was enraptured. It has been said, and truly, that no one who has not had the good fortune to be attracted to the *Faerie Queene* in boyhood can ever quite wholeheartedly and to the full enjoy it. The maturer student, appreciate as he may its innumerable beauties and noble ethical temper, can hardly fail to be critically conscious also of its arbitrary forms of rime and language, and sated by its melodious redundance: he will perceive its faults now of scholastic pedantry and now of flagging inspiration, the perplexity and discontinuousness of the allegory, and the absence of real and breathing humanity amidst all that luxuriance of symbolic and decorative invention, and prodigality of romantic incident and detail. It is otherwise with the greedy and indiscriminate imaginative appetite of boyhood. I speak as one of the fortunate who know by experience that for a boy there is no poetical revelation like the *Faerie Queene*, no pleasure equal to the pleasure of being rapt for the first time along that ever-buoyant stream of verse, by those rivers and forests of enchantment, glades and wildernesses alive with glancing figures of knight and lady, oppressor and champion, mage and Saracen, — with masque and combat, pursuit and rescue, the chivalrous shapes and hazards of the woodland, and beauty triumphant or in distress. Through the new world thus opened to him Keats went ranging with delight: 'ramping' is Cowden Clarke's word: he showed moreover his own instinct for the poetical art by fastening with critical enthusiasm on epithets of special felicity or power. For instance, says his friend, 'he hoisted himself up, and looked burly and dominant, as he said, "What an image that is — *sea-shouldering whales*!"'

Spenser has been often proved not only a great awakener of the love of poetry in youth, but a great fertilizer of the germs of original poetical power where they exist; and Charles Brown, Keats' most intimate companion during the two last years of his life, states positively that it was to the inspiration of the *Faerie Queene* that his first notion of attempting to write was due. 'Though born to be a poet, he was ignorant of his birthright until he had completed his eighteenth year. It was the *Faerie Queene* that awakened his genius. In Spenser's fairyland he was enchanted, breathed in a new world, and became another being; till enamoured of the stanza, he attempted to imitate it, and succeeded. This account of the sudden development of his poetic powers I first received from his brothers and afterwards from himself. This, his earliest attempt, the *Imitation of Spenser*, is in his first volume of poems, and it is peculiarly interesting to those acquainted with his history.' Cowden Clarke places the attempt two years earlier, but his memory for dates was, as he owns, the vaguest. We may fairly take Brown to be on this point the better informed of the two, and may assume that it was some time in the second year after he left school that the Spenser fever took hold on Keats, and with it the longing to be himself a poet. But it was not with Spenser alone, it was with other allegoric and narrative poets as well, his followers or contemporaries, that Keats was in these days gaining acquaintance. Not quite in his earliest, but still in his very early, attempts, we find clear traces of familiarity with the work both of William Browne of Tavistock and of Michael Drayton, and we can conceive how in that charming ingenuous retrospect of Drayton's on his boyish vocation to poetry, addressed to his friend Henry Reynolds, Keats will have smiled to find an utterance of the same passion that had just awakened in his own not very much maturer self.

Let it be remembered moreover that the years of Keats' school days and apprenticeship were also those of the richest and most stimulating outburst of the new poetry in England. To name only their chief products, — the *Lyrical Ballads* of Coleridge and Wordsworth had come while he was only a child: during his school days had appeared Wordsworth's still richer and not less challenging volumes of 1807, and the succession of Scott's romantic lays (but these last, in spite of their enormous public success, it was in circles influenced by Leigh Hunt not much the fashion to admire): during his apprentice years at Edmonton, the two first cantos of Byron's *Childe Harold* and the still more overwhelmingly successful series of his Eastern tales: and finally Wordsworth's *Excursion* , with which almost from the first Keats was profoundly impressed. But it was not, of course, only by reading poetry that he was learning to be a poet. Nature was quite as much his teacher as books; and the nature within easy reach of him, tame indeed and unimpressive in comparison with Wordsworth's lakes and mountains, had quite enough of vital English beauty to afford fair seed-time to his soul. Across the levels of the Lea valley, not then disfigured as they are now by factories and reservoir works and the squalor of sprawling suburbs, rose the softly shagged undulations of Epping forest, a region which no amount of Cockney frequentation or prosaic vicinity can ever quite strip of its primitive romance. Westward over Hornsey to the Highgate and Hampstead heights, north-westward through Southgate towards the Barnets, and thence in a sweep by the remains of Enfield Chase, was a rich tract of typically English country, a country of winding elm-shadowed lanes, of bosky hedge and thicket and undulating pasture-land charmingly diversified with parks and pleasaunces. Nearly such I can myself remember it some sixty years ago, and even now, off the tram-frequented highways and between the devastating encroachments of bricks and mortar, forlorn patches of its ancient pastoral self are still to be found lurking.

It was in his rambles afield in these directions and in his habitual afternoon and evening strolls to Enfield and back, that a delighted sense of the myriad activities of nature's life in wood and field and brook and croft and hedgerow began to possess Keats' mind, and to blend with the beautiful images that already peopled it from his readings in Greek mythology, and to be enhanced into a strange supernatural thrill by the recurring magic of moonlight. It is only in adolescence that such delights can be drunk in, not with conscious study and observation but passively and half unaware through all the pores of being, and no youth ever drank them in more deeply than Keats. Not till later came for him, or comes for any man, the time when the images so absorbed, and the emotions and sympathies so awakened, define and develop themselves in consciousness and discover with effort and practice the secret of rightly expressing themselves in words.

After Keats, under the stimulus of Spenser, had taken his first plunge into verse, he went on writing occasional sonnets and other pieces: secretly and shyly at first like all other young poets: at least it was not until some two years later, in the spring of 1815, that he showed anything that he had written to his friend and confidant Cowden Clarke. This was a sonnet on the release of Leigh Hunt after serving a two years' sentence of imprisonment for a political offence. Clarke relates how he was walking in to London from Enfield to call on and congratulate the ex-prisoner, whom he not only revered as a martyr in the cause of liberty but knew and admired personally, when Keats met him and turned back to accompany him part of the way. 'At the last field-gate, when taking leave, he gave me the sonnet entitled *Written on the day that Mr Leigh Hunt left prison* . This I feel to be the first proof I had received of his having committed himself in verse; and how clearly do I remember the conscious look and hesitation with which he offered it! There are some momentary glances by beloved friends that fade only with life.'

About a score of the pieces which Keats had written and kept secret during the preceding two years are preserved, and like the work of almost all beginners are quite imitative and conventional, failing to express anything original or personal to himself. They include the aforesaid Spenserian stanzas, which in fact echo the cadences of Thomson's *Castle of Indolence* much more than those of Spenser himself; an ode to Hope, quite in the square-toed manner of eighteenth century didactic verse, and another to Apollo, in which style and expression owe everything to Gray; a set of octosyllabics recording, this time with some touch of freshness, a momentary impression of a woman's beauty received one night at Vauxhall, and so intense that it continued to haunt his memory for years; two sets of verses addressed in a vein of polite parlour compliment to lady friends at the seaside; and several quite feeble sonnets in the Wordsworthian form, among them one on the peace of Paris in 1814, one on Chatterton and one on Byron.

Of Keats' outward ways and doings during these days when he was growing to manhood we know nothing directly except from Cowden Clarke, and can only gather a little more by inference. It is clear that he enjoyed a certain amount of liberty and holiday, more, perhaps, than would have fallen to the lot of a more zealous apprentice, and that he spent part of his free time in London in the society of his brother George, at this time a clerk in Mr Abbey's counting-house, and of friends to whom George made him known. Among these were the family of an officer of marines named Wylie, to whose charming daughter, Georgiana, George Keats a little later became engaged, and another family of prosperous tradespeople named Mathew. Here too there were daughters, Caroline and Ann, who made themselves pleasant to the Keats brothers, and to whom were addressed the pair of complimentary jingles already mentioned. One of the sisters, asked in later life for her recollections of the time, replied in a weariful strain of evangelical penitence for the frivolities of those days, and found nothing more to the purpose to say of Keats than this: — 'I cannot go further than say I always thought he had a very beautiful countenance and was very warm and enthusiastic in his character. He wrote a great deal of poetry at our house but I do not recollect whether I ever had any of it, I certainly have none now; Ann had many pieces of his.' A cousin of this family, one George Felton Mathew, was a youth of sensibility and poetical leanings, and became for a time an intimate friend of Keats, and next to his brothers and Cowden Clarke the closest confidant of his studies and ambitions. Their intimacy began in the Edmonton days and lasted through the earlier months of his student life in London. Looking back upon their relations after some thirty years, Mr Felton Mathew, then a supernumerary official of the Poor Law Board, struggling meekly under the combined strain of a precarious income, a family of twelve children, and a turn for the interpretation of prophecy, wrote as follows: —

Keats and I though about the same age, and both inclined to literature, were in many respects as different as two individuals could be. He enjoyed good health — a fine flow of animal spirits — was fond of company — could amuse himself admirably with the frivolities of life — and had great confidence in himself. I, on the other hand was languid and melancholy — fond of repose — thoughtful beyond my years — and diffident to the last degree. But I always delighted in administering to the happiness of others: and being one of a large family, it pleased me much to see him and his brother George enjoy themselves so much at our little domestic concerts and dances.... He was of the sceptical and republican school. An advocate for the innovations which were making progress in his time. A faultfinder with everything established. I, on the contrary, hated controversy and dispute — dreaded discord and disorder — loved the institutions of my country.... But I respected Keats' opinions, because they were sincere — refrained from subjects on which we differed, and only asked him to concede with me the imperfection of human knowledge, and the fallibility of human judgment: while he, on his part, would often express regret on finding that he had given pain or annoyance by opposing with ridicule or asperity the opinions of others.

Of Keats' physical appearance and poetical preferences the same witness writes further: —

A painter or a sculptor might have taken him for a study after the Greek masters, and have given him 'a station like the herald Mercury, new lighted on some heaven-kissing hill.' His eye admired more the external decorations than felt the deep emotions of the Muse. He delighted in leading you through the mazes of elaborate description, but was less conscious of the sublime and the pathetic. He used to spend many evenings in reading to me, but I never observed the tears in his eyes nor the broken voice which are indicative of extreme sensibility. These indeed were not the parts of poetry which he took pleasure in pointing out.

This last, it should be noted, seems in pretty direct contradiction with one of Cowden Clarke's liveliest recollections as follows: — 'It was a treat to see as well as hear him read a pathetic passage. Once when reading *Cymbeline* aloud, I saw his eyes fill with tears, and his voice faltered when he came to the departure of Posthumus, and Imogen saying she would have watched him —

Till the diminution
Of space had pointed him sharp as my needle;
Nay follow'd him till *he had melted from*
The smallness of a gnat to air ; and then
Have turn'd mine eye and wept.'

Early in the autumn of 1815, a few weeks before his twentieth birthday, Keats left the service of Mr Hammond, his indentures having apparently been cancelled by consent, and went to live in London as a student at the hospitals, then for teaching purposes united, of Guy's and St Thomas's. What befell him during the eighteen months that followed, and how his career as a student came to an end, will be told in the next two chapters.

Chapter II

OCTOBER 1815-MARCH 1817: HOSPITAL STUDIES: POETICAL AMBITIONS: LEIGH HUNT

The external and technical facts of Keats' life as a medical student are these. His name, as we have said, was entered at Guy's as a six months' student (surgeon's pupil) on October 1, 1815, a month before his twentieth birthday. Four weeks later he was appointed dresser to one of the hospital surgeons, Mr Lucas. At the close of his first six months' term, March 3, 1816, he entered for a further term of twelve months. On July 25, 1816, he presented himself for examination before the Court of Apothecaries and obtained their licence to practise. He continued to attend lectures and live the regular life of a student; but early in the spring of 1817, being now of age and on the eve of publishing his first volume of verse, he determined to abandon the pursuit of medicine for that of poetry, declared his intention to his guardian, and ceased attending the hospitals without seeking or receiving the usual certificate of proficiency. For the first two or three months of this period, from the beginning of October 1815 till about the new year of 1816, Keats lodged alone at 8 Dean Street, Borough, and then for half a year or more with several other students over the shop of a tallow chandler named Markham in St Thomas's Street. Thence, in the summer or early autumn of 1816, leaving the near neighbourhood of the hospitals, he went to join his brothers in rooms in The Poultry, over a passage leading to the Queen's Head Tavern. Finally, early in 1817, they all three moved for a short time to 76 Cheapside. For filling up this skeleton record, we have some traditions of the hospital concerning Keats' teachers, some recollections of fellow students, — of one, Mr Henry Stephens, in particular, — together with further reminiscences by Cowden Clarke and impressions recorded in after years by one and another of a circle of acquaintances which fast expanded. Moreover Keats begins during this period to tell something of his own story, in the form of a few poems of a personal tenor and a very few letters written to and preserved by his friends.

As to his hospital work, it is clear that though his heart was not in it and his thoughts were prone to wander, and though he held and declared that poetry was the only thing worth living for, yet when he chose he could bend his mind and will to the tasks before him. The operations which as dresser he performed or assisted in are said to have proved him no fumbler. When he went up for examination before the Court of Apothecaries he passed with ease and credit, somewhat to the surprise of his fellow students, who put his success down to his knowledge of Latin rather than of medicine. Later, after he had abandoned the profession, he was always ready to speak or act with a certain authority in cases of illness or emergency, and though hating the notion of practice evidently did not feel himself unqualified for it so far as knowledge went. He could not find in the scientific part of the study a satisfying occupation for his thoughts; and though a few years later, when he had realized that there is no kind of knowledge but may help to nourish a poet's mind, he felt unwilling to lose hold of what he had learned as apprentice and student, he was never caught by that special passion of philosophical curiosity which laid hold for a season on Coleridge and Shelley successively, and drew them powerfully towards the study of the mechanism and mysteries of the human frame. The practical responsibilities of the profession at the same time weighed upon him, and he was conscious of a kind of absent uneasy wonder at his own skill. Once when Cowden Clarke asked him about his prospects and feelings in regard to his profession, he frankly declared his own sense of his unfitness for it; with reasons such as this, that 'the other day, during the lecture, there came a sunbeam into the room, and with it a whole troop of creatures floating in the ray; and I was off with them to Oberon and fairyland.' 'My last operation,' he once told another friend, 'was the opening of a man's temporal artery. I did it with the utmost nicety, but reflecting on what passed through my mind at the time, my dexterity seemed a miracle, and I never took up the lancet again.'

The surgeon to whom he was specially assigned as pupil, Mr Lucas, seems to have had few qualifications as a teacher. We have the following lively character of him from a man afterwards highly honoured in the profession, John Flint South, who walked the hospitals at the same time as Keats: — 'A tall ungainly awkward man, with stooping shoulders and a shuffling walk, as deaf as a post, not overburdened with brains, but very good natured and easy, and liked by everyone. His surgical acquirements were very small, his operations generally very badly performed, and accompanied with much bungling, if not worse.' But the teacher from whom Keats will really, as all witnesses agree, have learnt the best of what he knew was the great dissector and anatomist, Astley Cooper, then almost in the zenith of his power as a lecturer and of his popular fame and practice. He is described as one of the handsomest and most ingratiating of men, as well as one of the most indefatigable and energetic, with an admirable gift of exposition made racy by a strong East Anglian accent; and it is on record that he took an interest in young Keats, and recommended him to the special care of his own dresser and namesake, George Cooper. It was in consequence of this recommendation that Keats left his solitary lodging in Dean Street and went to live as housemate in St Thomas's Street with three other students, the aforesaid George Cooper, one George Wilson Mackereth, and Henry Stephens, the last-named afterwards a surgeon in good repute as well as a dabbler in dramatic literature. It is from Stephens that we get much the fullest picture of Keats in these student days. I give the pith of his reminiscences, partly as quoted from his conversation by an intimate friend in the same profession, Sir Benjamin Ward Richardson, partly as written down by himself for Lord Houghton's information in 1847.

Whether it was in the latter part of the year 1815 or the early part of the year 1816 that my acquaintance with John Keats commenced I cannot say. We were both students at the united hospitals of St Thomas's and Guy's, and we had apartments in a house in St Thomas's Street, kept by a decent respectable woman of the name of Mitchell I think. [After naming his other fellow students, the witness goes on] —John Keats being alone, and to avoid the expense of having a sitting room to himself, asked to join us, which we readily acceded to. We were therefore constant companions, and the following is what I recollect of his previous history from conversation with him. Of his parentage I know nothing, for upon that subject I never remember his speaking, I think he was an orphan. He had been apprenticed to a Mr Hammond surgeon of Southgate from whence he came on the completion of his time to the hospitals. His passion, if I may so call it, for poetry was soon manifested. He attended lectures and went through the usual routine but he had no desire to excel in that pursuit.... He was called by his fellow students 'little Keats,' being at his full growth no more than five feet high.... In a room, he was always at the window, peering into space, so that the window-seat was spoken of by his comrades as Keats' place.... In the lecture room he seemed to sit apart and to be absorbed in something else, as if the subject suggested thoughts to him which were not practically connected with it. He was often in the subject and out of it, in a dreamy way.

He never attached much consequence to his own studies in medicine, and indeed looked upon the medical career as the career by which to live in a workaday world, without being certain that he could keep up the strain of it. He nevertheless had a consciousness of his own powers, and even of his own greatness, though it might never be recognised.... Poetry was to his mind the zenith of all his aspirations: the only thing worthy the attention of superior minds: so he thought: all other pursuits were mean and tame. He had no idea of fame or greatness but as it was connected with the pursuits of poetry, or the attainment of poetical excellence. The greatest men in the world were the poets and to rank among them was the chief object of his ambition. It may readily be imagined that this feeling was accompanied with a good deal of pride and conceit, and that amongst mere medical students he would walk and talk as one of the Gods might be supposed to do when mingling with mortals. This pride exposed him, as may be readily imagined, to occasional ridicule, and some mortification.

Having a taste and liking for poetry myself, though at that time but little cultivated, he regarded me as something a little superior to the rest, and would gratify himself frequently by showing me some lines of his writing, or some new idea which he had struck out. We had frequent conversation on the merits of particular poets, but our tastes did not agree. He was a great admirer of Spenser, his *Faerie Queene* was a great favourite with him. Byron was also in favour, Pope he maintained was no poet, only a versifier. He was fond of imagery, the most trifling similes appeared to please him. Sometimes I ventured to show him some lines which I had written, but I always had the mortification of hearing them condemned, indeed he seemed to think it presumption in me to attempt to tread along the same pathway as himself at however humble a distance.

He had two brothers, who visited him frequently, and they worshipped him. They seemed to think their brother John was to be exalted, and to exalt the family name. I remember a student from St Bartholomew's Hospital who came often to see him, as they had formerly been intimate, but though old friends they did not cordially agree. Newmarsh or Newmarch (I forget which was his name) was a classical scholar, as was Keats, and therefore they scanned freely the respective merits of the Poets of Greece and Rome. Whenever Keats showed Newmarch any of his poetry it was sure to be ridiculed and severely handled.

Newmarch was a light-hearted and merry fellow, but I thought he was rather too fond of mortifying Keats, but more particularly his brothers, as their praise of their brother John amounted almost to idolatry, and Newmarch and they frequently quarrelled. Whilst attending lectures he would sit and instead of copying out the lecture, would often scribble some doggrel rhymes among the notes of Lecture, particularly if he got hold of another student's syllabus. In my syllabus of chemical lectures he scribbled many lines on the paper cover. This cover has been long torn off, except one small piece on which is the following fragment of doggrel rhyme: —

Give me women, wine and snuff
Until I cry out, 'hold! enough'
You may do so, sans objection
Until the day of resurrection.

This is all that remains, and is the only piece of his writing which is now in my possession. He was gentlemanly in his manners and when he condescended to talk upon other subjects he was agreeable and intelligent. He was quick and apt at learning, when he chose to give his attention to any subject. He was a steady quiet and well behaved person, never inclined to pursuits of a low or vicious character.

The last words need to be read in the light of the convivial snatch of verse quoted just above. Keats in these days was no rake, indeed, but neither was he a puritan: his passions were strong in proportion to the general intensity of his being: and his ardent absorption in poetry and study did not save him from the risks and slips incident to appetite and hot blood.

Another fellow student relates: — 'even in the lecture room of St Thomas's I have seen Keats in a deep poetic dream; his mind was on Parnassus with the Muses. And here is a quaint fragment which he one evening scribbled in our presence, while the precepts of Sir Astley Cooper fell unheeded on his ear.' The fragment tells how Alexander the Great saw and loved a lady of surpassing beauty on his march through India, and reads like the beginning of an attempt to tell the story of the old French *Lai d'Aristote* in the style and spelling of an early-printed English prose romance, — possibly the *Morte d'Arthure*. Into his would-be archaic prose, luxuriantly describing the lady's beauty, Keats works in tags taken direct from Spenser and Shakespeare and Milton, all three. He no doubt knew this favourite mediæval tale — that of the Indian damsel whose charms enslaved first Alexander in the midst of his conquests and then his tutor Aristotle — either in the eighteenth-century prose version of Le Grand or the recent English verse translation by G. L. Way, who turns the tale in couplets of this style: —

At the first glance all dreams of conquest fade
And his first thought is of his Indian maid.

I cannot but think the Indian maiden of this story must have been still lingering in Keats' imagination when he devised the episode of that other Indian maiden in the fourth book of *Endymion*.

Besides these records, we have an actual tangible relic to show how Keats' attention in the lecture room was now fixed and now wandered, in the shape of a notebook in which some other student has begun to put down anatomy notes and Keats has followed. Beginning from both ends, he has made notes of an anatomical and also of a surgical course, which are not those of a lax or inaccurate student, but full and close as far as they go; only squeezed into the margins of one or two pages there are signs of flagging attention in the shape of sketches, rather prettily touched, of a pansy and other flowers.

After the first weeks of autumn gloom spent in solitary lodgings in the dingiest part of London, Keats expresses, in a rimed epistle to Felton Mathew, the fear lest his present studies and surroundings should stifle the poetic faculty in him altogether. About the same time he takes pains to get into touch again with Cowden Clarke, who had by this time left Enfield and was living with a brother-in-law in Clerkenwell. In a letter unluckily not dated, but certainly belonging to these first autumn weeks in London, Keats writes to Clarke: — 'Although the Borough is a beastly place in dirt, turnings, and windings, yet No 8, Dean Street, is not difficult to find; and if you would run the gauntlet over London Bridge, take the first turning to the right, and, moreover, knock at my door, which is nearly opposite a meeting, you would do me a charity, which, as St Paul saith, is the father of all the virtues. At all events, let me hear from you soon: I say, at all events, not excepting the gout in your fingers.' Clarke seems to have complied promptly with this petition, and before many months their renewed intercourse had momentous consequences. Keats' fear that the springs of poetry would dry up in him was not fulfilled, and he kept trying his prentice hand in various modes of verse. Some of the sonnets recorded to have belonged to the year 1815, as *Woman, when I behold thee, Happy is England*, may have been written in London at the close of that year: a number of others, showing a gradually strengthening touch, belong, we know, to the spring and early summer of the next. For his brother George to send to his *fiancée*, Miss Georgiana Wylie, on Valentine's day, Feb. 14, 1816, he wrote the pleasant set of heptasyllabics beginning 'Hadst thou lived in days of old.' In the same month was published Leigh Hunt's poem *The Story of Rimini*, and by this, working together with his rooted enthusiasm for Spenser, Keats was immediately inspired to begin an attempt at a chivalrous romance of his own, *Calidore*; which went no farther than an Induction and some hundred and fifty opening lines.

Cowden Clarke had kept up his acquaintance with Leigh Hunt, and was in the habit of going up to visit him at the cottage where he was now living at Hampstead, in the Vale of Health. Some time in the late spring of 1816 Clarke made known to Hunt first some of Keats' efforts in poetry and then Keats himself. Both Clarke and Hunt have told the story, both writing at a considerable, and Clarke at a very long, interval after the event. In their main substance the two accounts agree, but both are in some points confused, telescoping together, as memory is apt to do, circumstances really separated by an interval of months. One firm fact we have to start with, — that Hunt printed in his paper, the *Examiner*, for May 5th, 1816, Keats' sonnet, *O Solitude, if I with thee must dwell*. This was Keats' first appearance in print, and a decisive circumstance in his life. Clarke, it appears, had taken up the 'Solitude' sonnet and a few other manuscript verses of Keats to submit to Leigh Hunt for his opinion, and had every reason to be gratified at the result. Here is his story of what happened.

I took with me two or three of the poems I had received from Keats. I could not but anticipate that Hunt would speak encouragingly, and indeed approvingly, of the compositions — written, too, by a youth under age; but my partial spirit was not prepared for the unhesitating and prompt admiration which broke forth before he had read twenty lines of the first poem. Horace Smith happened to be there on the occasion, and he was not less demonstrative in his appreciation of their merits.... After making numerous and eager inquiries about him personally, and with reference to any peculiarities of mind and manner, the visit ended in my being requested to bring him over to the Vale of Health.

That was a 'red-letter day' in the young poet's life, and one which will never fade with me while memory lasts. The character and expression of Keats' features would arrest even the casual passenger in the street; and now they were wrought to a tone of animation that I could not but watch with interest, knowing what was in store for him from the bland encouragement, and Spartan deference in attention, with fascinating conversational eloquence, that he was to encounter and receive. As we approached the Heath, there was the rising and accelerated step, with the gradual subsidence of all talk. The interview, which stretched into three 'morning calls,' was the prelude to many after-scenes and saunterings about Caen Wood and its neighbourhood; for Keats was suddenly made a familiar of the household, and was always welcomed.

In connexion with this, take Hunt's own account of the matter, as given about ten years after the event in his volume, *Lord Byron and his Contemporaries* :

To Mr Clarke I was indebted for my acquaintance with him. I shall never forget the impression made upon me by the exuberant specimens of genuine though young poetry that were laid before me, and the promise of which was seconded by the fine fervid countenance of the writer. We became intimate on the spot, and I found the young poet's heart as warm as his imagination. We read and walked together, and used to write verses of an evening on a given subject. No imaginative pleasure was left unnoticed by us, or unenjoyed, from the recollections of the bards and patriots of old to the luxury of a summer's rain at our window or the clicking of the coal in winter-time.

Some inquirers, in interpreting these accounts, have judged that the personal introduction did not take place in the spring or early summer at all, but only after Keats' return from his holiday at the end of September. I think it is quite clear, on the contrary, that Clarke had taken Keats up to Hampstead by the end of May or some time in June. Unmistakeable impressions of summer strolls there occur in his poetry of the next few months. The 'happy fields' where he had been rambling when he wrote the sonnet to Charles Wells on June the 29th were almost certainly the fields of Hampstead, and there is no reason to doubt Hunt's statement that the 'little hill' from which Keats drank the summer view and air, as told at the opening of his poem *I stood tiptoe* , was one of the swells of ground towards the Caen wood side of the Heath. At the same time it would seem that their intercourse in these first weeks did not extend beyond a few walks and talks, and that it was not until after Keats' return from his summer holiday that the acquaintance ripened into the close and delighted intimacy which we find subsisting by the autumn.

For part of August and September he had been away at Margate, apparently alone. A couple of rimed epistles addressed during this holiday to his brother George and to Cowden Clarke breathe just such a heightened joy of life and happiness of anticipation as would be natural in one who had lately felt the first glow of new and inspiriting personal sympathies. To George, besides the epistle, he addressed a pleasant sonnet on the wonders he has seen, the sea, the sunsets, and the world of poetic glories and mysteries vaguely evoked by them in his mind. The epistle to George is dated August: that to Cowden Clarke followed in September. In it he explains, in a well-conditioned and affectionate spirit of youthful modesty, why he has hitherto been shy of addressing any of his own attempts in verse to a friend so familiar with the work of the masters; and takes occasion, in a heartfelt passage of autobiography, to declare all he has owed to that friend's guidance and encouragement.

> Thus have I thought; and days on days have flown
> Slowly, or rapidly — unwilling still
> For you to try my dull, unlearned quill.
> Nor should I now, but that I've known you long;
> That you first taught me all the sweets of song:
> The grand, the sweet, the terse, the free, the fine;
> What swell'd with pathos, and what right divine:

> Spenserian vowels that elope with ease,
> And float along like birds o'er summer seas;
> Miltonian storms, and more, Miltonian tenderness,
> Michael in arms, and more, meek Eve's fair slenderness.
> Who read for me the sonnet swelling loudly
> Up to its climax and then dying proudly?
> Who found for me the grandeur of the ode,
> Growing, like Atlas, stronger from its load?
> Who let me taste that more than cordial dram,
> The sharp, the rapier-pointed epigram?
> Show'd me that epic was of all the king,
> Round, vast, and spanning all like Saturn's ring?
> You too upheld the veil from Clio's beauty,
> And pointed out the patriot's stern duty;
> The might of Alfred, and the shaft of Tell;
> The hand of Brutus, that so grandly fell
> Upon a tyrant's head. Ah! had I never seen,
> Or known your kindness, what might I have been?
> What my enjoyments in my youthful years,
> Bereft of all that now my life endears?
> And can I e'er these benefits forget?
> And can I e'er repay the friendly debt?
> No doubly no; — yet should these rhymings please,
> I shall roll on the grass with twofold ease:
> For I have long time been my fancy feeding
> With hopes that you would one day think the reading
> Of my rough verses not an hour misspent;
> Should it e'er be so, what a rich content!

Some of these lines are merely feeble and boyish, but some show a fast ripening, nay an almost fully ripened, critical feeling for the poetry of the past. The couplet about Spenser's vowels could scarcely be happier, and the next on Milton anticipates, though without at all approaching in craftsmanship, the 'Me rather all that bowery loneliness' of Tennyson's famous alcaic stanzas to the same effect.

Coming back from the seaside about the end of September to take up his quarters with his brothers in their lodging in the Poultry, Keats was soon to be indebted to Clarke for another and invaluable literary stimulus: I mean his first knowledge of Chapman's translation of Homer. This experience, as every reader knows, was instantly celebrated by him in a sonnet, classical now almost to triteness, which is his first high achievement, and one of the masterpieces of our language in this form. The question of its exact date has been much discussed: needlessly, seeing that Keats himself signed and dated it in full, when it was printed in the *Examiner* for the first of December following, 'Oct'r 1816, John Keats.' The doubts expressed have been due partly to the overlooking of this fact and partly to a mistake in Cowden Clarke's account of the matter written many years later. After quoting Keats' invitation of October 1815 to come and find him at his lodging in the Borough, Clarke goes on: —

This letter having no date but the week's day, and no postmark, preceded our first symposium; and a memorable night it was in my life's career. A beautiful copy of the folio edition of Chapman's translation of *Homer* had been lent me. It was the property of Mr. Alsager, the gentleman who for years had contributed no small share of celebrity to the great reputation of the *Times* newspaper by the masterly manner in which he conducted the money-market department of that journal....

Well then, we were put in possession of the *Homer* of Chapman, and to work we went, turning to some of the 'famousest' passages, as we had scrappily known them in Pope's version. There was, for instance, that perfect scene of the conversation on Troy wall of the old Senators with Helen, who is pointing out to them the several Greek Captains; with the Senator Antenor's vivid portrait of an orator in Ulysses, beginning at the 237th line of the third book: —

> But when the prudent Ithacus did to his counsels rise,
> He stood a little still, and fix'd upon the earth his eyes,
> His sceptre moving neither way, but held it formally,
> Like one that vainly doth affect. Of wrathful quality,
> And frantic (rashly judging), you would have said he was;
> But when out of his ample breast he gave his great voice pass,
> And words that flew about our ears like drifts of winter's snow,
> None thenceforth might contend with him, though naught admired for show.

The shield and helmet of Diomed, with the accompanying simile, in the opening of the third book; and the prodigious description of Neptune's passage to the Argive ships, in the thirteenth book: —

> The woods and all the great hills near trembled beneath the weight
> Of his immortal-moving feet. Three steps he only took,
> Before he far-off Ægas reach'd, but with the fourth, it shook
> With his dread entry.

One scene I could not fail to introduce to him — the shipwreck of Ulysses, in the fifth book of the *Odysseis*, and I had the reward of one of his delighted stares, upon reading the following lines: —

> Then forth he came, his both knees falt'ring, both
> His strong hands hanging down, and all with froth
> His cheeks and nostrils flowing, voice and breath
> Spent to all use, and down he sank to death.
> *The sea had soak'd his heart through*; all his veins
> His toils had rack'd t'a labouring woman's pains.
> Dead-weary was he.
>
> On an after-occasion I showed him the couplet, in Pope's translation, upon the same passage: —
>
> From mouth and nose the briny torrent ran,
> And *lost in lassitude lay all the man*. (!!!)

Chapman supplied us with many an after-treat; but it was in the teeming wonderment of this his first introduction, that, when I came down to breakfast the next morning, I found upon my table a letter with no other enclosure than his famous sonnet, *On First Looking into Chapman's Homer*. We had parted, as I have already said, at day-spring, yet he contrived that I should receive the poem from a distance of, may be, two miles by ten o'clock.

The whole of the above is a typical case of what I have called the telescoping action of memory. Recollections not of one, but of many, Homer readings are here compressed into a couple of paragraphs. They will have been readings carried on at intervals through the autumn and winter of 1816-17: an inspiring addition to the other intellectual gains and pleasures which fell to Keats' lot during those months. There is no reason to doubt the exactness of Clarke's account of the first night the friends spent together over Chapman and its result in the shape of the sonnet which lay on his table the next morning. His error is in remembering these circumstances as having happened when he and Keats first foregathered in London in the autumn of 1815, whereas Keats' positive evidence above quoted shows that they did not really happen until a year later, after his return from his summer holiday in 1816. Before printing the Chapman sonnet, Leigh Hunt had the satisfaction of hearing his own opinion of it and of some other manuscript poems of Keats confirmed by good judges. I quote his words for the sake of the excellent concluding phrase. 'Not long afterwards, having the pleasure of entertaining at dinner Mr Godwin, Mr Hazlitt, and Mr Basil Montague, I showed them the verses of my young friend, and they were pronounced to be as extraordinary as I thought them. One of them was that noble sonnet on first reading Chapman's *Homer*, which terminates with so energetic a calmness, and which completely announced the new poet taking possession.' But by this time Keats had become an established intimate in the Leigh Hunt household, and was constantly backwards and forwards between London and the Hampstead cottage.

This intimacy was really the opening of a new chapter both in his intellectual and social life. At first it was a source of unmixed encouragement and pleasure, but seeing that it carried with it in the sequel disadvantages and penalties which gravely affected Keats' career, it is necessary that we should fix clearly in our mind Hunt's previous history and the place held by him in the literary and political life of the time. He was Keats' senior by eleven years: the son of an eloquent and elegant, self-indulgent and thriftless fashionable preacher, sprung from a family long settled in Barbadoes, who having married a lady from Philadelphia had migrated to England and exercised his vocation in the northern suburbs of London. Brought up at Christ's Hospital about a dozen years later than Lamb and Coleridge, Leigh Hunt gained at sixteen a measure of precocious literary reputation with a volume of juvenile poems which gave evidence of great fluency and, for a boy, of wide and eager reading. A few years later he came into notice as a theatrical critic, being then a clerk in the War Office: an occupation which he abandoned at twenty-four (in 1808) in order to take part in the conduct of the *Examiner* newspaper, then just founded by his brother John Hunt. For nearly five years the brothers Hunt, as manager and editor of that journal, helped to fight the losing battle of liberalism, in those days of tense grapple with the Corsican ogre abroad and stiff reaction and repression at home, with a dexterous brisk audacity and an unflinching sincerity of conviction. So far they had escaped the usual penalty of such courage. Several prosecutions directed against them failed, but at last, late in 1812, they were caught tripping. To go as far as was safely possible in satire of the follies and vices of the Prince Regent was a tempting exercise to the reforming spirits of the time. Provoked by the grovelling excesses of some of the Prince's flatterers, the *Examiner* at last broke bounds and denounced him as 'a violator of his word, a libertine over head and ears in disgrace, a despiser of domestic ties, the companion of gamblers and demireps, a man who had just closed half a century without one single claim on the gratitude of his country or the respect of posterity.' This attack followed within a few weeks of another almost as stinging contributed anonymously by Charles Lamb. Under the circumstances the result of a prosecution could not be doubtful: and the two Hunts were condemned to a fine of £500 each and two years imprisonment in separate jails. Leigh Hunt bore himself in his captivity with cheerful fortitude, suffering severely in health but flagging little in spirits or industry. He decorated his apartment in Horsemonger Lane Gaol with a rose-trellis paper and a ceiling to imitate a summer sky, so that it looked, said Charles Lamb, like a room in a fairy tale, and spent money which he had not got in converting its backyard into a garden of shrubs and flowers.

Very early in life Hunt had been received into a family called Kent at the instance of an elder daughter who greatly admired him. Not long afterwards he engaged himself to her younger sister, then almost a child, and married her soon after the *Examiner* was started. She proved a prolific, thriftless woman and ill housekeeper, but through all the rubs and pinches of his after years he was ever an affectionate husband and father. His wife was allowed to be with him in prison, and there they received the visits of many friends old and new. Liberal statesmen, philosophers, and writers, including characters so divers as Bentham and Byron, Brougham and Hazlitt, James Mill and Miss Edgeworth, Tom Moore and Wilkie the painter, pressed to offer this victim of political persecution their sympathy and society. Charles Lamb and his sister were the most constant of all his visitors. Tom Moore, who both before and after the sentence on the brothers Hunt managed in his series of verse skits, *The Twopenny Post Bag*, to go on playing with impunity the game of Prince-Regent-baiting, — the light-hearted Tom Moore joined in deepest earnest the chorus of sympathy with the prisoners: —

> Yet go — for thoughts as blessed as the air
> Of Spring or Summer flowers await you there:
> Thoughts such as He, who feasts his courtly crew
> In rich conservatories, *never* knew;
> Pure self-esteem — the smiles that light within —
> The Zeal, whose circling charities begin
> With the few lov'd ones Heaven has plac'd it near,
> And spread, till all Mankind are in its sphere;
> The Pride, that suffers without vaunt or plea,
> And the fresh Spirit, that can warble free,
> Through prison-bars, its hymn to Liberty!

Among ardent young men who brought their tributes was Cowden Clarke with a basket of fruit and flowers from his father's garden; and this was followed up by a weekly offering in the same kind. 'Libertas, the loved Libertas,' was the name found for Hunt by such fond young spirits and adopted by Keats.

During his captivity Hunt was allowed the full use of his library, and his chief reading was in the fifty volumes of the *Parnaso Italiano*. As a result he acquired and retained for life a really wide and familiar knowledge of Italian poetry. He continued to edit the *Examiner* from prison and occupied himself moreover with three small volumes in verse. One of these was *The Descent of Liberty, A Mask*, celebrating the downfall of Napoleon in 1814, and embodying gracefully enough the Liberal's hope against hope that with that catastrophe there might return to Europe not only peace but freedom. (We have told already how Keats at Edmonton tried his boyish hand at a sonnet on the same occasion and to the same purpose.) Another of his prison tasks was the writing of his poem, *The Story of Rimini*; a third, the recasting and annotating of his *Feast of the Poets*, an airily presumptuous trifle in verse first printed two years before and modelled on the precedent of several rimed skits of the Caroline age such as Suckling's *Session of the Poets* and the Duke of Buckinghamshire's *Election of a Poet Laureate*. It represented Apollo as convoking the contemporary British poets, or pretenders to the poetical title, to a session, or rather to a supper. Some of those who present themselves the god rejects with scorn, others he cordially welcomes, others he admits with reserve and admonition. In revising this skit while he was in prison, Hunt modified some of his earlier verdicts, but in the main he let them stand. Moore and Campbell fare the best; Southey and Scott are accepted but with reproof; Coleridge and Wordsworth admonished (but Wordsworth in much more lenient terms than in the first edition) and dismissed. Hunt's notes are of still living interest as setting forth, at that pregnant moment of our literary history, the considered judgments of a kindly and accomplished critic on his contemporaries. Seen at a distance of a hundred years they look short-sighted enough, as almost all contemporary judgments must, and are coloured as a matter of course with party feeling, though not so grossly as was the habit of the hour. Since Coleridge, Southey and Wordsworth had been transformed, first by the Terror and then by the aggressions of Bonaparte, from ardent revolutionary idealists into vehement partisans of reaction both at home and abroad, the bitterness of the 'Lost Leader' feeling, common to all liberals, accounts for much of Hunt's disparagement of them; while besides sharing the prejudice of his party in general against Scott as a known high Tory and friend to kings, he had ignorantly and peevishly conceived a special grudge against that great generous and chivalrous spirit on account of his lenient handling of Charles II in his *Life of Dryden*. Hunt in his new notes fully acknowledged the genius, while he condemned the defection and also what he thought the poetical perversities, of Wordsworth; but his treatment of Scott, as little more than a mere money-making manufacturer of pinchbeck northern lays in a sham antique ballad dialect, is idly flippant and patronizing. The point is of importance in Keats' history, for hence, as we shall see in the sequel, came probably a part at least of the peculiar and as it might seem paradoxical rancour with which the genial Hunt, and Keats as his friend and supposed follower, were by-and-by to be persecuted in Blackwood.

When Hunt's ordeal was over in the first days of February 1815, he issued from it a butt for savage and vindictive obloquy to the reactionary half of the lettered world, but little less than a hero and martyr to the reforming half. He retained the private friendship of many of those who had sought him out from public sympathy. Tall, straight, slender, charmingly courteous and vivacious, with glossy black hair, bright jet-black eyes, full, relishing nether lip, and 'nose of taste,' Leigh Hunt was one of the most winning of companions, full of kindly smiles and jests, of reading, gaiety, and ideas, with an infinity of pleasant things to say of his own and a beautiful caressing voice to say them in, yet the most sympathetic and deferential of listeners. To the misfortune of himself and his friends, he had no notion of even attempting to balance income and expenditure, and was perfectly light-hearted in the matter of money obligations, which he shrank neither from receiving nor conferring, — only circumstances made him almost invariably a receiver. But men of sterner fibre and better able to order their affairs have often been much more ready than he was to sacrifice conviction to advantage, and his friends found more to admire in his smiling steadfastness under obloquy and persecution than to blame in his chronic incapacity to pay his way. Hardly anyone had warmer well-wishers or requited them, so far as the depth of his nature went, with truer loyalty and kindness. His industry as a writer was incessant, hardly less than that of Southey himself. The titles he gave to the several journals he conducted, *The Examiner*, *The Reflector*, *The Indicator*, define accurately enough his true vocation as a guide to the pleasures of literature. His manner in criticism has at its best an easy penetration, and flowing unobtrusive felicity, most remote from those faults to which De Quincey and even the illustrious Coleridge, with their more philosophic powers and method, were subject, the faults of roundaboutness and over-laboured profundity.

The weakness of Leigh Hunt's style is of an opposite kind. 'Matchless,' according to Lamb's well-known phrase, 'as a fireside companion,' it was his misfortune to carry too much of a fireside or parlour tone, and sometimes, it must be owned, a very second-rate parlour tone, into literature. He could not walk by the advice of Polonius, and in aiming at the familiar was apt, rarely in prose but sadly often in verse, to slip into an underbred strain of airy and genteel vulgarity, hard to reconcile with what we are told of his acceptable social qualities in real life. He was as enthusiastic a student of our sixteenth and seventeenth century literature as Coleridge or Lamb, and though he had more appreciation than they of the characteristic excellencies of what he always persists in calling the 'French school,' the school of polished artifice and convention which came in after Dryden and swore by the precepts of Boileau, he was not less bent on seeing it overthrown. In English poetry his predilection was for the older writers from Chaucer to Dryden, and above all others for Spenser: in Italian for Boiardo, Ariosto, Pulci and the later writers of the chivalrous-fanciful epic style. He insisted that such writers were much better models for English poets to follow than the French, and fought as hard as anyone for the return of English poetry from the urbane conventions of the eighteenth century to the paths of nature and of freedom. But he had his own conception of the manner in which this return should be effected. He did not admit that Wordsworth with his rustic simplicities and his recluse philosophy had solved the problem. 'It was his intention,' he wrote in prison, 'by the beginning of next year to bring out a piece of some length... in which he would attempt to reduce to practice his own ideas of what is natural in style, and of the various and legitimate harmony of the English heroic.' The result of this intention was the *Story of Rimini*, begun before his prosecution and published a year after his release, in February or March, 1816. 'With the endeavour,' so he repeated himself in the preface, 'to recur to a freer spirit of versification, I have joined one of still greater importance, — that of having a free and idiomatic cast of language.'

We shall have to consider Hunt's effort to revive the old freedom of the English heroic metre when we come to the study of Keats' first volume, written much under Hunt's influence. As to his success with his 'ideas of what is natural in style,' and his free and idiomatic — or as he elsewhere says 'unaffected, contemporaneous' — cast of language to supersede the styles alike of Pope and Wordsworth, let us take a sample of *Rimini* at its best and worst. Relating the gradual obsession of Paolo's thoughts by the charm of his sister-in-law, —

> And she became companion of his thought;
> Silence her gentleness before him brought,
> Society her sense, reading her books,
> Music her voice, every sweet thing her looks,
> Which sometimes seemed, when he sat fixed awhile,
> To steal beneath his eyes with upward smile;
> And did he stroll into some lonely place,
> Under the trees, upon the thick soft grass,
> How charming, would he think, to see her here!
> How heightened then, and perfect would appear
> The two divinest things this world has got,
> A lovely woman in a rural spot!

The first few lines are skilfully modulated, and in an ordinary domestic theme might be palatable enough; but what a couplet, good heavens! for the last. At the climax, Hunt's version of Dante is an example of milk-and-water in conditions where milk-and-water is sheer poison: —

> As thus they sat, and felt with leaps of heart
> Their colour change, they came upon the part
> Where fond Genevra, with her flame long nurst,
> Smiled upon Launcelot when he kissed her first: —
> That touch, at last, through every fibre slid;
> And Paulo turned, scarce knowing what he did,
> Only he felt he could no more dissemble,
> And kissed her, mouth to mouth, all in a tremble.

The taste, we see, which guided Hunt so well in appreciating the work of others could betray him terribly in original composition. The passages of light narrative in *Rimini* are often vivacious and pleasant enough, those of nature description genuinely if not profoundly felt, and written with an eye on the object: but they are the only tolerable things in the poem. Hunt's idea of a true poetical style was to avoid everything strained, stilted, and conventional, and to lighten the stress of his theme with familiar graces and pleasantries in the manner of his beloved Ariosto. But he did not realize that while any style, from that of the *Book of Job* to that of Wordsworth's *Idiot Boy*, may become poetical if only there is strength and intensity of feeling behind it, nothing but the finest social instinct and tradition can impart the tact for such light conversational graces as he attempted, and that to treat a theme of high tragic passion in the tone and vocabulary of a suburban tea-party is intolerable. Contemporaries, welcoming as a relief any change from the stale conventions and tarnished glitter of eighteenth century poetic rhythm and diction, and perhaps sated for the moment with the rush and thrill of new romantic and exotic sensation they had owed in recent years, first to Scott's metrical tales of the Border and the Highlands, then to Byron's of Greece and the Levant, — contemporaries found something fresh and homefelt in Leigh Hunt's *Rimini*, and sentimental ladies and gentlemen wept over the sorrows of the hero and heroine as though they had been their own. No less a person than Byron, to whom the poem was dedicated, writes to Moore: — 'Leigh Hunt's poem is a devilish good one — quaint here and there, but with the substratum of originality, and with poetry about it that will stand the test. I do not say this because he has inscribed it to me.' And to Leigh Hunt himself Byron reports praise of the poem from Sir Henry Englefield the dilettante, 'a mighty man in the blue circles, and a very clever man anywhere,' from Hookham Frere 'and all the arch *literati*,' and says how he had left his own sister and cousin 'in fixed and delighted perusal of it.' Byron's admiration cooled greatly in the sequel, with or even before the cooling of his regard for the author. But it is an instructive comment on standards of taste and their instability that cultivated readers should at any time have endured to hear the story of Paolo and Francesca — Dante's Paolo and Francesca — diluted through four cantos in a style like that of the above quotations. When Keats and Shelley, with their immeasurably finer poetical gifts and instincts, successively followed Leigh Hunt in the attempt to add a familiar ease of manner to variety of movement in this metre, Shelley, it need not be said, was in no danger of falling into Hunt's faults of triviality and under-breeding: but Keats was only too apt to be betrayed into them.

Hunt had spent the first months after his release in London, but by the end of 1815, some time before the publication of *Rimini*, had settled at Hampstead, where he soon made himself a sort of self-crowned laureate of the beauties of the place, and continued to vary his critical and political labours with gossiping complimentary verses to his friends in the form both of sonnet and epistle. The gravest of the epistles is one addressed in a spirit of good-hearted loyalty to Byron in that disastrous April when, after four years spent in the full blaze of popularity and fashion, he was leaving England under the storm of obloquy aroused by the scandals attending his separation from his wife. This is in Hunt's reformed heroic couplet: the rest are in a chirruping and gossiping anapaestic sing-song which is perhaps the writer's most congenial vein. Here is a summer picture of Hampstead from a letter to Tom Moore: —

> And yet how can I touch, and not linger a while,
> On the spot that has haunted my youth like a smile?
> On its fine breathing prospects, its clump-wooded glades,
> Dark pines, and white houses, and long-allied shades,
> With fields going down, where the bard lies and sees
> The hills up above him with roofs in the trees?
> Now too, while the season, — half summer, half spring, —
> Brown elms and green oaks — makes one loiter and sing;
> And the bee's weighty murmur comes by us at noon,
> And the cuckoo repeats his short indolent tune,
> And little white clouds lie about in the sun,
> And the wind's in the west, and hay-making begun? —

and here an autumn night-sketch, from a letter expressing surprise that the wet weather has not brought a visit from Charles Lamb, that inveterate lover of walking in the rain: —

> We hadn't much thunder and lightning, I own;
> But the rains might have led you to walk out of town;
> And what made us think your desertion still stranger,
> The roads were so bad, there was really no danger;
> At least where I live; for the nights were so groping,
> The rains made such wet, and the paths are so sloping,
> That few, unemboldened by youth or by drinking,
> Came down without lanthorns, — nor then without shrinking.
> And really, to see the bright spots come and go,
> As the path rose or fell, was a fanciful shew.
> Like fairies they seemed, pitching up from their nooks,
> And twinkling upon us their bright little looks.

Such were Leigh Hunt's antecedents, and such his literary performances and reputation, when Keats at the age of twenty-one became his intimate. So far as opinions and public sympathies were concerned, those of Keats had already, as we have seen, been largely formed in boyhood by familiarity, under the lead of Cowden Clarke, with Leigh Hunt's writings in the *Examiner*. Hunt was a confirmed Voltairian and sceptic as to revealed religion, and supplied its place with a private gospel of cheerfulness, or system of sentimental optimism, inspired partly by his own invincibly sunny temperament and partly by the hopeful doctrines of eighteenth-century philosophy in France. Keats shared the natural sympathy of generous youth for Hunt's liberal and kind-hearted view of things, and he had a mind naturally unapt for dogma: ready to entertain and appreciate any set of ideas according as his imagination recognized their beauty or power, he could never wed himself to any as representing ultimate truth. In matters of poetic feeling and fancy the two men had up to a certain point not a little in common. Like Hunt, Keats at this time was given to 'luxuriating' too effusively and fondly over the 'deliciousness' of whatever he liked in art, books, or nature. To the everyday pleasures of summer and the English fields Hunt brought in a lower degree the same alertness of perception and acuteness of enjoyment which in Keats were intense beyond parallel. In his lighter and shallower way Hunt also truly felt with Keats the perennial charm and vitality of classic fable, and was scholar enough to produce about this time some agreeable translations of the Sicilian pastorals, and some, less adequate, of Homer. But behind such pleasant faculties in Hunt nothing deeper or more potent lay hidden. Whereas with Keats, as time went on, delighted sensation became more and more surely and instantaneously transmuted and spiritualized into imaginative emotion; his words and cadences came every day from deeper sources within him and more fully charged with the power of far-reaching and symbolic suggestion. Hence, as this profound and passionate young genius grew, he could not but be aware of what was shallow in the talent of his senior and cloying and distasteful in his ever-voluble geniality. But for many months the harmony of their relations was complete.

The 'little cottage' in the Vale of Health must have been fairly overcrowded, one would suppose, with Hunt's fast-growing family of young children, but a bed was made up for Keats on a sofa, 'in a parlour no bigger than an old mansion's closet,' says Hunt, which nevertheless served him for a library and had prints after Stothard hung on the walls and casts of the heads of poets and heroes crowning the bookshelves. Here the young poet was made always welcome. The sonnet beginning 'Keen, fitful gusts are whispering here and there' records a night of October or November 1816, when, instead of staying to sleep, he preferred to walk home under the stars, his head full of talk about Petrarch and the youth of Milton, to the city lodgings where he lived with his brothers the life affectionately described in that other pleasant sonnet written on Tom's birthday, November 18, beginning 'Small, busy flames play through the fresh-laid coals.' The well-known fifty lines at the end of *Sleep and Poetry*, a poem on which Keats put forth the best of his half-fledged strength this winter, give the fullest and most engaging account of the pleasure and inspiration he drew from Hunt's hospitality: —

> The chimes
> Of friendly voices had just given place
> To as sweet a silence, when I 'gan retrace
> The pleasant day, upon a couch at ease.
> It was a poet's house who keeps the keys
> Of pleasure's temple. Round about were hung
> The glorious features of the bards who sung
> In other ages — cold and sacred busts
> Smiled at each other. Happy he who trusts
> To clear Futurity his darling fame!
> Then there were fauns and satyrs taking aim
> At swelling apples with a frisky leap
> And reaching fingers, 'mid a luscious heap

> Of vine-leaves. Then there rose to view a fane
> Of liny marble, and thereto a train
> Of nymphs approaching fairly o'er the sward:
> One, loveliest, holding her white hand toward
> The dazzling sunrise: two sisters sweet
> Bending their graceful figures till they meet
> Over the trippings of a little child:
> And some are hearing, eagerly, the wild
> Thrilling liquidity of dewy piping.
> See, in another picture, nymphs are wiping
> Cherishingly Diana's timorous limbs; —
> A fold of lawny mantle dabbling swims
> At the bath's edge, and keeps a gentle motion
> With the subsiding crystal: as when ocean
> Heaves calmly its broad swelling smoothness o'er
> Its rocky marge, and balances once more
> The patient weeds; that now unshent by foam
> Feel all about their undulating home...
> Petrarch, outstepping from the shady green,
> Starts at the sight of Laura; nor can wean
> His eyes from her sweet face. Most happy they!
> For over them was seen a free display
> Of outspread wings, and from between them shone
> The face of Poesy: from off her throne
> She overlook'd things that I scarce could tell.

It is easy from the above and from some of Keats' later work to guess at most of the prints which had caught his attention on Hunt's walls and in his portfolios and worked on his imagination afterwards: — Poussin's 'Empire of Flora' for certain: several, probably, of his various 'Bacchanals,' with the god and his leopard-drawn car, and groups of nymphs dancing with fauns or strewn upon the foreground to right or left: the same artist's 'Venus and Adonis': Stothard's 'Bathers' and 'Vintage,' his small print of Petrarch as a youth first meeting Laura and her friend; Raphael's 'Poetry' from the Vatican; and so forth. These things are not without importance in the study of Keats, for he was quicker and more apt than any of our other poets to draw inspiration from works of art, — prints, pictures, or marbles, — that came under his notice, and it is not for nothing that he alludes in this same poem to

> — the pleasant flow
> Of words on opening a portfolio.

A whole treatise might be written on matters which I shall have to mention briefly or not at all, — how such and such a descriptive phrase in Keats has been suggested by this or that figure in a picture; how pictures by or prints after old masters have been partly responsible for his vision alike of the Indian maiden and the blind Orion; what various originals, paintings or antiques or both, we can recognize as blending themselves into his evocation of the triumph of Bacchus or his creation of the Grecian Urn.

On December the 1st, 1816, Hunt, as has been said, did Keats the new service of printing the Chapman sonnet as a specimen of his work in an essay in the *Examiner* on 'Young Poets,' in which the names of Shelley and Reynolds were bracketed with his as poetical beginners of high promise. With reference to the custom mentioned by Hunt of Keats and himself sitting down of an evening to write verses on a given subject, Cowden Clarke pleasantly describes one such occasion on December 30 of the same year, when the chosen theme was *The Grasshopper and the Cricket*: — 'The event of the after scrutiny was one of many such occurrences which have riveted the memory of Leigh Hunt in my affectionate regard and admiration for unaffected generosity and perfectly unpretentious encouragement. His sincere look of pleasure at the first line: —

> The poetry of earth is never dead.
>
> "Such a prosperous opening!" he said; and when he came to the tenth and eleventh lines: —
>
> On a lone winter morning, when the frost
> Hath wrought a silence —

"Ah that's perfect! Bravo Keats!" And then he went on in a dilatation on the dumbness of Nature during the season's suspension and torpidity.' The affectionate enthusiasm of the younger and the older man (himself, be it remembered, little over thirty) for one another's company and verses sometimes took forms which to the mind of the younger and wiser of the two soon came to seem ridiculous. One day in early spring (1817) the whim seized them over their wine to crown themselves 'after the manner of the elder bards.' Keats crowned Hunt with a wreath of ivy, Hunt crowned Keats with a wreath of laurel, and each while sitting so adorned wrote a pair of sonnets expressive of his feelings. While they were in the act of composition, it seems, three lady callers came in — conceivably the three Misses Reynolds, of whom we shall hear more anon, Jane, afterwards Mrs Thomas Hood, Marianne, and their young sister Charlotte. When visitors were announced Hunt took off his wreath and suggested that Keats should do the same: he, however, 'in his enthusiastic way, declared he would not take off his crown for any human being,' and accordingly wore it as long as the visit lasted. Here are Hunt's pair of sonnets, which are about as good as any he ever wrote, and which he not long afterwards printed: —

> A crown of ivy! I submit my head

> > To the young hand that gives it, — young, 'tis true,
> > But with a right, for 'tis a poet's too.
> > How pleasant the leaves feel! and how they spread
> > With their broad angles, like a nodding shed
> > Over both eyes! and how complete and new,
> > As on my hand I lean, to feel them strew
> > My sense with freshness, — Fancy's rustling bed!
> > Tress-tossing girls, with smell of flowers and grapes
> > Come dancing by, and downward piping cheeks,
> > And up-thrown cymbals, and Silenus old
> > Lumpishly borne, and many trampling shapes, —
> > And lastly, with his bright eyes on her bent,
> > Bacchus, — whose bride has of his hand fast hold.
> > It is a lofty feeling, yet a kind,
> > Thus to be topped with leaves; — to have a sense
> > Of honour-shaded thought, — an influence
> > As from great Nature's fingers, and be twined
> > With her old, sacred, verdurous ivy-bind,
> > As though she hallowed with that sylvan fence
> > A head that bows to her benevolence,
> > Midst pomp of fancied trumpets in the wind.
> > 'Tis what's within us crowned. And kind and great
> > Are all the conquering wishes it inspires, —
> > Love of things lasting, love of the tall woods,
> > Love of love's self, and ardour for a state
> > Of natural good befitting such desires,
> > Towns without gain, and haunted solitudes.

Keats had the good sense not to print his efforts of the day; they are of slight account poetically, but have a real biographical interest: —

ON RECEIVING A LAUREL CROWN FROM LEIGH HUNT

> Minutes are flying swiftly, and as yet
> Nothing unearthly has enticed my brain
> Into a delphic labyrinth — I would fain
> Catch an immortal thought to pay the debt
> I owe to the kind poet who has set
> Upon my ambitious head a glorious gain.
> Two bending laurel sprigs — 'tis nearly pain
> To be conscious of such a coronet.
> Still time is fleeting, and no dream arises
> Gorgeous as I would have it — only I see
> A trampling down of what the world most prizes,
> Turbans and crowns and blank regality;
> And then I run into most wild surmises
> Of all the many glories that may be.

TO THE LADIES WHO SAW ME CROWNED

> What is there in the universal earth
> More lovely than a wreath from the bay tree?
> Haply a halo round the moon — a glee
> Circling from three sweet pair of lips in mirth;
> And haply you will say the dewy birth
> Of morning roses — ripplings tenderly
> Spread by the halcyon's breast upon the sea —
> But these comparisons are nothing worth.
> Then there is nothing in the world so fair?
> The silvery tears of April? Youth of May?
> Or June that breathes out life for butterflies?
> No, none of these can from my favourite bear
> Away the palm — yet shall it ever pay
> Due reverence to your most sovereign eyes.

Here we have expressed in the first sonnet the same mood as in some of the holiday rimes of the previous summer, the mood of ardent expectancy for an inspiration that declines (and no wonder considering the circumstances) to come. It was natural that the call for an impromptu should bring up phrases already lying formed or half formed in Keats' mind, and the sestet of this sonnet is interesting as containing in its first four lines the germs of the well-known passage at the beginning of the third book of *Endymion* , —

> There are who lord it o'er their fellow-men
> With most prevailing tinsel —

and in its fifth a repetition of the 'wild surmise' phrase of the Chapman sonnet. The second sonnet has a happy line or two in its list of delights, and its opening is noticeable as repeating the interrogative formula of the opening lines of *Sleep and Poetry* , Keats' chief venture in verse this winter.

Very soon after the date of this scene of intercoronation (the word is Hunt's, used on a different occasion) Keats became heartily ashamed of it, and expressed his penitence in a strain of ranting verse (his own name for compositions in this vein) under the form of a hymn or palinode to Apollo: —

> God of the golden bow,
> And of the golden lyre,
> And of the golden hair,
> And of the golden fire,
> Charioteer
> Of the patient year,
> Where — where slept thine ire,
> When like a blank idiot I put on thy wreath,
> Thy laurel, thy glory,
> The light of thy story,
> Or was I a worm — too low crawling, for death?
> O Delphic Apollo!

And so forth: the same half-amused spirit of penitence is expressed in a letter of a few weeks later to his brother George: and later still he came to look back, with a smile of manly self-derision, on those days as a time when he had been content to play the part of 'A pet-lamb in a sentimental farce.'

Chapter III

WINTER 1816-1817: HAYDON: OTHER NEW FRIENDSHIPS: THE DIE CAST FOR POETRY

So much for the relations of Keats with Hunt himself in these first six months of their intimacy. Next of the other intimacies which he formed with friends to whom Hunt introduced him. One of the first of these, and for a while the most stimulating and engrossing, was with the painter Haydon. This remarkable man, now just thirty, had lately been victorious in one of the two great objects of his ambition, and had achieved a temporary semblance of victory in the other. For the last eight years he had fought and laboured to win national recognition for the deserts of Lord Elgin in his great work of salvage — for such under the conditions of the time it was — in bringing away the remains of the Parthenon sculptures from Athens. By dint of sheer justice of conviction and power of fight, and then only when he had been reinforced in the campaign by foreigners of indisputable authority like the archaeologist Visconti and the sculptor Canova, he had succeeded in getting the pre-eminence of these marbles among all works of the sculptor's art acknowledged, and their acquisition for the nation secured, in the teeth of powerful and bitterly hostile cliques. His opponents included both the sentimentalists who took their cue from Byron's *Curse of Minerva* in shrieking at Elgin as a vandal, and the dilettanti who, blinded to the true Greek touch by familiarity with smoothed and pumiced Roman copies, had declared the Parthenon sculptures to be works of the age of Hadrian.

Haydon's victory over these antagonists is his chief title, and a title both sound and strong, to the regard of posterity. His other and lifelong, half insane endeavour was to persuade the world to take him at his own estimate, as the man chosen by Providence to add the crown of heroic painting to the other glories of his country. His high-flaming energy and industry, his eloquence, vehemence, and social gifts, the clamour of his indomitable self-assertion and of his ceaseless conflict with the academic powers, even his unabashed claims for pecuniary support on friends, patrons, and society at large, had won for him much convinced or half convinced attention and encouragement, both in the world of art and letters and in that of dilettantism and fashion. His first and second great pictures, 'Dentatus' and 'Macbeth,' had been dubiously received; his third, the 'Judgment of Solomon,' with acclamation. This had been finished after his victory in the matter of the Elgin marbles. He was now busy on one larger and more ambitious than all, 'Christ's Entry into Jerusalem,' in which it was his purpose to include among the crowd of lookers-on portraits of many famous men both historical and contemporary. While as usual sunk deep in debt, he was perfectly confident of glory. Vain confidence — for he was in truth a man whom nature had endowed, as if maliciously, with one part of the gifts of genius and not the other. Its energy and voluntary power he possessed completely, and no man has ever lived at a more genuinely exalted pitch of feeling and aspiration. 'Never,' wrote he about this time, 'have I had such irresistible and perpetual urgings of future greatness. I have been like a man with air-balloons under his armpits, and ether in his soul. While I was painting, walking, or thinking, beaming flashes of energy followed and impressed me.... They came over me, and shot across me, and shook me, till I lifted up my heart and thanked God.' But for all his sensations and conviction of power, the other half of genius, the half which resides not in energy and will, but in faculties which it is the business of energy and will to apply, was denied to Haydon. Its vision and originality, its gift of 'heavenly alchemy' for transmuting and new-creating the materials offered it by experience, its sovereign inability to see with any eyes or create to any pattern but its own, were not in him. Except for a stray note here and there, an occasional bold conception, a trick of colour or craftsmanship not too obviously caught from greater men, the pictures with which he exultingly laid siege to immortality belong, as posterity has justly felt, to the kingdom not of true great art but of imitative pictorial posturing and empty pictorial bombast.

As a draughtsman especially, Haydon's touch is surprisingly loose, empty, and inexpressive. Even in drawing from the Elgin marbles, as he did with passionate industry, covering reams, he fails almost wholly to render the qualities which he so ardently perceived, and loses every distinction and every subtlety of the original. Infinitely better is his account of them in words: for in truth Haydon's chief intellectual power was as an observer, and his best instrument the pen. Readers of his journals and correspondence know how vividly and tellingly he can relate an experience or touch off a character. In this gift of striking out a human portrait in words he stood second in his age, if second, to Hazlitt alone, and in our later literature there has been no one to beat him except Carlyle. But passion and pugnacity, vanity and the spirit of self-exaltation, at the same time as they intensify vision, are bound to discolour and distort it; and the reader must always bear in mind that Haydon's pen portraits of his contemporaries are apt to be not less untrustworthy than they are unforgettable. Moreover in this, the literary, form of expression also, where he aims higher, leaving description and trying to become imaginative and impressive, we find only the same self-satisfied void turgidity, and proof of spiritual hollowness disguised by temperamental fervour, as in his paintings.

But it was the gifts and faculties which Haydon possessed, and not those he lacked, it was the ardour and enthusiasm of his character, and not his essential commonness of gift and faculty, that impressed his associates as they impressed himself. Sturdy, loud-voiced, eloquent, high of colour, with a bald perpendicular forehead surmounting a set of squarely compressed, pugnacious features, — eyes, lips and jaw all prominent and aggressive together, — he was a dominating, and yet a welcome, presence in some of the choicest circles of his day. Wordsworth and Wordsworth's firm ally, the painter-baronet Sir George Beaumont, Hazlitt, Horace Smith, Charles Lamb, Coleridge, Walter Scott, Mary Mitford, were among his friends. Some of them, like Wordsworth, held by him always, while his imperious and importunate egotism wore out others after a while. He was justly proud of his industry and strength of purpose: proud also of his religious faith and piety, and in the habit of thanking his maker effusively in set terms for special acts of favour and protection, for this or that happy inspiration in a picture, for deliverance from 'pecuniary emergencies,' and the like. 'I always rose up from my knees,' he says strikingly in a letter to Keats, 'with a refreshed fury, an iron-clenched firmness, a crystal piety of feeling that sent me streaming on with a repulsive power against the troubles of life.' And he was prone to hold himself up as a model to his friends in both particulars, lecturing them loftily on faith and conduct while he was living without scruple on their bounty.

In October 1816, the first month of Keats' intimacy with Hunt, Haydon also made a short stay at Hampstead. He and Hunt were already acquainted, and Hunt had published in the *Examiner* the very able, cogent and pungent letter with which Haydon a few months before had clenched the Elgin marble controversy and practically brought it to an end. Hunt had congratulated Haydon in a sonnet on the occasion, closing with a gentle hint that, fine as such a victory was, he was himself devoted to a mission finer still, as

One of the spirits chosen by heaven to turn
The sunny side of things to human eyes.

Their intercourse was now warmly resumed, though never without latent risk of antagonism and discord. The following letter of Haydon to Wilkie, more just and temperate than usual, is good for filling in our picture both of Hunt and of Haydon himself, as well as for adding another to the number of bewildering contemporary estimates of *Rimini*.

27 October, 1816.

I have been at Hampstead this fortnight for my eyes, and shall return with my body much stronger for application. The greater part of my time has been spent in Leigh Hunt's society, who is certainly one of the most delightful companions. Full of poetry and art, and amiable humour, we argue always with full hearts on everything but religion and Buonaparte, and we have resolved never to talk of these, particularly as I have been recently examining Voltaire's opinions concerning Christianity, and turmoiling my head to ascertain fully my right to put him into my picture!

Though Leigh Hunt is not deep in knowledge, moral, metaphysical, or classical, yet he is intense in feeling, and has an intellect for ever on the alert. He is like one of those instruments on three legs, which, throw it how you will, always pitches on two, and has a spike sticking for ever up and ever ready for you. He 'sets' at a subject with a scent like a pointer. He is a remarkable man, and created a sensation by his independence, his courage, his disinterestedness in public matters, and by the truth, acuteness, and taste of his dramatic criticisms he raised the rank of newspapers, and gave by his example a literary feeling to the weekly ones more especially.

As a poet, I think him full of the genuine feeling. His third canto in *Rimini* is equal to anything in any language of that sweet sort. Perhaps in his wishing to avoid the monotony of the Pope school, he may have shot into the other extreme, and his invention of obscure words to express obscure feelings borders sometimes on affectation. But these are trifles compared with the beauty of the poem, the intense painting of the scenery, and the deep burning in of the passion which trembles in every line. Thus far as a critic, an editor, and a poet. As a man, I know none with such an affectionate heart, if never opposed in his opinions. He has defects of course: one of his great defects is getting inferior people about him to listen, too fond of shining at any expense in society, and a love of approbation from the darling sex bordering on weakness; though to women he is delightfully pleasant, yet they seem more to dandle him as a delicate plant. I don't know if they do not put a confidence in him which to me would be mortifying.

He is a man of sensibility tinged with morbidity, and of such sensitive organisation of body that the plant is not more alive to touch than he. I remember once, walking in a field, we came to a muddy place concealed by grass. The moment Hunt touched it, he shrank back, saying, 'It's muddy!' as if he meaned that it was full of adders.... He is a composition, as we all are, of defects and delightful qualities, indolently averse to worldly exertion, because it harasses the musings of his fancy, existing only by the common duties of life, yet ignorant of them, and often suffering from their neglect.

A few days later, on October 31, we find Keats writing to Cowden Clarke of his pleasure at 'the thought of seeing so soon this glorious Haydon and all his creations.' The introduction was arranged to take place at Leigh Hunt's cottage, where they met for dinner. Haydon, the sublime egoist, could be rapturously sympathetic and genuinely kind to those who took him at his own valuation, and there was much to attract the spirits of eager youth about him as a leader. Keats and he were mutually delighted at first sight: each struck fire from the other, and they quickly became close friends and comrades. After an evening of high talk at the beginning of their acquaintance, on the 19th of November, 1816, the young poet wrote to Haydon as follows, joining his name with those of Wordsworth and Leigh Hunt: —

Last evening wrought me up, and I cannot forbear sending you the following: —

> Great spirits now on earth are sojourning:
> He of the cloud, the cataract, the lake,
> Who on Helvellyn's summit, wide awake,
> Catches his freshness from Archangel's wing:
> He of the rose, the violet, the spring,
> The social smile, the chain for Freedom's sake,
> And lo! whose steadfastness would never take
> A meaner sound than Raphael's whispering.
> And other spirits there are standing apart
> Upon the forehead of the age to come;
> These, these will give the world another heart,
> And other pulses. Hear ye not the hum
> Of mighty workings in some distant mart?
> Listen awhile, ye nations, and be dumb.

Haydon was at no time of his life unused to compliments of this kind. About the same time as Keats another young member of Hunt's circle, John Hamilton Reynolds, also wrote him a sonnet of eager sympathy and admiration; and the three addressed to him some years later by Wordsworth are well known. In his reply to Keats he proposed to hand on the above piece to Wordsworth — a proposal which 'puts me,' answers Keats, 'out of breath — you know with what reverence I would send my well-wishes to him.' Haydon suggested moreover the needless, and as it seems to me regrettable, mutilation of the sonnet by leaving out the words after 'workings' in the last line but one. The poet, however, accepted the suggestion, and his editors have respected his decision.

Some time after the turn of the year we find Keats presented with a copy of Goldsmith's *Greek History* 'from his ardent friend, B. R. Haydon.' All the winter and early spring the two met frequently, sometimes at Haydon's studio in Great Marlborough Street, sometimes in the rooms of the Keats brothers in the Poultry or in those of their common acquaintance, and discussed with passionate eagerness most things in heaven and earth, and especially poetry and painting. 'I have enjoyed Shakespeare,' declares Haydon, 'with John Keats more than with any other human being.' Both he and Keats' other painter friend, Joseph Severn, have testified that Keats had a fine natural sense for the excellencies of painting and sculpture. Both loved to take him to the British Museum and expatiate to him on the glories of the antique; and it would seem that through Haydon he must have had access also to the collection of one at least of the great dilettanti noblemen of the day. After a first visit to the newly acquired Parthenon marbles with Haydon at the beginning of March 1817, Keats tried to embody his impressions in a couple of sonnets, which Hunt promptly printed in the *Examiner*. It is characteristic of his unfailing sincerity with his art and with himself that he allows himself to break into no stock raptures, but strives faithfully to get into words the confused sensations of spiritual infirmity and awe that have overpowered him: —

> My spirit is too weak — mortality
> Weighs heavily on me like unwilling sleep.
> And each imagin'd pinnacle and steep
> Of godlike hardship, tells me I must die
> Like a sick Eagle looking at the sky.
> Yet 'tis a gentle luxury to weep
> That I have not the cloudy winds to keep,
> Fresh for the opening of the morning's eye.
> Such dim-conceived glories of the brain
> Bring round the heart an undescribable feud;
> So do these wonders a most dizzy pain,
> That mingles Grecian grandeur with the rude
> Wasting of old Time — with a billowy main —
> A sun — a shadow of a magnitude.

He sends this with a covering sonnet to Haydon asking pardon for its immaturity and justly praising the part played by Haydon in forcing the acceptance of the marbles upon the nation: —

> Haydon! forgive me that I cannot speak
> Definitely on these mighty things;
> Forgive me that I have not Eagle's wings —
> That what I want I know not where to seek;
> And think that I would not be over meek
> In rolling out upfollow'd thunderings,
> Even to the steep of Heliconian springs,
> Were I of ample strength for such a freak —
> Think too, that all those numbers should be thine;

> Whose else? In this who touch thy vesture's hem?
> For when men star'd at what was most divine
> With browless idiotism — o'erwise phlegm —
> Thou hadst beheld the Hesperian shine
> Of their star in the East, and gone to worship them.

Haydon's acknowledgment is of course enthusiastic, but betrays his unfortunate gift for fustian in the following precious expansion of Keats' image of the sick eagle: —

Many thanks, my dear fellow, for your two noble sonnets. I know not a finer image than the comparison of a poet unable to express his high feelings to a sick eagle looking at the sky, where he must have remembered his former towerings amid the blaze of dazzling sunbeams, in the pure expanse of glittering clouds; now and then passing angels, on heavenly errands, lying at the will of the wind with moveless wings, or pitching downward with a fiery rush, eager and intent on objects of their seeking....

In Haydon's journal about the same date there is an entry which reads with ironical pathos in the light of after events: — 'Keats is a man after my own heart. He sympathises with me, and comprehends me. We saw through each other, and I hope are friends for ever. I only know that, if I sell my picture, Keats shall never want till another is done, that he may have leisure for his effusions: in short he shall never want all his life.' To Keats himself, more hyperbolically still, and in terms still more suited to draw the pitying smile of the ironic gods, Haydon writes a little later: —

Consider this letter a sacred secret. — Often have I sat by my fire after a day's effort, as the dusk approached and a gauzy veil seemed dimming all things — and mused on what I had done, and with a burning glow on what I would do till filled with fury I have seen the faces of the mighty dead crowd into my room, and I have sunk down and prayed the great Spirit that I might be worthy to accompany these immortal beings in their immortal glories, and then I have seen each smile as it passes over me, and each shake his hand in awful encouragement. My dear Keats, the Friends who surrounded me were sensible to what talent I had, — but no one reflected my enthusiasm with that burning ripeness of soul, my heart yearned for sympathy, — believe me from my soul, in you I have found one, — you add fire, when I am exhausted, and excite fury afresh — I offer my heart and intellect and experience — at first I feared your ardor might lead you to disregard the accumulated wisdom of ages in moral points — but the feelings put forth lately have delighted my soul. God bless you! Let our hearts be buried on each other.

Familiar visitors at this time of Haydon in the Marlborough Street studio and of Hunt in the Hampstead cottage were two men of finer gift than either, William Hazlitt and Charles Lamb. With both of these seniors (Lamb was forty-one and Hazlitt thirty-eight) Keats now became acquainted without becoming intimate. Unluckily neither of them has left any but the slightest personal impression of the young poet, whose modesty probably kept him somewhat in the background when they were by. Haydon used to complain that it was only after Keats' death that he could get Hazlitt to acknowledge his genius; but Lamb, as we shall see, with his unerring critical touch, paid to Keats' best work while he was still living a tribute as splendid as it was just. Keats on his part, after the publication of Hazlitt's lectures on the characters of Shakespeare in 1817, reckoned his 'depth of taste' one of the things most to rejoice at in his age, and was a diligent attendant at his next course on the English poets. But he never frequented, presumably for lack of invitation, those Wednesday and Thursday evening parties at the Lambs of which Talfourd and B. W. Procter have left us such vivid pictures; and when he met some of the same company at the Novello's, the friends of his friend Cowden Clarke, he enjoyed it, as will appear later, less than one would have hoped. He has left no personal impression of Hazlitt, and of Lamb only the slightest and most casual. Fortunately we know them both so well from other sources that we can almost see and hear them: Hazlitt with his unkempt black hair and restless grey eyes, lean, slouching, splenetic, an Ishmaelite full of mistrust and suspicion, his habitual action of the hand within the waistcoat apt in his scowling moments to suggest a hidden dagger; but capable withal, in company where he felt secure, of throwing into his talk much the same fine mixture as distinguishes his writing of impetuous fullness and variety with incisive point and critical lucidity: Lamb noticeable in contrast by his neat, sombrely clad small figure on its spindle legs and his handsome romantic head; by his hurried, stammering utterance and too often, alas! his vinous flush and step almost as titubant as his tongue; but most of all by that airy genius of insight and caprice, of deep tenderness and freakish wisdom, quick to break from him in sudden, illuminating phrases at any moment and in any manner save the expected.

Yet another acquaintance brought about by Hunt in these days was that between Keats and Shelley, who was Keats' senior by only three years and with whom Hunt himself was now first becoming intimate. When Hunt was sentenced for sedition four years earlier, Shelley, then barely twenty, had been eager to befriend him and had sent him an offer of money help; which for once, not being then in immediate need, Hunt had honourably declined. Since then they had held only slight communication; but when Hunt included Shelley on the strength of his poem *Alastor*, among the young poets praised in his *Examiner* essay (December 1, 1816), a glowing correspondence immediately followed, and a few days later Shelley came up from Bath to stay at the Hampstead cottage. The result of a week's visit was an immediate intimacy and enthusiastic mutual regard, with a prompt determination on Shelley's part to rescue Hunt from the slough of debt (something like £1400) into which during and since his imprisonment he had cheerfully muddled himself.

It was the eve of the most harrowing crisis in Shelley's life, when his principle of love a law to itself entailed in action so dire a consequence, and his obedience to his own morality brought him into such harsh collision with the world's. First came the news of the suicide of his deserted wife Harriet (December 14) and three months later the sentence of Lord Eldon which deprived him of the custody of his and Harriet's children. On the day of the first tragic news he writes to Mary Godwin, whom he had left at Bath, 'Leigh Hunt has been with me all day, and his delicate and tender attentions to me, his kind speeches of you, have sustained me against the weight of horror of this event.' In the interval between the shock of Harriet's death and that of the judgment sequestering his children Shelley was a frequent guest in the Vale of Health, sometimes alone and sometimes with Mary, now legally his wife. Neither in these first days nor later could Hunt persuade his old intimates Hazlitt and Lamb to take kindly to his new friend Shelley either as man or poet. Lamb, who seems only to have seen him once, said after his death, 'his voice was the most obnoxious squeak I ever was tormented with'; of his poetry, that it was 'thin sown with profit or delight'; and of his 'theories and nostrums,' that 'they are oracular enough, but I either comprehend 'em not, or there is miching malice and mischief in 'em.' Hazlitt, opening the most studied of his several attacks on Shelley's poetry and doctrine, gives one of his vivid portraits, saying 'he has a fire in his eye, a fever in his blood, a maggot in his brain, a hectic flutter in his speech.... He is sanguine-complexioned, and shrill-voiced.... His bending, flexible form appears to take no strong hold of things, does not grapple with the world about him, but flows from it like a river.' Still less was a good understanding possible between Shelley and Haydon, who met him more than once in these early days at the Vale of Health. He tells how, on the evening of their first meeting, Shelley, looking hectically frail and girlish, opened the conversation at dinner with the words, 'as to that detestable religion, the Christian,' — and how he, Haydon, a man at all times stoutly and vociferously orthodox, waited till the meal was over and then, 'like a stag at bay and resolved to gore without mercy,' struck his hardest on behalf of the established faith, while Hunt in his airily complacent way kept skirmishing in on Shelley's side, until the contention grew hot and stormy. The heat and noise, Haydon owns, were chiefly on his side, and we might guess as much without his admission, for we have abundant evidence of the unfailing courtesy and sweetness of manner with which Shelley would in that high-pitched feminine voice of his advance the most staggering propositions and patiently encounter the arguments of his adversaries.

Such contentions, victorious as he always held himself to be in them, annoyed Haydon. The queer blend, in the atmosphere of the Hampstead cottage, of eager kindness and hospitality and a graceful, voluble enthusiasm for the 'luxuries' of poetry, art, and nature with slatternly housekeeping and a spirit of fervent or flippant anti-Christianity, became distasteful to him, and he afterwards dated from these days his gradual estrangement from Hunt and his circle. At the same time he began to try and draw away Keats from Hunt's influence.

Keats, we are told, though much inclining in these days towards the Voltairian views of his host, would take little part in such debates as that above narrated, and once even supported another young member of the circle, Joseph Severn, in a defence of Christianity against Hunt and Shelley. To Shelley himself, his senior by three years, his relation was from the first and remained to the end one of friendly civility and little more. He did not take to Shelley as kindly as Shelley did to him, says Hunt, and adds the comment: 'Keats, being a little too sensitive on the score of his origin, felt inclined to see in every man of birth a sort of natural enemy.' 'He was haughty, and had a fierce hatred of rank,' says Haydon in his unqualified way. Where his pride had not been aroused by anticipation, Keats, as we have seen, was eagerly openhearted to new friendships, and it may well be that the reserve he maintained towards Shelley was assumed at first by way of defence against the possibility of social patronage on the other's part. But he must soon have perceived that from Shelley, a gentleman of gentlemen, such an attitude was the last thing to be apprehended, and the cause of his standing off was much more likely his knowledge that nearly all Shelley's literary friends were his pensioners, — from Godwin, the greediest, to Leigh Hunt, the lightest-hearted, — and a fear that he too might be supposed to expect a similar bounty. It would seem that in his spirit of independence he gave Shelley the impression of being much better off than he was, — or possibly instances of his only too ready generosity in lending from his modest means to his intimates when they were hard pressed may have come to Shelley's knowledge: at all events a few months later we find Shelley casting about for persons able to help him in helping Hunt, and writing under a false impression, 'Keats certainly can.'

These two young poets, equally and conjointly beloved by posterity, were in truth at many points the most opposite-natured of men. Pride and sensitiveness apart, we can imagine that a full understanding was not easy between them. Keats, with the rich elements of earthly clay in his composition, his lively vein of everyday commonsense and humour, his keen, tolerant delight and interest in the aspects and activities of nature and human nature as he found them, may well have been as much repelled as attracted by Shelley, Shelley the 'Elfin knight,' the spirit all air and fire, with his passionate repudiation of the world's ways and the world's law, his passionate absorption in his vision of a happier scheme of things, a vision engendered in humanitarian dreams from his readings of Rousseau and Godwin and Plato, — or was it rather one brought with him from some ante-natal sojourn among the radiances and serenities of the sunset clouds? Leigh Hunt's way of putting it is this: — 'Keats, notwithstanding his unbounded sympathies with ordinary flesh and blood, and even the transcendental cosmopolitics of *Hyperion*, was so far inferior in universality to his great acquaintance, that he could not accompany him in his daedal rounds with nature, and his Archimedean endeavours to move the globe with his own hands.' Of the incidents and results of their intercourse at Hampstead we know little more than that Shelley, wisely enough in the light of his own headlong early experiments, tried to dissuade Keats from premature publication; and that Keats on his part declined, 'in order that he might have his own unfettered scope,' a cordial invitation from Shelley to come and stay with him at Great Marlow. Keats, though he must have known that he could learn much from Shelley's trained scholarship and fine literary sense, was doubtless right in feeling that whatever power of poetry might be in him must work its own way to maturity in freedom and not in leading-strings. To these scanty facts Shelley's cousin Medwin adds the statement that the two agreed to write in friendly rivalry the long poems each was severally meditating for his summer's work, Shelley *Laon and Cythna*, afterwards called *The Revolt of Islam*, and Keats *Endymion*. This may very well have been the case, but Medwin was a man so lax of memory, tongue, and pen that his evidence, unconfirmed, counts for little. Of the influence possibly exercised on

Keats by Shelley's first important poem, *Alastor*, or by his *Hymn to Intellectual Beauty* printed in the *Examiner* during the January of their intercourse at Hunt's, it will be time to speak later on.

A much closer intimacy sprang up between Keats and the other young poetic aspirant whom Hunt in his December essay in the *Examiner* had bracketed with him and Shelley. This was John Hamilton Reynolds, of whom we have as yet heard only the name. He was a handsome, witty, enthusiastic youth a year younger than Keats, having been born at Shrewsbury in September 1796. Part of his boyhood was spent in Devonshire near Sidmouth, a countryside to which he remained always deeply attached; but he was still quite young when his father came and settled in London as mathematical master and head writing master at Christ's Hospital. The elder Reynolds and his wife were people of literary leanings and literary acquaintance, and seem to have been characters in their way: both Charles Lamb and Leigh Hunt were frequenters of their house in Little Britain, and Mrs Reynolds is reported as holding her own well among the talkers at Lamb's evenings. Their son John was educated at St Paul's school and showed talent and inclinations which drew him precociously into the literary movement of the time. At eighteen he wrote an Eastern tale in verse in the Byronic manner, *Safie*, of which Byron acknowledged the presentation copy in a kind and careful letter several pages long. Two years later, just about the time of his first introduction to Keats at Leigh Hunt's, the youngster had the honour of receiving a similar attention from Wordsworth in reply to a presentation of another poem, *The Naiad* (November 1816). Neither of these two youthful volumes, nor yet a third, *The Eden of Imagination*, showed much more than a quick susceptibility to nature and romance, and a gift of falling in readily and gracefully now with one and now with another of the poetic fashions of the hour. Byron, Scott, Wordsworth, and Leigh Hunt were alternately his models.

The same gift of adaptiveness which Reynolds showed in serious work made him when he chose a deft, sometimes even a masterly, parodist in the humourous vein, and his work done in this vein a few years later in collaboration with Thomas Hood holds its own well beside that of his associate. Partly owing to the persuasions of the lady to whom he was engaged, Reynolds early gave up the hope of a literary career and went into business as a solicitor. In 1818 he inscribed a farewell sonnet to the Muses in a copy of Shakespeare which he gave to Keats, and in 1821 he writes again

As time increases
I give up drawling verse for drawing leases.

In point of fact he continued to write occasionally for some years, and in the end failed somewhat tragically to prosper in the profession of law. During these early years he was not only one of the warmest friends Keats had but one of the wisest, to whom Keats could open his innermost mind with the certainty of being understood, and who once at least saved him from a serious mistake. A sonnet written by him within three months of their first meeting proves with what warmth of affection as well as with what generosity of admiration the one young aspirant from the first regarded the other. Keats one day, calling on Cowden Clarke and finding him asleep over Chaucer, passed the time by writing on the blank space at the end of *The Floure and the Lefe*, a poem with which he was already familiar, the sonnet beginning 'This pleasant tale is like a little copse.' Reynolds's comment after reading it is as follows: —

> Thy thoughts, dear Keats, are like fresh-gathered leaves,
> Or white flowers pluck'd from some sweet lily bed;
> They set the heart a-breathing, and they shed
> The glow of meadows, mornings, and spring eyes,
> O'er the excited soul. — Thy genius weaves
> Songs that shall make the age be nature-led,
> And win that coronal for thy young head
> Which time's strange hand of freshness ne'er bereaves.
> Go on! and keep thee to thine own green way,
> Singing in that same key which Chaucer sung;

> Be thou companion of the summer day,
> Roaming the fields and older woods among: —
> So shall thy muse be ever in her May
> And thy luxuriant spirit ever young.

Reynolds had two sisters, Marianne and Jane, older than himself, and a third, Charlotte, several years younger. With the elder two Keats was soon on terms of almost brotherly intimacy and affection, seeing them often at the family home in Little Britain, exchanging lively letters with them in absence, and contributing to Jane's album sets of verses some of which have only through this means been preserved. A little later the piano-playing of the youngest sister, Charlotte, was often a source of great pleasure to him.

Outside his own family Reynolds had an inseparable friend with whom Keats also became quickly intimate: this was James Rice, a young solicitor of literary tastes and infinite jest, chronically ailing or worse in health, but always, in Keats' words, 'coming on his legs again like a cat'; ever cheerful and willing in spite of his sufferings, and indefatigable in good offices to those about him: 'dear noble generous James Rice,' records Dilke, — 'the best, and in his quaint way one of the wittiest and wisest men I ever knew.' It was through Rice that there presently came to Reynolds that uncongenial business opening which in worldly wisdom he held himself bound to accept. Besides Reynolds, another and more insignificant young versifying member, or satellite, of Hunt's set when Keats first joined it was one Cornelius Webb, remembered now, if remembered at all, by the derisory quotation in *Blackwood's Magazine* of his rimes on Byron and Keats, as well as by a disparaging allusion in one of Keats' own later letters. He disappeared early from the circle, but not before he had caught enough of its spirit to write sonnets and poetical addresses which might almost be taken for the work of Hunt, or even for that of Keats himself in his weak moments; and for some years afterwards served as press-reader in the printing-office of Messrs. Clowes, being charged especially with the revision of the *Quarterly* proofs.

To turn to other close associates of Keats during the same period, known to him not through Hunt but through his brothers, — a word may suffice for Charles Wells, to whom we find him addressing in the summer of 1816 a sonnet of thanks for a gift of roses. Wells had been a schoolmate of Tom Keats and R.H. Horne, and is described as in those days a small, red-headed, snub-nosed, blue-eyed youth of irrepressible animal spirits. Now or somewhat later he formed an intimacy, never afterwards broken, with Hazlitt. Keats' own regard for Wells was short-lived, being changed a year or so later into fierce indignation when Wells played off a heartless practical joke upon the consumptive Tom in the shape of a batch of pretended love-letters from an imaginary 'Amena.' It was after Keats' death that Wells earned a place of his own in literature with the poetic drama *Joseph and his Brethren*, dead-born in its first anonymous form and re-animated after many years, but still during the lifetime of its author, through the enthusiasm which its qualities of intellect and passion inspired in Rossetti and Swinburne.

Of far different importance were two other acquaintanceships, which Keats owed to his brother George and which in the same months were ripening into affection, one of them into an affection priceless in the sequel. The first was with a young solicitor called William Haslam (it is odd how high a proportion of Keats' intimates were of this profession). Of him no personal picture has come down to us, but in the coming days we find him, of all the set, the most prompt and serviceable on occasions of practical need or urgency: 'our oak friend' he is called in one such crisis by Joseph Severn. It was as the friend of Haslam, and through Haslam of his brother George, that Keats first knew Joseph Severn, whose name is now inseparable from his own. He was two years Keats' senior, the son of a music-master sprung from an old Gloucestershire stock and having a good connexion in the northern suburbs of London. The elder Severn seems to have been much of a domestic tyrant, and in all things headstrong and hot-headed, but blessed with an admirable wife whom he appreciated and who contrived to make the household run endurably if not comfortably. Joseph, the son, showing a precocious talent for drawing, was apprenticed to a stipple engraver, but the perpetual task of 'stabbing copper' irked him too sorely: his ambition was to be a painter, and against the angry opposition of his father he contrived to attend the Royal Academy schools, picking up meanwhile for himself what education in letters he could. He had a hereditary talent for music, an untrained love for books and poetry, and doubtless some touch already of that engaging social charm which Ruskin noted in him when they first met five and twenty years later in Rome. He was beginning to get a little practice as a miniature painter and to make private attempts in history-painting when he met the brilliant young poet-student of Guy's, with whom he was shy and timid at first, as with a sort of superior being. But before long he became used to drinking in with delight all that Keats, in communicative hours, was moved to pour out from the play of his imagination or the stores — infinite as to the innocent Severn they appeared — of his reading in poetry and history. What especially, he recorded in after life, used to enrapture him was Keats' talk on the meaning and beauty of the Greek polytheism as a 'religion of joy.' On his own part he was proud to act as cicerone to Keats in the British Museum or the British Institution (the National Gallery as yet was not), and deferentially to point out to him the glories of the antique or of Titian and Claude and Poussin.

Thus our obscurely-born and half-schooled young medical student, the orphan son of a Finsbury stable-keeper, found himself at twenty-one, before the end of his second winter in London, fairly launched in a world of art, letters, and liberal aspirations and living in familiar intimacy with some, and friendly acquaintance with others, of the most gifted spirits of his time. The power and charm of genius already shone from him, and impressed alike his older and his younger companions. Portraits of him verbal and other exist in abundance. A small, compact, well-turned figure, broad-chested for its height, which was barely an inch over five feet; a shapely head set off by thickly clustering gold-brown hair and carried with an eager upward and forward thrust from the shoulders; the features powerful, finished, and mobile, with an expression at once bold and sensitive; the forehead sloping and not high, but broad and strong: the brows well arched above hazel-brown, liquid flashing eyes, 'like the eyes of a wild gypsy maid in colour, set in the face of a young god,' Severn calls them. To the same effect Haydon, — 'an eye that had an inward look, perfectly divine, like a Delphian priestess who saw visions': and again Leigh Hunt, — 'the eyes mellow and glowing, large, dark, and sensitive. At the recital of a noble action or a beautiful thought, they would suffuse with tears and his mouth tremble.' In like manner George Keats, — 'John's eyes moistened and his lip quivered at the relation of any tale of generosity or benevolence or noble daring, or at sights of loveliness or distress.' And once more Haydon, — 'Keats was the only man I ever met who seemed and looked conscious of a high calling, except Wordsworth.... He was in his glory in the fields. The humming of a bee, the sight of a flower, the glitter of the sun, seemed to make his nature tremble, then his eyes flashed, his cheek glowed and his mouth quivered.' 'Nothing seemed to escape him,' — I now quote paragraphs compiled by the late Mr William Sharp from many jotted reminiscences of Severn's, —

Nothing seemed to escape him, the song of a bird and the undernote of response from covert or hedge, the rustle of some animal, the changing of the green and brown lights and furtive shadows, the motions of the wind — just how it took certain tall flowers and plants — and the wayfaring of the clouds: even the features and gestures of passing tramps, the colour of one woman's hair, the smile on one child's face, the furtive animalism below the deceptive humanity in many of the vagrants, even the hats, clothes, shoes, wherever these conveyed the remotest hint as to the real self of the wearer. Withal, even when in a mood of joyous observance, with flow of happy spirits, he would suddenly become taciturn, not because he was tired, not even because his mind was suddenly wrought to some bewitching vision, but from a profound disquiet which he could not or would not explain.

Certain things affected him extremely, particularly when 'a wave was billowing through a tree,' as he described the uplifting surge of air among swaying masses of chestnut or oak foliage, or when, afar off, he heard the wind coming across woodlands. 'The tide! the tide!' he would cry delightedly, and spring on to some stile, or upon the low bough of a wayside tree, and watch the passage of the wind upon the meadow grasses or young corn, not stirring till the flow of air was all around him, while an expression of rapture made his eyes gleam and his face glow till he 'would look sometimes like a wild fawn waiting for some cry from the forest depths,' or like 'a young eagle staring with proud joy before taking flight.'...

Though small of stature, not more than three-quarters of an inch over five feet, he seemed taller, partly from the perfect symmetry of his frame, partly from his erect attitude and a characteristic backward poise (sometimes a toss) of the head, and, perhaps more than anything else, from a peculiarly dauntless expression, such as may be seen on the face of some seamen....

The only time he appeared as small of stature was when he was reading, or when he was walking rapt in some deep reverie; when the chest fell in, the head bent forward as though weightily overburdened, and the eyes seemed almost to throw a light before his face....

The only thing that would bring Keats out of one of his fits of seeming gloomful reverie — the only thing, during those country-rambles, that would bring the poet 'to himself again' was the motion 'of the inland sea' he loved so well, particularly the violent passage of wind across a great field of barley. From fields of oats or barley it was almost impossible to allure him; he would stand, leaning forward, listening intently, watching with a bright serene look in his eyes and sometimes with a slight smile, the tumultuous passage of the wind above the grain. The sea, or thought-compelling images of the sea, always seemed to restore him to a happy calm.

In regard to Keats' social qualities, he is said, and owns himself, to have been not always quite well conditioned or at his ease in the presence of women, but in that of men all accounts agree that he was pleasantness itself: quiet and abstracted or brilliant and voluble by turns, according to his mood and company, but thoroughly amiable and unaffected. His voice was rich and low, and when he joined in discussion, it was usually with an eager but gentle animation, while his occasional bursts of fierce indignation at wrong or meanness bore no undue air of assumption, and failed not to command respect. 'In my knowledge of my fellow beings,' says Cowden Clarke, 'I never knew one who so thoroughly combined the sweetness with the power of gentleness, and the irresistible sway of anger, as Keats. His indignation would have made the boldest grave; and they who had seen him under the influence of injustice and meanness of soul would not forget the expression of his features — "the form of his visage was changed."'

In lighter moods his powers of mimicry and dramatic recital are described as great and never used unkindly. He loved the exhibition of any kind of energy, and was as almost as keen a spectator of the rough and violent as of the tender and joyous aspects and doings of life and nature. 'Though a quarrel in the streets,' he says, 'is a thing to be hated the energies displayed in it are fine; the commonest man shows a grace in his quarrel.' His yearning love for the old polytheism and instinctive affinity with the Greek spirit did not at all blunt his relish of actualities. To complete our picture and illustrate the wide and unfastidious range of his contact with life and interest in things, let us take Cowden Clarke's account of the way he could enjoy and re-enact such a scene of brutal sport and human low-life as our refinement no longer tolerates: —

His perception of humour, with the power of transmitting it by imitation, was both vivid and irresistibly amusing. He once described to me having gone to see a bear-baiting. The performance not having begun, Keats was near to, and watched, a young aspirant, who had brought a younger under his wing to witness the solemnity, and whom he oppressively patronized, instructing him in the names and qualities of all the magnates present. Now and then, in his zeal to manifest and impart his knowledge, he would forget himself, and stray beyond the prescribed bounds into the ring, to the lashing resentment of its comptroller, Mr William Soames, who, after some hints of a practical nature to 'keep back' began laying about him with indiscriminate and unmitigable vivacity, the Peripatetic signifying to his pupil. 'My eyes! Bill Soames giv' me sich a licker!' evidently grateful, and considering himself complimented upon being included in the general dispensation. Keats' entertainment with and appreciation of this minor scene of low life has often recurred to me. But his concurrent personification of the baiting, with his position, — his legs and arms bent and shortened till he looked like Bruin on his hind legs, dabbing his fore paws hither and thither, as the dogs snapped at him, and now and then acting the gasp of one that had been suddenly caught and hugged — his own capacious mouth adding force to the personation, was a remarkable and as memorable a display.

Thus stamped by nature, and moving in such a circle as we have described, Keats found among those with whom he lived nothing to check, but rather everything to foster, his hourly growing, still diffident and half awe-stricken, passion for the poetic life. Poetry and the love of poetry were at this period in the air. It was a time when even people of business and people of fashion read: a time of literary excitement, expectancy, discussion, and disputation such as England has not known since. Fortunes, even, had been made or were being made in poetry; by Scott, by Byron, by Moore, whose *Irish Melodies* were an income to him and who was known to have just received a cheque of £3000 in advance for *Lalla Rookh*. In such an atmosphere Keats, having enough of his inheritance left after payment of his school and hospital expenses to live on for at least a year or two, soon found himself induced to try his luck and his powers with the rest. The backing of his friends was indeed only too ready and enthusiastic. His brothers, including the business member of the family, the sensible and practical George, were as eager that John should become a famous poet as he was himself. So encouraged, he made up his mind to give up the pursuit of surgery for that of literature, and declared his decision, being now of age, firmly to his guardian; who naturally but in vain opposed it to the best of his power. The consequence was a quarrel, which Mr Abbey afterwards related, in a livelier manner than we should have expected from him, in the same document, now unfortunately gone astray, to which I have already referred as containing his character of the poet's mother. The die was cast. In the Marlborough Street studio, in the Hampstead cottage, in the City lodgings of the three brothers and the social gatherings of their friends, it was determined that John Keats (or according to his convivial *alias* 'Junkets') should put forth a volume of his poems. Leigh Hunt brought on the scene a firm of publishers supposed to be sympathetic, the brothers Charles and James Ollier, who had already published for Shelley and who readily undertook the issue. The volume was printed, and the last proof-sheets were brought one evening to the author amid a jovial company, with the intimation that if a dedication was to be added the copy must be furnished at once. Keats going to one side quickly produced the sonnet *To Leigh Hunt Esqr*, with its excellent opening and its weak conclusion: —

> Glory and Loveliness have pass'd away;
> For if we wander out in early morn,
> No wreathed incense do we see upborne
> Into the East to meet the smiling day:
> No crowd of nymphs soft-voiced and young and gay,
> In woven baskets bringing ears of corn,
> Roses and pinks, and violets, to adorn
> The shrine of Flora in her early May.
> But there are left delights as high as these,
> And I shall ever bless my destiny,
> That in a time when under pleasant trees
> Pan is no longer sought, I feel a free,
> A leafy luxury, seeing I could please,
> With these poor offerings, a man like thee.

With this confession of a longing retrospect towards the beauty of the old pagan world and of gratitude for present friendship, the young poet's first venture was sent forth, amid the applauding expectations of all his circle, in the first days of March 1817.

Chapter IV

THE 'POEMS' OF 1817

The note of Keats' early volume is accurately struck in the motto from Spenser which he prefixed to it: —
   What more felicity can fall to creature
   Than to enjoy delight with liberty?
The element in which his poetry moves is liberty, the consciousness of release from those conventions and restraints, not inherent in its true nature, by which the art had for the last hundred years been hampered. And the spirit which animates him is essentially the spirit of delight: delight in the beauty and activities of nature, in the vividness of sensation, in the charm of fable and romance, in the thoughts of friendship and affection, in anticipations of the future, and in the exercise of the art itself which expresses and communicates all these joys.

Technically considered, the volume consists almost entirely of experiments in two metrical forms: the one, the Italian sonnet of octave and sestet, not long fully reestablished in England after being disused, with some exceptions, since Milton: the other, the decasyllabic or five-stressed couplet first naturalized by Chaucer, revived by the Elizabethans in all manner of uses, narrative, dramatic, didactic, elegiac, epistolary, satiric, and employed ever since as the predominant English metre outside of lyric and drama. The only exceptions in the volume are the boyish stanzas in imitation of Spenser, — truly rather of Spenser's eighteenth century imitators; the *Address to Hope* of February 1815, quite in the conventional eighteenth century style and diction, though its form, the sextain stanza, is ancient; the two copies of verses *To some Ladies* and *On receiving a curious Shell from some Ladies*, composed for the Misses Mathew, about May of the same year, in the triple-time jingle most affected for social trifles from the days of Prior to those of Tom Moore; and the set of seven-syllabled couplets drafted in February 1816 for George Keats to send as a valentine to Miss Wylie. So far as their matter goes these exceptions call for little remark. Both the sea-shell verses and the valentine spring from a brain, to quote a phrase of Keats' own,
   — new stuff'd in youth with triumphs gay
   Of old romance, —
especially with chivalric images and ideas from Spenser. Of the second set of shell stanzas it may perhaps be noted that they seem to suggest an acquaintance with Oberon and Titania not only through the *Midsummer Night's Dream* but through Wieland's *Oberon*, a romance poem which Sotheby's translation had made well known in England and in which the fairy king and queen are divided by a quarrel far deeper and more durable than in Shakespeare's play.

Taking first the score or so of sonnets in the volume, we find that none of them are love-sonnets and that few are written in any high mood of passion or exaltation. They are for the most part of the class called 'occasional', — records of pleasant experience, addresses of friendly greeting or invocation, or compact meditations on a single theme. They bespeak a temper cordial and companionable as well as enthusiastic, manifest sincerity in all expressions of personal feeling, and contain here and there a passage of fine mature poetry. These, however, are seldom sustained for more than a single quatrain. The great exception of course is the sonnet, almost too well known to quote, — but I will quote it nevertheless, — on Chapman's *Homer*. That walk in the morning twilight from Clerkenwell to the Borough had enriched our language with what is by common consent one of its masterpieces in this form, having a close unsurpassed for the combined qualities of serenity and concentration: concentration twofold, first flashing on our mind's eye the human vision of the explorer and his companions with their looks and gestures, then symbolically evoking through that vision a whole world-wide range of the emotions of discovery.

> Much have I travell'd in the realms of gold,
> And many goodly states and kingdoms seen;
> Round many western islands have I been
> Which bards in fealty to Apollo hold.
> Oft of one wide expanse had I been told
> That deep-brow'd Homer rul'd as his demesne;
> Yet did I never breathe its pure serene
> Till I heard Chapman speak out loud and bold:
> Then felt I like some watcher of the skies
> When a new planet swims into his ken;
> Or like stout Cortez when with eagle eyes
> He star'd at the Pacific — and all his men
> Look'd at each other with a wild surmise —
> Silent, upon a peak in Darien.

The 'realms of gold' lines in the Chapman sonnet, recording Keats' range of reading in our older poetry, had been in a measure anticipated in this other, written six months earlier: —

> How many bards gild the lapses of time!
> A few of them have ever been the food
> Of my delighted fancy, — I could brood
> Over their beauties, earthly, or sublime:
> And often, when I sit me down to rhyme,
> These will in throngs before my mind intrude:
> But no confusion, no disturbance rude
> Do they occasion; 'tis a pleasing chime.
> So the unnumber'd sounds that evening store;
> The songs of birds — the whisp'ring of the leaves —
> The voice of waters — the great bell that heaves
> With solemn sound, — and thousand others more,
> That distance of recognizance bereaves,
> Make pleasing music, and not wild uproar.

Technical points worth attention here are the bold reversal of the regular accentual stress twice over in the first line, and the strained use of 'store' for 'fill' and 'recognizance' for 'recognition.' But the main interest of the sonnet is its comparison of the working of Keats' miscellaneous poetic reading in his mind and memory with the effect of the confused but harmonious sounds of evening on the ear, — a frank and illuminating comment by himself on those stray echoes and reminiscences of the older poets which we catch now and again throughout his work. Such echoes and reminiscences are always permitted to genius, because genius cannot help turning whatever it takes into something new of its own: and Keats showed himself from the first one of those chartered borrowers who have the right to draw inspiration as they please, whether direct from nature or, in the phrase of Wordsworth,

> From the great Nature that exists in works
> Of mighty poets.

Compare Shelley in the preface to *Prometheus Unbound* : — 'One great poet is a masterpiece of nature which another not only ought to study but must study.'

Most of the remaining sonnets can best be taken in groups, each group centering round a single theme or embodying a single mood or vein of feeling. One is what may be called the sex-chivalry group, including the sequence of three printed separately from the rest and beginning, 'Woman, when I behold thee flippant, vain'; that beginning 'Had I a man's fair form';

that addressed to Georgiana Wylie, with its admirable opening, 'Nymph of the downward smile, etc.,' and its rather lame conclusion; to which, as more loosely connected with the group, and touched in some degree with Byronic suggestion, may be added 'Happy is England, sweet her artless daughters.' That excellent critic, the late F.T. Palgrave, had a singular admiration for the set of three which I have placed at the head of this group: to me its chief interest seems not poetical but personal, inasmuch as in it Keats already defines with self-knowledge the peculiar blend in his nature of ardent, idealizing boyish worship of woman and beauty with an acute critical sensitiveness to flaws of character defacing his ideal in actual women: a sensitiveness which grew with his growth and many a time afterwards put him ill at ease with his company and himself.

A large proportion of the remaining sonnets centre themselves more or less closely about the figure of Leigh Hunt. Two introduce him directly by name and had the effect of definitely marking Keats down, in the minds of reactionary critics, as a victim to be swooped upon in association with Hunt whenever occasion offered. The two are the early sonnet composed on the day of Hunt's release from prison (February 5, 1815), and shown shyly as a first flight to Cowden Clarke immediately afterwards, and the dedicatory sonnet already quoted on the decay of the old pagan beauty, written almost exactly two years later. Intermediate in date between these two come two or three sonnets of May and June 1816 which, whether inspired directly or not by intercourse with Hunt, are certainly influenced by his writing, and express a townsman's enjoyment of country walks in a spirit and vocabulary near akin to his: — 'To one who has been long in city pent' (this opening comes with only the change of a word from *Paradise Lost*), 'O Solitude, if I with thee must dwell,' 'As late I rambled in the happy fields.' There is a memory of Wordsworth, and probably also of Epping Forest walks, in the cry to Solitude: —

> Let me thy vigils keep
> 'Mongst boughs pavillion'd, where the deer's swift leap
> Startles the wild bee from the foxglove bell.

Next comes the autumn group definitely recording the happiness received by the young poet from intercourse with Hunt and his friends, from the society of his brothers in London, and from walks between the Hampstead cottage and in their city lodgings: — 'Give me a golden pen,' 'Small, busy flames play through the fresh-laid coals,' 'Keen, fitful gusts are whispering here and there': to which may be added the sonnet *On the Grasshopper and Cricket* written in Hunt's house and in friendly competition with him.

A second new friend, Haydon, has a pair of sonnets in the volume all to himself, including that well-known one which brackets him with Wordsworth and Leigh Hunt among great spirits destined to give the world another heart and other pulses. A few of the sonnets stand singly apart from the rest by their subject or occasion. Such is the sonnet in honour of the Polish hero Kosciusko; and such again is that addressed to George Keats from Margate, with its fine ocean quatrain (Keats was always well inspired in writing of the sea): —

> The ocean with its vastness, its blue green,
> Its ships, its rocks, its caves, its hopes, its fears,
> Its voice mysterious, which whoso hears
> Must think on what will be, and what has been.

Now that we are posthumously acquainted with the other sonnets written by Keats in these early years it is a little difficult to see on what principle he made his choice of the specimens to be published in this 1817 volume. Among those excluded, he may well have thought the early attempts on the peace of 1814, on Chatterton, and on Byron, too feeble, though he has included others scarcely better. That headed 'As from the darkening gloom a silver dove' he may have counted too conventionally pious; and that satirizing the starched gloom of church-goers too likely on the other hand to give offence. The second Haydon pair, on visiting the Elgin marbles, and the recently discovered pair on receiving a laurel crown from Leigh Hunt, seem not to have been written (as that on the *Floure and the Lefe* certainly was not) until the book was passing, or had passed, the press. The last-named pair he would probably have had the good sense to omit in any case, as he has the sonnet celebrating a like laureation at the hands of a young lady at an earlier date. But why leave out 'After dark vapours' and 'Who loves to peer,' and above all why the admirable sonnet on Leander? The date of this was March 16, 1816, the occasion the gift by a lady of one of James Tassie's coloured paste reproductions of an engraved gem of the subject. 'Tassie's gems' were at this time immensely popular among lovers of Grecian taste, and were indeed delightful things, though his originals were too uncritically chosen and included but a small proportion of true antiques among a multitude of Renaissance and eighteenth-century imitations. Keats at one time proposed to make a collection of them for himself, and at another asked his young sister whether she would like a present of some. The sonnet opens with lines curiously recalling those invitations, or invocations, with which Dante begins some of his sonnets in the *Vita Nuova*. The last three lines are an example, hardly to be bettered, of condensed expression and of imagination kindling into instantaneous tragic vitality a cold and meagre image presented to the eye.

> Come hither all sweet maidens soberly,
> Down-looking aye, and with a chasten'd light
> Hid in the fringes of your eyelids white,
> And meekly let your fair hands joined be,
> As if so gentle that ye could not see,
> Untouch'd, a victim of your beauty bright,
> Sinking away to his young spirit's night, —
> Sinking bewilder'd 'mid the dreary sea:
> 'Tis young Leander toiling to his death;
> Nigh swooning, he doth purse his weary lips
> For Hero's cheek, and smiles against her smile.
> O horrid dream! see how his body dips
> Dead-heavy; arms and shoulders gleam awhile:
> He's gone: up bubbles all his amorous breath!

More than half the volume is taken up with epistles and meditative pieces (Drayton would have called them Elegies and Ben Jonson Epigrams) in the regular five-stressed or decasyllabic couplet. The earliest of these is the epistle to Felton Mathew from which I have already given a quotation. The form of the verse in this case is modelled pretty closely on Browne's *Britannia's Pastorals*. Keats, as has been said, was already familiar with the work of this amiable Spenserian allegorist, so thin and tedious in the allegorical part of his work proper, in romantic invention so poorly inspired, so admirable, genuine, and vivacious on the other hand in his scenes and similitudes from real west-country life and in notes of patriotism both local and national. By the following motto chosen from Browne's work Keats seems to put the group of *Epistles* in his volume under that poet's particular patronage: —

> Among the rest a shepheard (though but young
> Yet hartned to his pipe) with all the skill
> His few yeeres could, began to fit his quill.

But before coming to questions of the special influences which successively shaped Keats' aims both as to style and versification in poems of this form, I shall ask the reader to pause with me awhile and get freshly and familiarly into his ear and mind, what to special students is well known but to others only vaguely, the story of the chief phases which this most characteristic of English measures had gone through until the time when Keats tried to handle it in a spirit more or less revolutionary. Some of the examples I shall quote by way of illustration are passages which we know to have been specially familiar to Keats and to which we shall have occasion to recur. Let us first consider Chaucer's use, as illustrated in a part of the prayer of Emilia to Diana in the *Knightes Tale* : —

> O chastë goddesse of the wodës grene,
> To whom bothe hevene and erthe and see is sene,
> Quene of the regne of Pluto derk and lowe,
> Goddesse of maydens, that myn herte hast knowe
> Ful many a yeer, and woost what I desire,
> As keep me fro thy vengeance and thyn ire,
> That Attheon aboughtë cruelly.
> Chastë goddessë, wel wostow that I
> Desire to been a mayden al my lyf,
> Ne never wol I be no love ne wyf.
> I am, thou woost, yet of thy companye,
> A mayde, and love hunting and venerye,
> And for to walken in the wodës wilde,
> And noght to been a wyf, and be with childe.
> Noght wol I knowë companye of man.
> Now help me, lady, sith ye may and can,
> For tho thre formës that thou hast in thee.
> And Palamon, that hath swich love to me,
> And eek Arcite, that loveth me so sore,
> This grace I preyë thee with-outë more,
> As sendë love and pees bitwixte hem two;
> And fro me turne awey hir hertës so,
> That al hir hotë love, and hir desyr,
> And al hir bisy torment, and hir fyr
> Be queynt, or turnëd in another place;
> And if so be thou wolt not do me grace,
> Or if my destinee be shapen so,
> That I shal nedës have oon of hem two,
> As sende me him that most desireth me.

The rime-syllables with which Chaucer ends his lines are as a rule strong and followed by a pause, or at least by the grammatical possibility of a pause, though there are exceptions like the division of 'I | desire.' The general effect of the metre is that of a succession of separate couplets, though their separation is often slight and the sentence is allowed to run on with little break through several couplets divided from each other by no break of more than a comma. When a full stop comes and ends the sentence, it is hardly ever allowed to break a line by falling at any point except the end. On the other hand it is as often as not used to divide the couplet by falling at the end not of the second but of the first line, so that the ear has to wait a moment in expectancy until the second, beginning a new sentence, catches up the rime of the first like an echo. Other, slighter pauses fall quite variably where they will, and there is no regular breathing pause or caesura dividing the line after the second or third stress.

When the measure was revived by the Elizabethans two conflicting tendencies began to appear in its treatment. One was to end each line with a full and strong rime-syllable, noun or verb or emphatic adjective, and to let each couplet consist of a single sentence, or at any rate a single clause of a sentence, so as to be both grammatically and rhythmically almost independent of the next. Under this, which is called the closed or stopped couplet system, the rime-pattern and the sense or sentence-pattern, which together compose the formal elements in all rimed verse, are made strictly to coincide, and within the limits of a couplet no full break of the sense is allowed. Rhetorical and epigrammatical point and vigour are the special virtues of this system:

its weaknesses are monotony of beat and lack of freedom and variety in sentence structure. The other and opposite tendency is to suffer the sentence or period to develop itself freely, almost as in prose, running over as it will from one couplet into another, and coming to a full pause at any point in the line; and at the same time to let any syllable whatever, down to the lightest of prepositions or auxiliaries, serve at need as a rime-syllable. Under this system the sense and consequent sentence-pattern winds in and out of the rime-pattern variously and deviously, the rime-echo striking upon the ear now with emphasis, now lightly and fugitively, and being sometimes held up to follow a full pause and sometimes hurried on with the merest suggestion or insinuation of a possible pause, or with none at all. The virtues of this system are variety and freedom of movement; its special dangers are invertebrateness and a tendency to straggle and wind itself free of all real observance of rime-effect or metrical law.

Most of the Elizabethans used both systems interchangeably, now a string of closed couplets, and now a flowing period carried through a succession of couplets overrunning into one another. Spenser in *Mother Hubbard's Tale* and Marlowe in *Hero and Leander* were among the earliest and best revivers of the measure, and both inclined to the closed couplet system, Spenser the more strictly of the two, as the satiric and epigrammatic nature of his theme might naturally dictate. Let us take a well known passage from Marlowe: —

> It lies not in our power to love or hate,
> For will in us is over-ruled by fate.
> When two are stript, long ere the course begin,
> We wish that one should lose, the other win;
> And one especially do we affect
> Of two gold ingots, like in each respect:
> The reason no man knows; let it suffice,
> What we behold is censured by our eyes.
> Where both deliberate, the love is slight:
> Who ever loved, that loved not at first sight?
> He kneeled; but unto her devoutly prayed:
> Chaste Hero to herself thus softly said,
> 'Were I the saint he worships, I would hear him;'
> And, as she spake those words, came somewhat near him.
> He started up; she blushed as one ashamed;
> Wherewith Leander much more was inflamed.
> He touched her hand; in touching it she trembled:
> Love deeply grounded, hardly is dissembled.
> These lovers parlèd by the touch of hands:
> True love is mute, and oft amazèd stands.
> Thus while dumb signs their yielding hearts entangled,
> The air with sparks of living fire was spangled;
> And Night, deep-drenched in misty Acheron,
> Heaved up her head, and half the world upon
> Breathed darkness forth (dark night is Cupid's day).

The first ten lines, conveying moral saws or maxims, furnish almost a complete example of the closed couplet system, and not only of that, but of the division of single lines by a pause or caesura after the second or third stress. When the narrative begins, the verse moves still mainly in detached couplets (partly because a line of moral reflection is now and again paired with a line of narrative), but with a growing inclination to prolong the sentence and vary the rhythm, and with an abundant use, in the rimes, of the double or feminine ending, for which Chaucer affords precedent enough.

Drayton, a poet in whom Keats was well read, is commonly quoted as one who yielded habitually to the attraction of the closed couplet; and indeed he will often run on through page on page of twinned verses, or 'gemells' as he calls them, like these from the imaginary Epistle from Eleanor Cobham to Duke Humphrey: —

> Why, if thou wilt, I will myself deny,
> Nay, I'll affirm and swear, I am not I:
> Or if in that thy shame thou dost perceive,
> Lo, for thy dear sake, I my name will leave.
> And yet, methinks, amaz'd thou shouldst not stand,
> Nor seem so much appallèd at my hand;
> For my misfortunes have inur'd thine eye
> (Long before this) to sights of misery.
> No, no, read on, 'tis I, the very same,
> All thou canst read, is but to read my shame.
> Be not dismay'd, nor let my name affright;
> The worst it can, is but t' offend thy sight;
> It cannot wound, nor do thee deadly harm,
> It is no dreadful spell, no magic charm.

But Drayton is also very capable of the full-flowing period and the loose overrun of couplet into couplet, as witness the following from one of his epistles: —

> O God, though Virtue mightily do grieve
> For all this world, yet will I not believe
> But that she's fair and lovely and that she
> So to the period of the world will be;
> Else had she been forsaken (sure) of all,
> For that so many sundry mischiefs fall
> Upon her daily, and so many take
> Up arms against her, as it well might make
> Her to forsake her nature, and behind
> To leave no step for future time behind,
> As she had never been, for he that now
> Can do her most disgrace, him they allow
> The time's chief Champion — .

Turning to Keats' next favourite among the old poets, William Browne of Tavistock, here is a passage from *Britannia's Pastorals* which we know to have stuck in his memory, and which illustrates the prevailing tendency of the metre in Browne's hands to run in a succession of closed, but not too tightly closed, couplets, and to abound in double or feminine rime-endings which make a variation in the beat: —

> And as a lovely maiden, pure and chaste,
> With naked iv'ry neck, and gown unlaced,
> Within her chamber, when the day is fled,
> Makes poor her garments to enrich her bed:
> First, put she off her lily-silken gown,
> That shrieks for sorrow as she lays it down;
> And with her arms graceth a waistcoat fine,
> Embracing her as it would ne'er untwine.
> Her flaxen hair, ensnaring all beholders,
> She next permits to wave about her shoulders,
> And though she cast it back, the silken slips
> Still forward steal and hang upon her lips:
> Whereat she sweetly angry, with her laces
> Binds up the wanton locks in curious traces,

Whilst (twisting with her joints) each hair long lingers,
As loth to be enchain'd but with her fingers.
Then on her head a dressing like a crown;
Her breasts all bare, her kirtle slipping down,
And all things off (which rightly ever be
Call'd the foul-fair marks of our misery)
Except her last, which enviously doth seize her,
Lest any eye partake with it in pleasure,
Prepares for sweetest rest, while sylvans greet her,
And longingly the down bed swells to meet her.

Chapman, a poet naturally rugged of mind and speech and moreover hampered by having to translate, takes much greater liberties, constantly breaking up single lines with a full stop in the middle and riming on syllables too light or too grammatically dependent on the word next following to allow naturally any stress of after-pause, however slight; as thus in the sixth *Odyssey* : —

These, here arriv'd, the mules uncoach'd, and drave
Up to the gulfy river's shore, that gave
Sweet grass to them. The maids from coach then took
Their clothes, and steep'd them in the sable brook;
Then put them into springs, and trod them clean
With cleanly feet; adventuring wagers then,
Who should have soonest and most cleanly done.
When having throughly cleans'd, they spread them on
The flood's shore, all in order. And then, where
The waves the pebbles wash'd, and ground was clear,
They bath'd themselves, and all with glittering oil
Smooth'd their white skins; refreshing then their toil
With pleasant dinner, by the river's side;
Yet still watch'd when the sun their clothes had dried.
Till which time, having dined, Nausicaa
With other virgins did at stool-ball play,
Their shoulder-reaching head-tires laying by.

The other classical translation of the time with which Keats was most familiar was that of the *Metamorphoses* of Ovid by the traveller and colonial administrator George Sandys. As a rule Sandys prefers the regular beat of the self-contained couplet, but now and again he too breaks it uncompromisingly: for instance, —

Forbear yourselves, O Mortals, to pollute
With wicked food: fields smile with corn, ripe fruit
Weighs down their boughs; plump grapes their vines attire;
There are sweet herbs, and savory roots, which fire
May mollify, milk, honey redolent
With flowers of thyme, thy palate to content.
The prodigal earth abounds with gentle food;
Affording banquets without death or blood.
Brute beasts with flesh their ravenous hunger cloy:
And yet not all; in pastures horses joy:
So flocks and herds. But those whom Nature hath
Endued with cruelty, and savage wrath
(Wolves, bears, Armenian tigers, Lions) in

> Hot blood delight. How horrible a sin,
> That entrails bleeding entrails should entomb!
> That greedy flesh, by flesh should fat become!
> While by one creature's death another lives!

Contemporary masters of elegiac and epistolary verse often deal with the metre more harshly and arbitrarily still. Thus Donne, the great Dean of St Paul's, though capable of riming with fine sonority and richness, chooses sometimes to write as though in sheer defiance of the obvious framework offered by the couplet system; and the same refusal to stop the sense with the couplet, the same persistent slurring of the rime, the same broken and jerking movement, are plentifully to be matched from the epistles of Ben Jonson. In later and weaker hands this method of letting the sentence march or jolt upon its way in almost complete independence of the rime developed into a fatal disease and decay of the metre, analogous to the disease which at the same time was overtaking and corrupting dramatic blank verse. A signal instance, to which we shall have to return, is the *Pharonnida* of William Chamberlayne, (1659) a narrative poem not lacking momentary gleams of intellect and imagination, and by some insatiate students, including Southey and Professor Saintsbury, admired and praised in spite of its (to one reader at least) intolerable tedium and wretched stumbling, shuffling verse, which rimes indeed to the eye but to the ear is mere mockery and vexation. For example: —

> Some time in silent sorrow spent, at length
> The fair Pharonnida recovers strength,
> Though sighs each accent interrupted, to
> Return this answer: — 'Wilt, oh! wilt thou do
> Our infant love such injury — to leave
> It ere full grown? When shall my soul receive
> A comfortable smile to cherish it,
> When thou art gone? They're but dull joys that sit
> Enthroned in fruitless wishes; yet I could
> Part, with a less expense of sorrow, would
> Our rigid fortune only be content
> With absence; but a greater punishment
> Conspires against us — Danger must attend
> Each step thou tread'st from hence; and shall I spend
> Those hours in mirth, each of whose minutes lay
> Wait for thy life? When Fame proclaims the day
> Wherein your battles join, how will my fear
> With doubtful pulses beat, until I hear
> Whom victory adorns! Or shall I rest
> Here without trembling, when, lodged in thy breast,
> My heart's exposed to every danger that
> Assails thy valour, and is wounded at
> Each stroke that lights on thee — which absent I,
> Prompted by fear, to myriads multiply.'

The tendency which culminated in this kind of verse was met by a counteracting tendency in the majority of poets to insist on the regular emphatic rime-beat, and to establish the rime-unit — that is the separate couplet — as the completely dominant element in the measure, the 'heroic' measure as it had come to be called. The rule is nowhere so dogmatically laid down as by Sir John Beaumont, the elder brother of the dramatist, in an address to King James I: —

> In every language now in Europe spoke
> By nations which the Roman Empire broke,

> The relish of the Muse consists in rime:
> One verse must meet another like a chime.
> Our Saxon shortness hath peculiar grace
> In choice of words fit for the ending place,
> Which leave impression in the mind as well
> As closing sounds of some delightful bell.

Milton at nineteen, in a passage of his college *Vacation Exercise*, familiar to Keats and for every reason interesting to read in connexion with the poems expressing Keats' early aspirations, showed how the metre could still be handled nobly in the mixed Elizabethan manner: —

> Hail native Language, that by sinews weak
> Didst move my first endeavouring tongue to speak,
>
> ....
>
> I have some naked thoughts that rove about
> And loudly knock to have their passage out;
> And wearie of their place do only stay
> Till thou hast deck't them in thy best array;
> That so they may without suspect or fears
> Fly swiftly to this fair Assembly's ears;
> Yet I had rather if I were to chuse,
> Thy service in some graver subject use,
> Such as may make thee search thy coffers round,
> Before thou cloath my fancy in fit sound:
> Such where the deep transported mind may soare
> Above the wheeling poles, and at Heav'ns dore
> Look in, and see each blissful Deitie
> How he before the thunderous throne doth lie,
> Listening to what unshorn Apollo sings
> To th' touch of golden wires, while Hebe brings
> Immortal Nectar to her Kingly Sire:
> Then passing through the Spheres of watchful fire,
> And mistie Regions of wide air next under,
> And hills of Snow and lofts of piled Thunder,
> May tell at length how green-ey'd Neptune raves,
> In Heav'ns defiance mustering all his waves;
> Then sing of secret things that came to pass
> When Beldam Nature in her cradle was;
> And last of Kings and Queens and Hero's old,
> Such as the wise Demodocus once told
> In solemn Songs at King Alcinous feast,
> While sad Ulisses soul and all the rest
> Are held with his melodious harmonie
> In willing chains and sweet captivitie.

But the strictly closed system advocated by Sir John Beaumont prevailed in the main, and by the days of the Commonwealth and Restoration was with some exceptions generally established. Some poets were enabled by natural fineness of ear and dignity of soul to make it yield fine rich and rolling modulations: none more so than Andrew Marvell, as for instance in his noble poem on the death of Cromwell. The name especially associated in contemporary and subsequent criticism with the attainment of the admired quality of 'smoothness' (another name for clipped and even monotony of rime and rhythm) in this metre is Waller, the famous parliamentary and poetical turncoat who could adulate with equal unction first the Lord Protector and then the restored Charles. By this time, however, every rimer could play the tune, and thanks to the controlling and suggesting power of the metre itself, could turn out couplets with the true metallic and epigrammatic ring: few better than Katherine Philips ('the matchless Orinda'), who was a stickler for the strictest form of the couplet and wished even to banish all double endings. Take this from her elegy on the death of Elizabeth, Queen of Bohemia (1662): —

> Although the most do with officious heat
> Only adore the living and the great,
> Yet this Queen's merits Fame so far hath spread,
> That she rules still, though dispossest and dead.
> For losing one, two other Crowns remained;
> Over all hearts and her own griefs she reigned.
> Two Thrones so splendid as to none are less
> But to that third which she does now possess.
> Her heart and birth Fortune as well did know,
> That seeking her own fame in such a foe,
> She drest the spacious theatre for the fight:
> And the admiring World call'd to the sight:
> An army then of mighty sorrows brought,
> Who all against this single virtue fought;
> And sometimes stratagems, and sometimes blows,
> To her heroic soul they did oppose:
> But at her feet their vain attempts did fall,
> And she discovered and subdu'd them all.

Cowley in his long 'heroic' poem *The Davideis* admits the occasional Alexandrine or twelve-syllable line as a variation on the monotony of the rhythm. Dryden, with his incomparably sounder and stronger literary sense, saw the need for a richer variation yet, and obtained it by the free use both of triple rimes and of Alexandrines: often getting fine effects of sweeping sonority, although by means which the reader cannot but feel to be arbitrary, imported into the form because its monotony calls for relief rather than intrinsic and natural to it. Chaucer's prayer, above quoted, of Emilia to Diana runs thus in Dryden's 'translation': —

> O Goddess, Haunter of the Woodland Green,
> To whom both Heav'n and Earth and Seas are seen;
> Queen of the nether Skies, where half the Year
> Thy Silver Beams descend, and light the gloomy Sphere;
> Goddess of Maids, and conscious of our Hearts,
> So keep me from the Vengeance of thy Darts,
> Which Niobe's devoted Issue felt,
> When hissing through the Skies the feather'd Deaths were dealt:
> As I desire to live a Virgin-life,
> Nor know the Name of Mother or of Wife.
> Thy Votress from my tender Years I am,
> And love, like thee, the Woods and Sylvan Game.
> Like Death, thou know'st, I loath the Nuptial State,
> And Man, the Tyrant of our Sex, I hate,
> A lowly Servant, but a lofty Mate.
> Where Love is Duty on the Female Side,
> On theirs mere sensual Gust, and sought with surly Pride.
> Now by thy triple Shape, as thou art seen

> In Heav'n, Earth, Hell, and ev'ry where a Queen,
> Grant this my first Desire; let Discord, cease,
> And make betwixt the Rivals lasting Peace:
> Quench their hot Fire, or far from me remove
> The Flame, and turn it on some other Love.
> Or if my frowning Stars have so decreed,
> That one must be rejected, one succeed,
> Make him my Lord, within whose faithful Breast
> Is fix'd my Image, and who loves me best.

In serious work Dryden avoided double endings almost entirely, reserving them for playful and colloquial use in stage prologues, epilogues, and the like, thus: —

> I come, kind Gentlemen, strange news to tell ye;
> I am the Ghost of poor departed Nelly.
> Sweet Ladies, be not frighted; I'll be civil;
> I'm what I was, a little harmless Devil.
> For, after death, we Sprights have just such Natures,
> We had, for all the World, when human Creatures.

In the following generation Pope discarded, with the rarest exceptions, all these variations upon the metre and wrought up successions of separate couplets, each containing a single sentence or clause of a sentence complete, and each line having its breathing-pause or caesura almost exactly in the same place, to a pitch of polished and glittering elegance, of striking, instantaneous effect both upon ear and mind, which completely dazzled and subjugated not only his contemporaries but three full generations of rimers and readers after them. Everyone knows the tune; it is the same whether applied to purposes of pastoral sentiment or rhetorical passion or playful fancy, of Homeric translation or Horatian satire, of witty and plausible moral and critical reflection or of savage personal lampoon and invective. Let the reader turn in memory from Ariel's account of the duties of his subordinate elves and fays: —

> Some in the fields of purest ether play,
> And bask and whiten in the blaze of day:
> Some guide the course of wandering orbs on high,
> Or roll the planets through the boundless sky:
> Some, less refin'd, beneath the moon's pale light
> Pursue the stars that shoot athwart the night,
> Or suck the mists in grosser air below,
> Or dip their pinions in the painted bow,
> Or brew fierce tempests on the wintry main,
> Or o'er the glebe distil the kindly rain.
> Others, on earth, o'er human race preside,
> Watch all their ways, and all their actions guide, —

let the reader turn in memory from this to the familiarly known lines in which Pope congratulates himself

> That not in fancy's maze he wandered long,
> But stoop'd to truth, and moraliz'd his song;
> That not for fame, but virtue's better end,
> He stood the furious foe, the timid friend,
> The damning critic, half approving wit,
> The coxcomb hit, or fearing to be hit;
> Laughed at the loss of friends he never had,
> The dull, the proud, the wicked, and the mad;

> The distant threats of vengeance on his head,
> The blow unfelt, the tear he never shed;
> The tale revived, the lie so oft o'erthrown,
> The imputed trash, and dulness not his own, —

and again from this to his castigation of the unhappy Bayes: —

> Swearing and supperless the hero sate,
> Blasphem'd his gods, the dice, and damn'd his fate;
> Then gnaw'd his pen, then dash'd it on the ground,
> Sinking from thought to thought, a vast profound!
> Plung'd for his sense, but found no bottom there,
> Yet wrote and flounder'd on in mere despair.
> Round him much embryo, much abortion lay,
> Much future ode, and abdicated play;
> Nonsense precipitate, like running lead,
> That slipped through cracks and zigzags of the head.

The author thus brilliantly and evenly accomplished in one metre and so many styles ruled as a sovereign long after his death, his works being published in nearly thirty editions before the end of the century; and the measure as thus fixed and polished by him became for a full hundred years the settled norm and standard for English 'heroic' verse, the length and structure of periods, sentences and clauses having to be rigidly clipped to fit it. In this respect no change of practice came till after the whole spirit of English poetry had been changed. Almost from Pope's own day the leaven destined to produce what came afterwards to be called the romantic revolution was working, in the main unconsciously, in men's minds. Of conscious rebels or pioneers, two of the chief were that admirable, ridiculous pair of clerical brothers Joseph and Thomas Warton, Joseph long headmaster of Winchester, Thomas professor of poetry at Oxford and later poet laureate. Joseph Warton made at twenty-four, within two years of Pope's death, a formal protest against the reign of the polished and urbane moral essay in verse, and at all times stoutly maintained 'Invention and Imagination' to be the chief qualities of a poet; illustrating his views by what he called odes, to us sadly uninspired, of his own composition. His younger brother Thomas, with his passion for Gothic architecture, his masterly editing of Spenser, and his profound labours on the origin and history of our native English poetry, carried within him, for all his grotesque personality, many of the germs of the spirit that was to animate the coming age. As the century advanced, other signs and portents of what was to come were Chatterton's audaciously brilliant blunder of the Rowley forgeries, with the interest which it excited, the profound impression created by the pseudo-Ossian of Macpherson, and the enthusiastic reception of Percy's *Reliques*. But current critical taste did not recognize the meaning of these signs, and tacitly treated the breach between our older and newer literatures as complete. Admitting the older as a worthy and interesting subject of study and welcoming the labour of scholars — even those of pretended scholars — in collecting and publishing its remains or what purported to be such, criticism none the less expected and demanded of contemporary production that it should conform as a matter of course to the standards established since language and style had been 'polished' and reduced to 'correctness' by Dryden and Pope. Thomas Warton, wishing to celebrate in verse the glories of the Gothic architecture of Oxford, finds himself constrained to do so strictly in the dominant style and measure. His brother, the protesting Joseph, actually has to enrol himself among Pope's editors, and when for once he uses the heroic couplet and lets his fancy play upon the sight of a butterfly in Hackwood Park, must do so, he too, in this thoroughly Popeian wise: —

> Fair child of Sun and Summer, we behold
> With eager eyes thy wings bedropp'd with gold;
> The purple spots that o'er thy mantle spread,
> The sapphire's lively blue, the ruby's red,

> Ten thousand various blended tints surprise,
> Beyond the rainbow's hues or peacock's eyes:
> Not Judah's king in eastern pomp array'd,
> Whose charms allur'd from far the Sheban maid,
> High on his glitt'ring throne, like you could shine
> (Nature's completest miniature divine):
> For thee the rose her balmy buds renews,
> And silver lillies fill their cups with dews;
> Flora for thee the laughing fields perfumes,
> For thee Pomona sheds her choicest blooms.

William Blake, in his *Poetical Sketches* of 1784, poured scorn on the still reigning fashion for 'tinkling rhymes and elegances terse', and himself struck wonderful lyric notes in the vein of our older poetry: but nobody read or marked Blake: he was not for his own age but for posterity. Even those of the eighteenth century poets who in the main avoided the heroic couplet, and took refuge, like Thomson, in the Spenserian stanza or Miltonic blank verse, or confined themselves to lyric or elegiac work like Gray, — even they continued to be hampered by a strict conventional and artificial code of poetic style and diction. The first full and effective note of emancipation, of poetical revolution and expansion, in England was that struck by Coleridge and Wordsworth with the publication and defence of their *Lyrical Ballads* (1798, 1800). Both these young masters had written in the established mould in their quite earliest work, but afterwards disused it almost entirely (*The Happy Warrior* is of course a conspicuous exception); while their contemporary Walter Scott avoided it from the first.

The new poetry, whether cast in forms derived from or coloured by the old ballad literature of the country, or helping itself from the simplicities and directnesses of common everyday speech, or going back to Miltonic and pre-Miltonic tradition, fought its way to recognition now slowly, as in the case of Wordsworth, in whose style all these three elements play their part, now rapidly in the face of all opposition, as in the case of Scott with his dashing Border lays. But the heroic couplet on the Queen Anne model still held the field as the reigning and official form of verse; and among the most admired poets of Keats' day, Rogers, Campbell, and Crabbe in the older generation, each in his own manner, still kept sounding the old instrument essentially to the old tune, with Byron in the younger following, in *The Corsair* and *Lara*, at a pace more rapid and helter-skelter but with a beat even more monotonous and hammering than any of theirs. We have seen how Leigh Hunt declared his intention to try a reform of the measure, and how he carried out his promise in *Rimini*. He did little more than revive Dryden's expedients of the occasional triplet and Alexandrine, with a sprinkling of Elizabethan double-endings; failing withal completely to catch any touch either of the imaginative passion of the Elizabethans or of Dryden's fine virile energy and worldly good-breeding.

Rimini was not yet published, nor had Keats yet met its author, when Keats wrote his Epistle to Felton Mathew in November 1815. If, as is the case, his strain of social ease and sprightliness jars on us a little in the same manner as Hunt's, it is that there was really as he himself said on another occasion, something in common between them. At the same time it should be remembered that some of Keats' most Huntian-seeming rimes and phrases contain really an echo of the older masters. That William Browne was his earliest model in the handling of the metre will, I think, be apparent to any reader who will put the passage from *Britannia's Pastorals* above quoted (p. 98), with its easily flowing couplets varied at intervals by whole clusters or bunches of double endings, alongside of the following from Keats' first Epistle: —

> Too partial friend! fain would I follow thee
> Past each horizon of fine poesy;

    Fain would I echo back each pleasant note
As o'er Sicilian seas, clear anthems float
'Mong the light skimming gondolas far parted,
Just when the sun his farewell beam has darted:
But 'tis impossible; far different cares
Beckon me sternly from soft 'Lydian airs,'
And hold my faculties so long in thrall,
That I am oft in doubt whether at all
I shall again see Phoebus in the morning:
Or flush'd Aurora in the roseate dawning!
Or a white Naiad in a rippling stream;
Or a rapt seraph in a moonlight beam;
Or again witness what with thee I've seen,
The dew by fairy feet swept from the green,
After a night of some quaint jubilee
Which every elf and fay had come to see:
When bright processions took their airy march
Beneath the curved moon's triumphal arch.
But might I now each passing moment give
To the coy muse, with me she would not live
In this dark city, nor would condescend
'Mid contradictions her delights to lend.
Should e'er the fine-ey'd maid to me be kind,
Ah! surely it must be whene'er I find
Some flowery spot, sequester'd, wild, romantic,
That often must have seen a poet frantic;
Where oaks, that erst the Druid knew, are growing,
And flowers, the glory of one day, are blowing;
Where the dark-leav'd laburnum's drooping clusters
Reflect athwart the stream their yellow lustres,
And intertwin'd the cassia's arms unite,
With its own drooping buds, but very white.

This is artless enough as writing, but obviously sincere, and interesting as showing how early and instinctively both Greek and mediæval mythology had become to Keats symbols and incarnations, as living as in the days of their first creation, of the charm and power of nature. The piece ends with a queer Ovidian fancy about his friend, to the effect that he, Mathew, had once been a 'flowret blooming wild' beside the springs of poetry, and that Diana had plucked him and thrown him into the stream as an offering to her brother Apollo, who had turned him into a goldfinch, from which he was metamorphosed into a black-eyed swan fed by Naiads.

    The next experiments in this measure, the fragment of *Calidore* with its *Induction*, date from a few months later, after the publication of *Rimini*, and express the longing of the young aspirant to follow the example of Hunt, the loved Libertas, and tell, he too, a tale of chivalry. But the longing is seconded by scarce a touch of inspiration. The Gothic and nature descriptions are quite cheap and external, the figures of knights and ladies quite conventional, the whole thing a matter of plumes and palfreys and lances, shallow graces of costume and sentiment, much more recalling Stothard's sugared illustrations to Spenser than the spirit of Spenser himself, whose patronage Keats timorously invokes. He at the same time entreats Hunt to intercede with Spenser on his behalf: and in the result it seems as though Hunt had stepped bodily in between them. In the handling of the metre, indeed, there is nothing of Hunt's diluted Drydenism: there is the same direct though timid following of Elizabethan precedents as before, varied by an occasional echo of *Lycidas* in the use of the short six-syllable line: —

> Anon he leaps along the oaken floors
> Of halls and corridors.

But in the style and sentiment we trace Leigh Hunt, or those elements in Keats which were naturally akin to him, at every turn. We read, for instance, of trees that lean

> So elegantly o'er the waters brim
> And show their blossoms trim:

and of

> The lamps that from the high-roof'd hall were pendent
> And gave the steel a shining quite transcendent.

A few months later, on his August and September holiday at Margate, Keats resumes the measure again, in two familiar epistles, one to his brother George, the other to Cowden Clarke. To his brother he expresses frankly, and in places felicitously, the moods and aspirations of a youth passionately and justly conscious of the working of the poetic impulse in him, but not less justly dissatisfied with the present fruits of such impulse, and wondering whether any worth gathering will ever come to ripeness. He tells us of hours when all in vain he gazes at the play of sheet lightning or pries among the stars 'to strive to think divinely,' and of other hours when the doors of the clouds break open and show him visions of the pawing of white horses, the flashing of festal wine cups in halls of gold, and supernatural colours of dimly seen flowers. In such moods, he asks concerning an imagined poet: —

> Should he upon an evening ramble fare
> With forehead to the soothing breezes bare,
> Would he naught see but the dark silent blue
> With all its diamonds trembling through and through?
> Or the coy moon, when in the waviness
> Of whitest clouds she does her beauty dress,
> And staidly paces higher up, and higher,
> Like a sweet nun in holy-day attire?
> Ah, yes! much more would start into his sight —
> The revelries, and mysteries of night:
> And should I ever see them, I will tell you
> Such tales as needs must with amazement spell you.

But richer even than these privileges of the poet in his illuminated moments is the reward which he may look for from posterity. In a long passage, deeply pathetic considering the after-event, Keats imagines exultingly what must be a poet's deathbed feelings when he foresees how his name and work will be cherished in after times by men and women of all sorts and conditions — warrior, statesman, and philosopher, village May-queen and nursing mother (the best and most of the verses are those which picture the May-queen taking his book from her bosom to read to a thrilled circle on the village green). He might be happier, he admits, could he stifle all these ambitions. Yet there are moments when he already tastes the true delights of poetry; and at any rate he can take pleasure in the thought that his brother will like what he writes; and so he is content to close with an attempt at a quiet description of the Thanet scenery and surroundings whence he writes.

In addressing Cowden Clarke Keats begins with an odd image, likening the way in which poetic inspiration eludes him to the slipping away of drops of water which a swan vainly tries to collect in the hollows of his plumage. He would have written sooner, he tells his correspondent, but had nothing worthy to submit to one so familiar with the whole range of poetry and recently, moreover, privileged to walk and talk with Leigh Hunt, —

> One, who, of late, had ta'en sweet forest walks
> With him who elegantly chats, and talks —
> The wrong'd Libertas, — who has told you stories
> Of laurel chaplets, and Apollo's glories;
> Of troops chivalrous prancing through a city,
> And tearful ladies made for love, and pity.

(The allusion in the last three lines is of course to *The Feast of the Poets and Rimini*. The passage seems to make it certain that whatever intercourse Keats himself may up to this time have had with Hunt was slight.) Even now, he goes on, he would not show Clarke his verses but that he takes courage from their old friendship and from his sense of owing to it all he knows of poetry. Recurring to the pleasantness of his present surroundings, he says that they have inspired him to attempt the verses he is now writing for his friend, which would have been better only that they have been too long parted. Then follow the lines quoted farther back (p. 37) in affectionate remembrance of old Enfield and Edmonton days.

In these early attempts Keats again ventures some way, but not yet far, in the direction of breaking the fetters of the regular couplet. He runs his sentences freely enough through a succession of lines, but nine times out of ten with some kind of pause as well as emphasis on the rime-word. He deals freely in double endings, and occasionally, but not often (oftenest in the epistle to George) breaks the run of a line with a full stop in or near the middle. He is in like manner timid and sparing as yet in the use, to which a little later he was to give rein so fully, of Elizabethan word-forms, or forms modelled for himself on Elizabethan usage.

Somewhat more free and adventurous alike in metre and in diction are the two poems, *Sleep and Poetry* and '*I stood tip-toe*,' which Keats wrote after he came back to London in the autumn. These are the things which, together with two or three of the sonnets, give its real distinction and high promise to the volume. Both in substance and intention they are preludes merely, but preludes of genius, and, although marked by many immaturities, as interesting and attractive perhaps as anything which has ever been written by a poet of the same age about his art and his aspirations. In them the ardent novice communes intently with himself on his own hopes and ambitions. Possessed by the thrilling sense that everything in earth and air is full, as it were, of poetry in solution, he has as yet no clearness as to the forms and modes in which these suspended elements will crystallize for him. In *Sleep and Poetry* he tries to get into shape his conceptions of the end and aim of poetical endeavour, conjures up the difficulties of his task, counts over the new achievement and growing promise of the time in which he lives, and gives thanks for the encouragement by which he has been personally sustained. In '*I stood tip-toe*' he runs over the stock of nature-images which are his own private and peculiar delight, traces in various phases and aspects of nature a symbolic affinity, or spiritual identity, with various forms and kinds of poetry; tells how such a strain of verse will call up such and such a range of nature images, and conversely how this or that group of outdoor delights will inspire this or that mood of poetic invention; and finally goes on to speculate on the moods which first inspired some of the Grecian tales he loves best, and above all the tale of Endymion and Cynthia, the beneficent wonders of whose bridal night he hopes himself one day to retell.

Sleep and Poetry is printed at the end of the volume, '*I stood tip-toe*' at the beginning. It is hard to tell which of the two pieces was written first. *Sleep and Poetry* is the longer and more important, and has more the air of having been composed, so to speak, all of a piece. We know that '*I stood tip-toe*' was not finished until the end of December 1816. *Sleep and Poetry* cannot well have been written later, seeing that the book was published in the first days of the following March, and must therefore have gone to press early in the new year. What seems likeliest is that *Sleep and Poetry* was written without break during the first freshness of Keats' autumn intimacy at the Hampstead cottage; while '*I stood tip-toe*' may have been begun in the summer and resumed at intervals until the year's end. I shall take *Sleep and Poetry* first and let '*I stood tip-toe*' come after, as being the direct and express prelude to the great experiment, *Endymion*, which was to follow.

The scheme of *Sleep and Poetry* is to some extent that of *The Floure and the Lefe*, the pseudo-Chaucerian poem which, as we have seen, had so strongly caught Keats' fancy. Keats takes for his motto lines from that poem telling of a night wakeful but none the less cheerful, and avers that his own poem was the result of just such another night. An opening invocation sets the blessings of sleep above a number of other delightful things which it gives him joy to think of, and recounts the activities of Sleep personified, — 'Silent entangler of a beauty's tresses,' etc., — in lines charming and essentially characteristic, for it is the way of his imagination to be continually discovering active and dynamic qualities in things and to let their passive and inert properties be. But far higher and more precious than the blessings of sleep are those of something else which he will not name: —

    What is it? And to what shall I compare it?

It has a glory, and nought else can share it:
    The thought thereof is awful, sweet, and holy,
    Chasing away all worldliness and folly;
    Coming sometimes like fearful claps of thunder,
    Or the low rumblings earth's regions under;
    And sometimes like a gentle whispering
    Of all the secrets of some wond'rous thing
    That breathes about us in the vacant air;
    So that we look around with prying stare,
    Perhaps to see shapes of light, aerial limning,
    And catch soft floatings from a faint-heard hymning;
    To see the laurel wreath, on high suspended.
    That is to crown our name when life is ended.
    Sometimes it gives a glory to the voice,
    And from the heart up-springs, rejoice! rejoice!
    Sounds which will reach the Framer of all things,
    And die away in ardent mutterings.

Every enlightened spirit will guess, he implies, that this thing is poetry, and to Poetry personified he addresses his next invocation, declaring that if he can endure the overwhelming favour of her acceptance he will be admitted to 'the fair visions of all places' and will learn to reveal in verse the hidden beauty and meanings of things, in an ascending scale from the playing of nymphs in woods and fountains to 'the events of this wide world,' which it will be given him to seize 'like a strong giant.'

At this point a warning voice within him reminds him sadly of the shortness and fragility of life, to which an answering inward voice of gay courage and hope replies. Keats could only think in images, and almost invariably in images of life and action: those here conveying the warning and its reply are alike felicitous: —

    Stop and consider! life is but a day;
    A fragile dewdrop on its perilous way
    From a tree's summit; a poor Indian's sleep
    While his boat hastens to the monstrous steep
    Of Montmorenci. Why so sad a moan?
    Life is the rose's hope while yet unblown;
    The reading of an ever-changing tale;
    The light uplifting of a maiden's veil;
    A pigeon tumbling in clear summer air;

> A laughing schoolboy, without grief or care,
> Riding the springy branches of an elm.

Then follows a cry for length enough of years (he will be content with ten) to carry out the poetic schemes which float before his mind; and here he returns to his ascending scale of poetic ambitions and sets it forth and amplifies it with a new richness of figurative imagery. First the realms of Pan and Flora, the pleasures of nature and the country and the enticements of toying nymphs (perhaps with a Virgilian touch in his memory from schoolboy days — *Panaque Silvanumque senem nymphasque sorores* — certainly with visions from Poussin's Bacchanals in his mind's eye): then, the ascent to loftier regions where the imagination has to grapple with the deeper mysteries of life and experiences of the soul. Here again he can only shadow forth his ideas by evoking shapes and actions of visible beings to stand for and represent them symbolically. He sees a charioteer guiding his horses among the clouds, looking out the while 'with glorious fear,' then swooping downward to alight on a grassy hillside; then talking with strange gestures to the trees and mountains, then gazing and listening, 'awfully intent,' and writing something on his tablets while a procession of various human shapes, 'shapes of delight, of mystery and fear,' sweeps on before his view, as if in pursuit of some ever-fleeting music, in the shadow cast by a grove of oaks. The dozen lines calling up to the mind's eye the multitude and variety of figures in this procession —

> Yes, thousands in a thousand different waysM
> Flit onward —

contain less suggestion than we should have expected from what has gone before, of the events and tragedies of the world, 'the agonies, the strife of human hearts,' — and close with the vision of

> a lovely wreath of girls
> Dancing their sleek hair into tangled curls,

as if images of pure pagan joy and beauty would keep forcing themselves on the young aspirant's mind in spite of his resolve to train himself for the grapple with sterner themes.

This vision of the charioteer and his team remained in Keats' mind as a symbol for the imagination and its energies. For the moment, so his poem goes on, the vision vanishes, and the sense of everyday realities seems like a muddy stream bearing his soul into nothingness. But he clings to the memory of that chariot and its journey; and thereupon turns to consider the history of English poetry and the dearth of imagination from which it had suffered for so many years. Here comes the famous outbreak, first of indignant and then of congratulatory criticism, which was the most explicit battle-cry of the romantic revolution in poetry since the publication of Wordsworth's preface to the second edition of *Lyrical Ballads* seventeen years earlier: —

> Is there so small a range
> In the present strength of manhood, that the high
> Imagination cannot freely fly
> As she was wont of old? prepare her steeds,
> Paw up against the light, and do strange deeds
> Upon the clouds? Has she not shown us all?
> From the clear space of ether, to the small
> Breath of new buds unfolding? From the meaning
> Of Jove's large eyebrow, to the tender greening
> Of April meadows? Here her altar shone,
> E'en in this isle; and who could paragon
> The fervid choir that lifted up a noise

Of harmony, to where it aye will poise
Its mighty self of convoluting sound,
Huge as a planet, and like that roll round,
Eternally around a dizzy void?
Ay, in those days the Muses were nigh cloy'd
With honors; nor had any other care
Than to sing out and sooth their wavy hair.
Could all this be forgotten? Yes, a schism
Nurtured by foppery and barbarism,
Made great Apollo blush for this his land.
Men were thought wise who could not understand
His glories: with a puling infant's force
They sway'd about upon a rocking horse
And thought it Pegasus. Ah dismal soul'd!
The winds of heaven blew, the ocean roll'd
Its gathering waves — ye felt it not. The blue
Bared its eternal bosom, and the dew
Of summer nights collected still to make
The morning precious: beauty was awake!
Why were ye not awake? But ye were dead
To things ye knew not of, — were closely wed
To musty laws lined out with wretched rule
And compass vile: so that ye thought a school
Of dolts to smooth, inlay, and clip, and fit,
Till, like the certain wands of Jacob's wit,
Their verses tallied. Easy was the task:
A thousand handicraftsmen wore the mask
Of Poesy. Ill-fated, impious race!
That blasphemed the bright Lyrist to his face,
And did not know it, — no, they went about,
Holding a poor, decrepid standard out
Mark'd with most flimsy mottos, and in large
The name of one Boileau!

The two great elder captains of poetic revolution, Coleridge and Wordsworth, have expounded their cause, in prose, with full maturity of thought and language: Wordsworth in the austere contentions of his famous prefaces to his second edition (1800), Coleridge in the luminous retrospect of the *Biographia Literaria* (1816). In the interval a cloud of critics, including men of such gifts as Lamb, Hazlitt, and Leigh Hunt, were in their several ways champions of the same cause. But none of these has left any enunciation of theory having power to thrill the ear and haunt the memory like the rimes of this young untrained recruit, John Keats. It is easy, indeed, to pick his verses to shreds, if we choose to fix a prosaic and rational attention on their faults. What is it, for instance, that imagination is asked to do? Fly, or drive? Is it she, or her steeds, that are to paw up against the light? And why paw? Deeds to be done upon clouds by pawing can hardly be other than strange. What sort of a verb is 'I green, thou greenest?' Why should the hair of the muses require 'soothing'? — if it were their tempers it would be more intelligible. And surely 'foppery' belongs to civilization and not to 'barbarism': and a standard-bearer may be decrepit but not a standard, and a standard flimsy but not a motto. And so on without end, if we choose to let the mind assume that attitude and to resent the contemptuous treatment of a very finished artist and craftsman by one as yet obviously raw and imperfect. Byron, in his controversy with Bowles a year or two later, adopted this mode of attack effectively enough; his spleen against a contemporary finding as usual its most convenient weapon in an enthusiasm, partly real and partly affected, for the genius and the methods of Pope. But controversy apart, if we have in us a touch of instinct for the poetry of imagination and beauty, as distinct from that of taste and reason and 'correctness', — however clearly we may see the weak points of a passage like this, yet we cannot but feel that Keats touches truly the root of the matter: we cannot but admire the ring and power of his appeal to the elements, his fine spontaneous and effective turns of rhetoric, and the elastic life and variety of his verse.

So much for the indignant part of the passage. The congratulatory part repeats with different imagery the sense of the sonnet to Haydon beginning 'Great spirits now on earth are sojourning,' and declares that fine sounds are once more floating wild about the earth, wherefore the Muses are now glad and happy. But the congratulations, it next occurs to the young poet, need to be qualified. To some of the recent achievements of poetry he demurs, declaring that their themes of song are 'ugly clubs' and the poets who fling them Polyphemuses 'disturbing the grand sea of song' (Keats is here remembering the huge club which Ulysses and his companions, in the Homeric story, find in the cave of Polyphemus, and confusing it with the rocks which the blinded giant later tears up and hurls after them into the sea). The obvious supposition is that Keats is here referring to Byron's Eastern tales, with their clamour and heat and violence of melodramatic action and passion. Leigh Hunt, indeed, who ought to have known, asserts in his review of the volume that they are aimed against 'the morbidity which taints some of the productions of the poets of the Lake School.' I suspect that Hunt is here attributing to Keats some of his own poetical aversions. What productions can he mean? Southey's *Curse of Kehama*? Coleridge's *Ancient Mariner* or *Christabel*? Wordsworth's relatively few poems, or episodes, of tragic life — as the *Mad Mother*, *Ruth*, *Margaret*? For certainly the strained simplicities and trivialities of some of his country ballads, which were what Leigh Hunt and his friends most disliked in Wordsworth's work, could never be called thunders.

But these jarring things, Keats goes on, shall not disturb him. He will believe in and seek to enter upon the kingdom of poetry where all shall be gentle and soothing like a lawn beneath a myrtle tree,

> And they shall be accounted poet-kings
> Who simply sing the most heart-easing things.

Then a momentary terror of his own presumption seizes him; but he puts it away, defies despondency, and declares that for all his youth and lack of learning and wisdom, he has a vast idea before him, and a clear conception of the end and aim of poetry. Dare the utmost he will — and then once more the sense of the greatness of the task comes over him, and he falls back for support on thoughts of recent friendship and encouragement. A score of lines follow, recalling happy talks at Hunt's over books and prints: the memory of these calls up by association a string of the delights ('luxuries' as in Huntian phrase he calls them) of nature: thence he recurs to the pleasures of sleep, or rather of a night when sleep failed him for thinking over the intercourse he had been enjoying and the place where he now rested — that is on the couch in Hunt's library. Here follow the lines quoted above (p. 53) about the prints on the library walls: and the piece concludes: —

> The very sense of where I was might well
> Keep Sleep aloof: but more than that there came
> Thought after thought to nourish up the flame
> Within my breast; so that the morning light
> Surprised me even from a sleepless night;
> And up I rose refresh'd, and glad, and gay,
> Resolving to begin that very day
> These lines; and howsoever they be done,
> I leave them as a father does his son.

The best reason for thinking that the poem '*I stood tip-toe*,' though probably finished quite as late as *Sleep and Poetry*, was begun earlier, is that in it Keats again follows the practice which he had attempted in *Calidore* and its *Induction* but gave up in *Sleep and Poetry*, namely that of occasionally introducing a lyrical effect with a six-syllable line, in the manner used by Spenser in the *Epithalamion* and Milton in *Lycidas*, —

> Open afresh your round of starry folds,
> Ye ardent marigolds!

No conclusion as to the date when the piece was begun can be drawn from the scene of summer freshness with which it opens, or from Leigh Hunt's statement that this description was suggested by a summer's day when he stood at a certain spot on Hampstead Heath. This may be quite true, but in the mind of a poet such scenes ripen by recollection, and Keats may at any after day have evoked it for his purpose, which was to bring his imagination to the right taking-off place — to plant it, so to speak, on the right spring-board — from which to start on its flight through a whole succession of other and kindred images of natural beauty. Some of the series of evocations that follow are already almost in the happiest vein of Keats' lighter nature-poetry, especially the four lines about the sweet peas on tip-toe for a flight, and the long passage recalling his boyish delights by the Edmonton brookside and telling (in lines which Tennyson has remembered in his idyll of *Enid*) how the minnows would scatter beneath the shadow of a lifted hand and come together again. When in the course of his recapitulation there comes to him the image of the moon appearing from behind a cloud, he breaks off to apostrophize that goddess of his imaginative idolatry, that source at once and symbol, for such to his instinct she truly was, of poetic inspiration. But for the moment he does not pursue the theme: he pauses to trace the affinities between several kinds of nature-delight and corresponding moods of poetry, —

> In the calm grandeur of a sober line,
> We see the waving of the mountain pine;
> And when a tale is beautifully staid,
> We feel the safety of a hawthorn glade, —

and so forth. And then, having in his mind's eye, as I should guess, some of the mythological prints from Hunt's portfolios, he asks what moods or phases of nature first inspired the poets of old with the fables of Cupid and Psyche and of Pan and Syrinx, of Narcissus and Echo, and most beautiful of all, that of Cynthia and Endymion, — and for the remaining fifty lines of the poem moonlight and the Endymion story take full possession. The lines imagining the occasion of the myth's invention are lovely: —

> He was a Poet, sure a lover too,
> Who stood on Latmus' top, what time there blew
> Soft breezes from the myrtle vale below;
> And brought in faintness solemn, sweet, and slow
> A hymn from Dian's temple; while upswelling,
> The incense went to her own starry dwelling.
> But though her face was clear as infant's eyes,
> Though she stood smiling o'er the sacrifice,
> The Poet wept at her so piteous fate,
> Wept that such beauty should be desolate:
> So in fine wrath some golden sounds he won,
> And gave meek Cynthia her Endymion.

Then, treating the bridal night for the moment not as a myth but as a thing that actually happened, he recounts, in a strain of purely human tenderness which owes something to his hospital experience and which he was hardly afterwards to surpass, the sweet and beneficent influences diffused on that night about the world: —

> The breezes were ethereal and pure,
>
> And crept through half-closed lattices to cure
> The languid sick; it cool'd their fever'd sleep,
> And soothed them into slumbers full and deep.
> Soon they awoke clear eyed, nor burnt with thirsting,
> Nor with hot fingers, nor with temples bursting:
> And springing up, they met the wondering sight
> Of their dear friends, nigh foolish with delight;
> Who feel their arms and breasts, and kiss and stare,
> And on their placid foreheads part the hair.
> Young men and maidens at each other gaz'd
> With hands held back, and motionless, amaz'd
> To see the brightness in each other's eyes.

Then, closing, he asks himself the momentous question, 'Was there a poet born?' which he intended that his next year's work should answer.

In neither of these poems is the use of Elizabethan verbal forms, or the coinage of similar forms by analogy, carried nearly as far as we shall find it carried later on, especially in *Endymion*. The abstract nouns expressing qualities pleasant to the senses or the sensuous imagination, on the model of those in Chapman's *Hymn to Pan*, increase in number, and we get the 'quaint mossiness of aged roots,' the 'hurrying freshnesses' of a stream running over gravel, the 'pure deliciousness' of the Endymion story, the 'pillow silkiness' of clouds, the 'blue cragginess' of other clouds, and the 'widenesses' of the ocean of poetry. Once, evidently with William Browne's 'roundly form' in his mind, Keats invents, infelicitously enough, an adjective 'boundly' for 'bounden.' In the matter of metre, he is now fairly well at home in the free Elizabethan use of the couplet, letting his periods develop themselves unhampered, suffering his full pauses to fall at any point in the line where the sense calls for them, the rime echo to come full and emphatic or faint and light as may be, and the pause following the rime-word to be shorter or longer or almost non-existent on occasion. If his ear was for the moment attuned to the harmonies of any special master among the Elizabethans, it was by this time Fletcher rather than Browne: at least in *Sleep and Poetry* the double endings no longer come in clusters as they did in the earlier epistle, nor are the intervening couplets so nearly regular, while there is a marked preference for emphasizing an adjective by placing it at the end of a line and letting its noun follow at the beginning of the next, — 'the high | Imagination,' — 'the small | Breath of new buds unfolding.' The reader will best see my point if he will compare the movement of the passages in *Sleep and Poetry* where these things occur with the Endymion passage he will find quoted later on from the *Faithful Shepherdess* (p. 168).

As to contemporary influences apparent in Keats' first volume, enough has been said concerning that of Leigh Hunt. The influence of an incommensurably greater poet, of Wordsworth, is also to be traced in it. That Keats was by this time a diligent and critical admirer of Wordsworth we know: both of the earlier poems and of the *Excursion*, which had appeared when his passion for poetry was already at its height in the last year of his apprenticeship at Edmonton. There is a famous passage in the fourth book of *The Excursion* where Wordsworth treats of the spirit of Greek religion and imagines how some of its conceptions first took shape: —

> In that fair clime, the lonely herdsman, stretched
> On the soft grass through half a summer's day,
> With music lulled his indolent repose:

> And, in some fit of weariness, if he,
> When his own breath was silent, chanced to hear
> A distant strain, far sweeter than the sounds
> Which his poor skill could make, his fancy fetched,
> Even from the blazing chariot of the sun,
> A beardless Youth, who touched a golden lute,
> And filled the illumined groves with ravishment.
> The nightly hunter, lifting a bright eye
> Up towards the crescent moon, with grateful heart
> Called on the lovely wanderer who bestowed
> That timely light, to share his joyous sport:
> And hence, a beaming Goddess with her Nymphs,
> Across the lawn and through the darksome grove,
> Not unaccompanied with tuneful notes
> By echo multiplied from rock or cave,
> Swept in the storm of chase; as moon and stars
> Glance rapidly along the clouded heaven,
> When winds are blowing strong.

Keats, we know, was familiar with this passage, and a little later on we shall find him criticizing it in conversation with a friend. Leigh Hunt, in a review written at the time, hints that it was in his mind when he wrote the lines in '*I stood tip-toe*,' asking in what mood or under what impulse a number of the Grecian fables were first invented and giving the answers to his own questions. We may take Hunt's word for the fact, seeing that he was constantly in Keats' company at the time. Other critics have gone farther and supposed it was from Wordsworth that Keats first learned truly to understand Greek mythology. I do not at all think so. He would never have pored so passionately over the stories in the classical dictionaries as a schoolboy, nor mused on them so intently in the field walks of his apprentice days by sunset and moonlight, had not some inborn instinct made the world of ancient fable and the world of natural beauty each equally living to his apprehension and each equally life-giving to the other. Wordsworth's interpretations will no doubt have appealed to him profoundly, but not as something new, only as putting eloquently and justly what he had already felt and divined by native instinct.

Again, it has been acutely pointed out by Mr Robert Bridges how some of the ideas expressed by Keats in his own way in *Sleep and Poetry* run parallel with some of those expressed in a very different way by Wordsworth in *Tintern Abbey*, a poem which we know from other evidence to have been certainly much in Keats' mind a year and a half later. Wordsworth in *Tintern Abbey* defines three stages of his own emotional and imaginative development in relation to nature: first the stage of mere boisterous physical and animal pleasure: then that of intense and absorbing, but still unreflecting passion, —

> An appetite, a feeling and a love
> That had no need of a remoter charm
> By thought supplied, nor any interest
> Unborrowed from the eye, —

and lastly the higher, more humanized and spiritualized passion doubly enriched by the ever-present haunting of 'the still, sad music of humanity,' and by the

> sense sublime

> Of something far more deeply interfused,
> Whose dwelling is the light of setting suns,

> And the round ocean and the living air,
> And the blue sky, and in the mind of man:
> A motion and a spirit, that impels
> All thinking things, all objects of all thought,
> And rolls through all things.

Mr Bridges finds Wordsworth's conception of these three stages more or less accurately paralleled in various passages of Keats' *Sleep and Poetry*. One passage which he quotes, that in which Keats figures human life under the string of joyous images beginning, 'A pigeon tumbling in clear summer air', seems to me irrelevant, as being simply the answer of the poet's soul to certain melancholy promptings of its own. On the other hand there certainly is something that reminds us of Wordsworth's three stages in Keats' repeated indication of the ascending scale of theme and temper along which he hopes to work. And his long figurative passage beginning —

> And can I ever bid these joys farewell?
> Yes, I must pass them for a nobler life —

may fairly, at its outset, be compared with Wordsworth's final stage: only, as I have asked the reader to note, the procession of symbolic and enigmatic forms and actions which Keats summons up before our mind's eye, so far from having any fixed or increasing character of pensiveness or gravity, winds up with a figure of sheer animal happiness and joy of life.

Mr Bridges further notes, very justly, the striking contrast between the methods of the elder and the younger poet in these passages, defining Wordsworth's as a subjective and Keats' as an objective method. I should be inclined to describe the same difference in another way, and to say that both by gift and purpose it was the part of Wordsworth to meditate and expound, while the part of Keats was to imagine and evoke. Wordsworth, bringing strong powers of abstract thinking to bear on his intense and intensely realized personal experience, expounds the spiritual relations of man to nature as he conceives them, sometimes, as in *Tintern Abbey* and many passages of *The Prelude* and *Excursion*, with more revealing insight and a more exalted passion than any other poet has attained; sometimes, alas! quite otherwise, when his passion has subsided, and he must needs to go back upon his experiences and droningly and flatly analyse and explain them. Keats, on the other hand, had a mind constitutionally unapt for abstract thinking. When he conceives or wishes to express general ideas, his only way of doing so is by calling up, from the multitudes of concrete images with which his memory and imagination are haunted, such as strike him as fitted by their colour and significance, their quality of association and suggestion, to stand for and symbolize the abstractions working in his mind; and in this concrete and figurative fashion he will be found, by those who take the pains to follow him, to think coherently and purposefully enough. Again, Keats' sense of personal identity was ever ready to be dissolved and carried under by the strength of his imaginative sympathies. It is not the effect of nature on his personal self that he realizes and ponders over; what he does is with ever-participating joy and instantaneous instinct to go out into the doings of nature and lose himself in them. In the result he neither strives for or attains, as Mr Bridges truly points out, the sheer intellectual lucidity which Wordsworth in his most impassioned moments never loses. But as, in regard to nature, Wordsworth's is the genius of luminous exposition, so Keats', even among the immaturities of his first volume, is the genius of living evocation.

Chapter V

APRIL-DECEMBER 1817: WORK ON ENDYMION

Keats' first volume had been launched, to quote the words of Cowden Clarke, 'amid the cheers and fond anticipations of all his circle. Everyone of us expected (and not unreasonably) that it would create a sensation in the literary world.' The magniloquent Haydon words these expectations after his manner: — 'I have read your *Sleep and Poetry* — it is a flash of lightning that will rouse men from their occupations and keep them trembling for the crash of thunder that *will* follow.' Sonnets poured in on the occasion, and not from intimates only. I have already quoted (p. 75) one which Reynolds, familiar with the contents of the forthcoming book, wrote a few days before its publication to welcome it and at the same time to congratulate Keats on his sonnet written in Clarke's copy of the *Floure and the Lefe*. Leigh Hunt, always delighted to repay compliment with compliment, replied effusively in kind to the sonnet in which Keats had dedicated the volume to him. Richard Woodhouse, of whom we shall soon hear more but who was as yet a stranger, in the closing lines of a sonnet addressed to Apollo, welcomed Keats as the last born son of that divinity and the herald of his return to lighten the poetic darkness of the land: —

> Have these thy glories perish'd? or in scorn
> Of thankless man hath thy race ceased to quire?
> O no! thou hear'st! for lo! the beamèd morn
> Chases our night of song: and, from the lyre
> Waking long dormant sounds, Keats, thy last born,
> To the glad realm proclaims the coming of his sire.

Sonnets are not often addressed by publishers to their clients: but one has been found in the handwriting of Charles Ollier, and almost certainly composed by him, expressing admiration for Keats' work. The brothers Ollier, it will be remembered, were Shelley's publishers, and for a while also Leigh Hunt's and Lamb's, and Charles was the poetry-loving and enthusiastic brother of the two, and himself a writer of some accomplishment in prose and verse. But in point of fact, outside the immediate Leigh Hunt circle, the volume made extremely little impression, and the public was as far as possible from being roused from its occupations or made tremble. 'Alas!' continues Cowden Clarke, 'the book might have emerged in Timbuctoo with far stronger chance of fame and appreciation. The whole community as if by compact, seemed determined to know nothing about it.'

Clarke here somewhat exaggerates the facts. Leigh Hunt kept his own review of the volume back for some three months, very likely with the just idea that praise from him might prejudice Keats rather than serve him. At length it appeared, in three numbers of the *Examiner* for June and July, the first number setting forth the aims and tendencies of the new movement in poetry with a conscious clearness such as to those taking part in a collective, three-parts instinctive effort of the kind comes usually in retrospect only and not in the thick of the struggle. In the second and third notices Hunt speaks of the old graces of poetry reappearing, warns 'this young writer of genius' against disproportionate detail and a too revolutionary handling of metre, and after quotation winds up by calling the volume 'a little luxuriant heap of

> Such sights as youthful poets dream
> On summer eves by haunted stream.'

Two at least of the established critical reviews noticed the book at length, Constable's *Scots and Edinburgh Magazine*, and the *Eclectic Review*, the chief organ of lettered nonconformity, owned and edited by the busy dissenting poet and bookseller Josiah Conder. Both criticisms are of the preaching and admonishing kind then almost universally in fashion. The Scottish reviewer recognizes in the new poet a not wholly unsuccessful disciple of Spenser, but warns him against 'the appalling doom which awaits the faults of mannerism or the ambition of a sickly refinement,' and with reference to his association with the person and ideas of Hazlitt and Hunt declares that 'if Mr Keats does not forthwith cast off the uncleanness of this school, he will never make his way to the truest strain of poetry in which, taking him by himself, it appears he might succeed.' The preachment of the *Eclectic* is still more pompous and superior. There are mild words of praise for some of the sonnets, but none for that on Chapman's Homer. *Sleep and Poetry*, declares the critic, would seem to show of the writer that 'he is indeed far gone, beyond the reach of the efficacy of either praise or censure, in affectation and absurdity. Seriously, however, we regret that a young man of vivid imagination and fine talents should have fallen into so bad hands as to have been flattered into the resolution to publish verses, of which a few years hence he will be glad to escape from the remembrance.'

Notices such as this could not help a new writer to fame or his book to sale. But before they appeared Keats and his brothers, or they for him, had begun to fret at the failure of the volume and to impute it, as authors and their friends will, to some mishandling by the publishers. George in John's absence wrote to the Olliers taking them to task pretty roundly, and received the often-quoted reply drafted, let us hope, not by the sonneteer but by James Ollier, his business brother, and alleging of the work that —

By far the greater number of persons who have purchased it from us have found fault with it in such plain terms, that we have in many cases offered to take it back rather than be annoyed with the ridicule which has, time after time, been showered upon it. In fact, it was only on Saturday last that we were under the mortification of having our own opinion of its merits flatly contradicted by a gentleman, who told us he considered it 'no better than a take in.'

Meanwhile Keats had found other publishers ready to take up his next work, and destined to become his staunch and generous friends. These were Messrs Taylor and Hessey of 93 Fleet Street. John Taylor, the chief partner, was a man of high character and considerable attainments, who had come up from Nottinghamshire to open a business in London ten years earlier. He was already noted as an authority on Junius and was to be a little later the editor as well as publisher of the *London Magazine*, and the good friend and frequent entertainer (in the back parlour of the publishing house in Fleet Street) of his most distinguished contributors. How and through whom Keats was introduced to his firm is not quite clear: probably through Benjamin Bailey, a new acquaintance whom we know to have been a friend of Taylor's. Bailey was an Oxford man five years older than Keats. He had been an undergraduate of Trinity and was now staying up at Magdalen Hall to read for orders. He was an ardent student of poetry and general literature as well as of theology, a devout worshipper of Milton, and scarcely less of Wordsworth, with whom he had some personal acquaintance. Of his appetite for books Keats wrote when they had come to know each other well: 'I should not like to be pages in your way; when in a tolerably hungry mood you have no mercy. Your teeth are the Rock Tarpeian down which you capsize epic poems like mad. I would not for forty shillings be Coleridge's Lays [i.e. *Lay Sermons*] in your way.' Bailey was intimate with John Hamilton Reynolds and his family, and at this time a suitor for the hand of his sister Marianne. In the course of the winter 1816-17 Reynolds had written to him enthusiastically of Keats' poetical promise and personal charm. When at the beginning of March Keats' volume came out, Bailey was much struck, and on a visit to London called to make the new poet's acquaintance. Though it was not until a few months later that this acquaintance ripened into close friendship, it may well have been Bailey who recommended Keats and Taylor to each other.

Relations of business or friendship with Taylor necessarily involved relations with Richard Woodhouse, a lettered and accomplished young solicitor of twenty-nine who was an intimate friend of Taylor's and at this time apparently the regular reader and adviser to the firm. Woodhouse was sprung from an old landed stock in Herefordshire, some of whose members were now in the wine-trade (his father, it seems, was owner or part owner of the White Hart at

Bath). He had been educated at Eton but not at the university: his extant correspondence, as well as notes and version-books in his hand, show him to have been a good linguist in Spanish and Italian and a man of remarkably fine literary taste and judgment. He afterwards held a high position as a solicitor and was one of the founders of the Law Life Insurance Society.

These three new friendships, with Benjamin Bailey, John Taylor, and Richard Woodhouse, formed during the six weeks between the publication of his book (March 3) and the mid-April following, turned out to be among the most valuable of Keats' life, and were the best immediate results the issue of his first volume brought him. During this interval he and his brothers were lodging at 17 Cheapside, having left their old quarters in the Poultry. Some time in March it was decided, partly on Haydon's urging, that John should for the sake of quiet and self-improvement go and spend some time by himself in the country, and try to get to work upon his great meditated *Endymion* poem. He writes as much to Reynolds, concluding with an adaptation from Falstaff expressive of anxiety for the health of some of those dear to him — probably his brother Tom and James Rice: —

My brothers are anxious that I should go by myself into the country — they have always been extremely fond of me, and now that Haydon has pointed out how necessary it is that I should be alone to improve myself, they give up the temporary pleasure of living with me continually for a great good which I hope will follow. So I shall soon be out of Town. You must soon bring all your present troubles to a close, and so must I, but we must, like the Fox, prepare for a fresh swarm of flies. Banish money — Banish sofas — Banish Wine — Banish Music; but right Jack Health, honest Jack Health, true Jack Health — Banish Health and banish all the world.

On the 14th of April Keats took the night mail for Southampton, whence he writes next day a lively letter to his brothers. By the 17th, having looked at Shanklin and decided against it, he was installed in a lodging at Carisbrooke. Writing to Reynolds he gives the reasons for his choice, mentioning at the same time that he is feeling rather nervous from want of sleep, and enclosing the admirable sonnet *On the Sea* which he has just composed —

> It keeps eternal whisperings around
> Desolate shores, *etc.* —

It was the intense haunting of the lines in the scene on Dover Cliff in *King Lear* beginning 'Do you not hear the sea,' which moved him, he says, to this effort. He was reading and re-reading his Shakespeare with passion, and phrases from the plays come up continually in his letters, not only, as in the following extract, in the form of set quotations, but currently, as though they were part of his own mind and being. Having found in the lodging-house passage an engraved head of Shakespeare which pleased him and hung it up in his room (his landlady afterwards made him a present of it), he bethinks him of the approaching anniversary, April 23: —

I'll tell you what — on the 23d was Shakespeare born. Now if I should receive a letter from you, and another from my Brothers on that day 'twould be a parlous good thing. Whenever you write say a word or two on some Passage in Shakespeare that may have come rather new to you, which must be continually happening, notwithstanding that we read the same Play forty times — for instance, the following from the Tempest never struck me so forcibly as at present,

> Urchins
> *Shall, for the vast of night that they may work*,
> All exercise on thee —
> How can I help bringing to your mind the line —
> In the dark backward and abysm of time.

I find I cannot exist without Poetry — without eternal Poetry — half the day will not do — the whole of it — I began with a little, but habit has made me a Leviathan I had become all in a Tremble from not having written anything of late — the Sonnet overleaf did me good. I slept the better last night for it — this Morning, however, I am nearly as bad again. Just now I opened Spenser, and the first Lines I saw were these —

> The noble heart that harbours virtuous thought,
> And is with child of glorious great intent,
> Can never rest until it forth have brought
> Th' eternal brood of glory excellent.

'I shall forthwith begin my *Endymion*,' he adds, and looks forward to reading some of it out, when his correspondent comes to visit him, in a nook near the castle which he has already marked for the purpose.

But Haydon's prescription of solitude turned out the worst Keats could well have followed in the then state of his mind, fermenting with a thousand restless thoughts and inchoate imaginations and with the feverish conflict between ambition and self-distrust. The result at any rate was that he passed the time, to use his own words, 'in continual burning of thought, as an only resource,' and what with that and lack of proper food felt himself after a week or ten days 'not over capable in his upper stories' and in need of change and companionship. He made straight for his last year's lodging at Margate and got Tom to join him there. Thence in the second week of May he writes a long letter to Hunt and another to Haydon. To Hunt he criticizes some points in the last number of the *Examiner*, and especially, in his kind-hearted, well-conditioned way, deprecates a certain vicious allusion to grey hairs in an attack of Hazlitt upon Southey. Later on we shall have to tell of the critical savagery of *Blackwood* and the *Quarterly*, now long since branded and proverbial. But it should be borne in mind, as it by no means always is, that the Tories were far from having the savagery to themselves. When Hazlitt, for one, chose to strike on the liberal side, he could match Gifford or Lockhart or Wilson or Maginn with their own weapons. To realize the controversial atmosphere of the time, here is a passage, and not the fiercest, from the Hazlitt article in which Keats found too venomous a sting. Southey's first love, rails Hazlitt, had been the Republic, his second was Legitimacy, 'her more fortunate and wealthy rival': —

He is becoming uxorious in his second matrimonial connection; and though his false Duessa has turned out a very witch, a murderess, a sorceress, perjured, and a harlot, drunk with insolence, mad with power, a griping rapacious wretch, bloody, luxurious, wanton, malicious, not sparing steel, or poison, or gold, to gain her ends — bringing famine, pestilence, and death in her train — infecting the air with her thoughts, killing the beholders with her looks, claiming mankind as her property, and using them as her slaves — driving every thing before her, and playing the devil wherever she comes, Mr Southey sticks to her in spite of everything, and for very shame lays his head in her lap, paddles with the palms of her hands, inhales her hateful breath, leers in her eyes and whispers in her ears, calls her little fondling names, Religion, Morality, and Social Order, takes for his motto,

> Be to her faults a little blind,
> Be to her virtues very kind —

sticks close to his filthy bargain, and will not give her up, because she keeps him, and he is down in her will. Faugh!

It is fair to note that the mistress thus depicted as Southey's is an allegorical being, while the Blackwood scurrilities were often directly personal.

After asking how Hunt's own new poem, *The Nymphs*, is getting on, Keats tells how he has been writing some of *Endymion* every day the last fortnight, except travelling days, and how thoughts of the greatness of his ambition and the uncertainty of his powers have thrown him into a fit of gloom; hinting at such moods of bleak and blank despondency as we shall find now and again figuratively described in the text of *Endymion* itself.

I have asked myself so often why I should be a poet more than other men, seeing how great a thing it is,... that at last the idea has grown so monstrously beyond my seeming power of attainment that the other day I nearly consented with myself to drop into a Phaeton... I see nothing but continual uphill journeying. Now is there anything more unpleasant than to be so journeying and to miss the goal at last? But I intend to whistle all those cogitations into the sea, where I hope they will breed storms enough to block up all exit from Russia. Does Shelley go on telling strange stories of the deaths of kings? Tell him there are strange stories of the deaths of poets. Some have died before they were conceived.

The same evening Keats begins to answer a letter of encouragement and advice he had just had from Haydon. This is the letter of Haydon's from which I have already quoted the passage about the efficacy of prayer as Haydon had experienced it. Perfectly sincere and genuinely moved, he can never for a minute continuously steer clear of rant and fustian and self-praise at another's expense.

Never despair, he goes on, while the path is open to you. By habitual exercise you will have habitual intercourse and constant companionship; and at every want turn to the Great Star of your hopes with a delightful confidence that will never be disappointed. I love you like my own brother: Beware, for God's sake, of the delusions and sophistications that are ripping up the talents and morality of our friend. He will go out of the world the victim of his own weakness and the dupe of his own self-delusions, with the contempt of his enemies and the sorrow of his friends, and the cause he undertook to support injured by his own neglect of character. I wish you would come up to town for a day or two that I may put your head in my picture. I have rubbed in Wordsworth's, and advanced the whole. God bless you, my dear Keats! do not despair; collect incident, study character, read Shakespeare, and trust in Providence, and you will do, you must.

Keats in answer quotes the opening speech of the King in *Love's Labour's Lost*, —

> Let Fame, that all pant after in their lives
> Live registered upon our brazen tombs, etc.,

saying that he could not bear to think he had not the right to couple his own name with Haydon's in such a forecast, and acknowledging the occasional moods of depression which have put him into such a state of mind as to read over his own lines and hate them, though he has picked up heart again when he found some from Pope's Homer which Tom read out to him seem 'like Mice' to his own. He takes encouragement also from the notion that has visited him lately of some good genius — can it be Shakespeare? — presiding over him. Continuing the next day, he is downhearted again at hearing from George of money difficulties actual and prospective. 'You tell me never to despair — I wish it was as easy for me to deserve the saying — truth is I have a horrid morbidity of Temperament which has shown itself at intervals it is I have no doubt the greatest Enemy and stumbling block I have to fear — I may even say it is likely to be the cause of my disappointment.' Then referring to Haydon's warning in regard to Hunt, he goes half way in agreement and declares he would die rather than be deceived about his own achievements as Hunt is. 'There is no greater sin after the seven deadly,' he says, 'than to flatter oneself into the idea of being a great poet: the comfort is, such a crime must bring its own penalty, and if one is a self-deluder indeed accounts must one day be balanced.'

In the same week, moved no doubt by the difficulties George had mentioned about touching the funds due from their grandmother's estate, Keats writes to Taylor and Hessey, in a lively and familiar strain showing the terms of confidence on which he already stood with them, asking them to advance him an instalment of the agreed price for *Endymion*. He mentions in this letter that he is tired of Margate (he had already to another correspondent called it a 'treeless affair') and means to move to Canterbury. At this point there occurs an unlucky gap in Keats' correspondence. We know that he and Tom went to Canterbury from Margate as planned, but we do not know exactly when, nor how long he stayed there, nor what work he did (except that he was certainly going on with the first book of *Endymion*), nor what impressions he received.

It was his first visit to a cathedral city, and few in the world, none in England, are more fitted to impress. Chichester and Winchester he came afterwards to know, Winchester well and with affection; but it was with thoughts of Canterbury in his mind that he planned, some two years later, first a serious and then a frivolous verse romance having an English cathedral town for scene (*The Eve of St Mark*, *The Cap and Bells*). The heroine of both was to have been a maiden of Canterbury called Bertha; not, of course, the historic Frankish princess Bertha, daughter of Haribert and wife of Ethelbert king of Kent, who converted her husband and prepared his people for Christianity before the landing of Saint Augustin, and who sleeps in the ancient church of Saint Martin outside the walls: not she, but some damsel of the city, named after her in later days, whom Keats had heard or read of or invented, — I would fain know which; but I have found no external evidence of his studies or doings during this spring stay at Canterbury, and his correspondence is, as I have said, a blank.

Some time in June he returned and the three brothers were together again: not now in City lodgings but in new quarters to which they had migrated in Well Walk, Hampstead. Their landlord was one Bentley the postman, with whom they seem to have got on well except that Keats occasionally complains of the 'young carrots,' his children, now for making a 'horrid row,' now for smelling of damp worsted stockings. The lack of letters continues through these first summer months at Hampstead. The only exception is a laughingly apologetic appeal to his new publishers for a further advance of money, dated June 10th and ending with the words, — 'I am sure you are confident of my responsibility, and of the sense of squareness that is always in me.' For the rest, indirect evidence allows us to picture Keats in these months as working regularly at *Endymion*, having now reached the second book, and as living socially, not without a certain amount of convivial claret-drinking and racket, in the company of his brothers and of his friends and theirs. Leigh Hunt was still close by in the Vale of Health, and both in his circle and in Haydon's London studio Keats was as welcome as ever. Reynolds and Rice were still his close intimates, and Reynolds's sisters in Lamb's Conduit Street almost like sisters of his own. He was scarcely less at home in the family of his sister-in-law that was to be, Georgiana Wylie. The faithful Severn and the faithful Haslam came up eagerly whenever they could to join the Hampstead party. An acquaintance he had already formed at Hunt's with the Charles Dilkes and their friend Charles Brown, who lived as next-door neighbours at Wentworth Place, a double block of houses of their own building in a garden at the foot of the Heath, now ripened into friendship: that with Dilke rapidly, that with Brown, a Scotsman who by his own account held cannily aloof from Keats at first for fear of being thought to push, more slowly.

Charles Wentworth Dilke, by profession a clerk in the Navy Pay Office, by predilection a keen and painstaking literary critic and antiquary, had been stimulated by the charm of Lamb's famous volume of *Specimens* to work at the old English dramatic poets, and had recently (being now twenty-seven) brought out a set of volumes in continuation of Dodsley's *Old Plays*. In matters political and social he was something of a radical doctrinaire and 'Godwin-perfectibility man' (the label is Keats'), loving decision and positiveness in all things and being therein the very opposite of Keats, who by rooted instinct as well as choice allowed his mind to cherish uncertainties and to be a thoroughfare for all thoughts (the phrase is again his own). There were many but always friendly discussions between Keats and Dilke, and their mutual regard never failed. Charles Brown, Dilke's contemporary, schoolfellow, and close friend, was a man of Scottish descent born in Lambeth, who had in early youth joined a business set up by an elder brother in Petersburg. The business quickly failing, he had returned to London and after some years of struggle inherited a modest competence from another brother. A lively, cultivated, moderately successful amateur in literature, journalism, and drama, he was in person bald and spectacled, and portly beyond his years though active and robust; in habits much of a trencherman ('a huge eater' according to the abstemious Trelawny) and something of a *viveur* within his means; exactly strict in money matters, but otherwise far from a precisian in life or conversation; an ardent friend and genial companion, though cherishing some fixed unreasonable aversions:

in a word, a truly Scottish blend of glowing warmheartedness and 'thrawn' prejudice, of frank joviality and cautious dealing.

It was in these same weeks of June or July 1817, soon after the beginning of the Oxford vacation, that Benjamin Bailey again came to town and sought after and learned to delight in Keats' company. He meant to go back and read at Oxford for the latter part of the vacation, and invited Keats to spend some weeks with him there. Keats accepted, and the visit, lasting from soon after mid August until the end of September, proved a happiness alike to host and guest. At this point our dearth of documents ceases. Bailey's memoranda, though not put on paper till thirty years later, are vivid and informing, and Keats' own correspondence during the visit is fairly full. I will take Bailey's recollections first, and give them in his own words, seeing that they paint the writer almost as well as his subject; omitting only passages that seem to drag or interrupt. First comes the impression Keats made on him at the time of their introduction in the spring, and then his account of the days they spent together in Oxford.

I was delighted with the naturalness and simplicity of his character, and was at once drawn to him by his winning and indeed affectionate manner towards those with whom he was himself pleased. Nor was his personal appearance the least charm of a first acquaintance with the young poet. He bore, along with the strong impress of genius, much beauty of feature and countenance. His hair was beautiful — a fine brown, rather than auburn, I think, and if you placed your hand upon his head, the silken curls felt like the rich plumage of a bird. The eye was full and fine, and softened into tenderness, or beamed with a fiery brightness, according to the current of his thoughts and conversation. Indeed the form of his head was like that of a fine Greek statue: — and he realized to my mind the youthful Apollo, more than any head of a living man whom I have known.

At the commencement of the long vacation I was again in London, on my way to another part of the country: and it was my intention to return to Oxford early in the vacation for the purpose of reading. I saw much of Keats. And I invited him to return with me to Oxford, and spend as much time as he could afford with me in the silence and solitude of that beautiful place during the absence of the numerous members and students of the University. He accepted my offer, and we returned together. I think in August 1817. It was during this visit, and in my room, that he wrote the third book of *Endymion* .... His mode of composition is best described by recounting our habits of study for one day during the month he visited me at Oxford. He wrote, and I read, sometimes at the same table, and sometimes at separate desks or tables, from breakfast to the time of our going out for exercise, — generally two or three o'clock. He sat down to his task, — which was about 50 lines a day, — with his paper before him, and wrote with as much regularity, and apparently as much ease, as he wrote his letters.... Sometimes he fell short of his allotted task, but not often: and he would make it up another day. But he never forced himself. When he had finished his writing for the day, he usually read it over to me: and he read or wrote letters until we went for a walk. This was our habit day by day. The rough manuscript was written off daily, and with few erasures.

I remember very distinctly, though at this distance of time, his reading of a few passages; and I almost think I hear his voice, and see his countenance. Most vivid is my recollection of the following passage of the finest affecting story of the old man, Glaucus, which he read to me immediately after its composition: —

> The old man raised his hoary head and saw
> The wildered stranger — seeming not to see,
> The features were so lifeless. Suddenly
> He woke as from a trance; his snow white brows
> Went arching up, *and like two magic ploughs
> Furrowed deep wrinkles in his forehead large,
> Which kept as fixedly as rocky marge,
> Till round his withered lips had gone a smile.*

The lines I have italicised, are those which then forcibly struck me as peculiarly fine, and to my memory have 'kept as fixedly as rocky marge.' I remember his upward look when he read of the 'magic ploughs,' which in his hands have turned up so much of the rich soil of Fairyland.

When we had finished our studies for the day we took our walk, and sometimes boated on the Isis.... Once we took a longer excursion of a day or two, to Stratford upon Avon, to visit the birthplace of Shakespeare. We went of course to the house visited by so many thousands of all nations of Europe, and inscribed our names in addition to the 'numbers numberless' of those which literally blackened the walls. We also visited the Church, and were pestered with a commonplace showman of the place.... He was struck, I remember, with the simple statue there, which, though rudely executed, we agreed was most probably the best likeness of the many extant, but none very authentic, of Shakespeare.

His enjoyment was of that genuine, quiet kind which was a part of his gentle nature; deeply feeling what he truly enjoyed, but saying little. On our return to Oxford we renewed our quiet mode of life, until he finished the third Book of *Endymion*, and the time came that we must part; and I never parted with one whom I had known so short a time, with so much real regret and personal affection, as I did with John Keats, when he left Oxford for London at the end of September or the beginning of October 1817.

Living as we did for a month or six weeks together (for I do not remember exactly how long) I knew him at that period of his life, perhaps as well as any one of his friends. There was no reserve of any kind between us.... His brother George says of him that to his brothers his temper was uncertain; and he himself confirms this judgment of him in a beautiful passage of a letter to myself. But with his friends, a sweeter tempered man I never knew. Gentleness was indeed his proper characteristic, without one particle of dullness, or insipidity, or want of spirit. Quite the contrary. 'He was gentle but not fearful,' in the chivalric and moral sense of the term 'gentle.' He was pleased with every thing that occurred in the ordinary mode of life, and a cloud never passed over his face, except of indignation at the wrongs of others.

His conversation was very engaging. He had a sweet toned voice, 'an excellent thing' in *man* as well as 'in woman....' In his letters he talks of *suspecting* everybody. It appeared not in his conversation. On the contrary, he was uniformly the apologist for poor, frail human nature, and allowed for people's faults more than any man I ever knew, especially for the faults of his friends. But if any act of wrong or oppression, of fraud or falsehood, was the topic, he rose into sudden and animated indignation. He had a truly poetic feeling for women; and he often spoke to me of his sister, who was somehow withholden from him, with great delicacy and tenderness of affection. He had a soul of noble integrity: and his common sense was a conspicuous part of his character. Indeed his character was in the best sense manly.

Our conversation rarely or never flagged, during our walks, or boatings, or in the evening. And I have retained a few of his opinions on Literature and criticism which I will detail. The following passage from Wordsworth's Ode on Immortality was deeply felt by Keats, who however at this time seemed to me to value this great Poet rather in particular passages than in the full-length portrait, as it were, of the great imaginative and philosophic Christian Poet, which he really is, and which Keats obviously, not long afterwards, felt him to be.

> Not for these I raise
> The song of thanks and praise;
> But for those obstinate questionings
> Of sense and outward things,
> Fallings from us, vanishings;
> Blank misgivings of a creature
> Moving about in worlds not realized,
> *High instincts, before which our mortal nature*
> Did tremble like a guilty thing surprized.

The last lines he thought were quite awful in their application to a guilty finite creature, like man, in the appalling nature of the feeling which they suggested to a thoughtful mind. Again, we often talked of that noble passage in the lines on *Tintern Abbey* : —

> That blessed mood,
> In which *the burthen of the mystery* ,
> In which the heavy and the weary weight
> Of all this unintelligible world
> Is lightened.

And his references to this passage are frequent in his letters. — But in those exquisite stanzas,

> She dwelt among the untrodden ways,
> Beside the springs of Dove,
> ending, —
> She lived unknown and few could know
> When Lucy ceased to be;
> But she is in her grave, and oh,
> *The difference to me* .

The simplicity of the last line he declared to be the most perfect pathos.

Among the qualities of high poetic promise in Keats was, even at this time, his correct taste. I remember to have been struck with this by his remarks on that well known and often quoted passage of the *Excursion* upon the Greek Mythology — where it is said that

> Fancy fetched
> Even from the blazing chariot of the Sun
> A beardless youth who touched a golden lute,
> *And filled the illumined groves with ravishment* .

Keats said this description of Apollo should have ended at the 'golden lute,' and have left it to the imagination to complete the picture, *how* he 'filled the illumined groves.' I think every man of taste will feel the justice of the remark.

Every one now knows what was then known to his friends that Keats was an ardent admirer of Chatterton. The melody of the verses of the marvellous Boy who perished in his pride, enchanted the author of *Endymion* . Methinks I now hear him recite, or *chant* , in his peculiar manner, the following stanza of the Roundelay sung by the minstrels of Ella: —

> *Come with acorn cup and thorn*
> Drain my hertys blood away;
> Life and all its good I scorn;
> Dance by night or feast by day.

The first line to his ear possessed the great charm. Indeed his sense of melody was quite exquisite, as is apparent in his own verses; and in none more than in numerous passages of his *Endymion* .

Another object of his enthusiastic admiration was the Homeric character of Achilles — especially when he is described as 'shouting in the trenches.' One of his favourite topics of discourse was the principle of melody in verse, upon which he had his own notions, particularly in the management of open and close vowels. I think I have seen a somewhat similar theory attributed to Mr Wordsworth. But I do not remember his laying it down in writing. Be this as it may, Keats' theory was worked out by himself. It was, that the vowels should be so managed as not to clash one with another, so as to hear the melody, — and yet that they should be interchanged, like differing notes of music to prevent monotony....

Bailey here tries to reconstruct and illustrate from memory Keats' theory of vowel sounds, but his attempt falters and breaks down.

Keats' own first account of himself from Oxford is in a letter of September 5th to the Reynolds sisters, then on holiday at Littlehampton: a piece of mere lively foolery and rattle meant to amuse, in a taste which is not that of to-day. Five days later he writes the first of that series of letters to his young sister Fanny which acquaints us with perhaps the most loveable and admirable parts of his character. She was now just fourteen, and living under the close guardianship of the Abbeys, who had put her to a boarding school at Walthamstow. Keats shows a tender and considerate elder-brotherly anxiety to get into touch with her and know her feelings and likings: —

Let us now begin a regular question and answer — a little pro and con; letting it interfere as a pleasant method of my coming at your favourite little wants and enjoyments, that I may meet them in a way befitting a brother.

We have been so little together since you have been able to reflect on things that I know not whether you prefer the *History of King Pepin* to Bunyan's *Pilgrim's Progress* — or *Cinderella* and her glass slipper to Moor's *Almanack*. However in a few Letters I hope I shall be able to come at that and adapt my scribblings to your Pleasure. You must tell me about all you read if it be only six Pages in a Week and this transmitted to me every now and then will procure full sheets of Writing from me pretty frequently. — This I feel as a necessity for we ought to become intimately acquainted, in order that I may not only, as you grow up love you as my only Sister, but confide in you as my dearest friend. When I saw you last I told you of my intention of going to Oxford and 'tis now a Week since I disembark'd from his Whipship's Coach the Defiance in this place. I am living in Magdalen Hall on a visit to a young Man with whom I have not been long acquainted, but whom I like very much — we lead very industrious lives — he in general Studies and I in proceeding at a pretty good rate with a Poem which I hope you will see early in the next year. — Perhaps you might like to know what I am writing about. I will tell you. Many Years ago there was a young handsome Shepherd who fed his flocks on a Mountain's Side called Latmus he was a very contemplative sort of a Person and lived solitary among the trees and Plains little thinking that such a beautiful Creature as the Moon was growing mad in Love with him. — However so it was; and when he was asleep on the Grass she used to come down from heaven and admire him excessively for a long time; and at last could not refrain from carrying him away in her arms to the top of that high Mountain Latmus while he was a dreaming — but I dare say you have read this and all the other beautiful Tales which have come down from the ancient times of that beautiful Greece. If you have not let me know and I will tell you more at large of others quite as delightful. This Oxford I have no doubt is the finest City in the world — it is full of old Gothic buildings — Spires — towers — Quadrangles — Cloisters — Groves etc and is surrounded with more clear streams than ever I saw together. I take a Walk by the Side of one of them every Evening and, thank God, we have not had a drop of rain these days.

He goes on to tell her (herein echoing Hunt's opinion) how much better it would be if Italian instead of French were taught everywhere in schools, and winds up: —

Now Fanny you must write soon — and write all you think about, never mind what — only let me have a good deal of your writing — You need not do it all at once — be two or three or four days about it, and let it be a diary of your Life. You will preserve all my Letters and I will secure yours — and thus in the course of time we shall each of us have a good Bundle — which, hereafter, when things may have strangely altered and God knows what happened, we may read over together and look with pleasure on times past — that now are to come.

Next follows another letter to Jane Reynolds; partly making fun, much better fun than in the last, about Dilke's shooting and about the rare havoc he would like to make in Mrs Dilke's garden were he at Hampstead: partly grave in the high style into which he is apt at any moment to change from nonsense: —

Now let us turn to the seashore. Believe me, my dear Jane, it is a great happiness to see that you are, in this finest part of the year, winning a little enjoyment from the hard world. In truth, the great Elements we know of, are no means comforters: the open sky sits upon our senses like a sapphire crown — the Air is our robe of state — the Earth is our throne and the Sea a mighty minstrel playing before it — able, like David's harp, to make such a one as you forget almost the tempest cares of life. I have found in the ocean's music, — varying (tho' selfsame) more than the passion of Timotheus, an enjoyment not to be put into words; and, 'though inland far I be,' I now hear the voice most audibly while pleasing myself in the idea of your sensations.

To Reynolds Keats writes on September the 21st: —

For these last five or six days, we have had regularly a Boat on the Isis, and explored all the streams about, which are more in number than your eye-lashes. We sometimes skim into a Bed of rushes, and there become naturalized river-folks, — there is one particularly nice nest, which we have christened 'Reynolds's Cove,' in which we have read Wordsworth, and talked as may be; I think I see you and Hunt meeting in the Pit. — What a very pleasant fellow he is, if he would give up the sovereignty of a room pro bono. What evenings we might pass with him, could we have him from Mrs H. Failings I am always rather rejoiced to find in a man than sorry for; they bring us to a level.

Then follows a diatribe against the literary and intellectual pretensions of certain sets of ladies, from which he has felt an agreeable relief in some verses he has found on taking down from Bailey's shelves the poems of Katherine Philips, 'the matchless Orinda.' The verses which pleased him, truly of her best, are those *To M. A. at parting*, and Keats goes on to copy them in full. Had Orinda been a contemporary, he might not, indeed, have failed to recognize in her a true woman of letters: but would he not also have found something to laugh and chafe at in the poses of that high-flying coterie of mutual admirers, Silvander and Poliarchus, Lucasia and Rosania and Palæmon, of which she was the centre? This is one of the very few instances to be found in Keats' work or correspondence of interest in the poetry of the Caroline age.

Quite in the last days of his visit Keats, whose mind and critical power had been growing while he worked upon *Endymion*, and whom moreover the long effort of composition was clearly beginning to fatigue, confides to Haydon his dissatisfaction with what he has done: — 'You will be glad to hear that within these last three weeks I have written 1000 lines — which are the third Book of my Poem. My Ideas with respect to it I assure you are very low — and I would write the subject thoroughly again — but I am tired of it and think the time would be better spent in writing a new Romance which I have in my eye for next summer — Rome was not built in a day — and all the good I expect from my employment this summer is the fruit of Experience which I hope to gather in my next Poem.'

Coming back in the first week of October to Hampstead, whither his brothers had by this time also returned from a trip to Paris, Keats was presently made uncomfortable by evidences of discord among his friends and reports of what seemed like disloyalty on the part of one of them, Leigh Hunt, to himself. Haydon had now left the studio in Great Marlborough Street for one in Lisson Grove, and the Hunts, having come away from Hampstead and paid a long latesummer visit to the Shelleys at Marlow, were lodging near him in the same street. 'Everybody seems at loggerheads,' Keats writes to Bailey. 'There's Hunt infatuated — there's Haydon's picture in statu quo — There's Hunt walks up and down his painting-room — criticizing every head most unmercifully.' Both Haydon and Reynolds, he goes on, keep telling him tales of Hunt: How Hunt has been talking flippantly and patronizingly of *Endymion*, saying that if it is four thousand lines long now it would have been seven thousand but for him, and giving the impression that Keats stood to him in the relation of a pupil needing and taking advice. He declares in consequence that he is quite disgusted with literary men and will never know another except Wordsworth; and then, more coolly and sensibly, 'now, is not this a most paltry thing to think about?...This is, to be sure, the vexation of a day, nor would I say so many words about it to any but those whom I know to have my welfare and reputation at heart.'

During the six or seven autumn weeks spent at Hampstead after his return from Oxford Keats was getting on, a little flaggingly, with the fourth book of *Endymion* , besides writing an occasional lyric or two. Fresh from the steadying and sympathetic companionship of Bailey, he keeps up their intimacy by affectionate letters in which he discloses much of that which lay deepest and was best in him. Writing in the first days of November he congratulates Bailey on having got a curacy in Cumberland and promises some day to visit him there; says he is in a fair way to have finished *Endymion* in three weeks; mentions an idea he has of shipping his brother Tom, who has been looking worse, off to Lisbon for the winter and perhaps going with him; and gets in by a side wind a masterly criticism of Wordsworth's poem *The Gipsies* and also of Hazlitt's criticism of it in the *Round Table* . A fragment of another letter, dated November the 5th, alludes with annoyance, not for the first time, to some failure of Haydon's to keep his word or take trouble about a young man from Oxford named Cripps whom he had promised to receive as pupil and in whom Bailey and Keats were interested. The same fragment records the appearance in *Blackwood* (the *Endinburgh Magazine* , as Keats calls it) of the famous first article of the Cockney School series, attacking Hunt with a virulence far beyond even the accustomed licence of the time, and seeming by the motto prefixed to it (verses of Cornelius Webb coupling the names of Hunt and Keats) to threaten a similar handling of Keats later on. 'I don't mind the thing much,' says Keats, 'but if he should go to such lengths with me as he has done with Hunt, I must infallibly call him to an Account if he be a human being, and appears in Squares and Theatres, where we might possibly meet — I don't relish his abuse.'

Some time about mid-November Keats, his health and strength being steadier than in the spring, felt himself in the mood for a few weeks of solitude and went to spend them at Burford Bridge Inn, in the beautiful vale of Mickleham between Leatherhead and Dorking. The outing, he wrote, was intended 'to change the scene — change the air — and give me a spur to wind up my poem, of which there are wanting lines.' Keats dearly loved a valley: he loved even the sound of the names denoting one. In his marginal notes to a copy of *Paradise Lost* he gave a friend we find the following: —

> 'Or have ye chosen this place
> After the toil of battle to repose
> Your wearied virtue, for the ease you find
> To slumber here, as in the vales of Heaven?'

There is cool pleasure in the very sound of vale. The English word is of the happiest chance. Milton has put vales in heaven and hell with the very utter affection and yearning of a great Poet. It is a sort of Delphic Abstraction — a beautiful thing made more beautiful by being reflected and put in a Mist. The next mention of Vale is one of the most pathetic in the whole range of Poetry: —

> 'Others, more mild,
> Retreated in a silent valley, sing
> With notes angelical to many a harp
> Their own heroic deeds and hapless fall
> By doom of battle.'
> How much of the charm is in the valley!

There, from his inmost self, speaks a poet of another poet, and as if to and for poets, deep calling unto deep. But in his everyday vein of speech or writing Keats was always reticent in regard to the scenery of places he visited, disliking nothing more than the glib ecstasies of the tourist in search of the picturesque. When he has looked round him in his new quarters at Burford Bridge he says simply, writing to Reynolds on November the 22nd, 'I like this place very much. There is Hill and Dale and a little river. I went up Box Hill this evening after the moon — "you a' seen the Moon" — came down and wrote some lines.' 'Whenever I am separated from you,' he continues, 'and not engaged in a continuous Poem, every letter shall bring you a lyric — but I am too anxious for you to enjoy the whole to send you a particle:' the whole, that is, of *Endymion*. The sequel shows him to be just as deep and ardent in the study of Shakespeare as when he was beginning his poem at Carisbrooke in the spring. 'I never found so many beauties in the Sonnets — they seem to be full of fine things said unintentionally — in the intensity of working out conceits:' and he goes on to quote passages and phrases both from them and from *Venus and Adonis*. Next, with a sudden change of mind about letting Reynolds see a sample of *Endymion*, 'By the Whim-King! I'll give you a stanza, because it is not material in connexion, and when I wrote it I wanted you to give your vote, pro or con.' — The stanza he gives is from the song of the Constellations in the fourth book, certainly one of the weakest things in the poem: pity Reynolds had not been there indeed, to give his vote *contra*.

On the same day, November 22, Keats writes to Bailey a letter even richer in contents and more self-revealing than this to Reynolds. It gives the indispensable key both to much in his own character and much of the deeper speculative and symbolic meanings underlying his work, from *Endymion* to the *Ode on a Grecian Urn*. Beginning with a wise and tolerant reference to the Haydon trouble, and throwing out a passing hint of the distinction between men of Genius, who have not, and men of Power, who have, a proper individual self or determined character of their own, Keats passes at the close to an illuminating self-confession which is also a contrast between himself and his correspondent: —

You perhaps at one time thought there was such a thing as worldly happiness to be arrived at, at certain periods of time marked out, — you have of necessity from your disposition been thus led away — I scarcely remember counting upon any happiness — I look not for it if it be not in the present hour, — nothing startles me beyond the moment. The Setting Sun will always set me to rights, or if a Sparrow come before my Window, I take part in its existence and pick about the gravel. The first thing that strikes me on hearing a misfortune having befallen another is this — 'Well, it cannot be helped: he will have the pleasure of trying the resources of his Spirit' — and I beg now, my dear Bailey, that hereafter should you observe anything cold in me not to put it to the account of heartlessness, but abstraction — for I assure you I sometimes feel not the influence of a passion or affection during a whole Week — and so long this sometimes continues, I begin to suspect myself, and the genuineness of my feelings at other times — thinking them a few barren Tragedy Tears.

Readers of *Endymion* will recognize a symbolic embodiment of a mood akin to this in the Cave of Quietude in the fourth book. But the great value of the letter, especially great as a help to the study of *Endymion* in general, is in the long central passage setting forth his speculations as to the relation of imagination to truth, meaning truth ultimate or transcendental. He finds his clue in the eighth book of *Paradise Lost*, where Adam, recounting to Raphael his first experiences as new-created man, tells how twice over he fell into a dream and awoke to find it true: his first dream thus confirmed in the result being how 'One of shape divine' took him by the hand and led him into the garden of Paradise: his second, how the same glorious shape came to him and opened his side and from his rib fashioned a creature:

> Manlike, but different sex, so lovely fair,
> That what seem'd fair in all the World, seem'd now
> Mean, or in her sum'd up, in her contain'd
> And in her looks, which from that time infus'd
> Sweetness into my heart, unfelt before,
> And into all things from her Air inspir'd
> The spirit of love and amorous delight.
> She disappear'd, and left me dark, I wak'd
> To find her, or for ever to deplore
> Her loss, and other pleasures all abjure:
> When out of hope, behold her, not far off,
> Such as I saw her in my dream, adorn'd

> With what all Earth or Heaven could bestow
> To make her amiable.

It was no doubt this second of Adam's dreams that was chiefly in Keats' mind. His way of explaining his speculations to his friend is quite unstudied and inconsecutive; he is, as he says, 'continually running away from the subject,' or shall we say letting the stream of his ideas branch out into side channels from which he finds it difficult to come back? But yet their main current and purport will be found not difficult to follow, if only the reader will bear one thing well in mind: that when Keats in this and similar passages speaks of 'Sensations' as opposed to 'Thoughts' he does not limit the word to sensations of the body, of what intensity or exquisiteness soever or howsoever instantaneously transforming themselves from sensation into emotion: what he means are intuitions of the mind and spirit as immediate as these, as thrillingly convincing and indisputable, as independent of all consecutive stages and formal processes of thinking: almost the same things, indeed, as in a later passage of the same letter he calls 'ethereal musings.' And now let the poet speak for himself: —

O! I wish I was as certain of the end of all your troubles as that of your momentary start about the authenticity of the Imagination. I am certain of nothing but of the holiness of the Heart's affections, and the truth of Imagination. What the Imagination seizes as Beauty must be Truth — whether it existed before or not, — for I have the same idea of all our passions as of Love: they are all, in their sublime, creative of essential Beauty. In a Word you may know my favourite speculation by my first Book, and the little Song I sent in my last, which is a representation from the fancy of the probable mode of operating in these Matters. The Imagination may be compared to Adam's dream, he awoke and found it truth: — I am more zealous in this affair, because I have never yet been able to perceive how anything can be known for truth by consecutive reasoning — and yet it must be. Can it be that even the greatest Philosopher ever arrived at his Goal without putting aside numerous objections? However it may be, O for a life of Sensations rather than of Thoughts! It is 'a Vision in the form of Youth,' a shadow of reality to come — and this consideration has further convinced me, — for it has come as auxiliary to another favourite speculation of mine, — that we shall enjoy ourselves hereafter by having what we called happiness on Earth repeated in a finer tone. And yet such a fate can only befall those who delight in Sensation, rather than hunger as you do after Truth. Adam's dream will do here, and seems to be a Conviction that Imagination and its empyreal reflexion, is the same as human life and its spiritual repetition. But, as I was saying, the simple imaginative Mind may have its rewards in the repetition of its own silent Working coming continually on the Spirit with a fine Suddenness. To compare great things with small, have you never, by being surprised with an old Melody, in a delicious place by a delicious voice, *felt* over again your very speculations and surmises at the time it first operated on your soul? Do you not remember forming to yourself the Singer's face — more beautiful than it was possible, and yet, with the elevation of the Moment, you did not think so? Even then you were mounted on the Wings of Imagination, so high that the prototype must be hereafter — that delicious face you will see.

There is one sentence in the above which gives us special matter for regret. Keats speaks of 'the little Song I sent in my last, which is a representation from the fancy of the probable mode of operating in these matters.' Such a song, if we had it, would doubtless put forth clearly and melodiously in concrete imagery the ideas which Keats in his letter tries to expound in the abstract language of which he is by nature so much less a master. Of 'my last,' that is of his preceding letter to Bailey, unhappily but a fragment is preserved, and the song must have been lost with the sheet or sheets which went astray, seeing that none of Keats' preserved lyrics can be held to answer to his account of this one. His words have a further interest as proving that now in these days of approaching winter, with his long poem almost finished, he allowed himself to digress into some lyric experiments, as in its earlier stages he had not done. External testimony and reasonable inference enable us to identify some of these experiments. Two or three lightish love-lyrics, whether impersonal or inspired by passing adventures of his own, are among the number. That beginning 'Think not of it, sweet one, so,' dates definitely from November 11, before he left Hampstead. To nearly about the same time belongs almost certainly the very daintily finished stanzas 'Unfelt, unheard, unseen,' which one at least of Keats' subtlest critics considers (I cannot agree with her) the first of his technically faultless achievements. So also, I am convinced, does that much less happily wrought thing, the little love-plaint discovered only two years ago and beginning —

> You say you love, but with a voice
> Chaster than a nun's who singeth
> The soft vespers to herself
> When the chime-bell ringeth —
> O love me truly!
> You say you love; but with a smile
> Cold as sunrise in September,
> As you were St Cupid's nun,
> And kept his week of Ember.
> O love me truly! —

and so forth. Here again, it seems evident, we have an instance of an echo from one of the old Elizabethan poets (this time an anonymous song-writer) lingering like a chime in Keats' memory. Listen to the first three stanzas of *A Proper Wooing Song*, written to the tune of the *Merchant's Daughter* and printed in Clement Robinson's *Handful of Pleasant Delites*, 1584: —

> Maide will ye loue me yea or no?
> tell me the trothe and let me go.
> It can be no lesse than a sinful deed,
> trust me truly,
> To linger a Louer that lookes to speede,
> in due time duly.
> You maides that thinke yourselves as fine,
> as Venus and all the Muses nine:
> The Father Himselfe when He first made man,
> trust me truly,
> Made you for his helpe when the world began,
> in due time duly.
> Then sith God's will was even so
> why should you disdaine your Louer tho?
> But rather with a willing heart,
> loue him truly;
> For in so doing you do your part
> let reason rule ye.

The metrical form of Keats' verses is not, indeed, the same as that of the Elizabethan song, but I think he must certainly have had the cadence of its refrains more or less consciously in his mind's ear.

A definite and dated case of a lyrical experiment suggested to Keats at this time by an older model is the famous little 'drear-nighted December' song in which he re-embodies, with new and seasonable imagery, the ancient moral of the misery added to misery by the remembrance of past happiness. This was composed, as Woodhouse on the express testimony of Jane Reynolds informs us, in the beginning of this same December, 1817, when Keats was finishing *Endymion* at Burford Bridge. Any reader familiar with the aspect of the spot at that season, when the overhanging trees have shed their last gold, and spars of ice have begun to fringe the sluggish meanderings of the Mole, will realize how deeply the sentiment of the scene and season has sunk into Keats' verse. Well as the piece is known, I shall quote it entire, not in the form in which it is printed in the editions, but in that in which alone it exists in his own handwriting and in the transcripts by his friends Woodhouse and Brown: —

> In drear-nighted December,
> Too happy, happy tree,
> Thy branches ne'er remember
> Their green felicity:
> The north cannot undo them,
> With a sleety whistle through them;
> Nor frozen thawings glue them
> From budding at the prime.
> In drear-nighted December,
> Too happy, happy brook,
> Thy bubblings ne'er remember
> Apollo's summer look;
> But with a sweet forgetting,
> They stay their crystal fretting,
> Never, never petting
> About the frozen time.
> Ah! would 'twere so with many
> A gentle girl and boy!
> But were there ever any
> Writh'd not at passed joy?
> The feel of *not* to feel it,
> When there is none to heal it,
> Nor numbed sense to steel it,
> Was never said in rhyme.

Keats' model in this instance is a song from Dryden's *Spanish Fryar*, a thing rather beside his ordinary course of reading: can he perhaps have taken the volume containing it from Bailey's shelves, as he took the poems of Orinda? Here is a verse to show the tune as set by Dryden: —

> Farewell ungrateful Traitor,
> Farewell my perjured swain,
> Let never injured creature
> Believe a man again.
> The pleasure of possessing
> Surpasses all expressing,
> But 'tis too short a blessing,
> And Love too long a pain.

Do readers recall what the greatest of metrical magicians, who would be so very great a poet if metrical magic were the whole of poetry, or if the body of thought and imagination in his work had commonly half as much vitality as the verbal music which is its vesture, — do readers recall what Mr Swinburne made of this same measure when he took it up half a century later in the *Garden of Proserpine*?

But in attending to these incidental lyrics we risk losing sight of what was Keats' main business in these weeks, namely the bringing to a close his eight months' task upon *Endymion*. In finishing the poem he was only a little behind the date he had fixed when he wrote its opening lines at Carisbrooke: —

> Many and many a verse I hope to write,
> Before the daisies, vermeil rimm'd and white,

> Hide in deep herbage; and ere yet the bees
> Hum about globes of clover and sweet peas,
> I must be near the middle of my story.
> O may no wintry season, bare and hoary,
> See it half finish'd: but let Autumn bold,
> With universal tinge of sober gold,
> Be all about me when I make an end.

The gold had almost all fallen: in the passage in which Keats makes Endymion bid what he supposes to be his last farewell to his mortal love it is the season itself, the season and the autumnal scene, which speak, just as they spoke in the 'drear-nighted December' lyric: —

> The Carian
> No word return'd: both lovelorn, silent, wan,
> Into the vallies green together went.
> Far wandering, they were perforce content
> To sit beneath a fair lone beechen tree;
> Nor at each other gaz'd, but heavily
> Por'd on its hazle cirque of shedded leaves.

and again: —

> At this he press'd
> His hands against his face, and then did rest
> His head upon a mossy hillock green,
> And so remain'd as he a corpse had been
> All the long day; save when he scantly lifted
> His eyes abroad, to see how shadows shifted
> With the slow move of time, — sluggish and weary
> Until the poplar tops, in journey dreary,
> Had reach'd the river's brim. Then up he rose,
> And slowly as that very river flows,
> Walk'd towards the temple grove with this lament:
> 'Why such a golden eve? The breeze is sent
> Careful and soft, that not a leaf may fall
> Before the serene father of them all
> Bows down his summer head below the west.
> Now am I of breath, speech, and speed possest,
> But at the setting I must bid adieu
> To her for the last time. Night will strew
> On the damp grass myriads of lingering leaves,
> And with them shall I die; nor much it grieves
> To die, when summer dies on the cold sward.'

That point about making, as it were, a dial-hand of a certain group of poplars with their moving shadows would have a special local interest if one could find the place which suggested it. The sun sets early in this valley in the winter. I know not if there is any group of trees still standing that could be watched thus lengthening out its afternoon shadow to the river's edge.

Opposite the last line in the manuscript of *Endymion* Keats wrote the date November 28, whence it would appear that it had taken him some ten days at most to complete the required five hundred lines. He did not immediately leave Burford Bridge, but stayed on through the first week or ten days of December, setting to work at once, it would appear, on the revision of his long poem, and composing, we know, the 'drear-nighted December' lyric, and perhaps one or two others, before he returned to the fraternal lodgings at Hampstead. The scheme of a winter flight to Lisbon for the suffering Tom had been given up, and it had been arranged instead that George should take him to spend some months at Teignmouth. They were to be there by Christmas, and Keats timed his return so as to be with them for a week or two at Hampstead before they started. *Endymion* was not published until the following April, but inasmuch as with its completion there ends the first, the uncertain, experimental, now rapturously and now despondently expectant phase of Keats' mind and art, let us make this our opportunity for studying it.

Chapter VI

ENDYMION. — I. THE STORY: ITS SOURCES, PLAN, AND SYMBOLISM

Keats had long been in love with the Endymion story. The very music of the name, he avers, had gone into his being. We have seen how in the poem beginning 'I stood tiptoe,' finished at the end of 1816, he tried a kind of prelude or induction to the theme, and how, laying this aside, he determined to start fresh on a 'poetical romance' of Endymion on a great scale. When in April 1817, six weeks after the publication of the volume of *Poems*, he went off to the Isle of Wight to get firmly to work on his new task, it is clear that he had its main outlines and dimensions settled in his mind, but nothing more. He wrote to George soon after his departure: —

As to what you say about my being a Poet, I can return no Answer but by saying that the high Idea I have of poetical fame makes me think I see it towering too high above me. At any rate, I have no right to talk until *Endymion* is finished, it will be a test, a trial of my Powers of Imagination, and chiefly of my invention which is a rare thing indeed — by which I must make 4000 lines of one bare circumstance, and fill them with poetry — and when I consider that this is a great task, and that when done it will take me but a dozen paces towards the temple of fame — it makes me say — God forbid that I should be without such a task! I have Heard Hunt say, and I may be asked — why endeavour after a long Poem? To which I should answer, Do not the Lovers of Poetry like to have a little Region to wander in, where they may pick and choose, and in which the images are so numerous that many are forgotten and found new in a second Reading.... Besides, a long Poem is a test of invention, which I take to be the Polar Star of Poetry, as Fancy is the Sails — and Imagination the rudder. — Did our great Poets ever write Short Pieces? I mean in the shape of Tales. This same invention seems indeed of late years to have been forgotten as a Poetical excellence — But enough of this, I put on no Laurels till I shall have finished *Endymion*, and I hope Apollo is not angered at my having made a Mockery at Hunt's —

In his reiterated insistence on Invention and Imagination as the prime endowments of a poet, Keats closely echoes Joseph Warton's protest uttered seventy years before: is this because he had read and remembered it, or only because the same words came naturally to him in pleading the same cause? When his task was finished he confessed, in the draft of a preface afterwards cancelled, — 'Before I began I had no inward feel of being able to finish; and as I proceeded my steps were all uncertain.' But so far as the scale of the poem was concerned he adhered almost exactly to his original purpose, dividing it into four books and finding in himself resources enough to draw them out, all except the first, to a little over a thousand lines each.

Throughout Keats' work, the sources of his inspiration in his finest passages can almost always be recognized as dual, some special joy in the delights or sympathy with the doings of nature working together in him with some special stimulus derived from books. Of such a dual kind is the whole inspiration of *Endymion*. The poem is a joint outcome of his intense, his abnormal susceptibility to the spell of moonlight and of his pleasure in the ancient myth of the loves of the moon-goddess Cynthia and the shepherd-prince Endymion as made known to him through the earlier English poets.

The moon was to Keats a power very different from what she has always been to popular astrology and tradition. Traditionally and popularly she was the governess of floods, the presiding planet of those that ply their trade by sea, river, or canal, also of wanderers and vagabonds generally: the disturber and bewilderer withal of mortal brains and faculties, sending down upon men under her sway that affliction of lunacy whose very name was derived from her. For Keats it was her transmuting and glorifying power that counted, not her pallor but her splendour, the magic alchemy exercised by her light upon the things of earth, the heightened mystery, poetry, and withal unity of aspect which she sheds upon them. He can never keep her praises long out of his early poetry, and we have seen, in '*I stood tiptoe*,' what a range of beneficent activities he attributes to her. Now, as he settles down to work on *Endymion*, we shall find her, by reason of that special glorifying and unifying magic of her light, become for him, at first perhaps instinctively and unaware, but more and more consciously as he goes on, a definite symbol of Beauty itself — what he calls in a letter 'the principle of Beauty in all things,' the principle which binds in a divine community all such otherwise unrelated matters as those we shall find him naming together as things of beauty in the exordium of his poem. Hence the tale of the loves of the Greek shepherd-prince and the moon-goddess turns under his hand into a parable of the adventures of the poetic soul striving after full communion with this spirit of essential Beauty.

As to the literary associations which drew Keats to the Endymion story, there is scarce one of our Elizabethan poets but touches on it briefly or at length. Keats was no doubt acquainted with the *Endimion* of John Lyly, an allegorical court comedy in sprightly prose which had been among the plays edited, as it happened, by one of his new Hampstead friends, Charles Dilke: but in it he could have found nothing to his purpose. Marlowe is likely to have been in his mind, with

> — that night-wandering, pale, and watery star,
> When yawning dragons draw her thirling car
> From Latmus' mount up to the gloomy sky,
> Where, crowned with blazing light and majesty,
> She proudly sits.
> So will Shakespeare have been certainly, with the call —
> Peace, ho! the moon sleeps with Endymion,
> And would not be awaked,

uttered by Portia at the close of the most enchanting moonlight scene in all literature. Scarcely less familiar to Keats will have been the invocation near the end of Spenser's *Epithalamion*, or the reference to 'pale-changeful Cynthia' and her Endymion in Browne's *Britannia's Pastorals*; or those that recur once and again in the sonnets of Drummond of Hawthornden, or those he would have remembered from the masque in the *Maid's Tragedy* of Beaumont and Fletcher, or in translations of the love-elegies and heroical epistles of Ovid. But the two Elizabethans, I think, who were chiefly in his conscious or unconscious recollection when he meditated his theme are Fletcher and Michael Drayton. Here is the fine Endymion passage, delightfully paraphrased from Theocritus, and put into the mouth of the wanton Cloe, by Fletcher in the *Faithful Shepherdess*, that tedious, absurd, exquisitely written pastoral of which the measures caught and charmed Keats' ear in youth as they had caught and charmed the ear of Milton before him.

> Shepherd, I pray thee stay, where hast thou been?
> Or whither go'st thou? Here be Woods as green
> As any, air likewise as fresh and sweet,
> As where smooth *Zephyrus* plays on the fleet
> Face of the curled Streams, with Flowers as many
> As the young Spring gives, and as choise as any;
> Here be all new Delights, cool Streams and Wells,
> Arbors o'rgrown with Woodbinds, Caves, and Dells,
> Chuse where thou wilt, whilst I sit by, and sing,
> Or gather Rushes to make many a Ring
> For thy long fingers; tell thee tales of Love,
> How the pale *Phoebe* hunting in a Grove,
> First saw the Boy *Endymion*, from whose Eyes
> She took eternal fire that never dyes:
> How she convey'd him softly in a sleep,

> His temples bound with poppy, to the steep
> Head of old Latmus, where she stoops each night,
> Gilding the Mountain with her Brothers light,
> To kiss her sweetest.

In regard to Drayton's handling of the story there is more to note. In early life he wrote a poem in heroic couplets called *Endimion and Phoebe*. This he never reprinted, but introduced passages from it into a later piece in the same metre called the *Man in the Moone*. The volume containing Drayton's earlier *Endimion and Phoebe* became so rare that when Payne Collier reprinted it in 1856 only two copies were known to exist. It is unlikely that Keats should have seen either of these. But he possessed of his own a copy of Drayton's poems in Smethwick's edition of 1636 (one of the prettiest of seventeenth century books). The *Man in the Moone* is included in that volume, and that Keats was familiar with it is evident. In it, as in the earlier version, but with a difference, the poet, having enthroned his shepherd-prince beside Cynthia in her kingdom of the moon, weaves round him a web of mystical disquisition and allegory, in which popular fancies and superstitions are queerly jumbled up with the then current conceptions of the science of astronomy and the traditions of mediæval theology as to the number and order of the celestial hierarchies. In Drayton's earlier poem all this is highly serious and written in a rich and decorated vein of poetry intended, it might seem, to rival Marlowe's *Hero and Leander*: in his later, where the tale is told by a shepherd to his mates at the feast of Pan, the narrator lets down his theme with a satiric close in the vein of Lucian, recounting the human delinquencies nightly espied by Cynthia and her lover from their sphere.

The particular points in Keats' *Endymion* where I seem to find suggestions from Drayton's *Man in the Moone* are these. First the idea of introducing the story with the feast of Pan, — but as against this it may be said with truth that feasts of Pan are stock incidents in Elizabethan masques and pastorals generally. Second, his sending his hero on journeys beside or in pursuit of his goddess through manifold bewildering regions of the earth and air: for this antiquity affords no warrant, and the hint may have been partly due to the following passage in Drayton (which is also interesting for its exceptionally breathless and trailing treatment of the verse): —

> Endymion now forsakes
>
>> All the delights that shepherds do prefer,
>> And sets his mind so gen'rally on her
>> That, all neglected, to the groves and springs,
>> He follows Phoebe, that him safely brings
>> (As their great queen) unto the nymphish bowers,
>> Where in clear rivers beautified with flowers
>> The silver Naides bathe them in the brack.
>> Sometime with her the sea-horse he doth back,
>> Amongst the blue Nereides; and when,
>> Weary of waters, goddess-like again
>> She the high mountains actively assays,
>> And there amongst the light Oriades,
>> That ride the swift roes, Phoebe doth resort;
>> Sometimes amongst those that with them comport,
>> The Hamadriades, doth the woods frequent;
>> And there she stays not; but incontinent
>> Calls down the dragons that her chariot draw,
>> And with Endymion pleased that she saw,
>> Mounteth thereon, in twinkling of an eye,

Stripping the winds, beholding from the sky
The Earth in roundness of a perfect ball, —

the sequel is irrelevant, and the passage so loose in grammar and construction that it matters not where it is broken off.

Thirdly, we have the curious invention of the magic robe of Glaucus in Keats' third book. In it, we are told, all the rulers and all the denizens of ocean are figured and indued with magic power to dwindle and dilate before the beholder's eyes. Keats describes this mystic garment in a dozen lines which can scarcely be other than a summary and generalized recollection of a long passage of eighty in which Drayton describes the mantle of Cynthia herself, inwoven with figures of sea and storm and shipwreck and seabirds and of men fishing and fowling (crafts supposed to be subject to the planetary influence of the moon) in tidal or inland waters. And lastly, Keats in his second book has taken a manifest hint from Drayton where he makes Venus say archly how she has been guessing in vain which among the Olympian goddesses is Endymion's lover.

Not merely by delight in particular poets and familiarity with favourite passages, but by rooted instinct and by his entire self-training, Keats was beyond all his contemporaries, — and it is the cardinal fact to be borne in mind about him, — the lineal descendant and direct heir of the Elizabethans. The spirit of Elizabethan poetry was born again in him with its excesses and defects as well as its virtues. One general characteristic of this poetry is its prodigality and confusion of incidental, irrelevant, and superfluous beauties, its lack, however much it may revel in classical ideas and associations, of the classical instinct for clarity, simplicity, and selection. Another (I speak especially of narrative poetry) is its habitual wedding of allegory and romance, its love of turning into parable every theme, other than mere chronicle, which it touches. All the masters with whom Keats was at this time most familiar — Spenser of course first and foremost, William Browne and practically all the Spenserians, — were men apt to conceive alike of Grecian myth and mediæval romance as necessarily holding moral and symbolic under-meanings in solution. Again, it was from Ovid's *Metamorphoses*, as Englished by that excellent Jacobean translator, George Sandys, that Keats, more than from any other source, made himself familiar with the details of classic fable; and Sandys, in the fine Oxford folio edition of his book which we know Keats used, must needs conform to a fixed mediæval and Renaissance tradition by 'mythologizing' his text, as he calls it, with a commentary full not only of illustrative parallel passages but of interpretations half rationalist, half ethical, which Ovid never dreamt of. Neither must it be forgotten that among Keats' own contemporaries Shelley had in his first important poem, *Alastor*, set the example of embarking on an allegoric theme, and one shadowing forth, as we shall find that *Endymion* shadows forth though on different lines, the adventures and experiences of the poetic soul in man.

The bewildering redundance and intricacy of detail in *Endymion* are obvious, the presence of an underlying strain of allegoric or symbolic meaning harder to detect. Keats' letters referring to his poem contain only the slightest and rarest hints of the presence of such ideas in it, and in the execution they are so little obtruded or even made clear that they were wholly missed by two generations of his earlier readers. It is only of late years that they have yielded themselves, and even now none too definitely, to the scrutiny of students reading and re-reading the poem by the light of incidental utterances in his earlier and later poetry and in his miscellaneous letters. But the ideas are certainly there: they account for and give interest to much that, taken as mere narrative, is confusing or unpalatable: and the best way of finding a clue through the mazes of the poem is by laying and keeping hold upon them wherever we can.

For such a clue to serve the reader, he must have it in his hand from the beginning. Let it be borne in mind, then, that besides the fundamental idea of treating the passion of Endymion for Cynthia as a type of the passion of the poetic soul for essential Beauty, Keats wrote under the influence of two secondary moral ideas or convictions, inchoate probably in his mind when he began but gaining definiteness as he went on. One was that the soul enamoured of and pursuing Beauty cannot achieve its quest in selfishness and isolation, but to succeed must first be taken out of itself and purified by active sympathy with the lives and sufferings of others: the other, that a passion for the manifold separate and dividual beauties of things and beings upon earth is in its nature identical with the passion for that transcendental and essential Beauty: hence the various human love-adventures which befall the hero in dreams or in reality, and seem to distract him from his divine quest, are shown in the end to be in truth no infidelities but only attractions exercised by his celestial mistress in disguise.

In devising the adventures of his hero in accordance with these leading ideas, Keats works in part from his own mental experience. He weaves into his tale, in terms always of concrete imagery, all the complex fluctuations of joy and despondency, gleams of confident spiritual illumination alternating with faltering hours of darkness and self-doubt, which he had himself been undergoing since the ambition to be a great poet seized him. He cannot refrain from also weaving in a thousand and one irrelevant matters which the activity and ferment of his young imagination suggest, thus continually confusing the main current of his narrative and breaking the coherence of its symbolism. He draws out 'the one bare circumstance,' to use his own phrase, of the story into an endless chain of intricate and flowery narrative, leading us on phantasmagoric journeyings under the bowels of the earth and over the floor of ocean and through the fields of air. The scenery, indeed, is often not merely of a Gothic vastness and intricacy: there is something of Oriental bewilderment — an Arabian Night's jugglery with space and time — in the vague suddenness with which its changes are effected.

Critics so justly esteemed as Mr Robert Bridges and Professor de Sélincourt have sought a key to the organic structure of the poem in the supposition that each of its four books is intended to relate the hero's probationary adventures in one of the four elements, the first book being assigned to Earth, the second to Fire, the third to Water, the fourth to Air. I am convinced that this view is mistaken. The action of the first book passes on earth, no doubt, and that of the second beneath the earth. Now it is true that according to ancient belief there existed certain subterranean abodes or focuses of fire, — the stithy of Vulcan, the roots of Etna where the giants lay writhing, the river of bale rolling in flames around the city of the damned. But such things did not make the underworld, as the theory of these critics assumes, the recognized region of the element fire. According to the cosmology fully set forth by Ovid at the beginning of his first book, and therefore thoroughly familiar to Keats, the proper region or sphere of fire was placed above and outside that of air and farthest of all from earth. Not only had Keats therefore no ancient authority for thinking of the underworld as the special region of fire, he had explicit authority to the contrary. Moreover, if he had meant fire he would have given us fire, whereas in his underworld there is never a gleam of it, not a flicker of the flames of Phlegethon nor so much as a spark from the anvil of Vulcan; but instead, endless shadowy temple corridors, magical cascades spouting among prodigious precipices, and the gardens and bower of Adonis in their spring herbage and freshness. It is true, again, that the third book takes us and keeps us under sea. But the reason is the general one that Endymion, typifying the poetic soul of man in love with the principle of essential Beauty, has to leave habitual things behind him and

> wander far
> In other regions, past the scanty bar
> To mortal steps,

in order to learn secrets of life, death, and destiny necessary to his enlightenment and discipline. Where else should he learn such secrets if not in the mysterious hollows of the earth and on the untrodden floor of ocean? 'Our friend Keats,' Endymion is made to say in one of the poet's letters from Oxford, 'has been hauling me through the earth and sea with unrelenting perseverance': and in like manner in the poem itself the hero asks,

> Why am I not as are the dead,
> Since to a woe like this I have been led
> Through the dark earth, and through the wondrous sea?

But never a word to suggest any thought of the element fire — an element from which Keats' too often fevered spirit seems even to have shrunk, for except in telling of the blazing omens of *Hyperion's* downfall it is scarce mentioned in his poetry at all. Lastly, it is again true that in the fourth book Endymion and his earthly love are carried by winged horses on an ethereal excursion among the stars (though only for two hundred and seventy lines out of a thousand, the rest of the action passing, like that of the first book, on the soil of Caria). But this flight has nothing to do with the element air as such; it is the flight of the soul on the coursers of imagination through a region of dreams and visions destined afterwards to come true. Hints for such submarine and ethereal wanderings will no doubt have come into Keats' mind from various sources in his reading, — from the passage of Drayton above quoted, — from the *Arabian Nights*, — it may be from like incidents in the mediæval Alexander romances (in which the hero's crowning exploits are always a flight to heaven with two griffins and a plunge undersea in a glass case), or possibly even from the *Endimion* of Gombauld, a very wild and withal tiresome French seventeenth-century prose romance on Keats' own theme.

Book I. This book is entirely introductory, and carries us no farther than the exposition by the hero of the trouble in which he finds himself. For its exordium Keats uses a line, and probably a whole passage, which he had written many months before and kept by him. One day in 1816, while he was still walking the hospitals and sharing rooms in St Thomas's Street with his fellow students Mackereth and Henry Stephens, Keats called out to Stephens from his window-seat to listen to a new line he had just written, — 'A thing of beauty is a constant joy,' — and asked him how he liked it. Stephens indicating that he was not quite satisfied, Keats thought again and came out with the amended line, now familiar and proverbial even to triteness, 'A thing of beauty is a joy for ever.' Using this for the first line of his new poem, Keats runs on from it into a passage, which may or may not have been written at the same time, declaring the virtues of those things of beauty — sun, moon, trees, rivulets, flowers, tales of beauty and heroism indiscriminately — which make for health and quietude amidst the gloom and distemper of the world. Then he tells of his own happiness in setting about his cherished task in the prime of spring, and his hopes of finishing it before winter. He takes us to a Pan-haunted forest on Mount Latmos, with many paths leading to an open glade. The hour is dawn, the scene in part manifestly modelled on a similar one in the Chaucerian poem, *The Floure and Lefe*, in which he took so much pleasure. First a group of little children come in from the forest paths and gather round the altar, then a bevy of damsels, then a company of shepherds; priests and people follow, and last of all the young shepherd-prince and hero Endymion, now wan and pining from a new, unexplained soul-sickness.

The festival opens with a speech of thanksgiving and exhortation from the priest, followed by a choral hymn in honour of the god: then come dances and games and story-telling. Meantime Endymion and the priest sit apart among the elder shepherds, who pass the time imagining what happy tasks and ministrations it will be theirs to ply in their 'homes ethereal' after death. In the midst of such conversation Endymion goes off into a distressful trance, during which there comes to him his sister Peona (this personage and her name are inventions of Keats, the name perhaps suggested by that of Paeana in the fourth book of the *Faerie Queene*, or by the Paeon mentioned in Lemprière as a son of Endymion in the Elean version of the tale, or by Paeon the physician of the gods in the *Iliad*, whom she resembles in her quality of healer and comforter; or very probably by all three together). Peona wakes her brother from his trance, and takes him in a shallop to an arbour of her own on a little island in a lake. Here she lulls him to rest, the poet first pausing to utter a fine invocation to Sleep — his second, the first having been at the beginning of *Sleep and Poetry*. Endymion awakens refreshed, and promises to be of better cheer in future. She sings soothingly to the lute, and then questions him concerning his troubles: —

> Brother,'tis vain to hide
> That thou dost know of things mysterious,
> Immortal, starry; such alone could thus
> Weigh down thy nature.

When she has guessed in vain, he determines to confide in her: tells her how he fell asleep on a bed of poppies and other flowers which he had found magically new-blown on a place where there had been none before; how he dreamed that he was gazing fixedly at the stars shining in the zenith with preternatural glory, until they began to swim and fade, and then, dropping his eyes to the horizon, he saw the moon in equal glory emerging from the clouds; how on her disappearance he again looked up and there came down to him a female apparition of incomparable beauty (in whom it does not yet occur to him to recognize the moon-goddess); how she took him by the hand, and they were lifted together through mystic altitudes

> Where falling stars dart their artillery forth
> And eagles struggle with the buffeting north
> That balances the heavy meteor stone;

how thence they swooped downwards in eddies of the mountain wind, and finally how, clinging to and embracing his willing companion in a delirium of happiness, he alighted beside her on a flowery alp, and there fell into a dream-sleep within his sleep; from which awakening to reality, he found himself alone on the bed of poppies, with the breeze at intervals bringing him 'Faint fare-thee-wells and sigh-shrilled adieus,' and with disenchantment fallen upon everything about him: —

> All the pleasant hues
> Of heaven and earth had faded: deepest shades
> Were deepest dungeons: heaths and sunny shades
> Were full of pestilent light; and taintless rills
> Seem'd sooty, and o'erspread with upturn'd gills
> Of dying fish; the vermeil rose had blown
> In frightful scarlet, and its thorns outgrown
> Like spikèd aloe.

Here we have the first of those mystic dream-flights of Endymion and his celestial visitant in company, prefiguring the union of the soul with the spirit of essential Beauty, which have to come true before the end but of which the immediate result is that all other delights lose their savour and turn to ashes. The spirit of man, so the interpretation would seem to run, having once caught the vision of transcendental Beauty and been allowed to embrace it, must pine after it evermore and in its absence can take no delight in nature or mankind. Another way would have been to make his hero find in every such momentary vision or revelation a fresh encouragement, a source of joy and inspiration until the next: but this was not Keats' way. Peona listens with sisterly sympathy, but her powers of help, being purely human, cannot in this case avail. She can only try to rouse him by contrasting his present forlorn and languid state with his former virility and ambition: —

> Yet it is strange and sad, alas!
> That one who through this middle earth should pass
> Most like a sojourning demi-god, and leave
> His name upon the harp-string, should achieve
> No higher bard than simple maidenhood,
> Sighing alone, and fearfully, — how the blood
> Left his young cheek; and how he used to stray
> He knew not where; and how he would say, *Nay*,
> If any said 'twas love: and yet 'twas love;
> What could it be but love? How a ring-dove
> Let fall a sprig of yew-tree in his path;
> And how he died: and then, that love doth scathe
> The gentle heart, as Northern blasts do roses.

And then the ballad of his sad life closes
With sighs, and an alas! Endymion!

His reply in his own defence is long and much of it beautiful: but we follow the chain of thought and argument with difficulty, so hidden is it in flowers of poetry and so little are its vital links made obvious. A letter of Keats, containing one of his very few explanatory comments on work of his own, shows that he attached great importance to the passage and felt that its sequence and significance might easily be missed. Sending a correction of the proof to Mr Taylor, the publisher, he says — 'The whole thing must, I think, have appeared to you, who are a consecutive man, as a thing almost of mere words, but I assure you that when I wrote it, it was a regular stepping of the Imagination towards a truth. My having written that argument will perhaps be of the greatest service to me of anything I ever did. It set before me the gradations of happiness, even like a kind of pleasure thermometer, and is my first step towards the chief attempt in the drama.' The first ten lines offer little difficulty: —

> Peona! ever have I long'd to slake
> My thirst for the world's praises: nothing base,
> No merely slumberous phantasm, could unlace
> The stubborn canvas for my voyage prepar'd —
> Though now 'tis tatter'd; leaving my bark bar'd
> And sullenly drifting: yet my higher hope
> Is of too wide, too rainbow-large a scope,
> To fret at myriads of earthly wrecks.
> Wherein lies happiness? In that which becks
> Our ready minds to fellowship divine,
> A fellowship with essence; till we shine,
> Full alchemiz'd, and free of space. Behold
> The clear religion of heaven!

It seems clear that we have here shadowed forth the highest hope and craving of the poetic soul, the hope to be wedded in full communion or 'fellowship divine' — or shall we say with Wordsworth in love and holy passion? — with the spirit of essential Beauty in the world. In the next lines we shall find, if we read them carefully enough, that Keats, having thus defined his ultimate hope, breaks off and sets out again from the foot of a new ascending scale of poetical pleasure and endeavour which he asks us to consider. It differs from the ascending scale of the earlier poems inasmuch as it begins, not with the toying of nymphs in shady places and the like, but with thoughts of olden minstrelsy and romantic tales and prophecies. The verse here is of Keats' finest: —

> — hist, when the airy stress
> Of music's kiss impregnates the free winds,
> And with a sympathetic touch unbinds
> Æolian magic from their lucid wombs:
> Then old songs waken from enclouded tombs;
> Old ditties sigh above their father's grave;
> Ghosts of melodious prophecyings rave
> Round every spot where trod Apollo's foot;
> Bronze clarions awake, and faintly bruit,
> Where long ago a giant battle was;
> And, from the turf, a lullaby doth pass
> In every place where infant Orpheus slept.

It is impressed upon us in the next lines that this is a relatively unexalted phase of imaginative feeling, and our thoughts are directed to other experiences of the poetic soul more enthralling and more 'self-destroying' (that is more effectual in purging it of egotism), namely the experiences of friendship and love, those of love above all: —

> Aye, so delicious is the unsating food,
> That men, who might have tower'd in the van
> Of all the congregated world, to fan
> And winnow from the coming step of time
> All chaff of custom, wipe away all slime
> Left by men-slugs and human serpentry,
> Have been content to let occasion die,
> Whilst they did sleep in love's elysium.
> And, truly, I would rather be struck dumb,
> Than speak against this ardent listlessness:
> For I have ever thought that it might bless
> The world with benefits unknowingly;
> As does the nightingale, upperched high,
> And cloister'd among cool and bunched leaves —
> She sings but to her love, nor e'er conceives
> How tiptoe Night holds back her dark-grey hood.

If a man, next pleads Endymion, may thus reasonably give up even the noblest of worldly ambitions for the joys of a merely mortal love, how much more may he do so for those of an immortal. No, he reassures Peona in reply to her questioning glance, he is not fancy-sick: —

> no, no, I'm sure
> My restless spirit never could endure
> To brood so long upon one luxury,
> Unless it did, though fearfully, espy
> A hope beyond the shadow of a dream.

We have now been carried back to the top of the scale, and these lines again express, although vaguely, the aspirations of the poetic soul at their highest pitch, rising through thoughts and experiences of mortal love to the hope of communion with immortal Beauty. But that longed-for, loftiest phase of the imaginative life, that hope beyond the shadow of a dream, too vast and too rainbow-bright to be quenched by any fear of earthly disaster, Endymion cannot attempt to define, least of all to the practically-minded Peona. He can only try to convince her of its reality by telling her of later momentary visitations with which the divinity of his dreams has favoured him — her face reflected at him from a spring — her voice murmuring to him from a cave — and how miserably in the intervals he has pined and hungered for her. But now, he ends by assuring his sister, he will be patient and pine no longer. Yet it is but a sickly half-assurance after all.

> There is a paly flame of hope that plays
> Where'er I look: but yet, I'll say 'tis naught,
> And here I bid it die. Have I not caught,
> Already, a more healthy countenance?

And with this, as she rows him back from her island, the anxious sister must rest content.

Book II. opens with a renewed declamation on the power and glory of love, and the relative unimportance of the wars and catastrophes of history. Juliet leaning from her balcony, the swoon of Imogen, Hero wrongfully accused by Claudio, Spenser's Pastorella among the bandits, he declares,

>   Are things to brood on with more ardency
>   Than the death-day of empires.

The passage has caused some critics to reproach Keats as a mere mawkish amorist indifferent to the great affairs and interests of the world. But must one not believe that all poor flawed and fragmentary human loves, real or fabled, happy or miserable, are far off symbols and shadowings of that Love which, unless the universe is quite other than we have trusted, 'moves the sun and the other stars?' Are they not related to it as to their source and spring? It is quite true that Keats was not yet able to tell of such loves except in terms which you may call mawkish if you will (he called them so himself a little later). But being a poet he knew well enough their worth and parentage. And when the future looks back on today, even on today, a death-day of empires in a sterner and vaster sense than any world has known, will all the waste and hatred and horror, all the hope and heroism of the time, its tremendous issues and catastrophes, be really found to have eclipsed and superseded love as the thing fittest to fill the soul and inspire the songs of a poet?

The invocation ended, we set out with the hero on the adventures that await him. He gathers a wild-rose bud which on expanding releases a butterfly from its heart: the butterfly takes wing and he follows its flight with eagerness. At last they reach a fountain spouting near the mouth of a cave, and in touching the water the butterfly is suddenly transformed into a nymph of the fountain, who speaking to Endymion pities, encourages, and warns him in one breath. Endymion sits and soliloquizes beside the fountain, at first in wavering terms which express the ebb and flow of Keats' own inner aspirations and misgivings about his poetic calling. Anon he invokes the virgin goddess Cynthia to quell the tyranny of love in him (not yet guessing that his dream visitant is really she). But no, insensibility would be the worst of all; the goddess must, he is assured, know of some form of love higher and purer than the Cupids are concerned with; he prays to her to be propitious; dreams again that he is sailing through the sky with her; and makes a wild appeal to her which is answered by a voice from within the cavern bidding him descend 'into the sparry hollows of the world.' He obeys, (this plunge into a spring or fountain and thence into the underworld is a regular incident in a whole group of folk tales, one or another of which was no doubt in Keats' mind): and we follow him at first into a region

>   nor bright, nor sombre wholly,
>   But mingled up; a gleaming melancholy;
>   A dusky empire and its diadems;
>   One faint eternal eventide of gems.

A vein of gold sparkling with jewels serves him for path, and leads him through twilight vaults and passages to a ridge that towers over many waterfalls: and the lustre of a pendant diamond guides him further till he reaches a temple of Diana. What imaginative youth but has known his passive day-dreams haunted by visions, mysteriously impressive and alluring, of natural and architectural marvels, huge sculptured caverns and glimmering palace-halls in endless vista? To such imaginings, fed by his readings and dreamings on

>   Memphis, and Nineveh, and Babylon,

Keats in this book lets himself go without a check. Now we find ourselves in a temple, described as complete and true to sacred custom, with an image of Diana; and in a trice either we have passed, or the temple itself has dissolved, into a structure which by its 'abysmal depths of awe,' its gloomy splendours and intricacies of aisle and vault and corridor, its dimly gorgeous and most un-Grecian magnificence, reminds us of nothing so much as of Vathek and the halls of Eblis or some of the magical subterranean palaces of the *Arabian Nights*. (Beckford's *Vathek* and the *Thousand and One Nights* were both among Keats' familiar reading.) Endymion is miserable there, and appeals to Diana to restore him to the pleasant light of earth. Thereupon the marble floor breaks up beneath and before his footsteps into a flowery sward. Endymion walks on to the sound of a soft music which only intensifies his yearnings: is led by a light through the alleys of a myrtle grove; and comes to an embowered chamber where Adonis lies asleep among little ministering Loves, with Cupid himself, lute in hand, for their chief.

Here follows a long and highly wrought episode of the winter sleep of Adonis and the descent of Venus to awaken him. The original idea for the scene comes from Ovid, in part direct, in part through Spenser (*Faerie Queene*, iii, 6) and Shakespeare. But the detail is entirely Keats' own and on the whole is a happy example of his early luxuriant manner; especially the description of the entrance of Venus and the looks and presence of Cupid as bystander and interpreter. The symbolic meaning of the story is for him evidently much the same as it was to the ancients, — the awakening of nature to love and life after the sleep of winter, with all the ulterior and associated hopes implied by such a resurrection. The first embracements over, Endymion is about to intreat the favour of Venus for his quest when she anticipates him encouragingly, telling him that from her upper regions she has perceived his plight and has guessed (here is one of the echoes from Drayton to which I have referred above) that some goddess, she knows not which, has condescended to him. She bids her son be propitious to him, and she and Adonis depart. Endymion wanders on by miraculous grottoes and palaces, and then mounts by a diamond balustrade,

> Leading afar past wild magnificence,
> Spiral through ruggedst loopholes, and thence
> Stretching across a void, then guiding o'er
> Enormous chasms, where, all foam and roar,
> Streams subterranean teaze their granite beds;
> Then heighten'd just above the silvery heads
> Of a thousand fountains, so that he could dash
> The waters with his spear; but at the splash,
> Done heedlessly, those spouting columns rose
> Sudden a poplar's height, and 'gan to enclose
> His diamond path with fretwork, streaming round
> Alive, and dazzling cool, and with a sound,
> Haply, like dolphin tumults, when sweet shells
> Welcome the float of Thetis.

The fountains assume all manner of changing and interlacing imitative shapes which he watches with delight (this and much else on the underground journey seems to be the outcome of pure fancy and day-dreaming on the poet's part, without symbolic purpose). Then passing on through a dim tremendous region of vaults and precipices he has a momentary vision of the earth-goddess Cybele with her team of lions issuing from an arch below him. At this point the diamond balustrade suddenly breaks off in mid-space and ends in nothing. Endymion calls to Jove for help and rescue, and is taken up on the wings of an eagle, (is this the eagle of Dante in the *Purgatory* and of Chaucer in The *House of Fame* ?) who swoops down with him, — all this still happening, be it remembered, deep within the bowels of the earth, — to a place of sweet airs of flowers and mosses. He is deposited in a jasmine bower, wonders within himself who and what his unknown love may be, longs to force his way to her, but as that may not be, to sleep and dream of her. He sleeps on a mossy bed; she comes to him; and their endearments are related, unluckily in a very cloying and distasteful manner of amatory ejaculation. It was a flaw in Keats' art and a blot on his genius — or perhaps only a consequence of the rawness and ferment of his youth? — that thinking nobly as he did of love, yet when he came to relate a love-passage, even one intended as this to be symbolical of ideal things, he could only realize it in terms like these.

The visitant, whose identity is still unrecognized, again disappears; he resumes his quest, and next finds himself in a huge vaulted grotto full of sea treasures and sea sounds and murmurs. Here he goes over in memory his past life and aspirations,

> — the spur
> Of the old bards to mighty deeds: his plans
> To nurse the golden age 'mong shepherd clans:
> That wondrous night: the great Pan-festival:
> His sister's sorrow; and his wanderings all,
> Until into the earth's deep maw he rush'd:
> Then all its buried magic, till it flush'd
> High with excessive love. 'And now,' thought he,
> 'How long must I remain in jeopardy
> Of blank amazements that amaze no more?
> Now I have tasted her sweet soul to the core
> All other depths are shallow: essences,
> Once spiritual, are like muddy lees,
> Meant but to fertilize my earthly root,
> And make my branches lift a golden fruit
> Into the bloom of heaven: other light,
> Though it be quick and sharp enough to blight
> The Olympian eagle's vision, is dark,
> Dark as the parentage of chaos. Hark!
> My silent thoughts are echoing from these shells;
> Or they are but the ghosts, the dying swells
> Of noises far away? — list! —'

The poet seems here to mean that in the seeker's transient hour of union with his unknown divinity capacities for thought and emotion have been awakened in him richer and more spiritually illuminating than he has known before. The strange sounds which reach him are the rushing of the streams of the river-god Alpheus and the fountain-nymph Arethusa; Arethusa fleeing, Alpheus pursuing (according to that myth which is told most fully by Ovid and which Shelley's lyric has made familiar to all English readers); he entreating, she longing to yield but fearing the wrath of Diana. Endymion, who till now has had no thought of anything but his own plight, is touched by the pangs of these lovers and prays to his goddess to assuage them. We are left to infer that she assents: they plunge into a gulf and disappear: he turns to follow a path which leads him in the direction of a cooler light and a louder sound:

> — and lo!
> More suddenly than doth a moment go,
> The visions of the earth were gone and fled —
> He saw the giant sea above his head.

Throughout this second book Keats has been content to let the mystery and 'buried magic' of the underworld reveal itself in nothing of more original invention or of deeper apparent significance than the spring awakening of Adonis and the vision of the earth-goddess Cybele. His underworld is no Tartarus or Elysium, no place of souls: he attempts nothing like the calling-up of the ghosts of dead heroes by Ulysses in the *Odyssey*, still less like the mystic revelation of a future state of rewards and punishments in the sixth book of the *Aeneid*. Possibly the visit of the disguised Diana is meant to have a double meaning, and of her three characters as 'Queen of Earth, and Heaven, and Hell,' to refer to the last, that of a goddess of the underworld and of the dead, and at the same time to symbolize the power of the spirit of Beauty to visit the poet's soul with joy and illumination even among the 'dismal elements' of that nether sphere.

Into the rest of the underground scenery and incidents it is hard to read any symbolical meaning or anything but the uncontrolled and aimless-seeming play of invention. But in what is now to follow we are conscious of a fuller meaning and a stricter plan. That from Diana, conscious of her own weakness, indulgence for the weakness of her nymph Arethusa should be won by the prayer of Endymion, now for the first time wrought to sympathy with the sorrows of others, is a clear stage in the development of the poet's scheme. The next stage is more decisive and significant still.

Book III. Keats begins his third book with a denunciation of kings, conquerors, and worldly 'regalities' in general, amplifying in his least fortunate style the ideas contained in the sonnet 'On receiving a laurel crown from Leigh Hunt' written the previous March in the copy of his *Poems* which he gave to Reynolds (see above, p. 57). When Keats read this passage to Bailey at Oxford, Bailey very justly found fault with some forced expressions in it such as 'baaing vanities,' and also, he tells us, with what seemed to him an over-done defiance of the traditional way of handling the rimed couplet. From denunciation the verse passes into narrative with the question, 'Are then regalities all gilded masks?' The answer is, No, there are a thousand mysterious powers throned in the universe — cosmic powers, as we should now say — most of them far beyond human ken but a few within it; and of these, swears the poet, the moon is 'the gentlier-mightiest.' Having once more, in a strain of splendid nature-poetry, praised her, he resumes his tale, and tells how Cynthia, pining no less than Endymion, sends a shaft of her light down to him where he lies on an undersea bed of sand and pearls; how this comforts him, and how at dawn he resumes his fated journey. Here follows a description of the litter of the Ocean floor which, as we shall see later, is something of a challenge to Shakespeare and was in its turn something of an inspiration to Shelley. Endymion now in his own person takes up the inexhaustible theme of the moon's praise, asking her pardon at the same time for having lately suffered a more rapturous, more absorbing passion to come between him and his former youthful worship of her. At this moment the wanderer's attention is suddenly diverted, —

> For as he lifted up his eyes to swear
> How his own goddess was past all things fair,
> He saw far in the green concave of the sea
> An old man sitting calm and peacefully.
> Upon a weeded rock this old man sat,
> And his white hair was awful, and a mat
> Of weeds were cold beneath his cold thin feet.

The old man is Glaucus, and the rest of the book is taken up almost entirely with his story. Keats' reading of Ovid had made him familiar with this story: but he remodels it radically for his own ethical and symbolic purpose, giving it turns and a sequel quite unknown to antiquity, and even helping himself as he felt the need to certain incidents and machinery of Oriental magic from the *Arabian Nights*.

Glaucus at first sight of Endymion greets him joyfully, seeing in him his predestined deliverer from the spell of palsied age which binds him. But Endymion cannot endure the thought of being diverted from his own private quest, and meets the old man's welcome first with suspicious terror and then with angry defiance. The grey-haired creature weeps: whereupon Endymion, newly awakened to human sympathies, is struck with remorse.

> Had he then wrong'd a heart where sorrow kept?

....

> He had indeed, and he was ripe for tears.
> The penitent shower fell, as down he knelt
> Before that careworn sage.

They rise and proceed over the ocean floor together. Glaucus tells Endymion his history: how he led a quiet and kind existence as a fisherman long ago, familiar with and befriended by all sea-creatures, even the fiercest, until he was seized with the ambition to be free of Neptune's kingdom and able to live and breathe beneath the sea; how this desire being granted he loved and pursued the sea-nymph Scylla, and she feared and fled him; how then he asked the aid of the enchantress Circe, who made him her thrall and lapped him in sensual delights while Scylla was forgotten. How the witch, the 'arbitrary queen of sense,' one day revealed her true character, and 'specious heaven was changed to real hell.' (Is Keats here remembering the closing couplet of Shakespeare's great sonnet against lust —

> This all the world well knows; but none know well
> To shun the heaven that leads men to this hell?)

He came upon her torturing her crowd of spell-bound animals, once human beings, fled in terror at the sight, was overtaken, and with savage taunts driven back into his ocean-home. Here he found Scylla cold and dead, killed by Circe's arts. (In the original myth as told by Ovid and others Glaucus refuses the temptations of Circe, who in revenge inflicts on Scylla a worse punishment than death, transforming her into a sea-monster engirdled with a pack of ravening dogs and stationed as a terror to mariners at the Straits over against Charybdis). Glaucus then tells how he conveyed the body of his dead love to a niche in a vacant undersea temple, where she still remains. Then began the doom of paralysed and helpless senility which the enchantress had condemned him to endure for a thousand years and which still binds him fast, — a doom which inevitably reminds us of such stories as that of the Fisherman in the *Arabian Nights*, and of the spell laid by Suleiman upon the rebellious Djinn, whom he imprisoned for a thousand and eight hundred years in a bottle until the Fisherman released him.

Glaucus goes on to relate how once, in the course of his miserable spell-bound existence, he witnessed the drowning of a shipwrecked crew with agony at his own helplessness, and in trying vainly to rescue a sinking old man by the hand found himself left with a wand and scroll which the old man had held. Reading the scroll, he found in it comfortable words of hope and wisdom. (Note that it was through an attempted act of human succour that this wisdom came to him). If he would have patience, so ran the promise of the scroll, to probe all the depths of magic and the hidden secrets of nature — if moreover he would piously through the centuries make it his business to lay side by side in sanctuary all bodies of lovers drowned at sea — there would one day come to him a heaven-favoured youth to whom he would be able to teach the rites necessary for his deliverance. He recognizes the predestined youth in Endymion, who on learning the nature of the promise accepts joyfully his share in the prescribed duty, with the attendant risk of destruction to both if they fail. The young man and the old — or rather 'the young soul in age's mask' — go together to the submarine hall of burial where Scylla and the multitude of drowned lovers lie enshrined. As to the rites that follow and their effect, let us have them in the poet's own words: —

> 'Let us commence,'
> Whisper'd the guide, stuttering with joy, 'even now.'
> He spake, and, trembling like an aspen-bough,
> Began to tear his scroll in pieces small,
> Uttering the while some mumblings funeral.
> He tore it into pieces small as snow
> That drifts unfeather'd when bleak northerns blow;
> And having done it, took his dark blue cloak
> And bound it round Endymion: then struck
> His wand against the empty air times nine. —
> 'What more there is to do, young man, is thine:
> But first a little patience; first undo

This tangled thread, and wind it to a clue.
Ah, gentle! 'tis as weak as spider's skein;
And shouldst thou break it — What, is it done so clean
A power overshadows thee! O, brave!
The spite of hell is tumbling to its grave.
Here is a shell; 'tis pearly blank to me,
Nor mark'd with any sign or charactery —
Canst thou read aught? O read for pity's sake!
Olympus! we are safe! Now, Carian, break
This wand against yon lyre on the pedestal.'
'Twas done: and straight with sudden swell and fall
Sweet music breath'd her soul away, and sigh'd
A lullaby to silence. — 'Youth! now strew
These minced leaves on me, and passing through
Those files of dead, scatter the same around,
And thou wilt see the issue.' — 'Mid the sound
Of flutes and viols, ravishing his heart,
Endymion from Glaucus stood apart,
And scatter'd in his face some fragments light.
How lightning-swift the change! a youthful wight
Smiling beneath a coral diadem
Out-sparkling sudden like an upturn'd gem,
Appear'd, and, stepping to a beauteous corse,
Kneel'd down beside it, and with tenderest force
Press'd its cold hand, and wept, — and Scylla sigh'd!
Endymion, with quick hand, the charm apply'd —
The nymph arose: he left them to their joy,
And onward went upon his high employ,
Showering those powerful fragments on the dead.
And as he passed, each lifted up his head,
As doth a flower at Apollo's touch.
Death felt it to his inwards: 'twas too much:
Death fell a weeping in his charnel-house.
The Latmian persever'd along, and thus
All were re-animated. There arose
A noise of harmony, pulses and throes
Of gladness in the air — while many, who
Had died in mutual arms devout and true,
Sprang to each other madly; and the rest
Felt a high certainty of being blest.
They gaz'd upon Endymion. Enchantment
Grew drunken, and would have its head and bent.
Delicious symphonies, like airy flowers,
Budded, and swell'd, and, full-blown, shed full showers
Of light, soft, unseen leaves of sounds divine.
The two deliverers tasted a pure wine
Of happiness, from fairy-press ooz'd out.
Speechless they ey'd each other, and about
The fair assembly wander'd to and fro,
Distracted with the richest overflow
Of joy that ever pour'd from heaven.

The whole long Glaucus and Scylla episode filling the third book, and especially this its climax, has to many lovers and students of Keats proved a riddle hard of solution. And indeed at first reading the meaning of its strange incidents and imagery, beautiful as is much of the poetry in which they are told, looks obscure enough. Every definite clue to their interpretation seems to elude us as we lay hold of it, like the drowned man who sinks through the palsied grasp of Glaucus. But bearing in mind what we have recognized as the general scope and symbolic meaning of the poem, does not the main purport of the Glaucus book, on closer study, emerge clearly as something like this? The spirit touched with the divine beam of Cynthia — that is aspiring to and chosen for communion with essential Beauty — in other words the spirit of the Poet — must prepare itself for its high calling, first by purging away the selfishness of its private passion in sympathy with human loves and sorrows, and next by acquiring a full store alike of human experience and of philosophic thought and wisdom. Endymion, endowed by favour of the gods with the poetic gift and passion, has only begun to awaken to sympathy and acquire knowledge when he meets Glaucus, whose history has made him rich in all that Endymion yet lacks, including as it does the forfeiting of simple everyday life and usefulness for the exercise of a perilous superhuman gift; the desertion, under a spell of evil magic, of a pure for an impure love; the tremendous penalty which has to be paid for this plunge into sensual debasement; the painful acquisition of the gift of righteous magic, or knowledge of the secrets of nature and mysteries of life and death, by prolonged intensity of study, and the patient exercise of the duties of pious tenderness towards the bodies of the drowned. At the approach of Endymion the sage recognizes in him the predestined poet, and hastens to make over to him, as to one more divinely favoured than himself, all the dower of his dearly bought wisdom; in possession of which the poet is enabled to work miracles of joy and healing and to confer immortality on dead lovers.

As to the significance in detail of the rites by which the transfer of power is effected, we are again helped by remembering that Keats was mixing up with his classic myth ideas taken from the *Thousand and One Nights*. Let the student turn to the Glaucus and Circe episodes of Ovid's *Metamorphoses*, and then refresh his memory of certain Arabian tales, particularly that of Bebr Salim, with its kings and queens of the sea living and moving under water as easily as on land, its repeated magical transformations and layings on and taking off of enchantments, and the adventures of the hero with queen Lab, the Oriental counterpart of Circe, — let the student refresh his memory from these sources, and the proceedings of this episode will no longer seem so strange. In the Arabian tales, and for that matter in western tales of magic also, the commonest method of annulling enchantments is by sprinkling with water over which words of power have been spoken. Under sea you cannot sprinkle with water, so Keats makes Endymion use for sprinkling the shredded fragments of the scroll taken by Glaucus from the drowned man. First Glaucus tears the scroll, uttering 'some mumblings funeral' as he does so (compare the 'backward mutters of dissevering power' in Milton's *Comus*). Then follows a series of actions showing that the hour has come for him to surrender and make over his powers and virtues to the new comer. First he invests Endymion with his own magic robe. Then he waves his magic wand nine times in the air, — as a preliminary to the last exercise of its power? or as a sign that its power is exhausted? Nine is of course a magic number, and the immediate suggestion comes from the couplet in Sandys's Ovid where Glaucus tells how the sea-gods admitted him to their fellowship, —

Whom now they hallow, and with charms nine times
Repeated, purge me from my human crimes.

The disentangling of the skein and the perceiving and deciphering of runes on the shell which to Glaucus is a blank are evidently tests Endymion has to undergo before it is proved and confirmed that he is really the predestined poet, gifted to unravel and interpret mysteries beyond the ken of mere philosophy. The breaking of the philosopher's wand against the lyre suspended from its pedestal, followed by an outburst of ravishing music, is a farther and not too obscure piece of symbolism shadowing forth the surrender and absorption of the powers of study and research into the higher powers of poetic intuition and inspiration. And then comes the general disenchantment and awakening of the drowned multitude to life and happiness.

The parable breaks off at this point, and the book closes with a submarine pageant imagined, it would seem, almost singly for the pageant's sake; perhaps also partly in remembrance of Spenser's festival of the sea-gods at the marriage of Thames and Medway in the fourth book of the *Faerie Queene*. The rejuvenated Glaucus bids the whole beautiful multitude follow him to pay their homage to Neptune: they obey: the first crowd of lovers restored to life meets a second crowd on the sand, and some in either crowd recognize and happily pair off with their lost ones in the other. All approach in procession the palace of Neptune — another marvel of vast and vague jewelled and translucent architectural splendours — and find the god presiding on an emerald throne between Venus and Cupid. Glaucus and Scylla receive the blessing of Neptune and Venus respectively, and Venus addresses Endymion in a speech of arch encouragement, where the poet's style (as almost always in moments of his hero's prosperous love) turns common and tasteless. Dance and revelry follow, and then a hymn to Neptune, Venus, and Cupid. This is interrupted by the entrance of Oceanus and a train of Nereids. The presence of all these immortals is too much for Endymion's human senses: he swoons; a ring of Nereids lift and carry him tenderly away; he is aware of a message of hope and cheer from his goddess, written in starlight on the dark; and when he comes to himself, finds that he is restored to earth, lying on the grass beside a forest pool in his native Caria.

Book IV. In this book Endymion has to make his last discovery. He has to learn that all transient and secondary loves, which may seem to come between him and his great ideal pursuit and lure him away from it, are really, when the truth is known, but encouragements to that pursuit, visitations and condescensions to him of his celestial love in disguise. The narrative setting forth this discovery is pitched in a key which, following the triumphant close of the last book, seems curiously subdued and melancholy. An opening apostrophe by the poet to the Muse of his native land, long silent while Greece and Italy sang, but aroused in the fulness of time to happy utterance, begins joyously enough, but ends on no more confident note than this: —

> Great Muse, thou know'st what prison
> Of flesh and bone, curbs, and confines, and frets
> Our spirit's wings: despondency besets
> Our pillows; and the fresh tomorrow morn
> Seems to give forth its light in very scorn
> Of our dull, uninspir'd, snail-paced lives.
> Long have I said, how happy he who shrives
> To thee! But then I thought on poets gone,
> And could not pray: — nor could I now — so on
> I move to the end in lowliness of heart. —

Keats then tells how his hero, paying his vows to the gods, is interrupted by the plaint of a forsaken Indian damsel which reaches him through the forest undergrowth. (Such a damsel lying back on the grass with her arms among her hair had dwelt, I think, in the poet's mind's eye from pictures by or prints after Poussin ever since hospital and early Hunt days, and had been haunting him when he scribbled his attempted scrap of an Alexander romance in a fellow student's notebook). Endymion listens and approaches: the poet foresees and deplores the coming struggle between his hero's celestial love and this earthly beauty disconsolate at his feet. The damsel, speaking to herself, laments her loneliness, and tells how she could find it in her heart to love this shepherd youth, and how love is lord of all. Endymion falls to pitying and from pitying into loving her. Though without sense of treachery to his divine mistress, he is torn by the contention within him between this new earthly and his former heavenly flame. He goes on to declare the struggle is killing him, and entreats the damsel to sing him a song of India to ease his passing. Her song, telling of her desolation before and after she was swept from home in the train of Bacchus and his rout and again since she fell out of the march, is, in spite of one or two unfortunate blemishes, among the most moving and original achievements of English lyric poetry. Endymion is wholly overcome, and in a speech of somewhat mawkish surrender gives himself to the new earthly love, not blindly, but realizing fully what he forfeits. He bids the damsel —

> Do gently murder half my soul, and I
> Shall feel the other half so utterly.

A cry of 'Woe to Endymion!' echoing through the forest has no sooner alarmed the lovers than there is a sudden apparition of Mercury descending. The gods intend for Endymion an unexpected issue from his perplexities. Their messenger touches the ground with his wand and vanishes: two raven-black winged horses rise through the ground where he has touched, — the horses, no doubt, of the imagination, the same or of the same breed as those 'steeds with streamy manes' that paw up against the light and trample along the ridges of the clouds in *Sleep and Poetry*. Endymion mounts the damsel on one and himself mounts the other: they are borne aloft together,

> — unseen, alone,
> Among cool clouds and winds, but that the free,
> The buoyant life of song, can floating be
> Above their heads, and follow them untired.

The poet, seeming to realize that the most difficult part of his tale is now to tell, again invokes the native Muse, and relates how the lovers, couched on the wings of the raven steeds, enter on their flight a zone of mists enfolding the couch of Sleep, who has been drawn from his cave by the rumour of the coming nuptials of a goddess with a mortal. The narrative is here very obscure, but seems to run thus. Alike the magic steed and the lovers reclining on their wings yield to the influence of sleep, but still drift on their aerial course. As they drift, Endymion dreams that he has been admitted to Olympus. In his dream he drinks of Hebe's cup, tries the bow of Apollo and the shield of Pallas; blows a bugle which summons the Seasons and the Hours to a dance; asks whose bugle it is and learns that it is Diana's; the next moment she is there in presence; he springs to his now recognized goddess, and in the act he awakes, and it is a case of Adam's dream having come true; he is aware of Diana and the other celestials present bending over him. On the horse-plume couch beside him lies the Indian maiden: the conflict between his two loves is distractingly renewed within him, though some instinct again tells him that he is not really untrue to either. He embraces the Indian damsel as she sleeps; the goddess disappears; the damsel awakes; he pleads with her, says that his other love is free from all malice or revenge and that in his soul he feels true to both.

> What is this soul then? Whence
> Came it? It does not seem my own, and I
> Have no self-passion nor identity.

This charge, be it noted, is one which Keats in his private thoughts was constantly apt to bring against himself. Foreseeing disaster and the danger of losing both his loves and being left solitary, Endymion nevertheless rouses the steeds to a renewed ascent. He and the damsel are borne towards the milky way, in a mystery of loving converse: the crescent moon appears from a cloud, facing them: Endymion turns to the damsel at his side and finds her gone gaunt and cold and ghostly: a moment more and she is not there at all but vanished: her horse parts company from his, towers, and falls to earth. He is left alone on his further ascent, abandoned for the moment by both the objects of his passion, the celestial and the human. His spirit enters into a region, or phase, of involved and brooding misery and thence into one of contented apathy: he is scarcely even startled, though his steed is, by a flight of celestial beings blowing trumpets and proclaiming a coming festival of Diana. In a choral song they invite the signs and constellations to the festival: (the picture of the Borghese Zodiac in Spence's *Polymetis* has evidently given Keats his suggestion here). Then suddenly Endymion hears no more and is aware that his courser has in a moment swept him down to earth again.

He finds himself on a green hillside with the Indian maiden beside him, and in a long impassioned protestation renounces his past dreams, condemns his presumptuous neglect of human and earthly joys, and declares his intention to live alone with her for ever and (not forgetting to propitiate the Olympians) to shower upon her all the treasures of the pastoral earth: —

> O I have been
> Presumptuous against love, against the sky,
> Against all elements, against the tie
> Of mortals each to each, against the blooms
> Of flowers, rush of rivers, and the tombs
> Of heroes gone! Against his proper glory
> Has my own soul conspired: so my story
> Will I to children utter, and repent.
> There never liv'd a mortal man, who bent
> His appetite beyond his natural sphere,
> But starv'd and died. My sweetest Indian, here,
> Here will I kneel, for thou redeemed hast
> My life from too thin breathing: gone and past
> Are cloudy phantasms. Caverns lone, farewell!
> And air of visions, and the monstrous swell
> Of visionary seas! No, never more
> Shall airy voices cheat me to the shore
> Of tangled wonder, breathless and aghast.

Here Keats spins and puts into the mouth of Endymion wooing the Indian maiden a long, and in some at least of its verses exquisite, pastoral fantasia recalling, and no doubt partly founded on, the famous passage in Ovid, itself founded on one equally famous in Theocritus, where Polyphemus woos the nymph Galatea. Apparently, though it was through sympathy with the human sorrow of the Indian damsel that Endymion has first been caught, he proposes to enjoy her society now in detachment from all other human ties as well as from all transcendental dreams and ambitions.

But the damsel is aware of matters which prevent her from falling in with her lover's desires. She puts him off, saying that she has always loved him and longed and languished to be his, but that this joy is forbidden her, or can only be compassed by the present death of both (that is, to the mortal in love with the spirit of poetry and poetic beauty no life of mere human and earthly contentment is possible); and so she proposes to renounce him. Despondingly they wander off together into the forest.

The poet pauses for an apostrophe to Endymion, confusedly expressed, but vital to his whole meaning. His suffering hero, he says, had the tale allowed, should have been enthroned in felicity before now (the word is 'ensky'd,' from *Measure for Measure*). In truth he has been so enthroned for many thousand years (that is to say, the poetic spirit in man has been wedded in full communion to the essential soul of Beauty in the world): the poet, Keats himself, has had some help from him already, and with his farther help hopes ere long to sing of his 'lute-voiced brother': that is Apollo, to whom Endymion is called brother as being espoused to his sister Diana. This is the first intimation of Keats' intention to write on the story of Hyperion's fall and the advent of Apollo. But the present tale, signifies Keats, has not yet got to that point, and must now be resumed.

Endymion rests beside the damsel in a part of the forest where every tree and stream and slope might have reminded him of his boyish sports, but his downcast eyes fail to recognize them. Peona appears; he dreads their meeting, but without cause; interpreting things by their obvious appearance she sweetly welcomes the stranger as the bride her brother has brought home after his mysterious absence, and bids them both to a festival the shepherds are to hold tonight in honour of Cynthia, in whose aspect the soothsayers have read good omens. Still Endymion does not brighten; Peona asks the stranger why, and craves her help with him; Endymion with a great effort, 'twanging his soul like a spiritual bow', says that after all he has gone through he must not partake in the common and selfish pleasures of men, lest he should forfeit higher pleasures and render himself incapable of the services for which he has disciplined himself; that henceforth he must live as a hermit, visited by none but his sister Peona. To her care he at the same time commends the Indian lady: who consents to go with her, and remembering the approaching festival of Diana says she will take part in it and consecrate herself to that sisterhood and to chastity.

For a while they all three feel like people in sleep struggling with oppressive dreams and making believe to think them everyday experiences. Endymion tries to ease the strain by bidding them farewell. They go off dizzily, he stares distressfully after them and at last cries to them to meet him for a last time the same evening in the grove behind Diana's temple. They disappear; he is left in sluggish desolation till sunset, when he goes to keep his tryst at the temple, musing first with bitterness, then with a resigned prescience of coming death (the mood of the *Nightingale Ode* appearing here in Keats' work for the first time): then bitterly again: —

> I did wed
> Myself to things of light from infancy;
> And thus to be cast out, thus lorn to die
> Is sure enough to make a mortal man
> Grow impious. So he inwardly began
> On things for which no wording can be found;
> Deeper and deeper sulking, until drown'd
> Beyond the reach of music: for the choir
> Of Cynthia he heard not, though rough briar
> Nor muffling thicket interpos'd to dull
> The vesper hymn, far swollen, soft and full,
> Through the dark pillars of those sylvan aisles.
> He saw not the two maidens, nor their smiles,
> Wan as primroses gather'd at midnight
> By chilly finger'd spring. 'Unhappy wight!
> Endymion!' said Peona, 'we are here!
> What wouldst thou ere we all are laid on bier?'
> Then he embrac'd her, and his lady's hand
> Press'd saying: 'Sister, I would have command,
> If it were heaven's will, on our sad fate.'
> At which that dark-eyed stranger stood elate
> And said, in a new voice, but sweet as love,
> To Endymion's amaze: 'By Cupid's dove,
> And so thou shalt! and by the lily truth
> Of my own breast thou shalt, beloved youth!'
> And as she spake, into her face there came
> Light, as reflected from a silver flame:
> Her long black hair swell'd ampler, in display
> Full golden; in her eyes a brighter day
> Dawn'd blue and full of love. Aye, he beheld
> Phoebe, his passion!

And so the quest is ended, and the mystery solved. *Vera incessu patuit dea* : the forsaken Indian maiden had been but a disguised incarnation of Cynthia herself. Endymion's earthly passion, born of human pity and desire, was one all the while, had he but known it, with his heavenly passion born of poetic aspiration and the soul's thirst for Beauty. The two passions at their height and perfection are inseparable, and the crowned poet and the crowned lover are one. But these things are still a mystery to those who know not poetry, and when the happy lovers disappear the kind ministering sister Peona can only marvel: —

> Peona went
> Home through the gloomy wood in wonderment.

The poem ends on no such note of joy and triumph over the attained consummation as we might have expected and such as we found at the close of the third book, at the point where the faculty and vision of the poet had been happily enriched and completed by the gift of the learning and beneficence of the sage. The fourth book closes, as it began, in a minor key, leaving the reader, like Peona, in a mood rather musing than rejoicing. Is this because Keats had tired of his task before he came to the end, or because the low critical opinion of his own work which he had been gradually forming took the heart out of him, so that as he drew near the goal he involuntarily let his mind run on the hindrances and misgivings which beset the poetic aspirant on his way to victory more than on the victory itself? Or was it partly because of the numbing influence of early winter as recorded in the last chapter? We cannot tell.

But why take all this trouble, the reader may well have asked before now, to follow the argument and track the wanderings of Endymion book by book, when everyone knows that the poem is only admirable for its incidental beauties and is neither read nor well readable for its story? The answer is that the intricacy and obscurity of the narrative, taken merely as a narrative, are such as to tire the patience of many readers in their search for beautiful passages and to dull their enjoyment of them when found; but once the inner and symbolic meanings of the poem are recognized, even in gleams, their recognition gives it a quite new hold upon the attention. And in order to trace these meanings and disengage them with any clearness a fairly close examination and detailed argument are necessary. It is not with simple matters of personification, of the putting of initial capitals to abstract qualities, that we have to deal, nor yet with any obvious and deliberately thought-out allegory; still less is it with one purposely made riddling and obscure; it is with a vital, subtly involved and passionately tentative spiritual parable, the parable of the experiences of the poetic soul in man seeking communion with the spirit of essential Beauty in the world, invented and related, in the still uncertain dawn of his powers, by one of the finest natural-born and intuitively gifted poets who ever lived. This is a thing which stands almost alone in literature, and however imperfectly executed is worth any closeness and continuity of attention we can give it. Having now studied, to the best of our power, the sources and scheme of the poem, with its symbolism and inner meanings so far as they can with any confidence be traced, let us pass to the consideration of its technical and poetical qualities and its relation to the works of certain other poets and poems of Keats' time.

Chapter VII

ENDYMION. — II. THE POETRY: ITS QUALITIES AND AFFINITIES

Throughout the four books of *Endymion* we find Keats still working, more even than in his epistles and meditations of the year before, under the spell of Elizabethan and early Jacobean poetry. Spenser and the Spenserians, foremost among them William Browne; Drayton in his pastorals and elegies; Shakespeare, especially in his early poems and comedies; Fletcher and Ben Jonson in pastoral and lyrical work like *The Faithful Shepherdess* or *The Sad Shepherd*; Chapman's version of Homer, especially the *Odyssey* and the *Hymns*, and Sandys's of the *Metamorphoses* of Ovid; these are the masters and the models of whom we feel his mind and ear to be full. In their day the English language had been to a large extent unfixed, and in their instinctive efforts to enrich and expand and supple it, poets had enjoyed a wide range of freedom both in maintaining old and in experimenting with new usages. Many of the liberties they used were renounced by the differently minded age which followed them, and the period from the Restoration, roughly speaking, to the middle years of George III had in matters of literary form and style been one of steadily tightening restriction and convention. Then ensued the period of expansion, in which Wordsworth and Coleridge and Scott had been the most conspicuous leaders, each after his manner, in reconquering the freedom of poetry. Other innovators had followed suit, including Leigh Hunt in that slippered, sentimental, Italianate fashion of his own. And now came young Keats, not following closely along the paths opened by any of these, though closer to Leigh Hunt than to the others, but making a deliberate return to certain definite and long abandoned usages of the English poets during the illustrious half century from 1590-1640. He chose the heroic couplet, and in handling it reversed the settled practice of more than a century. He was even more sedulous than any of his Elizabethan or Jacobean masters to achieve variety of pause and movement by avoiding the regular beat of the closed couplet; while in framing his style he did not scruple to revive all or nearly all those licences of theirs which the intervening age had disallowed. There was a special rashness in his attempt considering the slightness of his own critical equipment, and considering also the strength of the long riveted fetters which he undertook to break and the charges of affectation and impertinence which such a revival of obsolete metrical and verbal usages — the marks of what Pope had denounced as 'our rustic vein And splay-foot verse' — was bound to bring against him.

First of his revolutionary treatment of the metre. He no longer uses double or feminine endings, as in his epistles of the year before, with a profusion like that of *Britannia's Pastorals*. They occur, but in moderation, hardly more than a score of them in any one of the four books. At the beginning he tries often, but afterwards gives up, an occasional trick of the Elizabethan and earlier poets in riming on the unstressed second syllables of words such as 'dancing' (rimed with 'string'), 'elbow' (with 'slow'), 'velvet' (with 'set'), 'purplish' (with 'fish'). On the other hand he regularly resolves the 'tion' or 'shion' termination into its full two syllables, the last carrying the rime, as — 'With speed of five-tailed exhalations:' 'Before the deep intoxication;' 'Vanish'd in elemental passion;' and the like. He admits closed couplets, but very grudgingly, as a general rule in the proportion of not more than one to eight or ten of the unclosed. He seldom allows himself even so much of a continuous run of them as this: —

> Moreover, through the dancing poppies stole
> A breeze most softly lulling to my soul;
> And shaping visions all about my sight
> Of colours, wings, and bursts of spangly light;
> The which became more strange, and strange, and dim,
> And then were gulph'd in a tumultuous swim:

Or this: —

> So in that crystal place, in silent rows,

> Poor lovers lay at rest from joys and woes. —
> The stranger from the mountains, breathless, trac'd
> Such thousands of shut eyes in order plac'd;
> Such ranges of white feet, and patient lips
> All ruddy, — for here death no blossom nips.
> He mark'd their brows and foreheads; saw their hair
> Put sleekly on one side with nicest care.

The essential principle of his versification is to let sentences, prolonged and articulated as freely and naturally as in prose, wind their way in and out among the rimes, the full pause often splitting a couplet by falling at the end of the first line, and oftener still (in the proportion of two or three times to one) breaking up a single line in the middle or at any point of its course. Sense and sound flow habitually over from one couplet to the next without logical or grammatical pause, but to keep the sense of metre present to the ear Keats commonly takes care that the second line of a couplet shall end with a fully stressed rime-word such as not only allows, but actually invites, at least a momentary breathing-pause to follow it. It is only in the rarest cases that he compels the breath to hurry on with no chance of stress or after-rest from a light preposition at the end of a line to its object at the beginning of the next ('on | His left,' 'upon | A dreary morning'), or from an auxiliary to its verb ('as might be | Remembered') or from a comparative particle to the thing compared ('sleeker than | Night-swollen mushrooms'); a practice in which Chapman, Ben Jonson, Fletcher, and their contemporaries indulged, as we have seen, freely, and which afterwards developed into a fatal disease of the metre. Keats' musical and metrical instincts were too fine, and his ear too early trained in the 'sweet-slipping' movement of Spenser, to let him fall often into this fault. To the other besetting fault of some of these masters, that of a harsh and jolting ruggedness, he was still less prone. Although he chooses to forgo that special effect of combined vigour and smoothness proper to the closed couplet, he always knows how to make a rich and varied music with his vowel sounds; while the same fine natural instinct for sentence-structure as distinguishes the prose of his letters makes itself felt in his verse, so that wherever he has need to place a full stop he can make his sentence descend upon it smoothly and skimmingly, like a seabird on the sea. The long passage quoted from Book III in the last chapter illustrates the narrative verse of *Endymion* in nearly all its moods and variations. Here is a characteristic example of its spoken or dramatic verse. Endymion supplicates his goddess from underground: —

> O Haunter chaste
> Of river sides, and woods, and heathy waste,
> Where with thy silver bow and arrows keen
> Art thou now forested? O Woodland Queen,
> What smoothest air thy smoother forehead woos?
> Where dost thou listen to the wide halloos
> Of thy disparted nymphs? Through what dark tree
> Glimmers thy crescent? Wheresoe'er it be,
> 'Tis in the breath of heaven: thou dost taste
> Freedom as none can taste it, nor dost waste
> Thy loveliness in dismal elements;
> But, finding in our green earth sweet contents,
> There livest blissfully. Ah, if to thee
> It feels Elysian, how rich to me,
> An exil'd mortal, sounds its pleasant name!
> Within my breast there lives a choking flame —
> O let me cool't the zephyr-boughs among!
> A homeward fever parches up my tongue —
> O let me slake it at the running springs!

> Upon my ear a noisy nothing rings —
> O let me once more hear the linnet's note!
> Before mine eyes thick films and shadows float —
> O let me 'noint them with the heaven's light!
> Dost thou now lave thy feet and ankles white?
> O think how sweet to me the freshening sluice!
> Dost thou now please thy thirst with berry-juice?
> O think how this dry palate would rejoice!
> If in soft slumber thou dost hear my voice,
> O think how I should love a bed of flowers! —

The first fifteen lines of the above are broken and varied much in Keats' usual way: in the following fourteen it is to be noted how he throws the speaker's alternate complaints of his predicament and prayers for release from it not into twinned but into split or parted couplets, making each prayer rime not with the complaint which calls it forth but with the new complaint which is to follow it: a bold and to my ear a happy sacrifice of obvious rhetorical effect to his predilection for the suspended or delayed rime-echo.

Rime is to some poets a stiff and grudging but to others an officious servant, overactive in offering suggestions to the mind; and no poet is rightly a master until he has learnt how to sift those suggestions, rejecting many and accepting only the fittest. Keats in *Endymion* has not reached nor come near reaching this mastery: in the flush and eagerness of composition he is content to catch at almost any and every suggestion of the rime, no matter how far-fetched and irrelevant. He had a great fore-runner in this fault in Chapman, who constantly, especially in the *Iliad*, wrenches into his text for the rime's sake ideas that have no kind of business there. Take the passage justly criticized by Bailey at the beginning of the third Book: —

> There are who lord it o'er their fellow-men
> With most prevailing tinsel: who unpen
> Their baaing vanities, to browse away
> The comfortable green and juicy hay
> From human pastures; or, O torturing fact!
> Who, through an idiot blink, will see unpack'd
> Fire-branded foxes to sear up and singe
> Our gold and ripe-ear'd hopes. With not one tinge
> Of sanctuary splendour, not a sight
> Able to face an owl's, they still are dight
> By the blear-ey'd nations in empurpled vests,
> And crowns, and turbans.

Here it is obviously the need of a rime to 'men' that has suggested the word 'unpen' and the clumsy imagery of the 'baaing sheep' which follows, while the inappropriate and almost meaningless 'tinge of sanctuary splendour' lower down has been imported for the sake of the foxes with fire-brands tied to their tails which 'singe' the metaphorical corn-sheaves (they come from the story of Samson in the Book of Judges). Milder cases abound, as this of Circe tormenting her victims: —

> appealing groans
> From their poor breasts went sueing to her ear
> In vain; *remorseless as an infant's bier*
> She whisk'd against their eyes the sooty oil.
> Does yonder thrush,
> Schooling its half-fledg'd little ones to brush
> About the dewy forest, whisper tales.

> Speak not of grief, young stranger, or *cold snails*
> *Will slime the rose tonight* .
> He rose: he grasp'd his stole,
> With convuls'd clenches waving it abroad,
> And in a voice of solemn joy, *that aw'd*
> *Echo into oblivion* , he said: —
> Yet hourly had he striven
> To hide the cankering venom, that had *riven*
> His fainting recollections.
> The wanderer
> Holding his forehead to keep off the *burr*
> Of smothering fancies.
> Endymion! the cave is secreter
> Than the isle of Delos. Echo hence shall *stir*
> No sighs but sigh-warm kisses, or light noise
> Of thy combing hand, the while it travelling *cloys*
> And trembles through my labyrinthine hair.

In some of these cases the trouble is, not that the rime drags in a train of far-fetched or intrusive ideas, but only that words are used for the rime's sake in inexact and inappropriate senses. Such laxity in the employment of words is one of the great weaknesses of Keats' style in *Endymion* , and is no doubt partly connected with his general disposition to treat language as though it were as free and fluid in his own day as it had been two hundred years earlier. The same disposition makes him reckless in turning verbs into nouns (a 'complain,' an 'exclaim,' a 'shine,' a 'pierce,' a 'quell') and nouns into verbs (to 'throe,' to 'passion,' to 'monitor,' to 'fragment up'); in using at his convenience active verbs as passive and passive verbs as active; and in not only reviving archaic participial forms ('dight,' 'fight,' 'raft,' etc.) but in giving currency to participles of the class Coleridge denounced as demoralizing to the ear, and as hybrids equivocally generated of noun-substantives ('emblem'd,' 'gordian'd,' 'mountain'd,' 'phantasy'd'), as well as to adjectives borrowed from Elizabethan use or new-minted more or less in accordance with it ('pipy,' 'paly,' 'ripply,' 'sluicy,' 'slumbery,' 'towery,' 'bowery,' 'orby,' 'nervy,' 'surgy,' 'sparry,' 'spangly).' It was these and such like technical liberties with language which scandalized conservative critics, and caused even De Quincey, becoming tardily acquainted with Keats' work, to dislike and utterly under-rate it. He himself came before long to condemn the style of 'the slipshod Endymion.' Nevertheless the consequence of his experiments in reviving or imitating the usages of the great Renaissance age of English poetry is only in part to be regretted. His rashness led him into almost as many felicities as faults, and the examples of the happier liberties in *Endymion* has done much towards enriching the vocabulary and diction of English poetry in the nineteenth century.

Other faults that more gravely mar the poem are not technical but spiritual: intimate failures of taste and feeling due partly to mere rawness and inexperience, partly to excessive intensity and susceptibility of temperament, partly to second-rateness of social training and association. A habit of cloying over-luxuriance in description, the giving way to a sort of swooning abandonment of the senses in contact with the 'deliciousness' of things, is the most besetting of such faults. Allied with it is Keats' treatment of love as an actuality, which in this poem is in unfortunate and distasteful contrast with his high conception of love in the abstract as the inspiring and ennobling power of the world and all things in it. Add the propensity to make Glaucus address Scylla as 'timid thing!' and Endymion beg for 'one gentle squeeze' from his Indian maiden, with many a like turn in the simpering, familiar mood which Keats at this time had caught from or naturally shared with Leigh Hunt. It should, however, be noted as a mark of progress in self-criticism that, comparing the drafts of the poem with the printed text, we find that in revising it for press he had turned out more and worse passages in this vein than he left in.

From flaws or disfigurements of one or other of these kinds the poem is never free for more than a page or two, and rarely for so much, at a time. But granting all weaknesses and immaturities whether of form or spirit, what a power of poetry is in *Endymion* : what evidence, unmistakeable, one would have said, to the blindest, of genius. Did any poet in his twenty-second year ever write with so prodigal an activity of invention, however undisciplined and unbraced, or with an imagination so penetrating to divine and so swift to evoke beauty? Were so many faults and failures ever interspersed with felicities of married sound and sense so frequent and absolute, and only to be matched in the work of the ripest masters? Lost as the reader may often feel himself among the phantasmagoric intricacies of the tale, cloyed by its amatory insipidities, bewildered by the redundancies of an invention stimulated into over-activity by any and every chance feather-touch of association or rime-suggestion, he can afford to be patient in the certainty of coming, from one page to another, upon touches of true and fresh inspiration in almost every strain and mode of poetry. Often the inspired poet and the raw cockney rimester come inseparably coupled in the limit of half a dozen lines, as thus in the narrative of Glaucus: —

> Upon a dead thing's face my hand I laid;
> I look'd — 'twas Scylla! Cursed, cursed Circe!
> O vulture-witch, hast never heard of mercy?
> Could not thy harshest vengeance be content,
> But thou must nip this tender innocent
> Because I loved her? — *Cold, O cold indeed*
> *Were her fair limbs, and like a common weed*
> *The sea-swell took her hair.*

or thus from the love-making of Cynthia: —

> Now I swear at once
> That I am wise, that Pallas is a dunce —
> Perhaps her love like mine is but unknown —
> O I do think that I have been alone
> In chastity: yes, Pallas has been sighing,
> *While every eve saw me my hair uptying,*
> *With fingers cool as aspen leaves* .

In like manner the unfortunate opening of Book III above cited leads on, as Mr de Sélincourt has justly observed, to a passage in praise of the moon which is among the very finest and best sustained examples of Keats' power in nature-poetry. For quotation I will take not this but a second invocation to the moon which follows a little later, for the reason that in it the raptures and longings which the poet puts into the mouth of his hero are really in a large measure his own: —

> What is there in thee, Moon! that thou shouldst move
> My heart so potently? When yet a child
> I oft have dry'd my tears when thou hast smil'd.
> Thou seem'dst my sister: hand in hand we went
> From eve to morn across the firmament.
> No apples would I gather from the tree,
> Till thou hadst cool'd their cheeks deliciously:
> No tumbling water ever spake romance,
> But when my eyes with thine thereon could dance:
> No woods were green enough, no bower divine,
> Until thou liftedst up thine eyelids fine:
> In sowing time ne'er would I dibble take,
> Or drop a seed, till thou wast wide awake;
> And, in the summer tide of blossoming,

> No one but thee hath heard me blythly sing
> And mesh my dewy flowers all the night.
> No melody was like a passing spright
> If it went not to solemnize thy reign.
> Yes, in my boyhood every joy and pain
> By thee were fashioned in the selfsame end;
> And as I grew in years, still didst thou blend
> With all my ardours: thou wast the deep glen;
> Thou wast the mountain-top — the sage's pen —
> The poet's harp — the voice of friends — the sun;
> Thou wast the river — thou wast glory won;
> Thou wast my clarion's blast — thou wast my steed —
> My goblet full of wine — my topmost deed: —
> Thou wast the charm of women, lovely Moon!
> O what a wild and harmonized tune
> My spirit struck from all the beautiful!

In the last two lines of the above Keats gives us the essential master key to his own poetic nature and being. The eight preceding, from 'As I grew in years' offer in their rhetorical form a curious parallel with a passage of similar purport in Drayton's *Endimion and Phoebe*: —

> Be kind (quoth he) sweet Nymph unto thy lover,
> My soul's sole essence and my senses' mover,
> Life of my life, pure Image of my heart,
> Impression of Conceit, Invention, Art.
> My vital spirit receives his spirit from thee,
> Thou art that all which ruleth all in me,
> Thou art the sap and life whereby I live,
> Which powerful vigour doth receive and give.
> Thou nourishest the flame wherein I burn,
> The North whereto my heart's true touch doth turn.

Was Keats, then, after all familiar with the rare volume in which alone Drayton's early poem had been printed, or does the similar turn of the two passages spring from some innate affinity between the two poets, — or perhaps merely from the natural suggestion of the theme?

In nature-poetry, and especially in that mode of it in which the poet goes out with his whole being into nature and loses his identity in delighted sympathy with her doings, Keats already shows himself a master scarcely excelled. Take the lines near the beginning which tell of the 'silent workings of the dawn' on the morning of Pan's festival: —

> Rain-scented eglantine
> Gave temperate sweets to that well-wooing sun;
> The lark was lost in him; cold springs had run
> To warm their chilliest bubbles in the grass;
> Man's voice was on the mountains; and the mass
> Of nature's lives and wonders puls'd tenfold,
> To feel this sunrise and its glories old.

The freshness and music and felicity of the first two lines are nothing less than Shakespearean: in the rest note with how true an instinct the poet evokes the operant magic and living activities of the dawn, single instances first and then in a sudden outburst the sum and volume of them all: how he avoids word-painting and palette-work, leaving all merely visible beauties, the stationary world of colours and forms, as they should be left, to the painter, and dealing, as poetry alone is able to deal, with those delights which are felt and divined rather than seen, delights which the poet instinctively attributes to nature as though she were as sentient as himself. It is like Keats here so to place and lead up to the word 'old' as to make it pregnant with all the meanings which it bore to him: that is with all the wonder and romance of ancient Greece, and at the same time with a sense of awe, like that expressed in the opening chorus of Goethe's *Faust*, at nature's eternal miracle of the sun still rising 'glorious as on creation's day.'

It is interesting to note how above all other nature-images Keats, whose blood, when his faculties were at their highest tension, was always apt to be heated even to fever-point, prefers those of nature's coolness and refreshment. Here are two or three out of a score of instances. Endymion tells how he had been gazing at the face of his unknown love smiling at him from the well: —

> I started up, when lo! refreshfully,
> There came upon my face in plenteous showers
> Dewdrops, and dewy buds, and leaves, and flowers,
> Wrapping all objects from my smothered sight,
> Bathing my spirit in a new delight.

Coming to a place where a brook issues from a cave, he says to himself —

> 'Tis the grot
> Of Proserpine, when Hell, obscure and hot,
> Doth her resign; and where her tender hands
> She dabbles on the cool and sluicy sands:

A little later, and

> Now he is sitting by a shady spring,
> And elbow-deep with feverous fingering,
> Stems the upbursting cold.

For many passages where the magic of nature is mingled instinctively and inseparably with the magic of Greek mythology, the prayer of Endymion to Cynthia above quoted (p. 210) may serve as a sample: and all readers of poetry know the famous lines where the beautiful evocation of a natural scene melts into one, more beautiful still, of a scene of ancient life and worship which comes floated upon the poet's inner vision by an imagined strain of music from across the sea: —

> It seem'd he flew, the way so easy was;
> And like a new-born spirit did he pass
> Through the green evening quiet in the sun,
> O'er many a heath, through many a woodland dun,
> Through buried paths, where sleepy twilight dreams
> The summer time away. One track unseams
> A wooded cleft, and, far away, the blue
> Of ocean fades upon him; then, anew,
> He sinks adown a solitary glen,
> Where there was never sound of mortal men,
> Saving, perhaps, some snow-light cadences
> Melting to silence, when upon the breeze
> Some holy bark let forth an anthem sweet,
> To cheer itself to Delphi.

Often in thus conjuring up visions of the classic past, Keats effects true master strokes of imaginative concentration. Do we not feel half the romance of the *Odyssey*, with the spell that is in the sound of the vowelled place-names of Grecian story, and the breathing mystery of moonlight falling on magic islands of the sea, distilled into the one line —

> Aeaea's isle was wondering at the moon?
> And again in the pair of lines —
> Like old Deucalion mountain'd o'er the flood
> Or blind Orion hungry for the morn,

do not the two figures evoked rise before us full-charged each with the vital significance of his story? Mr de Sélincourt is no doubt right in suggesting that in the Orion line Keats' vision has been stimulated by the print from that picture of Poussin's which Hazlitt has described in so rich a strain of eulogy.

One of the great symptoms of returning vitality in the imagination of Europe, as the eighteenth century passed into the nineteenth, was its re-awakening to the significance and beauty of the Greek mythology. For a hundred years and more the value of that mythology for the human spirit had been forgotten. There never had been a time when the names of the ancient, especially the Roman, gods and goddesses were used so often in poetry, but simply in cold obedience to tradition and convention; merely as part of the accepted mode of speech of persons classically educated, and with no more living significance than belonged to the trick of personifying abstract forces and ideas by putting capital initials to their names. So far as concerned any real effect upon men's minds, it was tacitly understood and accepted that the Greek mythology was 'dead.' As if it could ever die; as if the 'fair humanities of old religion,' in passing out of the transitory state of things believed into the state of things remembered and cherished in imagination, had not put on a second life more enduring and more fruitful than the first. Faiths, as faiths, perish one after another; but each in passing away bequeaths for the enrichment of the after-world whatever elements it has contained of imaginative or moral truth or beauty. The polytheism of ancient Greece, embodying the instinctive effort of the brightliest gifted human race to explain its earliest experiences of nature and civilization, of the thousand moral and material forces, cruel or kindly, which environ and control the life of man on earth, is rich beyond measure in such elements; and if the modern world at any time fails to value them, it is the modern mind which is in so far dead and not they. Some words of Johnson's written forty years before Keats' time may help us to realize the full depth of the deadness from which in this respect it had to be awakened: —

He (Waller) borrows too many of his sentiments and illustrations from the old Mythology, for which it is in vain to plead the example of ancient poets: the deities, which they introduced so frequently, were considered as realities, so far as to be received by the imagination, whatever sober reason might even then determine. But of these images time has tarnished the splendour. A fiction, not only detected but despised, can never afford a solid basis to any position, though sometimes it may furnish a transient allusion, or slight illustration.

To rescue men's minds from this mode of deadness was part of the work of the English poetical revival of 1800 and onwards, and Keats was the poet who has contributed most to the task. Wordsworth could understand and expound the spirit of Grecian myths, and on occasion, as in his cry for a sight of Proteus and a sound of old Triton's horn, could for a moment hanker after its revival. Shelley could feel and write of Apollo and Pan and Proserpine, of Alpheus and Arethusa, with ardent delight and lyric emotion. But it was the gift of Keats to make live by imagination, whether in few words or many, every ancient fable that came up in his mind. The couple of lines telling of the song with which Peona tries to soothe her brother's pining are a perfect example alike of appropriate verbal music and of imagination following out a classic myth, that of the birth and nurture of Pan, from a mere hint to its recesses and finding the human beauty and tenderness that lurk there: —

> 'Twas a lay
> More subtle cadencèd, more forest wild
> Than Dryope's lone lulling of her child:

Even in setting before us so trite a personification as the god of love, Keats manages to escape the traditional and the merely decorative, and to endow him with a new and subtle vitality —

> awfully he stands;
> A sovereign quell is in his waving hands;
> No sight can bear the lightning of his bow;
> His quiver is mysterious, none can know
> What themselves think of it; from forth his eyes
> There darts strange light of varied hues and dyes:
> A scowl is sometimes on his brow, but who
> Look full upon it feel anon the blue
> Of his fair eyes run liquid through their souls.

Keats in one place defines his purpose in his poem, if only he can find strength to carry it out, as a

> striving to uprear
> Love's standard on the battlements of song.

His actual love scenes, as we have said, are the weakest, his ideal invocations to and celebrations of love among the strongest, things in the poem. One of these, already quoted, comes near the end of the first book: the second book opens with another: in the third book the incident of the moonlight spangling the surface of the sea and penetrating thence to the undersea caverns where Endymion lies languishing is used to point an essential moral of the narrative: —

> O love! how potent hast thou been to teach
> Strange journeyings! Wherever beauty dwells,
> In gulph or aerie, mountains or deep dells,
> In light, in gloom, in star or blazing sun,
> Thou pointest out the way, and straight 'tis won.

When the poet interrupts for a passing moment his tale of the might and mysteries of love, celestial or human, and turns to images of war, we find, him able to condense the whole tragedy of the sack of Troy into three potent lines, —

> The woes of Troy, towers smothering o'er their blaze,
> Stiff-holden shields, far-piercing spears, keen blades,
> Struggling, and blood, and shrieks.

From a passage like the following any reasonably sympathetic reader of Keats' day, running through the poem to find what manner and variety of promise it might contain, should have augured well of another kind of power, the dramatic and ironic, to be developed in due time. The speaker is the detected witch Circe uttering the doom of her revolted lover Glaucus: —

> 'Ha! ha! Sir Dainty! there must be a nurse
> Made of rose leaves and thistledown, express,
> To cradle thee, my sweet, and lull thee: yes,
> I am too flinty-hard for thy nice touch:
> My tenderest squeeze is but a giant's clutch.
> So, fairy-thing, it shall have lullabies
> Unheard of yet: and it shall still its cries
> Upon some breast more lily-feminine.
> Oh, no — it shall not pine, and pine, and pine
> More than one pretty, trifling thousand years.

> ...Mark me! Thou hast thews
> Immortal, for thou art of heavenly race:
> But such a love is mine, that here I chase
> Eternally away from thee all bloom
> Of youth, and destine thee towards a tomb.
> Hence shalt thou quickly to the watery vast;
> And there, ere many days be overpast,
> Disabled age shall seize thee: and even then
> Thou shalt not go the way of aged men;
> But live and wither, cripple and still breathe
> Ten hundred years: which gone, I then bequeath
> Thy fragile bones to unknown burial.
> Adieu, sweet love, adieu!'

A vein very characteristic of Keats at this stage of his mind's growth is that of figurative confession or self-revelation. Many passages in *Endymion* give poetical expression to the same alternating moods of ambition and humility, of exhilaration, depression, or apathy, which he confides to his friends in his letters. One of the most striking and original of these pieces of figurative psychology studied from his own moods is the description of the Cave of Quietude in Book IV: —

> There lies a den,
> Beyond the seeming confines of the space
> Made for the soul to wander in and trace
> Its own existence, of remotest glooms.
> Dark regions are around it, where the tombs
> Of buried griefs the spirit sees, but scarce
> One hour doth linger weeping, for the pierce
> Of new-born woe it feels more inly smart:
> And in these regions many a venom'd dart
> At random flies; they are the proper home
> Of every ill: the man is yet to come
> Who hath not journeyed in this native hell.
> But few have ever felt how calm and well
> Sleep may be had in that deep den of all.
> There anguish does not sting; nor pleasure pall:
> Woe-hurricanes beat ever at the gate,
> Yet all is still within and desolate.
> ...Enter none
> Who strive therefore: on the sudden it is won.

To the student of *Endymion* there are few things more interesting than to observe Keats' technical and spiritual relations to his Elizabethan models in those places where he has one or another of them manifestly in remembrance. Here is the passage in Sandys's *Ovid* which tells how Cybele, the Earth-Mother, punished the pair of lovers Hippomenes and Atalanta for the pollution of her sanctuary by turning them into lions and yoking them to her car: —

> The Mother, crown'd
> With towers, had struck them to the Stygian sound,
> But that she thought that punishment too small.
> When yellow manes on their smooth shoulders fall;
> Their arms, to legs; their fingers turn to nails;
> Their breasts of wondrous strength: their tufted tails

> Whisk up the dust; their looks are full of dread;
> For speech they roar: the woods become their bed.
> These Lions, fear'd by others, Cybel checks
> With curbing bits, and yokes their stubborn necks.

This is a typical example of Ovid's brilliantly clever, quite unromantic, unsurprised, and as it were unblinking way of detailing the marvels of an act of transformation. Keats' recollection of it — and probably also of a certain engraving after a Roman altar-relief of Cybele and her yoked lions — inspires a vision of intense imaginative life expressed in verse of a noble solemnity and sonority: —

> Forth from a rugged arch, in the dusk below,
> Came mother Cybele! alone — alone —
> In sombre chariot; dark foldings thrown
> About her majesty, and front death-pale,
> With turrets crown'd. Four maned lions hale
> The sluggish wheels; solemn their toothed maws,
> Their surly eyes brow-hidden, heavy paws
> Uplifted drowsily, and nervy tails
> Cowering their tawny brushes. Silent sails
> This shadowy queen athwart, and faints away
> In another gloomy arch.

The four lions instead of two must be a whim of Keats' imagination, and finds no authority either from Ovid or from ancient sculpture. Should any reader wish to pursue farther the comparison between Ovid in the *Metamorphoses* and Keats in *Endymion*, let him turn to the passage of Ovid where Polyphemus tells Galatea what rustic treasures he will lavish upon her if she will be his, — the same passage from which is derived the famous song in Handel's *Acis and Galatea* : let him turn to this and compare it with the list of similar delights offered by Endymion to the Indian maiden when he is bent on forgoing his dreams of a celestial union for her sake, and he will see how they are dematerialized and refined yet at the same time made richer in colour and enchantment.

But let us for our purpose rather take, as illustrating the relations of Keats to his classic and Elizabethan sources, two of the incidental lyrics in his poem. There are four such lyrics in *Endymion* altogether. Two of them are of small account, — the hymn to Neptune and Venus at the end of the third book, and the song of the Constellations in the middle of the fourth. The other two, the hymn to Pan in Book I and the song of the Indian maiden in Book IV, are among Keats' very finest achievements. The hymn to Pan is especially interesting in comparison with two of Keats' Elizabethan sources, Chapman's translation of the Homeric hymn and Ben Jonson's original hymns in his masque of *Pan's Anniversary*. Here is part of the Homeric hymn according to Chapman: —

> Sing, Muse, this chief of Hermes' love-got joys,
> Goat-footed, two-horn'd, amorous of noise,
> That through the fair greens, all adorn'd with trees,
> Together goes with Nymphs, whose nimble knees
> Can every dance foot, that affect to scale
> The most inaccessible tops of all
> Uprightest rocks, and ever use to call
> On Pan, the bright-haired God of pastoral;
> Who yet is lean and loveless, and doth owe
> By lot all loftiest mountains crown'd with snow;
> All tops of hills, and cliffy highnesses,

All sylvan copses, and the fortresses
Of thorniest queaches here and there doth rove,
And sometimes, by allurement of his love,
Will wade the wat'ry softnesses. Sometimes
(In quite oppos'd *capriccios*) he climbs
The hardest rocks, and highest, every way
Running their ridges. Often will convey
Himself up to a watch-tow'r's top, where sheep
Have their observance. Oft through hills as steep
His goats he runs upon, and never rests.
Then turns he head, and flies on savage beasts,
Mad of their slaughters...
(When Hesp'rus calls to fold the flocks of men)
From the green closets of his loftiest reeds
He rushes forth, and joy with song he feeds.
When, under shadow of their motions set,
He plays a verse forth so profoundly sweet,
As not the bird that in the flow'ry spring,
Amidst the leaves set, makes the thickets ring
Of her sour sorrows, sweeten'd with her song,
Runs her divisions varied so and strong.

And here are two of the most characteristic strophes from Ben Jonson's hymns:

—

Pan is our all, by him we breathe, we live,
We move, we are; 'tis he our lambs doth rear,
Our flocks doth bless, and from the store doth give
The warm and finer fleeces that we wear.
He keeps away all heats and colds,
Drives all diseases from our folds:
Makes every where the spring to dwell,
The ewes to feed, their udders swell;
But if he frown, the sheep (alas)
The shepherds wither, and the grass.
Strive, strive to please him then by still increasing thus
The rites are due to him, who doth all right for us.

....

Great Pan, the father of our peace and pleasure,
Who giv'st us all this leisure,
Hear what thy hallowed troop of herdsmen pray
For this their holy-day,
And how their vows to thee they in Lycæum pay.
So may our ewes receive the mounting rams,
And we bring thee the earliest of our lambs:
So may the first of all our fells be thine,
And both the breastning of our goats and kine.
As thou our folds dost still secure,
And keep'st our fountains sweet and pure,
Driv'st hence the wolf, the tod, the brock,
Or other vermin from the flock.

> That we preserv'd by thee, and thou observ'd by us,
> May both live safe in shade of thy lov'd Maenalus.

Comparing these strophes with the hymn in *Endymion*, we shall realize how the Elizabethan pastoral spirit, compounded as it was of native English love of country pleasures and Renaissance delight in classic poetry, emerged after near two centuries' occultation to reappear in the poetry of Keats, but wonderfully strengthened in imaginative reach and grasp, richer and more romantic both in the delighted sense of nature's blessings and activities and in the awed apprehension of a vast mystery behind them. The sense of such mystery is nowhere else expressed by Keats with such brooding inwardness and humbleness as where he invokes Pan no longer as a shepherd's god but as a symbol of the World-All. Wordsworth, when Keats at the request of friends read the piece to him, could see, or would own to seeing, nothing in it but a 'pretty piece of paganism,' though indeed in the more profoundly felt and imagined lines, such as those with which the first and fifth strophes open, the inspiration can be traced in great part to the influence of Wordsworth himself: —

> O Thou, whose mighty palace roof doth hang
> From jagged trunks, and overshadoweth
> Eternal whispers, glooms, the birth, life, death
> Of unseen flowers in heavy peacefulness;
> Who lov'st to see the hamadryads dress
> Their ruffled locks where meeting hazels darken;
> And through whole solemn hours dost sit, and hearken
> The dreary melody of bedded reeds —
> In desolate places, where dank moisture breeds
> The pipy hemlock to strange overgrowth;
> Bethinking thee, how melancholy loth
> Thou wast to lose fair Syrinx — do thou now,
> By thy love's milky brow!
> By all the trembling mazes that she ran,
> Hear us, great Pan!
> O thou, for whose soul-soothing quiet, turtles
> Passion their voices cooingly 'mong myrtles,
> What time thou wanderest at eventide
> Through sunny meadows, that outskirt the side
> Of thine enmossed realms: O thou, to whom
> Broad leaved fig trees even now foredoom
> Their ripen'd fruitage; yellow girted bees
> Their golden honeycombs; our village leas
> Their fairest blossom'd beans and poppied corn;
> The chuckling linnet its five young unborn,
> To sing for thee; low creeping strawberries
> Their summer coolness; pent up butterflies
> Their freckled wings; yea, the fresh budding year
> All its completions — be quickly near,
> By every wind that nods the mountain pine,
> O forester divine!
> Thou, to whom every faun and satyr flies
> For willing service; whether to surprise
> The squatted hare while in half sleeping fit;
> Or upward ragged precipices flit
> To save poor lambkins from the eagle's maw;
> Or by mysterious enticement draw

Bewildered shepherds to their path again;
Or to tread breathless round the frothy main,
And gather up all fancifullest shells
For thee to tumble into Naiads' cells,
And being hidden, laugh at their out-peeping;
Or to delight thee with fantastic leaping,

The while they pelt each other on the crown
With silvery oak apples, and fir cones brown —
By all the echoes that about thee ring,
Hear us, O satyr king!
O Hearkener to the loud clapping shears,
While ever and anon to his shorn peers
A ram goes bleating: Winder of the horn,
When snouted wild-boars routing tender corn
Anger our huntsmen: Breather round our farms,
To keep off mildews, and all weather harms:
Strange ministrant of undescribed sounds,
That come a swooning over hollow grounds,
And wither drearily on barren moors:
Dread opener of the mysterious doors
Leading to universal knowledge — see,
Great son of Dryope,
The many that are come to pay their vows
With leaves about their brows!
Be still the unimaginable lodge
For solitary thinkings; such as dodge
Conception to the very bourne of heaven,
Then leave the naked brain; be still the leaven,
That spreading in this dull and clodded earth
Gives it a touch ethereal — a new birth:
Be still a symbol of immensity;
A firmament reflected in a sea;
An element filling the space between;
An unknown — but no more: we humbly screen
With uplift hands our foreheads, lowly bending,
And giving out a shout most heaven rending,
Conjure thee to receive our humble Paean,
Upon thy Mount Lycean!

The song of the Indian maiden in the fourth book is in a very different key from this, more strikingly original in form and conception, and but for a weak opening and one or two flaws of taste would be a masterpiece. Keats' later and more famous lyrics, though they have fewer faults, yet do not, to my mind at least, show a command over such various sources of imaginative and musical effect, or touch so thrillingly so many chords of the spirit. A mood of tender irony and wistful pathos like that of the best Elizabethan love-songs; a sense as keen as Heine's of the immemorial romance of India and the East; a power like that of Coleridge, and perhaps partly caught from him, of evoking the remotest weird and beautiful associations almost with a word; clear visions of Greek beauty and wild wood-notes of northern imagination; all these elements come here commingled, yet in a strain perfectly individual. Keats calls the piece a 'roundelay,' — a form which it only so far resembles that its opening measures are repeated at the close. It begins by invoking and questioning sorrow in a series of dreamy musical stanzas of which the imagery embodies, a little redundantly and confusedly, the idea expressed elsewhere by Keats with greater perfection, that it is Sorrow which confers upon beautiful things their richest beauty. From these the song passes to tell what has happened to the singer: —

> To Sorrow,
> I bade good-morrow,
> And thought to leave her far away behind;
> But cheerly, cheerly,
> She loves me dearly;
> She is so constant to me, and so kind:
> I would deceive her
> And so leave her,
> But ah! she is so constant and so kind.
> Beneath my palm tree, by the river side,
> I sat a weeping: in the whole world wide
> There was no one to ask me why I wept, —
> And so I kept
> Brimming the water-lily cups with tears
> Cold as my fears.
> Beneath my palm trees, by the river side,
> I sat a weeping: what enamour'd bride,
> Cheated by shadowy wooer from the clouds,
> But hides and shrouds
> Beneath dark palm trees by a river side?

It is here that we seem to catch an echo, varied and new-modulated but in no sense weakened, from Coleridge's *Kubla Khan* , —

> A savage place, as holy as enchanted
> As e'er beneath the waning moon was haunted
> By woman wailing for her demon lover.

Then, with another change of measure comes the deserted maiden's tale of the irruption of Bacchus on his march from India; and then, arranged as if for music, the challenge of the maiden to the Maenads and satyrs and their choral answers: —

> 'Whence came ye, merry Damsels! Whence came ye!
> So many and so many, and such glee?
> Why have ye left your bowers desolate,
> Your lutes, and gentler fate?'
> 'We follow Bacchus! good or ill betide,
> We dance before him thorough kingdoms wide:
> Come hither, lady fair, and joined be
> To our wild minstrelsy!'
> 'Whence came ye jolly Satyrs! Whence came ye!
> So many, and so many, and such glee?
> Why have ye left your forest haunts, why left
> Your nuts in oak-tree cleft?'
> 'For wine, for wine we left our kernel tree;
> For wine we left our heath, and yellow brooms,
> And cold mushrooms;
> For wine we follow Bacchus through the earth;
> Great God of breathless cups and chirping mirth!
> Come hither, lady fair, and joined be

To our mad minstrelsy!'
'Over wide streams and mountains great we went,
And save when Bacchus kept his ivy tent,
Onward the tiger and the leopard pants,
With Asian elephants:
Onward these myriads — with song and dance,
With zebras striped, and sleek Arabians' prance,
Web-footed alligators, crocodiles,
Bearing upon their scaly backs, in files,
Plump infant laughers mimicking the coil
Of seamen, and stout galley-rowers' toil:
With toying oars and silken sails they glide,
Nor care for wind and tide.
Pl. V

'Onward the tiger and the leopard pants
With Asian elephants'

FROM A SARCOPHAGUS RELIEF AT WOBURN ABBEY

It is usually said that this description of Bacchus and his rout was suggested by Titian's famous picture of Bacchus and Ariadne (after Catullus) which is now in the National Gallery, and which Severn took Keats to see when it was exhibited at the British Institution in 1816. But this will account for a part at most of Keats' vision. Tiger and leopard panting along with Asian elephants on the march are not present in that picture, nor anything like them. Keats might have found suggestions for them in the text both of Godwin's little handbook just quoted and in Spence's *Polymetis* : but it would have been much more like him to work from something seen with his eyes: and these animals, with Indian prisoners mounted on the elephants, are invariable features of the triumphal processions of Bacchus through India as represented on a certain well-known type of ancient sarcophagus. From direct sight of such sarcophagus reliefs or prints after such Keats, I feel sure, must have taken them, while the children mounted on crocodiles may have been drawn from the plinth of the famous ancient recumbent statue of the Nile, and the pigmy rowers, in all likelihood, from certain reliefs which Keats will have noticed in the Townley collection at the British Museum: so that the whole brilliant picture is a composite (as we shall see later was the case with the Grecian Urn) which had shaped itself from various sources in Keats' imagination and become more real than any reality to his mind's eye. But I am holding up the reader, with this digression as to sources, from the fine rush of verse with which the lyric sweeps on to tell how the singer dropped out of the train of Bacchus to wander alone into the Carian forest, and finally, returning to the opening motive, ends as it began with an exquisite strain of lovelorn pathos: —

Come then, sorrow!
Sweetest sorrow!
Like an own babe I nurse thee on my breast:
I thought to leave thee,
And deceive thee,
But now of all the world I love thee best.
There is not one,
No, no, not one
But thee to comfort a poor lonely maid;
Thou art her mother
And her brother,
Her playmate, and her wooer in the shade.

An intensely vital imaginative feeling, such as can afford to dispense with scholarship, for the spirit of Greek and Greco-Asiatic myths and cults inspires these lyrics respectively; and strangely enough the result seems in neither case a whit impaired by the fact that the nature-images Keats invokes in them are almost purely English. Bean-fields in blossom and poppies among the corn, hemlock growing in moist places by the brookside, field mushrooms with the morning dew upon them, cowslips and strawberries and the song of linnets, oak, hazel and flowering broom, holly trees smothered from view under the summer leafage of chestnuts, these are the things of nature that he has loved and lived with from a child, and his imagination cannot help importing the same delights not only into the forest haunts of Pan but into the regions ranged over by Bacchus with his train of yoked tiger and panther, of elephant, crocodile and zebra.

Contemporary influences as well as Elizabethan and Jacobean are naturally discernible in the poem. The strongest and most permeating is that of Wordsworth, not so much to be traced in actual echoes of his words, though these of course occur, as in adoptions of his general spirit. We have recognized a special instance in that deep and brooding sense of mystery, of 'something far more deeply interfused,' of the working of an unknown spiritual force behind appearances, which finds expression in the hymn to Pan. Endymion's prayer to Cynthia from underground in the second book will be found to run definitely and closely parallel with Wordsworth's description of the huntress Diana in his account of the origin of Greek myths (see above, pp. 125-6). When Keats likens the many-tinted mists enshrouding the litter of Sleep to the fog on the top of Skiddaw from which the travellers may

> With an eye-guess towards some pleasant vale
> Descry a favourite hamlet faint and far,

we know that his imagination is answering to a stimulus supplied by Wordsworth. But it is for the undercurrent of ethical symbolism in *Endymion* that Keats will have owed the most to that master. Both Shelley and he had been profoundly impressed by the reading of *The Excursion* , published when Shelley was in his twenty-second year and Keats in his nineteenth, and each in his own way had taken deeply to heart Wordsworth's inculcation, both in that poem and many others, of the doctrine that a poet must learn to go out of himself and to live and feel as a man among fellow men, — that it is a kind of spiritual suicide for him to attempt to live apart from human sympathies,

Housed in a dream, at distance from the Kind!

A large part of *Endymion* , as we have seen, is devoted to the symbolical setting forth of this conviction. For the rest, that essential contrast between the mental processes and poetic methods of the elder and the younger man which we have noted in discussing Keats' first volume continues to strike us in the second. In interpreting the relations of man to the natural world, Wordsworth's poetry is intensely personal and 'subjective,' Keats' intensely impersonal and 'objective.' Wordsworth expounds, Keats evokes: the mind of Wordsworth works by strenuous after-meditation on his experiences of life and nature and their effect upon his own soul and consciousness: the mind of Keats works by instantaneous imaginative participation, instinctive and self-oblivious, in nature's doings and beings, especially those which make for human refreshment and delight.

The second contemporary influence to be considered is that of Shelley. Shelley's *Alastor*, it will be remembered, published early in 1816, had been praised by Hunt in *The Examiner* for December of that year, and in the following January Hunt printed in the same paper Shelley's *Hymn to Intellectual Beauty* . In the course of that same December and January Keats had seen a good deal of Shelley at Hunt's and taken part with him in many talks on poetry. It is certain that Keats read and was impressed by *Alastor* : doubtless he also read the *Hymn* . How much did either or both influence him in the composition of *Endymion* ? Mr Andrew Bradley thinks he sees evidence that *Alastor* influenced him strongly. That poem is a parable, as *Endymion* is, of the adventures of a poet's soul; and it enforces, as much of *Endymion* does, the doctrine that a poet cannot without ruin to himself live in isolation from human sympathies. But there the resemblance between the two conceptions really ends. In *Alastor* the poet, having lived in solitary communion 'with all that is most beautiful and august in nature and in human thought and the world's past' (the words are Shelley's own prose summary of the imagined experiences which the first part of the poem relates in splendid verse), is suddenly awakened, by a love-vision which comes to him in a dream, to the passionate desire of finding and mating with a kindred soul, the living counterpart of his dream, who shall share with him the delight of such communion. The desire, ever unsatisfied, turns all his former joys to ashes, and drives him forth by unheard-of ways through monstrous wildernesses until he pines and dies, or in the strained Shelleyan phrase, 'Blasted by his disappointment, he descends into an untimely grave.' The essence of the theme is the quest of the poetic soul for perfect spiritual sympathy and its failure to discover what it seeks. Shelley does not make it fully clear whether the ideal of his poet's dream is a purely abstract entity, an incarnation of the collective response which he hopes, but fails, to find from his fellow creatures at large; or whether, or how far, he is transcendentally expressing his own personal longing for an ideally sympathetic soul-companion in the shape of woman. Both strains no doubt enter into his conception; so far as the private strain comes in, many passages of his life furnish a mournfully ironic comment on his dream. But in any case his conception is fundamentally different from that of Keats in *Endymion*. The essence of Keats' task is to set forth the craving of the poet for full communion with the essential spirit of Beauty in the world, and the discipline by which he is led, through the exercise of the active human sympathies and the toilsome acquisition of knowledge, to the prosperous and beatific achievement of his quest.

It is rather the preface to *Alastor* than the poem itself which we can trace as having really worked in the mind of Keats. In it the evil fate of those who shut themselves out from human sympathies is very eloquently set forth, in a passage which is only partly relevant to the design of the poem, inasmuch as its warning is addressed not only to the poet in particular but to human beings in general. The passage may have had some influence on Keats when he framed the scheme of *Endymion* : what is certain is that we shall find its thoughts and even its words recurring forcibly to his mind in an hour of despondency some thirty months later: let us therefore postpone its consideration until then. For the rest, it is not difficult to show correspondence between some of the descriptive passages of *Alastor* and *Endymion*, especially those telling of the natural and architectural marvels amid which the heroes wander. Endymion's wanderings we are fresh from tracing. Alastor before him had wandered —

> where the secret caves
> Rugged and dark, winding amid the springs
> Of fire and poison, inaccessible
> To avarice or pride, their starry domes
> Of diamond and of gold expand above
> Numerous and immeasurable halls,
> Frequent with crystal columns, and clear shrines
> Of pearl, and thrones radiant with chrysolite.

But these are the kind of visions which may rise spontaneously in common in the minds of almost any pair of youthful dreamers. Shelley's poetic style is of course as much sounder and less experimental than that of Keats at this time as his range and certainty of penetrating and vivifying imagination are, to my apprehension at least, less: he had a trained and scholarly feeling both for the resources of the language and for its purity, and Keats might have learnt much from him as to what he should avoid. But as we have seen, Keats was firmly on his guard against letting any outside influence affect his own development, and would not visit Shelley at Marlow during the composition of *Endymion*, in order 'that he might have his own unfettered scope' and that the spirit of poetry might work out its own salvation in him.

As to the *Hymn to Intellectual Beauty*, written though it was by Shelley under the fresh impression of the glory of the Alps and also in the first flush of his acquaintance with and enthusiasm for Plato, I think Keats would have felt its strain of aspiration and invocation too painful, too near despair, to make much appeal to him, and that Shelley's

> Spirit of Beauty, that dost consecrate
> With thine own hues all thou dost shine upon,

would have seemed to him something abstract, remote, and uncomforting. His own imagination insisted on the existence of something in the ultimate nature of the universe to account for what he calls the 'wild and harmonised tune' which he found his spirit striking from all the scattered and broken beauties of the world. Vague and floating his conception of that something might be, but it was extraordinarily intense, partaking of the concentrated essence of a thousand thrilling joys of perception and imagination. He had read no Plato, though he was of course familiar enough with Spenser's mellifluous dilution of Platonic and neo-Platonic doctrine in his four *Hymns*. In *Endymion*, as in the speculative passages of the letters we have quoted, his mind has to go adventuring for itself among those ancient, for him almost uncharted, mysteries of Love and Beauty. He does not as yet conceive himself capable of anything more than steppings, to repeat his own sober phrase, of the imagination towards truth. He does not light, he does not expect to light, upon revelations of truth abstract or formal, and seems to waver between the Adam's dream idea of finding in some transcendental world all the several modes of earthly happiness 'repeated in a finer tone' but yet retaining their severalness, and an idea, nearer to the Platonic, of a single principle of absolute or abstract Beauty, the object of a purged and perfected spiritual contemplation, from which all the varieties of beauty experienced on earth derive their quality and oneness. But in his search he strikes now and again, for the attentive reader, notes of far reaching symbolic significance that carry the mind to the verge of the great mysteries of things: he takes us with him on exploratory sweeps and fetches of figurative thought in regions almost beyond the reach of words, where we gain with him glimmering adumbrations of the super-sensual through distilled and spiritualized remembrance of the joys of sense-perception at their most intense.

So much for Keats' possible debt to Shelley in regard to *Endymion*. There is an interesting small debt to be recorded on the other side, which critics, I think, have hitherto failed to notice. Shelley, notwithstanding his interest in Keats, did not read *Endymion* till a year or more after its publication. He had in the meantime gone to live in Italy, and having had the volume sent out to him at Leghorn, writes: 'much praise is due to me for having read it, the author's intention appearing to be that no person should possibly get to the end of it. Yet it is full of the highest and finest gleams of poetry: indeed, everything seems to be viewed by the mind of a poet which is described in it. I think if he had printed about fifty pages of fragments from it, I should have been led to admire Keats as a poet more than I ought, of which there is now no danger.' Nothing can be more just; and in the same spirit eight months later, in May 1820, he writes, 'Keats, I hope, is going to show himself a great poet; like the sun, to burst through the clouds, which, though dyed in the finest colours of the air, obscured his rising.' About the same time, having heard of Keats' hæmorrhage and sufferings and of their supposed cause in the hostility of the Tory critics, Shelley drafted, but did not send, his famous indignant letter to the editor of the *Quarterly Review*. In this draft he shows himself a careful student of *Endymion* by pointing out particular passages for approval. One of these passages is that near the beginning of the third book describing the wreckage seen by the hero as he traversed the ocean floor before meeting Glaucus. Everybody knows, in Shakespeare's *Richard III*, Clarence's dream of being drowned and of what he saw below the sea: —

> What dreadful noise of waters in mine ears!
> What ugly sights of death within mine eyes!
> Methought I saw a thousand fearful wrecks;
> Ten thousand men that fishes gnaw'd upon;
> Wedges of gold, great anchors, heaps of pearl,

Inestimable stones, unvalued jewels,
All scatter'd in the bottom of the sea.

Keats, no doubt remembering, and in a sense challenging, this passage, wrote, —

Far had he roam'd,
With nothing save the hollow vast, that foam'd,
Above, around, and at his feet; save things
More dead than Morpheus' imaginings:
Old rusted anchors, helmets, breastplates large
Of gone sea-warriors; brazen beaks and targe;
Rudders that for a hundred years had lost
The sway of human hand; gold vase emboss'd
With long-forgotten story, and wherein
No reveller had ever dipp'd a chin
But those of Saturn's vintage; mouldering scrolls,
Writ in the tongue of heaven, by those souls
Who first were on the earth; and sculptures rude
In ponderous stone, developing the mood
Of ancient Nox; — then skeletons of man,
Of beast, behemoth, and leviathan,
And elephant, and eagle, and huge jaw
Of nameless monster.

Jeffrey in his review of the *Lamia* volume has a fine phrase about this passage. It 'comes of no ignoble lineage,' he says, 'nor shames its high descent.' How careful Shelley's study of the passage had been, and how completely he had assimilated it, is proved by his, doubtless quite unconscious, reproduction and amplification of it in the fourth act of *Prometheus Unbound*, which he added as an afterthought to the rest of the poem in December 1819. The wreckage described is not that of the sea, but that which the light flashing from the forehead of the infant Earth-spirit reveals at the earth's centre.

The beams flash on
And make appear the melancholy ruins
Of cancelled cycles; anchors, beaks of ships;
Planks turned to marble; quivers, helms, and spears,
And gorgon-headed targes, and the wheels
Of scythèd chariots, and the emblazonry
Of trophies, standards, and armorial beasts,
Round which death laughed, sepulchred emblems
Of dead destruction, ruin within ruin!
The wrecks beside of many a city vast,
Whose population which the earth grew over
Was mortal, but not human; see, they lie,
Their monstrous works, and uncouth skeletons,
Their statues, homes and fanes; prodigious shapes
Huddled in gray annihilation, split,
Jammed in the hard, black deep; and over these,
The anatomies of unknown wingèd things,
And fishes which were isles of living scale,
And serpents, bony chains, twisted around
The iron crags, or within heaps of dust
To which the tortuous strength of their last pangs
Had crushed the iron crags; and over these
The jaggèd alligator, and the might

> Of earth-convulsing behemoth, which once
> Were monarch beasts.

The derivation of this imagery from the passage of Keats seems evident alike from its general conception and sequence and from details like the anchors, beaks, targes, the prodigious primeval sculptures, the skeletons of behemoth and alligator and antediluvian monsters without name. Another possible debt of Shelley to *Endymion* has also been suggested in the list of delights which the poet, in the closing passage of *Epipsychidion*, proposes to share with his spirit's mate in their imagined island home in the Ægean. If Shelley indeed owes anything to *Endymion* here, he has etherealized and transcendentalized his original even more than Keats did Ovid. Possibly, it may also be suggested, it may have been Shelley's reading of *Endymion* that led him at this time to take two of the myths handled in it by Keats as subjects for his own two lyrics, *Arethusa* and the *Hymn to Pan* (both of 1820); but he may just as well have thought of these subjects independently; and in any case they are absolutely in his own vein, nor was their exquisite leaping and liquid lightness of rhythm a thing at any time within Keats' compass. It would be tempting to attribute to a desire of emulating and improving on Keats Shelley's beautifully accomplished use of the rimed couplet with varied pause and free overflow in the *Epistle to Maria Gisborne* (1819) and *Epipsychidion* (1820), but that he had already made a first experiment in the same kind with *Julian and Maddalo*, written before his copy of *Endymion* had reached him, so that we must take his impulse in the matter to have been drawn not intermediately through Keats but direct from Leigh Hunt.

Chapter VIII

DECEMBER 1817-JUNE 1818: HAMPSTEAD AND TEIGNMOUTH: EMIGRATION OF GEORGE KEATS

From finishing *Endymion* at Burford Bridge Keats returned some time before mid-December to his Hampstead lodging. The exact date is uncertain; but it was in time to see Kean play *Richard III* at Drury Lane on the 15th — the actor's first performance after a break of some weeks due to illness. J. H. Reynolds had gone to Exeter for a Christmas holiday, and Keats, acting as his substitute, wrote four dramatic criticisms for the *Champion* : the first, printed on December 21, on Kean in general and his reappearance as Richard III in particular; a second on a hash of the three parts of Shakespeare's *Henry VI* produced under the title *Richard Duke of York* , with Kean in the name-part and probably Kean also as compiler; a third on a tragedy of small account by one Dillon, called *Retribution* , or the *Chieftain's Daughter* , in which the young Macready played the part of the villain; and a fourth on a pantomime of *Don Giovanni*. No one, least of all one living in Keats' circle, could well attempt stage criticism at this time without trying to write like Hazlitt. Keats acquits himself on the whole rather youthfully and crudely. In one point he is cruder than one would have expected, and that is where, after re-reading the three parts of *Henry VI* for his purpose, he retracts what he had begun to say about them and declares that they are 'perfect works,' apparently without any suspicion that Shakespeare's part in them is at most that of a beginner of genius touching up the hackwork of others with a fine passage here and there.

It is only in the notice of Kean as Richard III that the genius in Keats really kindles. Here his imagination teaches him phrases beyond the reach of Hazlitt, to express (there is nothing more difficult) the specific quality and very thrill of the actor's voice and utterance. The whole passage is of special interest, both what is groping in it and what is masterly, and alike for itself and for such points as its familiar use of tags from the then recent *Christabel* and *Siege of Corinth* : —

A melodious passage in poetry is full of pleasures both sensual and spiritual. The spiritual is felt when the very letters and points of charactered language show like the hieroglyphics of beauty; the mysterious signs of our immortal free-masonry! 'A thing to dream of, not to tell'! The sensual life of verse springs warm from the lips of Kean and to one learned in Shakespearian hieroglyphics — learned in the spiritual portion of those lines to which Kean adds a sensual grandeur; his tongue must seem to have robbed the Hybla bees and left them honeyless! There is an indescribable *gusto* in his voice, by which we feel that the utterer is thinking of the past and future while speaking of the instant. When he says in *Othello* , 'Put up your bright swords, for the dew will rust them,' we feel that his throat had commanded where swords were as thick as reeds. From eternal risk, he speaks as though his body were unassailable. Again, his exclamation of 'blood, blood, blood!' is direful and slaughterous to the deepest degree; the very words appear stained and gory. His nature hangs over them, making a prophetic repast. The voice is loosed on them, like the wild dog on the savage relics of an eastern conflict; and we can distinctly hear it 'gorging and growling o'er carcase and limb.' In Richard, 'Be stirring with the lark tomorrow, gentle Norfolk!' comes from him as through the morning atmosphere towards which he yearns.... Surely this intense power of anatomizing the passions of every syllable, of taking to himself the airings of verse, is the means by which he becomes a storm with such fiery decision; and by which, with a still deeper charm, he does his spiriting gently. Other actors are continually thinking of their sum-total effect throughout a play. Kean delivers himself up to the instant feeling, without a shadow of a thought about anything else. He feels his being as deeply as Wordsworth, or any other of our intellectual monopolists. From all his comrades he stands alone, reminding us of him, whom Dante has so finely described in his Hell:

and sole apart retir'd the Soldan fierce.

Although so many times he has lost the battle of Bosworth Field, we can easily conceive him really expectant of victory, and a different termination of the piece.

Keats was by this time left alone in Well Walk, having seen his brothers off for Teignmouth, whither George carried the invalid Tom for change of climate. His regular occupation for the next two months was revising and copying out *Endymion* for press. Regular also was his attendance at Hazlitt's evening lectures on the English Poets at the Surrey Institution. Of the lectures on Shakespeare which Coleridge was in the same weeks delivering in Fetter Lane Keats makes no mention, and it is clear that he made no effort to go and hear them, though the distance of the lecture-hall from his Hampstead lodging was so much less. The reader who would fain conjure up for himself the contrasted personalities and styles in public discourse of these two master critics, the shy and saturnine, yet vigorously straight-hitting and trenchantly effective Hazlitt, and the ramblingly mellifluous, sometimes beautifully inspired and sometimes painfully drug-beclouded Coleridge, can draw but a faint and tantalized satisfaction from the diaries of Henry Crabb Robinson, that assiduous friend and satellite of men of genius, who punctually records his attendance at both courses, but lacked the touch that should have made his record live.

Keats' letters to his brothers in these winter months, with a few more to Bailey and Reynolds, give us lively glimpses of his social doings, and others, interesting in the extreme, of the inward growth and workings of his mind. He tells of a certain amount of commonplace conviviality: an absurd dance and rackety supper at one Redhall's; noisy Saturday 'concerts' at his own rooms, which means that two or three intimates came to early afternoon dinner and spent the rest of the day drinking claret and keeping up a concerted racket, each in imitation of some musical instrument (Keats himself of the bassoon); but of this pastime he soon got tired and rather ashamed. His social relations began to extend themselves more than he much cared about, or thought consistent with proper industry. We find him dining with Shelley's friend, the genial and admirable stockbroker and man of letters Horace Smith, in company with some fashionable wits, concerning whom he reflects: — 'They only served to convince me how superior humour is to wit, in respect to enjoyment. These men say things which make one start, without making one feel; they are all alike; they all know fashionables; they have all a mannerism in their eating and drinking, in their mere handling a decanter. They talked of Kean and his low company. "Would I were with that company instead of yours," said I to myself.' Sunday evenings were for a while set apart for dining with Haydon, and here, on the last Sunday of the year, Keats met Wordsworth for the first time.

Wordsworth was on one of his rare visits to London, and had been staying since the beginning of December with his brother Christopher at Lambeth rectory. According to Crabb Robinson, he seems to have been in these weeks in one of his stiffest and most domineering moods of egotism, much ruffled by the moderate strictures of Coleridge in *Biographia Literaria* on certain qualities in his work and not at all appeased by the splendid praise which so much out-balanced them. One evening in conversation he went so far as to treat that great helpless genius, his old bosom-friend and inspirer, with a rudeness of contradiction which even the devoted Robinson found it hard to forgive. Near about the same time, hearing that the next Waverley novel was to be about Rob Roy, he took down his ballad so named, read it aloud, and said 'I do not know what more Mr Scott can have to say on the subject.' Keats promptly had full experience of Wordsworth's egotism, but also saw more genial aspects of his character. Quite coolly and briefly he mentions those circumstances of their first meeting which Haydon, in a famous passage of his autobiography, thrusts before us in the insistent colour and illumination of a magic-lantern picture. 'I think,' writes Keats, 'Ritchie is going to Fezan in Africa; thence to proceed if possible like Mungo Park. Then there was Wordsworth, Lamb, Monkhouse, Landseer, and your humble servant. Lamb got tipsy and blew up Kingston — proceeding so far as to take the candle across the room, hold it to his face, and show us what a soft fellow he was.' It should be explained that Ritchie was a young explorer whom Tom had met the summer before on his run to Paris, and Kingston a thick-witted, thick-skinned, intrusive but kindly gentleman of lion-hunting proclivities, who as Comptroller of Stamps had had some correspondence with Wordsworth and on the strength of this invited himself to join Haydon's party in the poet's honour. Now for Haydon: —

On December 28th the immortal dinner came off in my painting-room, with Jerusalem towering up behind us as a background. Wordsworth was in fine cue, and we had a glorious set-to, — on Homer, Shakespeare, Milton and Virgil. Lamb got exceedingly merry and exquisitely witty; and his fun in the midst of Wordsworth's solemn intonations of oratory was like the sarcasm and wit of the fool in the intervals of Lear's passion. He made a speech and voted me absent, and made them drink my health. 'Now,' said Lamb, 'you old lake poet, you rascally poet, why do you call Voltaire dull?' We all defended Wordsworth, and affirmed there was a state of mind when Voltaire would be dull. 'Well,' said Lamb, 'here's to Voltaire — the Messiah of the French nation, and a very proper one too.'

He then, in a strain of humour beyond description, abused me for putting Newton's head into my picture, — 'a fellow,' said he, 'who believed nothing unless it was as clear as the three sides of a triangle. And then he and Keats agreed he had destroyed all the poetry of the rainbow by reducing it to the prismatic colours. It was impossible to resist him, and we all drank 'Newton's health, and confusion to mathematics.' It was delightful to see the good-humour of Wordsworth in giving in to all our frolics without affectation and laughing as heartily as the best of us.

By this time other friends joined, amongst them poor Ritchie who was going to penetrate by Fezzan to Timbuctoo. I introduced him to all as 'a gentleman going to Africa.' Lamb seemed to take no notice; but all of a sudden he roared out, 'Which is the gentleman we are going to lose?' We then drank the victim's health, in which Ritchie joined.

In the morning of this delightful day, a gentleman, a perfect stranger, had called on me. He said he knew my friends, had an enthusiasm for Wordsworth and begged I would procure him the happiness of an introduction. He told me he was a comptroller of stamps, and often had correspondence with the poet. I thought it a liberty; but still, as he seemed a gentleman, I told him he might come.

When we retired to tea we found the comptroller. In introducing him to Wordsworth I forgot to say who he was. After a little time the comptroller looked down, looked up and said to Wordsworth, 'Don't you think, sir, Milton was a great genius?' Keats looked at me, Wordsworth looked at the comptroller. Lamb who was dozing by the fire turned round and said, 'Pray, sir, did you say Milton was a great genius?' 'No, sir; I asked Mr Wordsworth if he were not.' 'Oh,' said Lamb, 'then you are a silly fellow.' 'Charles! my dear Charles!' said Wordsworth; but Lamb, perfectly innocent of the confusion he had created, was off again by the fire.

After an awful pause the comptroller said, 'Don't you think Newton a great genius?' I could not stand it any longer; Keats put his head into my books. Ritchie squeezed in a laugh. Wordsworth seemed asking himself, 'Who is this?' Lamb got up, and taking a candle, said, 'Sir, will you allow me to look at your phrenological development?' He then turned his back on the poor man, and at every question of the comptroller he chaunted —

Diddle diddle dumpling, my son John
Went to bed with his breeches on.

The man in office, finding Wordsworth did not know who he was, said in a spasmodic and half-chuckling anticipation of assured victory, 'I have had the honour of some correspondence with you, Mr Wordsworth.' 'With me, sir?' said Wordsworth, 'not that I remember.' 'Don't you, sir? I am a comptroller of stamps.' There was a dead silence; — the comptroller evidently thinking that was enough. While we were waiting for Wordsworth's reply, Lamb sung out

Hey diddle diddle,
The cat and the fiddle.

'My dear Charles!' said Wordsworth, —
Diddle diddle dumpling, my son John,

chaunted Lamb, and then rising, exclaimed, 'Do let me have another look at that gentleman's organs.' Keats and I hurried Lamb into the painting-room, shut the door and gave way to inextinguishable laughter. Monkhouse followed and tried to get Lamb away. We went back but the comptroller was irreconcilable. We soothed and smiled and asked him to supper. He stayed though his dignity was sorely affected. However, being a good-natured man, we parted all in good humour, and no ill effects followed.

All the while, until Monkhouse succeeded, we could hear Lamb struggling in the painting-room and calling at intervals, 'Who is that fellow? Allow me to see his organs once more.'

It was indeed an immortal evening. Wordsworth's fine intonation as he quoted Milton and Virgil, Keats' eager inspired look, Lamb's quaint sparkle of lambent humour, so speeded the stream of conversation, that in my life I never passed a more delightful time. All our fun was within bounds. Not a word passed that an apostle might not have listened to. It was a night worthy of the Elizabethan age, and my solemn Jerusalem flashing up by the flame of the fire, with Christ hanging over us like a vision, all made up a picture which will long glow upon —

that inward eye
Which is the bliss of solitude.

Keats made Ritchie promise he would carry his *Endymion* to the great desert of Sahara and fling it in the midst.

To complete our impression of Wordsworth at this time of his winter visit to London in his forty-eighth year, let us turn for a moment to Leigh Hunt's recollections of his looks and ways about the same time.

Certainly I never beheld eyes that looked so inspired or supernatural. They were like fires half burning, half smouldering, with a sort of acrid fixture of regard, and seated at the end of two caverns. One might imagine Ezekiel or Isaiah to have had such eyes.... He had a dignified manner, with a deep roughish but not unpleasing voice, and an exalted mode of speaking. He had a habit of keeping his left hand in the bosom of his waistcoat; and in this attitude, except when he turned round to take one of the subjects of his criticism from the shelves, he was dealing forth his eloquent but hardly catholic judgments.

Hazlitt, in words written a few years later, gives a nearly similar portrait: —

He is above the middle size, with marked features, and an air somewhat stately and Quixotic. He reminds one of some of Holbein's heads, grave, saturnine, with a slight indication of sly humour.... He has a peculiar sweetness in his smile, and great depth and manliness and a rugged harmony in the tones of his voice. His manner of reading his own poetry is particularly imposing, and in his favourite passages his eye beams with preternatural lustre, and the meaning labours slowly up from his swelling breast.

Although the great man could praise or care for no contemporary poetry save his own, and had none of the sympathetic or encouraging criticism to bestow on Keats which to that ardent young spirit would have meant so much, he nevertheless showed him no little personal kindness, receiving him when he called and inviting him several times to dine or sup. On his first visit Keats was kept waiting till the poet bustled in, full dressed in stiff stock and knee breeches, in haste to keep a dinner appointment with one of his official chiefs. This experience proved no check to their acquaintance: neither did Wordsworth's chilling comment when Keats was induced to read to him the hymn to Pan from *Endymion* . 'A very pretty piece of Paganism,' he remarked and that was all. Severn was present at the gathering in Haydon's studio where this reading took place. The evening's talk, he relates, ran much on the virtues of a vegetable diet, which was for the moment, through the vehement advocacy of Shelley, so much in vogue in Leigh Hunt's circle that even the ruddy and robust Haydon gave himself out for a proselyte like the rest, until friends one day caught him coming privily smacking his lips out of a chop-house.

Wordsworth was in a jocular mood, and asked his herbivorous friends whether they did not welcome such a succulent morsel of animal food as a chance caterpillar in their cabbage. Was it on the same occasion that the sage and seer condescended to a pun, telling Haydon that if he ever took the name of another artist, as some of the old masters used to do, it should be Teniers, seeing that he had been ten years working on his great picture, still unfinished, of Christ's Entry into Jerusalem, in which Wordsworth and other leading personages of the time were to figure among the crowd of lookers on?

A fortnight after their first meeting Keats re-affirms to his brother the view he had formerly expressed to Haydon that 'If there were three things superior in the modern world they were *The Excursion*, Haydon's Pictures, and Hazlitt's depth of Taste.' About the same time, that is in the course of January, he writes of having 'seen Wordsworth frequently': and again 'I have seen a good deal of Wordsworth.' A later allusion implies that he has seen him 'with his beautiful wife and his enchanting sister.' At one meeting Keats must have heard talk or reading that delighted him, for Severn tells how while he was toiling late one night over his miniature painting, Keats burst into his lodging fresh from Wordsworth's company and in a state of eager elation over his experience. It is hard to refrain from conjecture as to what had happened. What one would like to think is that Wordsworth had been reading Keats some of those great passages in the *Prelude* without which the master cannot truly be more than half known and which remained unpublished until the year of his death. Or may we possibly trace a clue to the evening's enjoyment in this further note of Hazlitt's on a phase of Wordsworth's conversation? —

It is fine to hear him talk of the way in which certain subjects should have been treated by eminent poets, according to his notions of the art. Thus he finds fault with Dryden's description of Bacchus in the *Alexander's Feast*, as if he were a mere good-looking youth, or boon companion

> Flushed with a purple grace,
> He shows his honest face —

Instead of representing the god returning from the conquest of India, crowned with vine-leaves, and drawn by panthers, and followed by troops of satyrs, of wild men and animals that he had tamed. You would think, in hearing him speak on this subject, that you saw Titian's picture of the meeting of Bacchus and Ariadne — so classic were his conceptions, so glowing his style.

It is tempting to seek some kind of connexion between Keats in his great Bacchic ode in *Endymion* and Wordsworth in this vein of talk. Had we not known that *Endymion* was finished before the elder and the younger poet met, we might have been inclined to attribute to Wordsworth's eloquence some part of Keats' inspiration. And even as it is such possibility remains open, for it must be remembered that Keats carefully recopied the several cantos of his poem during the spring, the fourth canto not until March, at Teignmouth, and it is conceivable, though unlikely, that the triumph of Bacchus might have been an addition made in recopying.

It was most likely a result of the interest taken by Wordsworth in Keats that the young poet received at this time a friendly call, of which he makes passing mention, from Crabb Robinson.

But the more Keats saw of Wordsworth himself, the more critically, as his letters show, he came gradually to look upon him. He disliked the idea of a man so revered dining with the foolish Kingston, and refused to dine and meet him there. He regrets, after Wordsworth has gone, that he has 'left a bad impression wherever he has visited in town by his egotism, Vanity, and bigotry;' adding, 'yet he is a great poet if not a philosopher.' The fullest expression of this critical attitude occurs in a letter written to Reynolds at the beginning of February. Keats is for the moment out of conceit with the poets of his own time; particularly with Wordsworth, whom he had always devoutly reverenced from a distance, and with Hunt, next to Cowden Clarke his earliest encourager and sympathiser, whom to his disappointment he had lately found more ready to carp than praise when he read him the early books of *Endymion*. It seems Hunt would have liked the talk of Endymion and Peona to come nearer his own key of simpering triviality in *Rimini*. 'He says,' writes Keats 'the conversation is unnatural and too high-flown for Brother and Sister — says it should be simple, forgetting do ye mind that they are both overshadowed by a supernatural Power and perforce could not talk like Francesca in the *Rimini*. He must first prove that Caliban's poetry is unnatural. This with me completely overturns his objections.' In revising *Endymion* for press Keats proved his wise adherence to his own point of view by cutting out some of the passages most infected with the taint of Hunt's familiar tea-party manner. The words in which he expresses his impatience of the several dogmatisms of Wordsworth and Hunt are vital in relation to his own conception of poetry and of its right aim and working: —

It may be said that we ought to read our contemporaries, that Wordsworth etc., should have their due from us. But, for the sake of a few fine imaginative or domestic passages, are we to be bullied into a certain Philosophy engendered in the whims of an Egotist? Every man has his speculations, but every man does not brood and peacock over them till he makes a false coinage and deceives himself. Many a man can travel to the very bourne of Heaven, and yet want confidence to put down his half-seeing. Sancho will invent a Journey heavenward as well as anybody. We hate poetry that has a palpable design upon us, and, if we do not agree, seems to put its hand into its breeches pocket. Poetry should be great and unobtrusive, a thing which enters into one's soul, and does not startle or amaze it with itself, but with its subject. How beautiful are the retired flowers! how would they lose their beauty were they to throng into the highway crying out, 'Admire me, I am a violet! Dote upon me, I am a primrose!' Modern poets differ from the Elizabethans in this: each of the moderns like an Elector of Hanover governs his petty state, and knows how many straws are swept daily from the Causeways in all his dominions, and has a continual itching that all the Housewives should have their coppers well scoured. The ancients were Emperors of vast Provinces, they had only heard of the remote ones and scarcely cared to visit them. I will cut all this — I will have no more of Wordsworth or Hunt in particular.... I don't mean to deny Wordsworth's grandeur and Hunt's merit, but I mean to say we need not be teazed with grandeur and merit when we can have them uncontaminated and unobtrusive.

These winter letters of Keats are full of similar first fruits of young reflection, thoughts forming or half-forming themselves in absolute sincerity as he writes, intuitions of his first-endeavouring mind on the search for vital truths of art and nature and humanity. Imperfect, half-wrought phrases often come from him which prove, when you have lived with them, to be more sufficient as well as more suggestive than if they had been chiselled into precision by longer study and a more confident mind. For instance: 'the excellence of every art is its intensity, capable of making all disagreeables evaporate from their being in close relationship with Beauty and Truth': a sentence worth whole treatises and fit, sketchy as it is, to serve as text to all that can justly be discoursed concerning problems of art in its relation to nature, — of realism, romance, and the rest. Or this: —

Brown and Dilke walked with me and back to the Christmas pantomime. I had not a dispute, but a disquisition, with Dilke upon various subjects; several things dove-tailed in my mind, and at once it struck me what quality went to form a man of achievement, especially in literature, and which Shakespeare possessed so enormously — I mean *Negative Capability*, that is, when a man is capable of being in uncertainties, mysteries, doubts, without any irritable reaching after fact and reason. Coleridge, for instance, would let go by a fine isolated verisimilitude caught from the Penetralium of mystery, from being incapable of remaining content with half-knowledge. This pursued through volumes would perhaps take us no further than this, that with a great poet the sense of Beauty overcomes every other consideration, or rather obliterates all consideration.

Or this: —

In poetry I have a few axioms, and you will see how far I am from their centre.

1st. I think poetry should surprise by a fine excess, and not by singularity; it should strike the reader as a wording of his own highest thoughts, and appear almost a remembrance.

2nd. Its touches of beauty should never be halfway, thereby making the reader breathless, instead of content. The rise, the progress, the setting of Imagery should, like the sun, come natural to him, shine over him, and set soberly, although in magnificence, leaving him in the luxury of twilight.

But it is easier to think what poetry should be, than to write it. And this leads me to another axiom — That if poetry comes not as naturally as the leaves to a tree, it had better not come at all. However it may be with me, I cannot help looking into new countries with 'O for a muse of Fire to ascend!' If *Endymion* serves me as a pioneer, perhaps I ought to be content — I have great reason to be content, for thank God I can read, and perhaps understand Shakespeare to his depths; and I have I am sure many friends, who, if I fail will attribute any change in my life and temper to humbleness rather than pride — to a cowering under the wings of great poets, rather than to a bitterness that I am not appreciated.

Cogitations of this cast, not less fresh than deep, and often throwing a clear retrospective light on the moods and aims which governed him in writing *Endymion*, are interspersed at the beginning of the year with regrets at dissensions rife among his friends. The strain between Haydon and Hunt had increased since the autumn, and now, over a sordid matter of money borrowed by Mrs Hunt — by all accounts the most unabashed of petty spongers — and not repaid, grew into an active quarrel. Another still fiercer quarrel broke out between Haydon and Reynolds, who with all his fine qualities seems to have been quick and touchy, and whom we find later in open breach with his admirable brother-in-law Thomas Hood. Keats was not involved. With his distinguished good sense and good heart in matters of friendship, he knew how to keep in close and affectionate touch with what was loveable or likeable in each of the disputants severally. His comments are the best key to the best part of himself, and show him as the true great spirit, by character not less than by gift, among the group.

Things have happened lately of great perplexity — you must have heard of them — Reynolds and Haydon retorting and recriminating, and parting for ever — the same thing has happened between Haydon and Hunt. It is unfortunate — Men should bear with each other: there lives not the Man who may not be cut up, aye lashed to pieces on his weakest side. The best of men have but a portion of good in them — a kind of spiritual yeast in their frames, which creates the ferment of existence — by which a Man is propelled to act, and strive, and buffet with Circumstance. The sure way, Bailey, is first to know a Man's and then be passive — if after that he insensibly draws you towards him then you have no power to break the link. Before I felt interested in either Reynolds or Haydon, I was well read in their faults; yet, knowing them, I have been cementing gradually with both. I have an affection for them both, for reasons almost opposite — and to both must I of necessity cling, supported always by the hope that, when a little time, a few years, shall have tried me more fully in their esteem, I may be able to bring them together. The time must come, because they have both hearts and they will recollect the best parts of each other, when this gust is overblown.

Of Haydon himself and of his powers as a painter Keats continued to think as highly as ever, seeing in his pictures, as the friends and companions of every ardent and persuasive worker in the arts are apt to see, not so much the actual performance as the idea he had preconceived of it in the light of his friend's enthusiastic ambition and eloquence. Severn repeatedly insists on Keats' remarkably keen natural instinct for and understanding of the arts both of music and painting. Cowden Clarke's piano-playing had been one of the chief pleasures of his school-days: as to the capacity he felt in himself for judging the works of painting, here is his own scrupulously modest and sincere estimate expressed to Haydon a little later:

Believe me Haydon your picture is part of myself — I have ever been too sensible of the labyrinthian path to eminence in Art (judging from Poetry) ever to think I understood the emphasis of painting. The innumerable compositions and decompositions which take place between the intellect and its thousand materials before it arrives at that trembling delicate and snail-horn perception of beauty. I know not your many havens of intenseness — nor ever can know them: but for this I hope nought you achieve is lost upon me: for when a Schoolboy the abstract idea I had of an heroic painting — was what I cannot describe. I saw it somewhat sideways, large, prominent, round, and colour'd with magnificence — somewhat like the feel I have of Anthony and Cleopatra. Or of Alcibiades leaning on his Crimson Couch in his Galley, his broad shoulders imperceptibly heaving with the Sea.

With Hunt also, in spite of the momentary causes of annoyance we have seen, Keats' intercourse continued frequent, while with Reynolds his intimacy grew daily closer. At Hunt's he again saw something of Shelley. 'The Wednesday before last Shelley, Hunt, and I, wrote each a sonnet on the river Nile,' he tells his brothers on the 16th of February, 1818. The sonnets are preserved. They were to be written, it was agreed, in a quarter of an hour. Shelley and Keats were up to time, but Hunt had to sit up half the night to finish his. It was worth the pains, and with it for once the small poet outdid the two great. 'I have been writing,' continues Keats, 'at intervals, many songs and sonnets, and I long to be at Teignmouth to read them over to you.' With the help of his manuscripts or of the transcripts made from them by his friends, it is possible to retrace the actual order of many of these fugitive pieces. On the 16th of January was written the sonnet on Mrs Reynolds's cat, perhaps Keats' best thing in the humorous vein; on the 21st, after seeing in Leigh Hunt's possession a lock of hair reputed to be Milton's, the address to that poet beginning 'Chief of organic numbers!' which he sends to the prime Milton enthusiast among his friends, Benjamin Bailey, with the comment, 'This I did at Hunt's, at his request, — perhaps I should have done something better alone and at home.' The first two lines, —

> Chief of organic numbers,
> Old scholar of the spheres!

read like an anticipation in the rough of the first stanza of Tennyson's masterly set of alcaics already referred to, beginning 'O mighty-mouthed inventor of harmonies.' To the 22nd belongs the sonnet, 'O golden tongued Romance with serene lute,' in which Keats bids himself lay aside (apparently) his Spenser, in order to read again the more rousing and human-passionate pages of *Lear*. This is one of the last of his sonnets written in the Petrarchan form as followed by Milton and Wordsworth, and from henceforth he follows the Shakespearean form almost exclusively. On the 31st he writes to Reynolds in a rollicking mood, and sends him the lines to Apollo beginning 'Hence Burgundy, Claret, and Port,' part rant (the word is his own) pure and simple, part rant touched with genius, and giving words to a very frequent and intense phase of feeling in himself: —

> Aye, when the soul is fled
> Too high above our head,
> Affrighted do we gaze
> After its airy maze,
> As doth a mother wild,
> When her young infant child
> Is in an eagle's claws —
> And is not this the cause
> Of madness? — God of Song,
> Thou bearest me along
> Through, sights I scarce can bear:
> O let me, let me share
> With the hot lyre and thee,
> The staid Philosophy.
> Temper my lonely hours,
> And let me see thy bowers
> More unalarm'd!

By way of a sober conclusion to the same letter, he adds the very fine and profoundly felt sonnet in the Shakespearean form beginning 'When I have fears that I may cease to be,' which be calls his last. On the 3rd of February he sends two spirited sets of verses in the favourite four-beat measure, heptasyllable varied with octosyllable, of the later Elizabethans and the youthful Milton, namely those to Robin Hood (suggested by a set of sonnets by Reynolds on Sherwood Forest) and those on the Mermaid Tavern. On the 4th comes another Shakespearean sonnet, that beginning 'Time's sea has been five years at its slow ebb,' in which he recalls the memory of an old, persistent, haunting love-fancy. The two sonnets of January 31 and February 4 should be read strictly together: —

> When I have fears that I may cease to be
> Before my pen has glean'd my teeming brain,
> Before high-piled books, in charact'ry,
> Hold like full garners the full-ripen'd grain;
> When I behold, upon the night's starr'd face,
> Huge cloudy symbols of a high romance,
> And think that I may never live to trace
> Their shadows, with the magic hand of chance;
> And when I feel, fair creature of an hour!
> That I shall never look upon thee more,
> Never have relish in the faery power
> Of unreflecting love! — then on the shore
> Of the wide world I stand alone, and think,
> Till Love and Fame to nothingness do sink.
> Time's sea hath been five years at its slow ebb;
> Long hours have to and fro let creep the sand;
> Since I was tangled in thy beauty's web,
> And snared by the ungloving of thine hand.
> And yet I never look on midnight sky,
> But I behold thine eyes' well memoried light;
> I cannot look upon the rose's dye,
> But to thy cheek my soul doth take its flight;
> I cannot look on any budding flower,
> But my fond ear, in fancy at thy lips,
> And hearkening for a love-sound, doth devour
> Its sweets in the wrong sense: — Thou dost eclipse
> Every delight with sweet remembering,
> And grief unto my darling joys dost bring.

The former is far the richer in contents, and in the light of the tragedy to come its two first quatrains now seem to thrill with prophetic meaning. But what is singular is that in the third quatrain should be recalled, in the same high strain of emotion, the vision of a beauty seen but not even accosted three-and-a-half years earlier (not really five) in the public gardens at Vauxhall, and then (August, 1814) addressed in what are almost the earliest of Keats' dated verses, those in which he calls for a 'brimming bowl,' —

> From my despairing heart to charm
> The Image of the fairest form
> That e'er my reveling eyes beheld,
> That e'er my wandering fancy spell'd....

Such, Woodhouse assures us, is the case, and the same memory fills the second sonnet: but this it might be possible to take rather as a fine Shakespearean exercise than as an expression of profound feeling. On the 5th, Keats sends another sonnet postponing compliance for the present with an invitation of Leigh Hunt's to compose something in honour, or in emulation, of Spenser; and on the 8th, the sonnet in praise of the colour blue composed by way of protest against one of Reynolds preferring black, at least in the colouring of feminine eyes. About the same time he agreed with Reynolds that they should each write some metrical tales from Boccaccio, and publish them in a joint volume; and began at once for his own part with the first few stanzas of *Isabella* or the *Pot of Basil*. A little later in this so prolific month of February we find him rejoicing in the song of the thrush and blackbird, and melted into feelings of indolent pleasure and receptivity under the influence of spring winds and dissolving rain. He theorizes pleasantly in a letter to Reynolds on the virtues and benefits of this state of mind, translating the thrush's music into some blank-verse lines of subtle and haunting cadence, in which, disowning for the nonce his habitual doctrine of the poet's paramount need of knowledge, he makes the thrush say,

> O fret not after knowledge — I have none,
> And yet my song comes native with the warmth,
> O fret not after knowledge — I have none,
> And yet the evening listens.

In the course of the next fortnight we find him in correspondence with Taylor about the corrections to *Endymion*; and soon afterwards making a clearance of borrowed books, and otherwise preparing to flit. His brother George, who had been taking care of Tom at Teignmouth since December, was now obliged to come to town, bent on a scheme of marriage and emigration; and Tom's health having made a momentary rally, Keats was unwilling that he should leave Teignmouth, and determined to join him there. He started in the second week of March, and stayed almost two months. It was an unlucky season for weather, — the soft-buffeting sheets and misty drifts of Devonshire rain renewing themselves wave on wave, in the inexhaustible way all lovers of that country know, throughout almost the whole spring, and preventing him from getting more than occasional tantalizing snatches of enjoyment in the beauty of the scenery, the walks, and flowers. His letters are full of whimsical objurgations not only against the climate, but against the male inhabitants, whose fibre he chooses to conceive relaxed by it: —

You may say what you will of Devonshire: the truth is, it is a splashy, rainy, misty, snowy, foggy, haily, floody, muddy, slipshod county. The hills are very beautiful, when you get a sight of 'em — the primroses are out, but then you are in — the Cliffs are of a fine deep colour, but then the Clouds are continually vieing with them — the women like your London people in a sort of negative way — because the native men are the poorest creatures in England — because Government never have thought it worth while to send a recruiting party among them. When I think of Wordsworth's Sonnet, 'Vanguard of Liberty! ye men of Kent!' the degenerated race about me are Pulvis ipecac. simplex — a strong dose. Were I a corsair, I'd make a descent on the south coast of Devon; if I did not run the chance of having Cowardice imputed to me. As for the men, they'd run away into the Methodist meeting-houses, and the women would be glad of it.... Such a quelling Power have these thoughts over me that I fancy the very air of a deteriorating quality. I fancy the flowers, all precocious, have an Acrasian spell about them — I feel able to beat off the Devonshire waves like soapfroth. I think it well for the honour of Britain that Julius Caesar did not first land in this County. A Devonshirer standing on his native hills is not a distinct object — he does not show against the light — a wolf or two would dispossess him.

A man of west-country descent should have known better. Why did not the ghost of William Browne of Tavistock arise and check Keats' hand, and recite for his rebuke the burst in praise of Devon from *Britannia's Pastorals*, with its happy echo of the Virgilian *Salve magna parens* and *Haec genus acre virum* ? —

> Hail thou my native soil: thou blessed plot
> Whose equal all the world affordeth not!
> Shew me who can so many christall rills,

Such sweet-clothed vallies, or aspiring hills,
Such wood-ground, pastures, quarries, wealthy mines,

Such rocks in whom the diamond fairly shines:
And if the earth can shew the like again;
Yet will she fail in her sea-ruling men.
Time never can produce men to o'er-take
The fames of Grenville, Davies, Gilbert, Drake,
Or worthy Hawkins or of thousands more
That by their power made the Devonian shore
Mock the proud Tagus.

Of the Devonshire girls Keats thought better than of their menkind, and writes and rimes on them with a certain skittishness of admiration. With one local family, a Mrs Jeffrey and her daughters, he and his brothers were on terms of warm friendship, as is shown by his correspondence with them a year later. One of the daughters married afterwards a Mr Prowse, and published two volumes of very tolerable sentimental verse: some of their contents, as interpreted (says Mr Buxton Forman) by Teignmouth tradition, would indicate that her heart had been very deeply touched by the young poet during his stay: but of responsive feelings on his own part his letters give no hint, and it was only a few weeks later that he wrote how his love for his brothers had hitherto stifled any impression that a woman might have made on him.

Besides his constant occupation in watching and cheering the invalid Tom, who had a relapse just after he came down, Keats was busy during these Devonshire days seeing through the press the last sheets of *Endymion*. He also composed, with the exception of the few verses he had begun at Hampstead, the whole of *Isabella* or *The Pot of Basil*, the first of his longer poems written with real maturity of art and certainty of touch. At the same time, no doubt with his great intended effort, *Hyperion*, in mind, he was studying and appreciating Milton as he had never done before. He had been steeped since boyhood in the charm of the minor poems, from the *Vacation Exercise* to *Lycidas*, and had read but not greatly cared for *Paradise Lost*, until first Severn, and then more energetically Bailey, had insisted that this was a reproach to him: and he now threw himself upon that poem, and penetrated with the grasp and swiftness of genius, as his marginal criticisms show, into the very essence of its power and beauty. His correspondence with his friends, particularly Bailey and Reynolds, is during this same time unusually sustained and full. Sometimes his vein is light and titterly (to use a word of his own) as I have indicated, and sometimes he masks an anxious heart beneath a lively manner, as thus: —

But ah Coward! to talk at this rate to a sick man, or, I hope, to one that was sick — for I hope by this you stand on your right foot. If you are not — that's all, — I intend to cut all sick people if they do not make up their minds to cut Sickness — a fellow to whom I have a complete aversion, and who strange to say is harboured and countenanced in several houses where I visit — he is sitting now quite impudent between me and Tom — he insults me at poor Jem Rice's — and you have seated him before now between us at the Theatre, when I thought he looked with a longing eye at poor Kean. I shall say, once for all, to my friends, generally and severally, cut that fellow, or I cut you.

On another day he recurs to the mood of half real half mock impatience against those who rub the bloom off things of beauty by over-commenting and over-interpreting them, a mood natural to a spirit dwelling so habitually and intuitively at the heart of beauty as his: —

It has as yet been a Mystery to me how and where Wordsworth went. I can't help thinking he has returned to his Shell — with his beautiful Wife and his enchanting Sister. It is a great Pity that People should by associating themselves with the finest things, spoil them. Hunt has damned Hampstead and masks and sonnets and Italian tales. Wordsworth has damned the lakes. Milman has damned the old drama — West has damned wholesale. Peacock has damned satire — Ollier has damn'd Music — Hazlitt has damned the bigoted and the blue-stockinged;

how durst the Man? he is your only good damner, and if ever I am damn'd — damn me if I shouldn't like him to damn me.

Once, writing to Reynolds, he resumes his habit of a year and a half earlier, and casts his fancies and reflections into rime. Beginning playfully, he tells of an odd jumble of incongruous images that had crossed his brain, a kind of experience expressed by him elsewhere in various strains of verse, *e.g.* the finished poem *Fancy* and the careless lines beginning 'Welcome Joy, and welcome Sorrow.' He supposes that some people are not subject to such freaks of the mind's eye, but have it consistently haunted by fine things such as he next proceeds to conjure up from memory, —

> Some Titian colours touch'd into real life, —
> The sacrifice goes on; the pontiff knife
> Gleams in the Sun, the milk-white heifer lows,
> The pipes go shrilly, the libation flows;
> A white sail shows above the green-head cliff,
> Moves round the point, and throws her anchor stiff;
> The mariners join hymn with those on land.

There exists no such picture of a sacrifice by Titian, and what Keats was thinking of, I feel sure, was the noble 'Sacrifice to Apollo' by Claude from the Leigh Court collection, which he had seen at the British Institution in 1816 (hung, as it happened, next to Titian's Europa from Cobham Hall), and which evidently worked deeply on his mind. To memory of it is probably due that magic vision of a little town emptied of its folk on a morning of sacrifice, which he evoked a year later in the ode on a Grecian Urn. It shows to the right an altar in front of a temple of Apollo, and about the altar a group including king and priest and a young man holding down a victim ox by the horns; people with baskets and offerings coming up from behind the temple; and to the left tall trees with a priest leading in another victim by the horns, and a woman with a jar bringing in libation; a little back, two herdsmen with their goats; a river spanned by a bridge and winding towards a sea-bay partly encircled by mountains which close the view, and on the edge of the bay the tower and roofs of a little town indistinctly seen. Recollection of this Claude leads Keats on quickly to that of another, the famous 'Enchanted Castle,' which he partly mixes up with it, and partly transforms by fantasy into something quite different from what it really is. He forgets the one human figure in the foreground, describes figures and features of the landscape which are not there, and remembering that the architecture combines ancient Roman with mediæval castellated and later Palladian elements, invents for it far-fetched origins and associations which in a more careless fashion almost remind one of those invented by Pope for his Temple of Fame. (A year later, all this effervescence of the imagination about the picture had subsided, and the distilled and concentrated essence of its romance was expressed — so at least I conceive — in the famous 'magic casement' phrase at the end of the Nightingale ode).

> From this play of fancy about two half-remembered pictures Keats turns suddenly to reflections, which he would like to banish but cannot, on the 'eternal fierce destruction' which is part of nature's law: —

> But I saw too distinct into the core
> Of an eternal fierce destruction,
> And so from happiness I far was gone.
> Still am I sick of it, and tho', to-day,
> I've gathered young spring-leaves, and flowers gay
> Of periwinkle and wild strawberry,
> Still do I that most fierce destruction see,
> The Shark at savage prey, — the Hawk at pounce, —

> The gentle Robin, like a Pard or Ounce,
> Ravening a worm, — Away, ye horrid moods!
> Moods of one's mind!

The letters of this date should be read and re-read by all who want to get to the centre of Keats' mind or to hold a key to the understanding of his deepest poetry. The richest of them all is that in which he sends the fragments of an ode to Maia written on May day with the (alas! unfulfilled) promise to finish it 'in good time.' The same letter contains the reassertion of a purpose declared in a letter of a week before to Mr Taylor in the phrases, 'I find I can have no enjoyment in the world but the continual drinking of knowledge. I find there is no worthy pursuit but the idea of doing some good to the world.... There is but one way for me. The road lies through application, study and thought. I will pursue it.' The mood of the verses interpreting the song of the thrush a few weeks earlier has passed, the reader will note, clean out of the poet's mind. To Reynolds his words are: —

An extensive knowledge is needful to thinking people — it takes away the heat and fever; and helps, by widening speculation, to ease the Burden of the Mystery, a thing which I begin to understand a little, and which weighed upon you in the most gloomy and true sentence in your letter. The difference of high Sensations with and without knowledge appears to me this: in the latter case we are falling continually ten thousand fathoms deep and being blown up again, without wings, and with all [the] horror of a bare-shouldered creature — in the former case, our shoulders are fledged, and we go through the same air and space without fear.

Let it never be forgotten that 'sensations' contrasted with 'thoughts' mean for Keats not pleasures and experiences of the senses as opposed to those of the mind, but direct intuitions of the imagination as opposed to deliberate processes of the understanding; and that by 'philosophy' he does not mean metaphysics but knowledge and the fruits of reading generally.

The same letter, again, contains an interesting meditation on the relative qualities of genius in Milton and Wordsworth as affected by the relative stages of history at which they lived, and on the further question whether Wordsworth was a greater or less poet than Milton by virtue of being more taken up with human passions and problems. This speculation leads on to one of Keats' finest passages of life-wisdom: —

And here I have nothing but surmises, from an uncertainty whether Milton's apparently less anxiety for Humanity proceeds from his seeing further or not than Wordsworth: And whether Wordsworth has in truth epic passion, and martyrs himself to the human heart, the main region of his song. In regard to his genius alone — we find what he says true as far as we have experienced and we can judge no further but by larger experience — for axioms in philosophy are not axioms until they are proved upon our pulses. We read fine things, but never feel them to the full until we have gone the same steps as the author. — I know this is not plain; you will know exactly my meaning when I say that now I shall relish *Hamlet* more than I have ever done — Or, better — you are sensible no man can set down Venery as a bestial or joyless thing until he is sick of it, and therefore all philosophising on it would be mere wording. Until we are sick, we understand not; in fine, as Byron says, 'Knowledge is sorrow'; and I go on to say that 'Sorrow is wisdom' — and further for aught we can know for certainty 'Wisdom is folly.'

Presently follows the famous chain of images by which Keats, searching and probing for himself along pathways of the spirit parallel to those followed by Wordsworth in the *Lines composed a few miles above Tintern Abbey*, renders account to himself of the stage of development to which his mind has now reached: —

Well — I compare human life to a large Mansion of many apartments, two of which I can only describe, the doors of the rest being as yet shut upon me. The first we step into we call the Infant, or Thoughtless Chamber, in which we remain as long as we do not think. We remain there a long while, and notwithstanding the doors of the second Chamber remain wide open, showing a bright appearance, we care not to hasten to it; but are at length imperceptibly impelled by the awakening of the thinking principle within us — we no sooner get into the second Chamber, which I shall call the Chamber of Maiden-Thought, than we become intoxicated with the light and the atmosphere, we see nothing but pleasant wonders, and think of delaying there for ever in delight. However among the effects this breathing is father of is that tremendous one of sharpening one's vision into the heart and nature of Man — of convincing one's nerves that the world is full of Misery and Heartbreak, Pain, Sickness, and oppression — whereby this Chamber of Maiden Thought becomes gradually darkened, and at the same time, on all sides of it, many doors are set open — but all dark — all leading to dark passages. We see not the balance of good and evil; we are in a mist, *we* are now in that state, we feel the 'Burden of the Mystery.' To this point was Wordsworth come, as far as I can conceive, when he wrote *Tintern Abbey*, and it seems to me that his genius is explorative of those dark Passages. Now if we live, and go on thinking, we too shall explore them.

Here is a typical case of the method of evocation as against the method of exposition. Wordsworth's lines are written with a high, almost an inspired, power of describing and putting into direct words the successive moods of a spirit gradually ripening and deepening in the power of communion with nature, and through nature, with all life. But Keats, fully as he has pondered them, cannot be satisfied that they fit his own case until he has called up the history of his similar experiences in the form natural to him, the form, that is, of concrete similitudes or visions of the imagination — the Thoughtless Chamber, the Chamber of Maiden Thought with its gradual darkening and its many outlets standing open to be explored. It is significant that such visions should still be of architecture, of halls and chambers in an imagined mysterious building.

Apart from his growing sense of the darker sides of human existence and of the mysteries of good and evil, Keats was suffering at this time from the pain of a family break-up now imminent. George Keats had made up his mind to emigrate to America, and embark his capital, or as much of it as he could get possession of, in business there. Besides the wish to push his own fortunes, a main motive of this resolve on George's part was the desire to be in a position as quickly as possible to help or if need be support, his poet-brother. He persuaded the girl to whom he had long been attached, Miss Georgiana Wylie, to share his fortunes, and it was settled that they were to be married and sail early in the summer. Some of Keats' letters during the last weeks of his stay at Teignmouth are taken up with his plans for the time immediately following this change. He wavered for a while between two incompatible purposes. One was to go for a summer's walking tour through Scotland with Charles Brown. 'I have many reasons,' he writes to Reynolds, 'for going wonder-ways; to make my winter chair free from spleen; to enlarge my vision; to escape disquisitions on poetry, and Kingston-criticism; to promote digestion and economize shoe-leather.' (How 'economize,' one wonders?) 'I'll have leather buttons and belt, and if Brown hold his mind, "over the hills we go." If my books will keep me to it, then will I take all Europe in turn, and see the kingdoms of the earth and the glory of them.' Here we find Keats in his turn caught by the romance of wild lands and of travel which had in various ways been so much of an inspiration to Byron and Shelley before him. A fortnight later we find him inclining to give up this purpose under an overmastering sense of the inadequacy of his own attainments, and of the necessity of acquiring knowledge, and ever more knowledge, to sustain the flight of poetry.

The habit of close self-observation and self-criticism is in most natures that possess it allied with vanity and egoism; but it was not so in Keats, who without a shadow of affectation judges himself, both in his strength and weakness, as the most clear-sighted and disinterested friend might judge. He is inclined, when not on the defensive against what he felt to be foolish criticism, to under-rate rather than to overrate his own work, and in his correspondence of the previous year we have found him perfectly aware that in writing *Endymion* he has rather been working off a youthful ferment of the mind than producing a sound or satisfying work of poetry. And when the time comes to write a preface to the poem, he in a first draft makes confession to the public of his 'non-opinion of himself' in terms both a little too intimate and too fidgeting and uneasy. Reynolds seeing the draft at once recognised that it would not do, and in criticizing it to Keats seems to have told him that it was too much in the manner of Leigh Hunt. In deference to his judgment Keats at once abandoned it, and a second attempt says briefly, with perfect dignity and taste, all that can justly be said in dispraise of his work. He warns the reader to expect 'great inexperience, immaturity, and every error denoting a feverish attempt, rather than a deed accomplished,' and adds most unboastfully: — 'it is just that this youngster should die away: a sad thought for me, if I had not some hope that while it is dwindling I may be plotting, and fitting myself for verses fit to live.'

Keats and Tom, the latter for the moment easier in health, were back at Hampstead in the last week of May, in time for the marriage of their brother George with Miss Georgiana Wylie. This was the young lady to whom Keats had rimed a valentine for his brother two years earlier (the lines beginning 'Hadst thou liv'd in days of old') and to whom he had also on his own account addressed the charming sonnet, 'Nymph of the downward smile and sidelong glance.' With no other woman or girl friend was he ever on such easy and cordial terms of intimacy. The wedding took place 'a week ago,' writes Keats on June 4, and about the same date, in order that he may not miss seeing as much of the young couple as possible before their departure, he declines a warm invitation from Bailey to visit him again at Oxford. Writing, as usual to this correspondent, with absolute openness, Keats shows that he is suffering from one of his moods of overmastering depression. First it takes the form of apathy. Bailey had written eagerly and judiciously in praise of *Endymion* in the *Oxford Herald*. Keats replies on June 1: —

My intellect must be in a degenerating state — it must be — for when I should be writing about — God knows what — I am troubling you with moods of my own mind, or rather body, for mind there is none. I am in that temper that if I were under water I would scarcely kick to come up to the top — I know very well 'tis all nonsense. In a short time I hope I shall be in a temper to feel sensibly your mention of my book. In vain have I waited till Monday to have any Interest in that, or anything else. I feel no spur at my Brother's going to America, and am almost stony-hearted about his wedding. All this will blow over. All I am sorry for is having to write to you in such a time — but I cannot force my letters in a hotbed. I could not feel comfortable in making sentences for you.

Nine days later the mood has deepened to one of positive despondency, but it is the despondency of a great and generous spirit: —

Were it in my choice, I would reject a Petrarchal coronation — on account of my dying day, and because women have cancers. I should not by right speak in this tone to you for it is an incendiary spirit that would do so. Yet I am not old enough or magnanimous enough to annihilate self — and it would perhaps be paying you an ill compliment. I was in hopes some little time back to be able to relieve your dulness by my spirits — to point out things in the world worth your enjoyment — and now I am never alone without rejoicing that there is such a thing as death — without placing my ultimate in the glory of dying for a great human purpose. Perhaps if my affairs were in a different state, I should not have written the above — you shall judge: I have two brothers; one is driven, by The 'burden of Society,' to America; the other, with an exquisite love of life, is in a lingering state. My love for my Brothers, from the early loss of our parents, and even from earlier misfortunes, has grown into an affection 'passing the love of women.' I have been ill-tempered with them — I have vexed them — but the thought of them has always stifled the impression that any woman might otherwise have made upon me. I have a sister too, and may not follow them either to America or to the grave. Life must be undergone, and I certainly derive some consolation from the thought of writing one or two more poems before it ceases.

Meanwhile his fluctuations of purpose between a plunge into a life of solitude and study and an excursion in Brown's company to Scotland had been decided in favour of the Scottish tour. George and his bride having to set out for Liverpool on June 22, it was arranged that Keats and Brown should accompany them so far on their way to the north. The coach started from the Swan and two Necks in Lad Lane, and on the first day stopped for dinner at Redbourne near St Albans, where Keats' friend of medical student days, Mr Stephens, was in practice. He came to shake hands with the travelling party at the poet's request, and many years afterwards wrote an account of the interview, the chief point of which is a description of Mrs George Keats. 'Rather short, not what might be called strictly handsome, but looked like a being whom any man of moderate sensibility might easily love. She had the imaginative poetical cast. Somewhat singular and girlish in her attire.... There was something original about her, and John seemed to regard her as a being whom he delighted to honour, and introduced her with evident satisfaction.'

Chapter IX

JUNE-AUGUST 1818: THE SCOTTISH TOUR

The farewells at Liverpool over, Keats and Brown went on by coach to Lancaster, thence to begin their tour on foot. Keats took for his reading one book only, the miniature three-volume edition of Cary's Dante. Brown, it would appear, carried a pocket Milton. They found the town of Lancaster in an uproar with the preparations for a contested election and were glad to leave it. Rising at four in the morning (June 25th) to make a start before breakfast, they were detained by a downpour, during which Brown preached patience from *Samson Agonistes*; at seven they set out in a still dripping mist; breakfasted at Bolton-le-Sands; stopped to dine at the village of Burton-in-Kendal, and found the inns crowded, to their hosts' distraction, with soldiers summoned by the Lowther interest to keep order at the election. This was the famous contest where Brougham had the effrontery, as his opponents considered it, to go down and challenge for the first time the power of that great family in their own country. The same state of things prevailed farther down the road. Hearing that they could not hope to find a bed at Kendal, they slept in a mean roadside inn at End Moor, taking interested note of a sad old dog of a drunkard, fallen from better days, whom they found there; and the next morning walked on, passing Kendal on their way, as far as Bowness on Windermere. As they dropped down the hill and came in sight of the lake the weather yielded fine effects of clearance after rain; and Brown, in the account compiled twenty years later from his diaries written at the time, expatiates in full romantic vein on the joy and amazement with which Keats and he drank in the beauties of the varied and shifting scene before them: —

On the next morning, after reaching Kendal, we had our first really joyous walk of nine miles towards the lake of Windermere. The country was mild and romantic, the weather fine, though not sunny, while the fresh mountain air, and many larks about us, gave us unbounded delight. As we approached the lake the scenery became more and more grand and beautiful, and from time to time we stayed our steps, gazing intently on it. Hitherto, Keats had witnessed nothing superior to Devonshire; but, beautiful as that is, he was now tempted to speak of it with indifference. At the first turn from the road, before descending to the hamlet of Bowness, we both simultaneously came to a full stop. The lake lay before us. His bright eyes darted on a mountain-peak, beneath which was gently floating on a silver cloud; thence to a very small island, adorned with the foliage of trees, that lay beneath us, and surrounded by water of ? glorious hue, when he exclaimed — 'How can I believe in that a — surely it cannot be!' He warmly asserted that no view in the world could equal this — that it must beat all Italy — yet, having moved onward but a hundred yards — catching the further extremity of the lake, he thought it 'more and more wonderfully beautiful!' The trees far and near, the grass immediately around us, the fern and the furze in their most luxuriant growth, all added to the charm. Not a mist, but an imperceptible vapour bestowed a mellow, softened tint over the immense mountains on the opposite side and at the further end of the lake.

After a bathe and a midday meal at Bowness the friends walked on with ever increasing delight to Ambleside. Spending the night there they scrambled about the neighbouring waterfalls, and endured as patiently as they could the advances of a youth lately from Oxford, touring knapsack on back like themselves but painfully bent on showing himself off for a scholar and buck about town, airing his pedigree and connexions while affecting to make light of them. The next day they went on by Grasmere to Rydal, where they paused that Keats might call and pay his respects to Wordsworth. But the poet was away at Lowther Castle electioneering (he had been exerting himself vigorously in the Tory and Lowther interest since the spring in prospect of this contest). Complete want of sympathy with the cause of his absence made Keats' disappointment the keener; and finding none of the family at home he could do no more than leave a note of regret. The same afternoon the travellers reached the hamlet of Wythburn and slept there as well as fleas would allow, intending to climb Helvellyn the next morning. Heavy rain interfering, they pursued their way by Thirlmere to Keswick, made the circuit of Derwentwater, visited the Druids' Circle and the Falls of Lodore, and set out at four the next morning to climb Skiddaw. A cloud-cap settling down compelled them to stop a little short of the summit, and they resumed their tramp by Bassenthwaite into the relatively commonplace country lying between the lakes and Carlisle, making their next night's resting-place at the old market town of Ireby.

I have shown by a specimen how Brown, working from his diaries of the tour, expatiates on his and his companion's enthusiasm over the romantic scenes they visited. Keats in his own letters says comparatively little about the scenery, and that quite simply and quietly, not at all with the descriptive enthusiasm of the picturesque tourist: hardly indeed with so much of that quality as the sedate and fastidious Gray had shown in his itineraries fifty years before. Partly, no doubt, a certain instinctive reticence, a restraining touch of the Greek ±0'ÎÂ, keeps him from fluent words on the beauties that most deeply moved him: his way rather is to let them work silently in his being until at the right moment, if the right moment comes, their essence and vital power shall distil themselves for him into a phrase of poetry. Partly, also, the truth is that an intensely active, intuitive genius for nature like his hardly needs the stimulus of nature's beauties for long or at their highest power, but on a minimum of experience can summon up and multiply for itself spirit sunsets, and glories of dream lake and mountain, richer and more varied than the mere receptive lover of scenery can witness and register in memory during a lifetime of travel and pursuit. In this respect Keats' letters written on his northern tour seem more essentially the letters of a poet than Shelley's from Switzerland and Italy. Shelley pours out long, set, detailed descriptions, written as any cultivated and enthusiastic observer visiting such scenes for the first time might write, only with more beauty and resource of language, rather than as one made by imagination a born partner and co-creator with nature herself, free by birthright of her glories and knowing them all, as it were, beforehand. Keats' way of telling about his travels is quite familiar and unstrained. Here is a paragraph from his first letter to his brother Tom, written at Keswick after walking round Derwentwater and climbing Skiddaw: —

I had an easy climb among the streams, about the fragments of Rocks, and should have got I think to the summit, but unfortunately I was damped by slipping one leg into a squashy hole. There is no great body of water, but the accompaniment is delightful; for it oozes out from a cleft in perpendicular Rocks, all fledged with ash and other beautiful trees. It is a strange thing how they got there. At the south end of the Lake the Mountains of Borrowdale are perhaps as fine as anything we have seen. On our return from this circuit, we ordered dinner, and set forth about a mile and a half on the Penrith road, to see the Druid temple. We had a fag up hill, rather too near dinner-time, which was rendered void by the gratification of seeing those aged stones on a gentle rise in the midst of the Mountains, which at that time darkened all around, except at the fresh opening of the Vale of St. John. We went to bed rather fatigued, but not so much so as to hinder us getting up this morning to mount Skiddaw. It promised all along to be fair, and we had fagged and tugged nearly to the top, when, at half-past six, there came a Mist upon us, and shut out the view. We did not, however, lose anything by it: we were high enough without mist to see the coast of Scotland — the Irish Sea — the hills beyond Lancaster — and nearly all the large ones of Cumberland and Westmoreland, particularly Helvelleyn and Scawfell. It grew colder and colder as we ascended, and we were glad, at about three parts of the way, to taste a little rum which the Guide brought with him, mixed, mind ye, with Mountain water. I took two glasses going and one returning. It is about six miles from where I am writing to the top. So we have walked ten miles before Breakfast to-day. We went up with two others, very good sort of fellows. All felt, on arising into the cold air, that same elevation which a cold bath gives one — I felt as if I were going to a Tournament.

For an instant only, the poet in Keats speaks vividly in the tournament touch; and farther back, illustrating what I have said about his instinct for distillation rather than description, will be found the germs of two famous passages in his later verse, the 'dark-clustered trees' that

Fledge the wild-ridged mountains steep by steep
in the *Ode to Psyche*, and the lines in *Hyperion* about the
dismal cirque
Of Druid stones, upon a forlorn moor
When the chill rain begins at shut of eve,
In dull November, and their chancel vault,
The Heaven itself, is blinded throughout night.

A change, it should be added, was coming over Keats' thoughts and feelings whereby natural scenery in general was beginning to interest him less and his fellow creatures more. In the acuteness of childish and boyish sensation, among the suburban fields or on seaside holidays, he had instinctively, as if by actual partnership with and self-absorption into nature, gained enough delighted knowledge of her ways and doings for his faculties to work on through a lifetime of poetry; and now, in his second chamber of Maiden-thought, the appeal of nature, even at its most thrilling, yields in his mind to that of humanity. 'Scenery is fine,' he had already written from Devonshire in the spring, 'but human nature is finer.' So far as concerns shrewd and interested observation of human types encountered by the way, he had a sympathetic companion in Brown, whose diary sets effectively before us alike the sodden, wheedling old toper, staggering with hanging arms like a bear on its hind feet, in the inn at End Moor, and the vulgar, uneasy gentlemanhood of the flash Oxford man at Ambleside. Here is Brown's account of what they saw at Ireby: —

It is a dull, beggarly looking place. Our inn was remarkably clean and neat, and the old host and hostess were very civil and prepossessing — but, heyday! what were those obstreperous doings overhead? It was a dancing school under the tuition of a travelling master! Folks here were as partial to dancing as their neighbours, the Scotch; and every little farmer sent his young ones to take lessons. We went upstairs to witness the skill of these rustic boys and girls — fine, healthy, clean-dressed, and withal perfectly orderly, as well as serious in their endeavours. We noticed some among them quite handsome, but the attention of none was drawn aside to notice us. The instant the fiddle struck up, the slouch in the gait was lost, the feet moved, and gracefully, with complete conformity to the notes; and they wove the figure, sometimes extremely complicated to my inexperienced eyes, without an error, or the slightest pause. There was no sauntering, half-asleep country dance among them; all were inspired.

And here is the same scene as touched by Keats: —

We were greatly amused by a country dancing-school holden at the Tun, it was indeed 'no new cotillon fresh from France.' No, they kickit and jumpit with mettle extraordinary, and whiskit, and friskit, and toed it and go'd it, and twirl'd it, and whirl'd it, and stamped it, and sweated it, tattooing the floor like mad. The difference between our country dances and these Scottish figures is about the same as leisurely stirring a cup o' Tea and beating up a batter-pudding. I was extremely gratified to think that, if I had pleasures they knew nothing of, they had also some into which I could not possibly enter. I hope I shall not return without having got the Highland fling. There was as fine a row of boys and girls as you ever saw; some beautiful faces, and one exquisite mouth. I never felt so near the glory of Patriotism, the glory of making by any means a country happier. This is what I like better than scenery.

From Ireby the friends walked by way of Wigton to Carlisle, arriving there on the last day of June. From Carlisle they took coach to Dumfries, having heard that the intervening country was not interesting: neither did Keats much admire what he saw of it. Besides the familiar beauties of the home counties of England, two ideals of landscape had haunted and allured his imagination almost equally, that of the classic south, harmonious and sunned and gay, and that of the shadowed, romantic and adventurous north; and the Scottish border, with its bleak and moorish rain-swept distances, its 'huddle of cold old grey hills' (the phrase is Stevenson's) struck him somehow as answering to neither. 'I know not how it is, the clouds, the sky, the houses, all seem anti-Grecian and anti-Charlemagnish.'

So writes Keats from Dumfries, where they visited the tomb of Burns and the ruins of Lincluden College, and where Keats expressed his sense of foreignness and dreamlike discomfort in a sonnet interesting as the record of a mood but of small merit poetically. Brown also, a Scotsman from the outer Hebrides, as he believed, by descent, but by habit and education purely English, felt himself at first an alien in the Scottish Lowlands. On this stage of the walk they were both unpleasurably struck by the laughterless gravity and cold greetings of the people, ('more serious and solidly inanimated than necessary' Brown calls them) and by the lack of anything like the English picturesque and gardened snugness in villages and houses: Brown also by the barefoot habit of the girls and women, but this Keats liked, expatiating to his friend on the beauty of a lassie's natural uncramped foot and its colour against the grass.

From Dumfries they started on July 2 south-westward for Galloway, a region not overmuch frequented even now, and then hardly at all, by tourists: even Wordsworth on his several Scottish trips passed it by unexplored. Our travellers broke the journey first at Dalbeattie: thence on to Kirkcudbright, with a long morning pause for breakfast and letter-writing by the wayside near Auchencairn. Approaching the Kirkcudbrightshire coast, with its scenery at once wild and soft, its embosomed inlets and rocky tufted headlands, its high craggy moors towering inland, and its backward views over the glimmering Solway to the Cumberland fells or the hazier hills of Man, they began to enjoy themselves to the full. Brown bethought him that this was Guy Mannering's country, and fell talking to Keats about Meg Merrilies. Keats, who according to the fashion of his circle was no enthusiast for Scott's poetry, and of the Waverley novels, at this time guessed but not known to be Scott's, had read *The Antiquary* (to which he whimsically preferred Smollett's *Humphrey Clinker*) but not *Guy Mannering*, was much struck by what he heard.

I enjoyed the recollection of the events [writes Brown] as I described them in their own scenes. There was a little spot, close to our pathway, where, without a shadow of doubt, old Meg Merrilies had often boiled her kettle, and, haply, cooked a chicken. It was among fragments of rock, and brambles, and broom, and most tastefully ornamented with a profusion of honeysuckle, wild roses, and foxglove, all in the very blush and fullness of blossom. While finishing breakfast, and both employed in writing, I could not avoid noticing that Keats' letter was not running in regular prose. He told me he was writing to his little sister, and giving a ballad on old Meg for her amusement. Though he called it too much a trifle to be copied, I soon inserted it in my journal. It struck me as a good description of that mystic link between mortality and the weird sisters; and, at the same time, in appropriate language to the person addressed.

> Old Meg she was a Gipsy,
> And liv'd upon the Moors:
> Her bed it was the brown heath turf
> And her house was out of doors.
> Her apples were swart blackberries,
> Her currants pods o' broom;
> Her wine was dew of the wild white rose,
> Her book a churchyard tomb.
> Her Brothers were the craggy hills,
> Her Sisters larchen trees —
> Alone with her great family
> She liv'd as she did please.
> No breakfast had she many a morn,
> No dinner many a noon,
> And 'stead of supper she would stare
> Full hard against the Moon.

But every morn of woodbine fresh
She made her garlanding,
And every night the dark glen Yew
She wove, and she would sing.
And with her fingers old and brown
She plaited Mats o' Rushes,
And gave them to the Cottagers
She met among the Bushes.
Old Meg was brave as Margaret Queen
And tall as Amazon:
An old red blanket cloak she wore;
A chip hat had she on.
God rest her aged bones somewhere —
She died full long agone!

Keats had in this 'trifle,' using the ballad form for the first time, handled it with faultless tact, and though leaving out the tragic features of Scott's creation, had been able to evoke of his own an instantaneous vision of her in vitally conceived spiritual relation with her surroundings. He copied the piece out in letters written in pauses of their walk both to his young sister and to his brother Tom. The letter to Fanny Keats is full of fun and nonsense, with a touch or two which shows that he was fully sensitive to the charm of the Galloway coast scenery. 'Since I scribbled the Meg Merrilies song we have walked through a beautiful country to Kirkcudbright — at which place I will write you a song about myself.' Then follows the set of gay doggrel stanzas telling of various escapades of himself as a child and since, — 'There was a naughty boy;' and then the excuse for them, — 'My dear Fanny, I am ashamed of writing you such stuff, nor would I if it were not for being tired after my day's walking, and ready to tumble into bed so fatigued that when I am in bed you might sew my nose to my great toe and trundle me round the town, like a Hoop, without waking me.' It was his way on his tour, and indeed always, thus to keep by him the letters he was writing and add scraps to them as the fancy took him. The systematic Brown, on the other hand, wrote regularly and uniformly in the evenings. 'He affronts my indolence and luxury,' says Keats, 'by pulling out of his knapsack, first his paper; secondly his pens; and last, his ink. Now I would not care, if he would change a little. I say now, why not take out his pens first sometimes? But I might as well tell a hen to hold up her head before she drinks, instead of afterwards.'

From Kirkcudbright they walked on July 5, — taking the beautiful coast road from Gatehouse of Fleet and passing where Cairnsmore heaves a huge heathered shoulder above the fertile farmlands of the Cree valley, — as far as Newton Stewart: thence across the low-rolling Wigtownshire country by Glenluce to Stranraer and Portpatrick. Here they took the packet for Donaghadee on the opposite coast of Ireland, with the intention of seeing the Giant's Causeway, but finding the distances and expense much exceed their calculation, contented themselves with a walk to Belfast, and crossed back again to Portpatrick on the third day. In a letter to his brother Tom written during and immediately after this excursion, Keats has some striking passages of human observation and reflection. The change of spirit between one generation and another is forcibly brought home to us when we think of Johnson, setting forth on his Scottish tour forty-five years earlier with the study of men, manners and social conditions in his mind as the one aim worthy of a serious traveller, (he had spoken scoffingly, not long before, of the 'prodigious noble wild prospects' which Scotland, he understood, shared with Lapland), yet forced now and again by the power of scenery to break, as it were half ashamedly, into stiff but striking phrases of descriptive admiration; and when now we find Keats, carried northward by the romantic passion and fashion of a later day for nature and scenery, compelled in his turn by his innate human instincts to forget the landscape and observe and speculate upon problems of society and economics and racial character: —

These Kirk-men have done Scotland good. They have made men, women; old men, young men; old women, young women; boys, girls; and all infants careful; so that they are formed into regular Phalanges of savers and gainers. Such a thrifty army cannot fail to enrich their Country, and give it a greater appearance of comfort than that of their poor rash neighbourhood [meaning Ireland]. These Kirk-men have done Scotland harm; they have banished puns, and laughing, and kissing, etc., (except in cases where the very danger and crime must make it very gustful). I shall make a full stop at kissing,...and go on to remind you of the fate of Burns poor, unfortunate fellow! his disposition was Southern! How sad it is when a luxurious imagination is obliged, in self-defence, to deaden its delicacy in vulgarity and in things attainable, that it may not have leisure to go mad after things that are not!...I have not sufficient reasoning faculty to settle the doctrine of thrift, as it is consistent with the dignity of human Society — with the happiness of Cottagers. All I can do is by plump contrasts; were the fingers made to squeeze a guinea or a white hand? — were the lips made to hold a pen or a kiss? and yet in Cities man is shut out from his fellows if he is poor — the cottager must be very dirty, and very wretched, if she be not thrifty — the present state of society demands this, and this convinces me that the world is very young, and in a very ignorant state. We live in a barbarous age — I would sooner be a wild deer, than a girl under the dominion of the Kirk; and I would sooner be a wild hog, than be the occasion of a poor Creature's penance before those execrable elders.

Here is an impression received in Ireland, followed by a promise, which was fulfilled a few days later with remarkable shrewdness and insight, of further considerations on the contrasts between the Irish character and the Scottish: —

On our return from Belfast we met a sedan — the Duchess of Dunghill. It was no laughing matter though. Imagine the worst dog-kennel you ever saw, placed upon two poles from a mouldy fencing. In such a wretched thing sat a squalid old woman, squat like an ape half-starved from a scarcity of biscuit in its passage from Madagascar to the Cape, with a pipe in her mouth and looking out with a round-eyed, skinny-lidded inanity, with a sort of horizontal idiotic movement of her head: squat and lean she sat, and puffed out the smoke, while two ragged, tattered girls carried her along. What a thing would be a history of her life and sensations; I shall endeavour when I have thought a little more, to give you my idea of the difference between the Scotch and Irish.

From Stranraer the friends made straight for Burns's country, walking along the coast by Ballantrae, Girvan, Kirkoswald and Maybole (the same walk that Stevenson took the reverse way in the winter of 1876) to Ayr. Brown grows especially lyrical, and Keats more enthusiastic than usual, over the beauty of the first day's walk from Stranraer by Cairn Ryan and Glen App, with Ailsa Craig suddenly looming up through showers after they topped the pass: —

When we left Cairn [writes Keats] our Road lay half way up the sides of a green mountainous shore, full of clefts of verdure and eternally varying — sometimes up sometimes down, and over little Bridges going across green chasms of moss, rock and trees — winding about everywhere. After two or three Miles of this we turned suddenly into a magnificent glen finely wooded in Parts — seven Miles long — with a Mountain stream winding down the Midst — full of cottages in the most happy situations — the sides of the Hills covered with sheep — the effect of cattle lowing I never had so finely. At the end we had a gradual ascent and got among the tops of the Mountains whence in a little time I descried in the Sea Ailsa Rock feet high — it was 15 Miles distant and seemed close upon us. The effect of Ailsa with the peculiar perspective of the Sea in connection with the ground we stood on, and the misty rain then falling gave me a complete Idea of a deluge. Ailsa struck me very suddenly — really I was a little alarmed.

Less vivid than the above is the invocatory sonnet, apparently showing acquaintance with the geological theory of volcanic upheaval, which Keats was presently moved to address *To Ailsa Rock*. Coming down into Ballantrae in blustering weather, the friends met a country wedding party on horseback, and Keats tried a song about it in the Burns dialect, for Brown to palm off on Dilke as an original: 'but it won't do,' he rightly decides. From Maybole he writes to Reynolds with pleased anticipation of the visit to be paid the next day to Burns's cottage. 'One of the pleasantest means of annulling self is approaching such a shrine as the cottage of Burns — we need not think of his misery — that is all gone — bad luck to it — I shall look upon it all with unmixed pleasure, as I do upon my Stratford-on-Avon day with Bailey.' On the walk from Maybole to Ayr Keats has almost the only phrase which escapes him during the whole tour to indicate a sense of special inspiring power in mountain scenery for a poet: — 'The approach to it [Ayr] is extremely fine — quite outwent my expectations — richly meadowed, wooded, heathed, and rivuleted — with a Grand Sea view terminated by the black mountains of the Isle of Arran. As soon as I saw them so nearly I said to myself, "How is it they did not beckon Burns to some grand attempt at an Epic."' Nearing Kirk Alloway, Keats had been delighted to find the first home of Burns in a landscape so charming. 'I endeavoured to drink in the Prospect, that I might spin it out to you, as the Silkworm makes silk from Mulberry leaves — I cannot recollect it.' But his anticipations were deceived, the whole scene disenchanted, and thoughts of Burns's misery forced on him in his own despite, by the presence and chatter of the man in charge of the poet's birthplace: —

The Man at the Cottage was a great Bore with his Anecdotes — I hate the rascal — his life consists in fuz, fuzzy, fuzziest. He drinks glasses five for the Quarter and twelve for the hour — he is a mahogany-faced old Jackass who knew Burns. He ought to have been kicked for having spoken to him. He calls himself 'a curious old Bitch' — but he is a flat old dog — I should like to employ Caliph Vathek to kick him. O the flummery of a birthplace! Cant! cant! cant! It is enough to give a spirit the guts-ache. Many a true word, they say, is spoken in jest — this may be because his gab hindered my sublimity: the flat dog made me write a flat sonnet. My dear Reynolds — I cannot write about scenery and visitings — Fancy is indeed less than a present palpable reality, but it is greater than remembrance — you would lift your eyes from *Homer* only to see close before you the real Isle of Tenedos — you would rather read *Homer* afterwards than remember yourself. One song of Burns's is of more worth to you than all I could think for a whole year in his native country. His Misery is a dead weight upon the nimbleness of one's quill — I tried to forget it — to drink Toddy without any Care — to write a merry sonnet — it won't do — he talked with Bitches — he drank with blackguards, he was miserable. We can see horribly clear, in the works of such a Man his whole life, as if we were God's spies. What were his addresses to Jean in the latter part of his life?

A little farther back Keats had written, 'my head is sometimes in such a whirl in considering the million likings and antipathies of our Moments that I can get into no settled strain in my Letters.' But their straggling, careless tissue is threaded with such strands of genius and fresh human wisdom that one often wonders whether they are not legacies of this rare young spirit equally precious with the poems themselves. Certainly their prose is better than most of the verse which he had strength or leisure to write during this Scottish tour. As the two friends tramped among the Highland mountains some days later Keats composed with considerable pains (as Brown particularly mentions) the lines beginning 'There is a charm in footing slow across a silent plain,' intended to express the temper in which his pilgrimage through and beyond the Burns country had been made. They are written in the long iambic fourteeners of Chapman's *Iliad*, a metre not touched by Keats elsewhere, and perhaps chosen to convey a sense of the sustained continuous trudge of his wayfaring. They are very interesting as an attempt to capture and fix in words certain singular, fluctuating intensities of the poet's mood — the pressure of a great and tragic memory absorbing his whole consciousness and deadening all sense of outward things as he nears the place of pilgrimage — and afterwards his momentary panic lest the spell of mighty scenery and associations may be too overpowering and drag his soul adrift from its moorings of everyday habit and affection — from the ties of 'the sweet and bitter world' — 'of Brother's eyes, of Sister's brow.' In some of the lines expressing these obscure disturbances of the soul there is a deep smouldering fire, but hardly ever that touch of absolute felicity which is the note of Keats' work when he is quite himself. The best, technically speaking, are those which tell of the pilgrim's absorbed mood of expectant approach to his goal: —

Light heather-bells may tremble then but they are far away;
Wood-lark may sing from sandy fern, — the Sun may hear his lay;
Runnels may kiss the grass on shelves and shallows clear,
But their low voices are not heard, though come on travels drear;
Blood-red the Sun may set behind black mountain peaks;
Blue tides may sluice and drench their time in caves and weedy creeks;
Eagles may seem to sleep wing-wide upon the air;
Ring-doves may fly convuls'd across to some high-cedar'd lair;
But the forgotten eye is still fast lidded to the ground,
As Palmer's, that with weariness, mid-desert shrine hath found.
At such a time the soul's a child, in childhood is the brain;
Forgotten is the worldly heart — alone, it beats in vain. —

Keats makes it clear that he did not write these lines until some days after he had left Burns's country and was well on into the heart of the Highlands, and we get what reads like the prose of some of them in a letter written to Tom on the last stage of his walk before reaching Oban. Meantime the friends had passed through Glasgow, of which they had nothing to say except that they were taken, not for the first time, for pedlars by reason of their knapsacks, and Brown in particular for a spectacle-seller by reason of his glasses, and that the whole population seemed to have turned out to stare at them. A drunken man in the street, accosting Keats with true Glaswegian lack of ceremony, vowed he had seen all kinds of foreigners but never the like o' *him* : a remark perhaps not to be wondered at when we recall Mrs Dilke's description of Keats' appearance when he came home (see the end of this chapter) and Brown's account of his own weird toggery as follows: — 'a thick stick in my hand, the knapsack on my back, "with spectacles on nose," a white hat, a tartan coat and trousers and a Highland plaid thrown over my shoulders.' From Glasgow they walked by Dumbarton through the Loch Lomond country, round the head of Loch Fyne to Inverary, thence down the side and round the south-west end of Loch Awe and so past the head of Loch Craignish to the coast. At his approach to the lower end of Loch Lomond Keats had thought the scene 'precious good;' but his sense of romance was disturbed by finding it so frequented. 'Steamboats on Loch Lomond and Barouches on its sides take a little from the pleasure of such romantic chaps as Brown and I.' If the scene were to be peopled he would prefer that it were by another kind of denizen. 'The Evening was beautiful nothing could surpass our fortune in the weather — yet was I worldly enough to wish for a fleet of chivalry Barges with Trumpets and Banners just to die away before me into that blue place among the mountains' — and here follows a little sketch of the narrow upper end of the lake from near Tarbet, just to show where the blue place was. At Inverary Keats has a word about the woods which reminds one of Coleridge's *Kubla Khan* — 'the woods seem old enough to remember two or three changes in the Crags above them' — and then goes on to tell how he has been amused and exasperated by a performance of *The Stranger* to an accompaniment of bagpipe music. Bathing in Loch Fyne the next morning, he got horribly bitten by gad-flies, and vented his smart in a set of doggrel rhymes. Of all these matters he gossips gaily for the entertainment of the invalid Tom. Turning on the same day to write to Benjamin Bailey, the most serious-minded of his friends, he proceeds in a strain of considerate self-knowledge to confess and define some of the morbid elements in his own nature. That Bailey may be warned against taking any future complainings of his too seriously, 'I carry all matters,' he says, 'to an extreme — so that when I have any little vexation, it grows in five minutes into a theme for Sophocles.' And then by way of accounting for his having failed of late to see much of the Reynolds sisters in Little Britain, he lays bare his reasons for thinking himself unfit for ordinary society and especially for the society of women: —

I am certain I have not a right feeling towards women — at this moment I am striving to be just to them, but I cannot. Is it because they fall so far beneath my boyish imagination? When I was a schoolboy I thought a fair woman a pure Goddess, my mind was a soft nest in which some one of them slept, though she knew it not. I have no right to expect more than their reality — I thought them ethereal above men — I find them perhaps equal — great by comparison is very small. Insult may be inflicted in more ways than by word or action. One who is tender of being insulted does not like to think an insult against another. I do not like to think insults in a lady's company — I commit a crime with her which absence would not have known.... I must absolutely get over this — but how? the only way is to find the root of the evil, and so cure it 'with backward mutters of disseering power' — that is a difficult thing; for an obstinate Prejudice can seldom be produced but from a gordian complication of feelings, which must take time to unravel, and care to keep unravelled.

And then, as to his present doings and impressions: —

I should not have consented to myself these four months tramping in the highlands, but that I thought it would give me more experience, rub off more prejudice, use me to more hardships, identify finer scenes, load me with grander mountains, and strengthen more my reach in Poetry, than would stopping at home among books, even though I should reach *Homer*. By this time I am comparatively a Mountaineer. I have been among wilds and mountains too much to break out much about their grandeur. I have fed upon oat-cake — not long enough to be very much attached to it. — The first mountains I saw, though not so large as some I have since seen, weighed very solemnly upon me. The effect is wearing away — yet I like them mainly.

The word 'identify' in the above is noticeable, as seeming to imply that the fruit of his travel was not discovery, but only the recognition of scenes already fully preconceived in his imagination. Resuming his letter to Tom at a later stage, he tells of things that have impressed him: how in Glencroe they had been pleased with the noise of shepherds' sheep and dogs in the misty heights close above them, but could see none of them for some time, till two came in sight 'creeping among the crags like Emmets,' yet their voices plainly audible: how solemn was the first sight of Loch Awe as they approached it 'along a complete mountain road' (that is by way of Glen Aray) 'where if one listened there was not a sound but that of mountain streams'; how they tramped twenty miles by the loch side and how the next day they had reached the coast within view of Long Island (that is Luing; the spot was probably Kilmelfort). It is at this point we get the prose of some of the lines quoted above from the verses expressing the temper of his pilgrimage: —

Our walk was of this description — the near Hills were not very lofty but many of them steep, beautifully wooded — the distant Mountains in the Hebrides very grand, the Saltwater Lakes coming up between Crags and Islands full tide and scarcely ruffled — sometimes appearing as one large Lake sometimes as three distinct ones in different directions. At one point we saw afar off a rocky opening into the main sea. — We have also seen an Eagle or two. They move about without the least motion of Wings when in an indolent fit.

At the same point occur for the first time complaints, slight at first, of fatigue and discomfort. At the beginning of his tour Keats had written to his sister of its effects upon his appetite: 'I get so hungry a ham goes but a very little way and fowls are like larks to me.... I can eat a bull's head as easily as I used to do bull's eyes.' Some days later he writes that he is getting used to it, and doing his twenty miles or more a day without inconvenience. But now, in the remoter parts of the Highlands, the hard accommodation and monotonous diet and rough journeys and frequent drenchings begin to tell upon both him and Brown: —

Last night poor Brown with his feet blistered and scarcely able to walk, after a trudge of 20 Miles down the side of Loch Awe had no supper but Eggs and oat Cake — we have lost the sight of white bread entirely — Now we had eaten nothing but eggs all day — about 10 a piece and they had become sickening — To-day we have fared rather better — but no oat Cake wanting — we had a small chicken and even a good bottle of Port but altogether the fare is too coarse — I feel it a little.

Our travellers seem to have felt the hardships of the Highlands more than either Wordsworth and his sister Dorothy when they visited the same scenes just fifteen years earlier, or Lockhart and his brother in their expedition, only three years before, to the loneliest wilds of Lochaber.

But then the Wordsworth party only walked when they wished, and drove much of the way in their ramshackle jaunting-car; and the Lockharts, being fishermen, had their rods, and had besides brought portable soup with them and a horse to carry their kit. Lockhart's account of his experience is in curious contrast with those of Keats and Brown: —

We had a horse with us for the convenience of carrying baggage — but contemning the paths of civilized man, we dared the deepest glens in search of trout. There is something abundantly delightful in the warmheartedness of the Highland people. Bating the article of inquisitiveness, they are as polite as courtiers. The moment we entered a cottage the wife began to bake her cakes — and having portable soup with us, our fare was really excellent. What think you of porritch and cream for breakfast? trout, pike, and herrings for dinner, and right peat-reek whisky?

Arrived at Oban by way of the Melfort pass and Glen Euchar, the friends undertook one journey in especial which proved too much for Keats' strength. Finding the regular tourist route by water to Staffa and Iona too expensive for their frugal scheme of travel, they were persuaded to take the ferry to the isle of Kerrera and thence on to the hither shore of Mull. Did Keats in crossing Kerrera hear of — he would scarcely have travelled out of his way to visit — the ruins of the castle of Goylen on its precipice above the sea, with its legend of the girl-child, unaccountably puny as was thought, who turned out to be really the fairy mistress of a gentleman of Ireland, and being detected as such threw herself headlong from the window into the waves? and was this scene with its story in his mind when he wrote of forlorn fairy lands where castle casements open on the foam of perilous seas? From the landing place in Mull they had to take a guide and traverse on foot the whole width of the island to the extreme point of the Ross of Mull opposite Iona: a wretched walk, as Keats calls it, of some thirty-seven miles, over difficult ground and in the very roughest weather, broken by one night's rest in a shepherd's hut at a spot he calls Dun an Cullen, — perhaps for Derrynacullen. Having crossed the narrow channel to Iona and admired the antiquities of that illustrious island (the epithet is Johnson's), they chartered a fresh boat for the trip to Staffa and thence up Loch na Keal, so landing on the return journey in the heart of Mull and shortening their walk back across the island by more than half. By the power of the past and its associations among the monastic ruins of Iona, and of nature's architecture in building and scooping the basaltic columns of Fingal's Cave, Keats shows himself naturally impressed. In this instance, and once or twice afterwards, he exerts himself to write a full and precise description for the benefit of his brother Tom. In doing so he uses a phrase which indicates a running of his thoughts upon his projected poem, *Hyperion* : —

The finest thing is Fingal's cave — it is entirely a hollowing out of Basalt Pillars. Suppose now the Giants who rebelled against Jove had taken a whole Mass of black Columns and bound them together like bunches of matches — and then with immense Axes had made a cavern in the body of these Columns — of course the roof and floor must be composed of the broken ends of the Columns — such is Fingal's cave except that the Sea has done the work of excavations and is continually dashing there — so that we walk along the sides of the cave on the pillars which are left as if for convenient stairs — the roof is arched somewhat gothic-wise and the length of some of the entire side-pillars is 50 feet.... The colour of the columns is a sort of black with a lurking gloom of purple therein. For solemnity and grandeur it far surpasses the finest Cathedral.

More characteristically than this description, some verses he sends at the same time tell how Fingal's cave and its profanation by the race of tourists affected him: I mean those beginning 'Not Aladdin Magian,' written in the seven-syllable metre which he handled almost as well as his sixteenth and seventeenth century masters, from Fletcher and Ben Jonson to the youthful Milton. Avoiding word-painting and description, like the born poet he is, he begins by calling up for comparison visions of other fanes or palaces of enchantment, and then, bethinking himself of Milton's cry to Lycidas,

> where'er thy bones are hurl'd,
> Whether beyond the stormy Hebrides —

he imagines that lost one to have been found by the divinity of Ocean and put by him in charge of this cathedral of his building. In his priestly character Lycidas tells his latter-day visitant of the religion of the place, complains of the violation of its solitude, and then dives suddenly from view. In the six lines which tell of the scene's profanation the style sinks with the theme into flat triviality: —

> So for ever will I leave
> Such a taint and soon unweave
> All the magic of the place,
> Tis now free to stupid face,
> To cutters and to Fashion boats,
> To cravats and to Petticoats: —
> The great sea shall war it down,
> For its fame shall not be blown
> At each farthing Quadrille dance.
> So saying with a Spirit glance
> He dived —.

Keats evidently, and no wonder, did not like those six lines from 'Tis now free' to 'dance': in transcripts by his friends they are dropped out or inserted only in pencil: but he apparently did not see his way to mend them, and Brown tells us he could never persuade him to finish or resume the poem. In the broken close as he left it there is after all an appropriate abruptness which may content us.

From the exertion and exposure which he underwent on his Scottish tour, and especially in this Mull expedition, are to be traced the first distinct and settled symptoms of failure in Keats' health, which by reason of his muscular vigour had to his friends hitherto seemed so robust, and of the development of his hereditary tendency to consumption. In the same letter to his brother Tom which contains the transcript of the Fingal poem he speaks of a 'slight sore throat,' — Brown calls it a violent cold, — which compelled him to rest for a day or two at Oban. Thence they pushed on in broken weather by Ballachulish and the shore of Loch Linnhe to Fort William, and from thence groped and struggled up Ben Nevis, a toilsome climb at best, in a dissolving mist. Once again Keats makes an exceptional endeavour to realise the scene in words for his brother's benefit, telling of the continual shifting and opening and closing and re-opening of the cloud veils about them; and to clench his effect adds, 'There is not a more fickle thing than the top of a Mountain — what would a Lady give to change her headdress as often and with as little trouble?' Seated, so Brown tells us, almost on the edge of a precipice of fifteen hundred feet drop, Keats composed a sonnet, above his worst but much below his best, turning the experience of the hour into a simple enough symbol of his own mental state in face of the great mysteries of things: —

> Read me a lesson, Muse, and speak it loud
> Upon the top of Nevis, blind in mist!
> I look into the chasms, and a shroud
> Vap'rous doth hide them, — just so much I wist
> Mankind do know of hell; I look o'erhead,
> And there is sullen mist, — even so much
> Mankind can tell of heaven; mist is spread
> Before the earth, beneath me, — even such,
> Even so vague is man's sight of himself!
> Here are the craggy stones beneath my feet, —
> Thus much I know that, a poor witless elf,
> I tread on them, — that all my eye doth meet

> Is mist and crag, not only on this height,
> But in the world of thought and mental might!

Hearing of a previous ascent by a Mrs Cameron, 'the fattest woman in all Invernesshire,' he had the energy to compose also for Tom's amusement a comic dialogue in verse between the mountain and the lady, much more in Brown's vein than in his own. By the 6th of August the travellers had reached Inverness, having tramped, as Brown calculates, six hundred and forty-two miles since leaving Lancaster.

Keats' throat had for some time been getting worse: the ascent, and especially the descent, of Ben Nevis had, as he confesses, shaken and tried him: feverish symptoms set in, and the doctor whom he consulted at Inverness thought his condition seriously threatening, and forbad him to continue his tour. Accordingly he gave up the purpose with which he had set out of footing it southward by a different route, seeing Edinburgh, and on his way home visiting Bailey at his curacy in Cumberland, and decided to take passage at once for London by the next packet from Cromarty. Dilke had in the meantime felt compelled to write and recall him on account of a sudden change for the worse in the condition of the invalid Tom, so that his tour with Brown would have been cut short in any case. On their way round the head of Beauly Firth to Cromarty the friends did not miss the opportunity of visiting the ruins of Beauly Abbey. The interior was then and for long afterwards used as a burial place and receptacle for miscellaneous rubbish. Their attention being drawn to a heap of skulls which they took, probably on the information of some local guide, for skulls of ancient monks of the Abbey, they jointly composed upon them a set of verses in Burns's favourite measure (but without, this time, any attempt at his dialect). Unluckily Brown wrote the lion's share of the piece and set the tone of the whole. To the sixteen stanzas Keats contributed, as he afterwards informed Woodhouse, only the first line-and-a-half of the first stanza, with three of the later stanzas entire. As the piece has never been published and is a new document in the history of the tour, it seems to call for insertion here: but in view of its length and lack of quality (for it has nowhere a touch of Keats' true magic) I choose rather to relegate it to an appendix.

It was on the eighth or ninth of August that the smack for London put out from Cromarty with Keats on board, and Brown, having bidden him goodbye, was left to finish the tour alone — 'much lamenting,' says he, 'the loss of his beloved companionship at my side.' Keats in some degree picked up strength during a nine days' sea passage, the humours of which he afterwards described pleasantly in a letter to his brother George. But his throat trouble, the premonitory sign of worse, never really or for any length of time left him afterwards. On the 18th of August he arrived at Hampstead, and made his appearance among his friends the next day, 'as brown and as shabby as you can imagine,' writes Mrs Dilke, 'scarcely any shoes left, his jacket all torn at the back, a fur cap, a great plaid, and his knapsack. I cannot tell what he looked like.' When he found himself seated, for the first time after his hardships, in a comfortable stuffed chair, we are told how he expressed a comic enjoyment of the sensation, quoting at himself the words in which Quince the carpenter congratulates his gossip the weaver on his metamorphosis.

Chapter X

SEPTEMBER-DECEMBER 1818: BLACKWOOD AND THE QUARTERLY

On the first of September, within a fortnight of Keats' return from the North, appeared the threatened attack on him in Blackwood's *Edinburgh Magazine*. Much as has been said and written on the history and effect of the 'Cockney School' articles, my task requires that the story should be retold, as accurately and fairly as may be, in the light of our present knowledge.

The Whig party in politics and letters had held full ascendency for half a generation in the periodical literature of Scotland by means of the *Edinburgh Review*, published by Archibald Constable and edited at this time by Jeffrey. The Tory rival, the *Quarterly*, was owned and published also by a Scotsman, but a Scotsman migrated to London, John Murray. Early in 1817 William Blackwood, an able Tory bookseller in Edinburgh, projected a new monthly review which should be a thorn in the side of his astute and ambitious trade rival, Constable, and at the same time should hold up the party flag against the blue and yellow Whig colours in the North, and show a livelier and lustier fighting temper than the Quarterly. The first number appeared in March under the title of *The Edinburgh Monthly Magazine*. The first editors were two insignificant men who proved neither competent nor loyal, and flat failure threatening the enterprise, Blackwood after six months got rid of the editors and determined to make a fresh start. He added his own name to the title of the magazine and called to his aid two brilliant young men who had been occasional contributors, John Wilson and John Gibson Lockhart, both sound Oxford scholars and Lockhart moreover a well-read modern linguist, both penmen of extraordinary facility and power of work, both at this period of their lives given, in a spirit partly of furious partisanship partly of reckless frolic, to a degree of licence in controversy and satire inconceivable to-day. Wilson, by birth the son of a rich Glasgow manufacturer but now reduced in fortune, was in person a magnificent, florid, blue-eyed athlete of thirty, and in literature the bully and Berserker of the pair. Lockhart, the scion of an ancient Lanarkshire house, a dark, proud, handsome and graceful youth of twenty-three, pensive and sardonically reserved, had a deadly gift of satire and caricature and a lust for exercising it which was for a time uncontrollable like a disease. Wilson had lived on Windermere in the intimacy of Wordsworth and his circle, and already made a certain mark in literature with his poem *The Isle of Palms*. Lockhart had made a few firm friends at Oxford and after his degree had frequented the Goethe circle at Weimar, but was otherwise without social or literary experience. Blackwood was the eager employer and unflinching backer of both. The trio were determined to push the magazine into notoriety by fair means or foul. Its management was informally divided between them, so that no one person could be held responsible. Of Wilson and Lockhart, each was at one time supposed to be editor, but neither ever admitted as much or received separate payment for editorial work. They were really chief contributors and trusted and insistent chief advisers, but Blackwood never let go his own control, and took upon himself, now with effrontery, now with evasion, occasionally with compromise made and satisfaction given, all the risks and rancours which the threefold management chose to incur.

Wilson's obstreperousness, even when he had in some degree sobered down as a university professor, was at all times irresponsible and irrepressible, but for some of the excesses of those days he expressed regret and tried to make atonement; while Lockhart, the vitriol gradually working out of his nature in the sunshine of domestic happiness and of Scott's genial and paternal influence, sincerely repented them when it was too late. But they lasted long enough to furnish one of the most deplorable chapters in our literary history. The fury of political party spirit, infesting the whole field of letters, accounts for, without excusing much. It was a rough unscrupulous time, the literary as well as the political atmosphere thick, as we have seen, with the mud and stones of controversy, flung often very much at random. The *Quarterly*, as conducted by the acrid and deformed pedant Gifford, had no mercy for opponents:

and one of the harshest of its contributors was the virtuous Southey. On the other side the Edinburgh, under the more urbane and temperate Jeffrey, could sneer spitefully at all times and abuse savagely enough on occasion, especially when its contributor was Hazlitt. If a notorious Edinburgh attack on Coleridge's *Christabel* volume was really by Hazlitt, as Coleridge always believed and Hazlitt never denied, he in that instance added unpardonable personal ingratitude to a degree of critical blindness amazing in such a man. Even Leigh Hunt, in private life one of the most amiable of hearts, could in controversy on the liberal side be almost as good a damner (to use Keats' phrase) as his ally, the same Hazlitt himself. But nowhere else were such felon strokes dealt in pure wantonness of heart as in the early numbers of Blackwood. The notorious first number opened with an article on Coleridge's *Biographia Literaria* even more furiously insulting than the aforesaid Edinburgh article on *Christabel* attributed to Hazlitt. But for Hazlitt Coleridge was in politics an apostate not to be pardoned, while for the Blackwood group he was no enemy but an ally. Why treat him thus unless it were merely for the purpose of attracting a scandalized attention? More amazing even than the virulence of Blackwood was its waywardness and inconsistency. Will it be believed that less than three years later the same Coleridge was being praised and solicited — and what is more, successfully solicited — for contributions? Again, nothing is so much to the credit of Wilson and Lockhart in those days as their admiration for Wordsworth. The sins of their first number are half redeemed by the article in Wordsworth's praise, a really fine, eloquent piece of work in Wilson's boisterous but not undiscriminating manner of laudation. But not even Wordsworth could long escape the random swash of Wilson's bludgeon, and a very few years later his friends were astonished to read a ferocious outbreak against him in one of the *Noctes* by the same hand. In regard even to the detested Hazlitt the magazine blew in some degree hot and cold, printing through several numbers a series of respectful summaries, supplied from London by Patmore, of his Surrey Institution lectures; in another number a courteous enough estimate of his and Jeffrey's comparative powers in criticism; and a little later taking him to task on one page rudely, but not quite unjustly, for his capricious treatment of Shakespeare's minor poems and on another page addressing to him an insulting catechism full of the vilest personal imputations.

The only contemporary whose treatment by the Blackwood trio is truly consistent was Leigh Hunt, and of him it was consistently blackguardly. To return to the first number of the new series, three articles were counted on to create an uproar. First, the aforesaid emptying of the critical slop-pail on Coleridge. Second, the *Translation from an ancient Chaldee Manuscript*, being a biting personal satire, in language parodied from the Bible, on noted Edinburgh characters, including the Blackwood group themselves, disguised under transparent nicknames that stuck, Blackwood as Ebony, Wilson as the Leopard, Lockhart as the Scorpion that delighteth to sting the faces of men. Third, the article on the Cockney School of Poetry, numbered as the first of the series, headed with a quotation from Cornelius Webb, and signed with the initial 'Z.' As a thing to hang gibes on, the quotation from the unlucky Webb is aptly enough chosen: —

> Our talk shall be (a theme we never tire on)
> Of Chaucer, Spenser, Shakespeare, Milton, Byron,
> (Our England's Dante) — Wordsworth, Hunt, and Keats,
> The Muses' son of promise, and what feats
> He yet may do —

Nor are the gibes themselves quite unjustified so far as they touch merely the underbred insipidities of Leigh Hunt's tea-party manner in *Rimini*. But they are as outrageously absurd as they are gross and libellous when they go on to assail both poem and author on the score of immorality.

The extreme moral depravity of the Cockney School is another thing which is for ever thrusting itself upon the public attention, and convincing every man of sense who looks into their productions, that they who sport such sentiments can never be great poets. How could any man of high original genius ever stoop publicly, at the present day, to dip his fingers in the least of those glittering and rancid obscenities which float on the surface of Mr Hunt's *Hippocrene* ? His poetry is that of a man who has kept company with kept-mistresses. He talks indelicately like a tea-sipping milliner girl. Some excuse for him there might have been, had he been hurried away by imagination or passion. But with him indecency is a disease, as he speaks unclean things from perfect inanition. The very concubine of so impure a wretch as Leigh Hunt would be to be pitied, but alas! for the wife of such a husband! For him there is no charm in simple seduction; and he gloats over it only when accompanied with adultery and incest.

Such is the manner in which these censors set about showing their superior breeding and scholarship. 'Z' was in most cases probably a composite and not a single personality, but the respective shares of Wilson and Lockhart can often be confidently enough disentangled by those who know their styles.

The scandal created by the first number exceeded what its authors had hoped or expected. All Edinburgh was in a turmoil about the *Chaldee Manuscript*, the victims writhing, their enemies chuckling, lawsuits threatening right and left. In London the commotion was scarcely less. The London agents for the sale of the Magazine protested strongly, and Blackwood had to use some hard lying in order to pacify them. Murray, who had a share in the magazine, soon began remonstrating against its scurrilities, and on their continuance withdrew his capital. Leigh Hunt in the *Examiner* retorted upon 'Z' with natural indignation and a peremptory demand for the disclosure of his name. The libellers hugged their anonymity, and at first showed some slight movement of panic. In a second edition of the first number the *Chaldee Manuscript* was omitted and the assault on Hunt made a little less gross and personal. For a while Hunt vigorously threatened legal proceedings, but after some time desisted, whether from lack of funds or doubt of a verdict or inability to identify his assailant we do not know, and declared, and stuck to the declaration, that he would take no farther notice. The attacks were soon renewed more savagely than ever. The second of the 'Z' papers alone is scholarly and relatively reasonable. Its phrase, 'the genteel comedy of incest,' fitly enough labels *Rimini* in contrast with the tragic treatment of kindred themes by real masters, as Sophocles, Dante, Ford, Alfieri, Schiller, even Byron in *Manfred* and *Parisina*. The third article, and two other attacks in the form of letters addressed directly to Hunt with the same signature, are merely rabid and outrageous. Correspondents having urged in protest that Hunt's domestic life was blameless, the assailant says in effect, so much the greater his offence for writing a profligate and demoralizing poem; and to this preposterous charge against one of the mildest pieces of milk-and-water sentimentality in all literature he returns (or they return) with furious iteration.

The reasons for this special savagery against Hunt have never been made fully clear. He and his circle used to think it was partly due to his slighting treatment of Scott in the *Feast of the Poets* : nay, they even idly imagined for a moment that Scott himself had been the writer, — Scott, than whom no man was ever more magnanimously and humorously indifferent to harsh criticism or less capable of lifting a finger to resent it. But some of Scott's friends and idolaters in Edinburgh were sensitive on his behalf as he never was on his own. Even for the Blackwood assault on Coleridge one rumoured reason was that Coleridge had rudely denounced a play, the *Bertram* of Maturin, admired and recommended to Drury Lane by Scott; and it is, as a matter of fact, conceivable that a similar excess of loyalty may have had something to do with the rancour of the 'Z' articles.

Looking back on the way in which the name of this great man got mixed up in some minds with matters so far beneath him, it seems worth while to set forth exactly what were his relations at this time to Blackwood and the Blackwood group. About 1816-1817 the two rival publishers Blackwood and Constable, were hot competitors for Scott's favour, and Constable had lately scored a point in the game in the matter of the *Tales of my Landlord*. It became in the eyes of Blackwood and his associates a vital matter to secure some kind of countenance from Scott for their new venture. They knew they would never attach him as a partisan or secure a monopoly of his favours, and the authors of the *Chaldee Manuscript* divined his attitude wittily and shrewdly when they represented him as giving precisely the same answer to each of the two publishers who courted him, thus. (The man in plain apparel is Blackwood and the Jordan is the Tweed): —

44. Then spake the man clothed in plain apparel to the great magician who dwelleth in the old fastness, hard by the river Jordan, which is by the Border. And the magician opened his mouth, and said, Lo! my heart wisheth thy good, and let the thing prosper which is in thy hands to do it.

45. But thou seest that my hands are full of working and my labour is great. For lo I have to feed all the people of my land, and none knoweth whence his food cometh, but each man openeth his mouth, and my hand filleth it with pleasant things.

46. Moreover, thine adversary also is of my familiars.

47. The land is before thee, draw thou up thy hosts for the battle in the place of Princes, over against thine adversary, which hath his station near the mount of the Proclamation; quit ye as men, and let favour be shewn unto him which is most valiant.

48. Yet be thou silent, peradventure will I help thee some little.

More shrewdly still, Blackwood bethought himself of the one and only way of practically enlisting Scott, and that was by promising permanent work on the magazine for his friend, tenant, and dependent, William Laidlaw, whom he could never do enough to help. So it was arranged that Laidlaw should regularly contribute a chronicle on agricultural and antiquarian topics, and that Scott should touch it up and perhaps occasionally add a paragraph or short article of his own. In point of fact the peccant first number contains such an article, an entertaining enough little skit 'On the alarming Increase of Depravity among Animals.' After the number had appeared Scott wrote to Blackwood in tempered approval, but saying that he must withdraw his support if satire like that of the *Chaldee Manuscript* was to continue. He had been pleased and tickled with the prophetic picture of his own neutrality, but strongly disapproved the sting and malice of much of the rest.

One cannot but wish he had put his foot down in like manner about the 'Cockney school' and other excesses: but home — that is Edinburgh — affairs and personages interested him much more than those of London. Lockhart he did not yet personally know. They first met eight months later, in June 1818: the acquaintance ripened rapidly into firm devotion on Lockhart's part — for this young satirist could love as staunchly as he could stab unmercifully — a devotion requited with an answering warmth of affection on the part of Scott. At an early stage of their relations Scott, recognizing with regret that his young friend was 'as mischievous as a monkey,' got an offer for him of official work which would have freed him of his ties to Blackwood. In like manner two years later Scott threw himself heart and soul into the contest on behalf of Wilson for the Edinburgh chair of moral philosophy, not merely as the Tory candidate, but in the hope — never fully realized — that the office would tame his combative extravagances as well as give scope for his serious talents. And when the battle was won and Lockhart, now Scott's son-in-law, crowed over it in a set of verses which Scott thought too vindictive, he remonstrated in a strain of admirable grave and affectionate wisdom: —

I have hitherto avoided saying anything on this subject, though some little turn towards personal satire is, I think, the only drawback to your great and powerful talents, and I think I may have hinted as much to you. But I wished to see how this matter of Wilson's would turn, before making a clean breast upon this subject.... Now that he has triumphed I think it would be bad taste to cry out — 'Strike up our drums — pursue the scattered stray.' Besides, the natural consequence of his situation must be his relinquishing his share in these compositions — at least, he will injure himself in the opinion of many friends, and expose himself to a continuation of galling and vexatious disputes to the embittering of his life, should he do otherwise. In that case I really hope you will pause before you undertake to be the Boaz of the Maga; I mean in the personal and satirical department, when the Jachin has seceded.

Besides all other objections of personal enemies, personal quarrels, constant obloquy, and all uncharitableness, such an occupation will fritter away your talents, hurt your reputation both as a lawyer and a literary man, and waste away your time in what at best will be but a monthly wonder. What has been done in this department will be very well as a frolic of young men, but let it suffice.... Remember it is to the *personal* satire I object, and to the horse-play of your raillery.... Revere yourself, my dear boy, and think you were born to do your country better service than in this species of warfare. I make no apology (I am sure you will require none) for speaking plainly what my anxious affection dictates.... I wish you to have the benefit of my experience without purchasing it; and be assured, that the consciousness of attaining complete superiority over your calumniators and enemies by the force of your general character, is worth a dozen of triumphs over them by the force of wit and raillery.

It took a longer time and harder lessons to cure Lockhart of the scorpion habit and wean him from the seductions of the 'Mother of Mischief,' as Scott in another place calls *Blackwood's Magazine*. Meantime he had in the case of Keats done as much harm as he could. He had not the excuse of entire ignorance. His intimate friend Christie (afterwards principal in the John Scott duel) was working at the bar in London and wrote to Lockhart in January 1818 that he had met Keats and been favourably impressed by him. In reply Lockhart writes: 'What you say of Keates (sic) is pleasing, and if you like to write a little review of him, in admonition to leave his ways, etc., and in praise of his natural genius, I shall be greatly obliged to you.' Later Benjamin Bailey had the opportunity of speaking with Lockhart in Keats' behalf. Bailey had by this time taken orders, and after publishing a friendly notice of *Endymion* in the *Oxford Herald* for June, had left the University and gone to settle in a curacy in Cumberland. In the course of the summer he staid at Stirling, at the house of Bishop Gleig; whose son, afterwards the well-known writer and chaplain-general to the forces, was his friend, and whose daughter he soon afterwards married. Here Bailey met Lockhart, and anxious to save Keats from the sort of treatment to which Hunt had already been exposed, took the opportunity of telling him in a friendly way Keats' circumstances and history, explaining at the same time that his attachment to Leigh Hunt was personal and not political; pleading that he should not be made an object of party denunciation; and ending with the request that at any rate what had been thus said in confidence should not be used to his disadvantage. To which Lockhart replied that certainly it should not be so used by *him*. Within three weeks the article appeared, making use to all appearance, and to Bailey's great indignation, of the very facts he had thus confidentially communicated.

'That amiable but infatuated bardling, Mister John Keats,' had received a certain amount of attention from 'Z' already, both in the quotation from Cornelius Webb prefixed to the Cockney school articles, and in allusion to Hunt's pair of sonnets on the intercoronation scene which he had printed in his volume, *Foliage*, since the 'Z' series began. When now Keats' own turn came, in the fourth article of the series, his treatment was almost mild in comparison with that of his supposed leader. 'This young man appears to have received from nature talents of an excellent, perhaps even of a superior, order — talents which, devoted to the purposes of any useful profession, must have rendered him a respectable, if not an eminent citizen.' But, says the critic, he has unfortunately fallen a victim to the *metromania* of the hour; the wavering apprentice has been confirmed in his desire to quit the gallipots by his admiration for 'the most worthless and affected of all the versifiers of our time.' 'Mr Hunt is a small poet, but he is a clever man, Mr Keats is a still smaller poet, and he is only a boy of pretty abilities which he has done everything in his power to spoil.' And so on; and so on; not of course omitting to put a finger on real weaknesses, as lack of scholarship, the use of Cockney rimes like *higher*, *Thalia* ; *ear*, *Cytherea* ; *thorn*, *fawn* ; deriding the Boileau passage in *Sleep and Poetry*, and perceiving nothing but laxity and nervelessness in the treatment of the metre. In the conceit of academic talent and training, the critic shows himself open-eyed to all the faults and stone-blind to all the beauty and genius and promise, and ends with a vulgarity of supercilious patronage beside which all the silly venial faults of taste in Leigh Hunt seem like good breeding itself.

And now, good-morrow to 'the Muses' son of Promise;' as for 'the feats he yet may do,' as we do not pretend to say like himself, 'Muse of my native land am I inspired,' we shall adhere to the safe old rule of *pauca verba*. We venture to make one small prophecy, that his bookseller will not a second time venture £50 upon any thing he can write. It is a better and a wiser thing to be a starved apothecary than a starved poet; so back to the shop Mr John, back to 'plasters, pills, and ointment boxes,' *etc*. But, for Heaven's sake, young Sangrado, be a little more sparing of extenuatives and soporifics in your practice than you have been in your poetry.

There is a lesson in these things. I remember the late Mr Andrew Lang, one of the most variously gifted and richly equipped critical minds of our time, and under a surface vein of flippancy essentially kind-hearted, — I remember Mr Andrew Lang, in a candid mood of conversation, wondering whether in like circumstances he might not have himself committed a like offence, and with no *Hyperion* or *St Agnes' Eve* or *Odes* yet written and only the 1817 volume and *Endymion* before him, have dismissed Keats fastidiously and scoffingly. Who knows? — and let us all take warning. But now-a-days the errors of criticism are perhaps rather of an opposite kind, and any rashness and rawness of undisciplined novelty is apt to find itself indulged and fostered rather than repressed. What should at any time have saved *Endymion* from harsh judgment, if the quality of the poetry could not save it, was the quality of the preface. How could either carelessness or rancour not recognize, not augur the best from, its fine spirit of manliness and modesty and self-knowledge?

The responsibility for the gallipots article, as for so many others in the Blackwood of the time, may have been in some sort collective. But that Lockhart had the chief share in it is certain. According to Dilke, he in later life owned as much. To those who know his hand, he stands confessed not only in the general gist and style but in particular phrases. One is the use of Sangrado for doctor, a use which both Scott and Lockhart had caught from *Gil Blas*. Others are the allusions to the *Métromanie* of Piron and the *Endymion* of Wieland, particularly the latter. Wieland's *Oberon*, as we have seen, had made its mark in England through Sotheby's translation, but no other member of the Blackwood group is the least likely to have had any acquaintance with his untranslated minor works except Lockhart, whose stay at Weimar had given him a familiar knowledge of contemporary German literature. In the *Mad Banker of Amsterdam*, a comic poem in the vein of Frere's *Whistlecraft* and Byron's *Beppo*, contributed by him at this time to Blackwood under one of his Protean pseudonyms, as 'William Wastle Esq.,' Lockhart sketches his own likeness as follows: —

> Then touched I off friend Lockhart (Gibson John),
> So fond of jabbering about Tieck and Schlegel,
> Klopstock and *Wieland*, Kant and Mendelssohn,
> All High Dutch quacks, like Spurzheim or Feinagle —
> Him the Chaldee yclept the Scorpion. —
> The claws, but not the pinions, of the eagle,
> Are Jack's, but though I do not mean to flatter,
> Undoubtedly he has strong powers of satire.

Bailey to the end of his life never forgave Lockhart for what he held to be a base breach of faith after their conversation above mentioned, and his indignation communicated itself to the Keats circle and afterwards, as we shall see, to Keats himself. Mr Andrew Lang, in his excellent *Life* of Lockhart, making such defence as is candidly possible for his hero's share in the Blackwood scandals, urges justly enough that the only matter of fact divulged about Keats by 'Z' is that of his having been apprenticed to a surgeon ('Z' prefers to say an apothecary) and that thus much Lockhart could not well help knowing independently, either from his own friend Christie or from Bailey's friend and future brother-in-law Gleig, then living at Edinburgh and about to become one of Blackwood's chief supporters. When in farther defence of 'Z's' attacks on Hunt Mr Lang quotes from Keats' letters phrases in dispraise of Hunt almost as strong as those used by 'Z' himself, he forgets the world of difference there is between the confidential criticism, in a passing mood or whim of impatience, of a friend by a friend to a friend and the gross and reiterated public defamation of a political and literary opponent.

Lockhart in after life pleaded the rawness of youth, and also that in the random and incoherent violences of the early years of Blackwood there had been less of real and settled malice than in the *Quarterly Review* as at that time conducted. The plea may be partly admitted, but to forgive him we need all the gratitude which is his due for his filial devotion to and immortal biography of Scott, as well as all the allowance to be made for a dangerous gift and bias of nature.

The Quarterly article on *Endymion* followed in the last week of September (in the number dated April, — such in those days was editorial punctuality). It is now known to have been the work of John Wilson Croker, a man of many sterling gifts and honourable loyalties, unjustly blackened in the eyes of posterity by Macaulay's rancorous dislike and Disraeli's masterly caricature, but in literature as in politics the narrowest and stiffest of conservative partisans. Like his editor Gifford, he was trained in strict allegiance to eighteenth century tradition and the school of Pope. His brief review of *Endymion* is that of a man insensible to the higher charm of poetry, incapable of judging it except by mechanical rule and precedent, and careless of the pain he gives. He professes to have been unable to read beyond the first canto, or to make head or tail of that, and what is worse, turns the frank avowals of Keats' preface foolishly and unfairly against him. At the same time, like Lockhart, he does not fail to point out and exaggerate real weaknesses of Keats' early manner, and the following, from the point of view of a critic who sees no salvation outside the closed couplet, is not unreasonable criticism: —

He seems to us to write a line at random, and then he follows not the thought excited by this line, but that suggested by the *rhyme* with which it concludes. There is hardly a complete couplet inclosing a complete idea in the whole book. He wanders from one subject to another, from the association, not of ideas but of sounds, and the work is composed of hemistichs which, it is quite evident, have forced themselves upon the author by the mere force of the catchwords on which they turn.

In another of the established reviews, *The British Critic*, a third censor came out with a notice even more contemptuous than those of Blackwood and the Quarterly. For a moment Keats' pride winced, as any man's might, under the personal insults of the critics, and dining in the company of Hazlitt and Woodhouse with Mr Hessey, the publisher, he seems to have declared in Woodhouse's hearing that he would write no more. But he quickly recovered his balance, and in a letter to Dilke of a few days later, speaking of Hazlitt's wrath against the Blackwood scribes, is silent as to their treatment of himself. Meantime some of his friends and more than one stranger were actively sympathetic and indignant on his behalf. A just and vigorous expostulation appeared in the *Morning Chronicle* under the initials J.S., — those in all likelihood of John Scott, then editor of the *London Magazine*, not long afterwards killed by Lockhart's friend Christie in a needless and blundering duel arising out of these very Blackwood brawls. Bailey, being in Edinburgh, had an interview with Blackwood and pleaded to be allowed to contribute a reply to his magazine; and this being refused, sought out Constable, who besides the *Edinburgh Review* conducted the monthly periodical which had been kind to Keats' first volume, and proposed to publish in it an attack on Blackwood and the 'Z' articles: but Constable would not take the risk. Reynolds published in a west-country paper, the *Alfred*, a warm rejoinder to the *Quarterly* reviewer, containing a judicious criticism in brief of Keats' work, with remarks very much to the point on the contrast between his and the egotistical (meaning Wordsworth's) attitude to nature. This Leigh Hunt reprinted with some introductory words in the *Examiner*, and later in life regretted that he had not done more. But he could not have done more to any purpose. He was not himself an enthusiastic admirer of *Endymion*, had plainly said so to Keats and to his friends, and would have got out of his depth if he had tried to appreciate the intensity and complexity of symbolic and spiritual meaning which made that poem so different from his own shallow, self-pleasing metrical versions of classic or Italian tales. Reynolds's piece, which he reprinted, was quite effective and to the point as far as it went; and moreover any formal defence of Keats by Hunt would only have increased the virulence of his enemies, as they both perfectly well knew. Privately at the same time Reynolds, who had just been reading *The Pot of Basil* in manuscript, wrote to his friend with affectionate wisdom as follows: —

As to the poem, I am of all things anxious that you should publish it, for its completeness will be a full answer to all the ignorant malevolence of cold, lying Scotchmen and stupid Englishmen. The overweening struggle to oppress you only shows the world that so much of endeavour cannot be directed to nothing. Men do not set their muscles and strain their sinews to break a straw. I am confident, Keats, that the 'Pot of Basil' hath that simplicity and quiet pathos which are of a sure sovereignty over all hearts. I must say that it would delight me to have you prove yourself to the world what we know you to be — to have you annul *The Quarterly Review* by the best of all answers. One or two of your sonnets you might print, I am sure. And I know that I may suggest to you which, because you can decide as you like afterward. You will remember that we were to print together. I give over all intention, and you ought to be alone. I can never write anything now — my mind is taken the other way. But I shall set my heart on having you high, as you ought to be. Do *you* get Fame, and I shall have it in being your affectionate and steady friend.

Woodhouse, in a correspondence with the unceasingly kind and loyal publishers Taylor and Hessey, shows himself as deeply moved as anyone, and Taylor in the course of the autumn sought to enlist on behalf of the victim the private sympathies of one of the most cultivated and influential Liberal thinkers and publicists of the time, Sir James Mackintosh. Sending him a copy of *Endymion*, Taylor writes: — 'Its faults are numberless, but there are redeeming features in my opinion, and the faults are those of real Genius. Whatever this work is, its Author is a true poet.' After a few words as to Keats' family and circumstances he adds, 'These are odd particulars to give, when I am introducing the work and not the man to you, — but if you knew him, you would also feel that strange personal interest in all that concerns him. — Mr Gifford forgot his own early life when he tried to bear down this young man. Happily, it will not succeed. If he lives, Keats will be the brightest ornament of this Age.' In concluding Taylor recommends particularly to his correspondent's attention the hymn to Pan, the Glaucus episode, and above all the triumph of Bacchus.

Proud in the extreme, Keats had no irritable vanity; and aiming in his art, if not always steadily, yet always at the highest, he rather despised than courted such successes as he saw some of his contemporaries — Thomas Moore, for instance, with *Lalla Rookh* — enjoy. 'I hate,' he says, 'a mawkish popularity.' Wise recognition and encouragement would no doubt have helped and cheered him, but even in the hopes of permanent fame which he avowedly cherished, there was nothing intemperate or impatient; and he was conscious of perceiving his own shortcomings at least as clearly as his critics. Accordingly he took his treatment at their hands more coolly than older and more experienced men had taken the like. Hunt, as we have seen, had replied indignantly to his Blackwood traducers, repelling scorn with scorn, and he and Hazlitt were both at first red-hot to have the law of them. Keats after the first sting with great dignity and simplicity treated the annoyance as one merely temporary, indifferent, and external. When early in October Mr Hessey sent for his encouragement the extracts from the papers in which he had been defended, he wrote: —

I cannot but feel indebted to those gentlemen who have taken my part. As for the rest, I begin to get a little acquainted with my own strength and weakness. Praise or blame has but a momentary effect on the man whose love of beauty in the abstract makes him a severe critic on his own works. My own domestic criticism has given me pain without comparison beyond what 'Blackwood' or the 'Quarterly' could possibly inflict — and also when I feel I am right, no external praise can give me such a glow as my own solitary reperception and ratification of what is fine. J. S. is perfectly right in regard to the slipshod *Endymion*. That it is so is no fault of mine. No! — though it may sound a little paradoxical. It is as good as I had power to make it — by myself. Had I been nervous about its being a perfect piece, and with that view asked advice, and trembled over every page, it would not have been written; for it is not in my nature to fumble — I will write independently. — I have written independently *without Judgment*. I may write independently, and *with Judgment*, hereafter. The Genius of Poetry must work out its own salvation in a man: It cannot be matured by law and precept, but by sensation and watchfulness in itself. That which is creative must create itself. In *Endymion* I leaped headlong into the sea, and thereby have become better acquainted with the Soundings, the quicksands, and the rocks, than if I had stayed upon the green shore, and piped a silly pipe, and took tea and comfortable advice. I was never afraid of failure; for I would sooner fail than not be among the greatest. But I am nigh getting into a rant.

Two or three weeks later, in answer to a similar encouraging letter from Woodhouse, he explains, in sentences luminous with self-knowledge, what he calls his own chameleon character as a poet, and the variable and impressionable temperament such a character implies. 'Where then,' he adds, 'is the wonder that I should say I would write no more? Might I not at that very instant have been cogitating on the characters of Saturn and Ops?... I know not whether I make myself wholly understood: I hope enough to make you see that no dependence is to be placed on what I said that day.' And again about the same time to his brother and sister-in-law: —

There have been two letters in my defence in the 'Chronicle,' and one in the 'Examiner,' copied from the Exeter paper, and written by Reynolds. I don't know who wrote those in the 'Chronicle.' This is a mere matter of the moment: I think I shall be among the English Poets after my death. Even as a matter of present interest, the attempt to crush me in the 'Quarterly' has only brought me more into notice, and it is a common expression among bookmen, 'I wonder the "Quarterly" should cut its own throat.'

It does me not the least harm in Society to make me appear little and ridiculous: I know when a man is superior to me and give him all due respect — he will be the last to laugh at me and as for the rest I feel that I make an impression upon them which ensures me personal respect while I am in sight whatever they may say when my back is turned.

Since these firm expressions of indifference to critical attack have been before the world, it has been too confidently assumed that Shelley and Byron were totally misled and wide of the mark when they believed that *Blackwood* and the *Quarterly* had killed Keats or even much hurt him. But the truth is that not they, but their consequences, did in their degree help to kill him. It must not be supposed that such words of wisdom and composure, manifestly sincere as they are, represent the whole of Keats, or anything like the whole. They represent, indeed, the admirably sound and manly elements which were a part of him: they show us the veins of what Matthew Arnold calls flint and iron in his nature uppermost. But he was no Wordsworth, to remain all flint and iron in indifference to derision and in the scorn of scorn. He had not only in a tenfold degree the ordinary acuteness of a poet's feelings: he had the variable and chameleon temperament of which he warns Woodhouse while in the very act of reassuring him: he had along with the flint and iron a strong congenital tendency, against which he was always fighting but not always successfully, to fits of depression and self-torment. Moreover the reviews of those days, especially the *Edinburgh* and *Quarterly*, had a real power of barring the acceptance and checking the sale of an author's work. What actually happened was that when a year or so later Keats began to realise the harm which the reviews had done and were doing to his material prospects, these consequences in his darker hours preyed on him severely and conspired with the forces of disease and passion to his undoing.

For the present and during the first stress of the *Blackwood* and *Quarterly* storms, he was really living under the pressure of another and far more heartfelt trouble. His friends the Dilkes, before they heard of his intended return from Scotland, had felt reluctantly bound to write and summon him home on account of the alarming condition of his brother Tom, whom he had left behind in their lodgings at Well Walk. In fact the case was desperate, and for the next three months Keats' chief occupation was the harrowing one of watching and ministering to this dying brother. In a letter written to Dilke in the third week of September, he speaks thus of his feelings and occupations: —

I wish I could say Tom was better. His identity presses upon me so all day that I am obliged to go out — and although I had intended to have given some time to study alone, I am obliged to write and plunge into abstract images to ease myself of his countenance, his voice, and feebleness — so that I live now in a continual fever. It must be poisonous to life, although I feel well.

Imagine 'the hateful siege of contraries' — if I think of fame, of poetry, it seems a crime to me, and yet I must do so or suffer.'

And again about the same time to Reynolds: —

I never was in love, yet the voice and shape of a Woman has haunted me these two days — at such a time when the relief, the feverish relief of poetry, seems a much less crime. This morning poetry has conquered — I have relapsed into those abstractions which are my only life — I feel escaped from a new, strange, and threatening sorrow, and I am thankful for it. There is an awful warmth about my heart, like a load of immortality.

What he calls the abstractions into which he had plunged for relief were the conceptions of the fallen Titans, 'the characters of Saturn and Ops' at the beginning of *Hyperion*. Those conceptions were just beginning to clothe themselves in his mind in the verses which every English reader knows, verses of a cadence as majestic and pathetic almost as any in the language, yet scarcely more charged with high emotion or more pregnant with the sense and pressure of destiny than some of the prose of his familiar letters written about the same time. His only other attempt in poetry during those weeks was a translation from a sonnet of Ronsard, whose works Taylor had lent him and from whom he got some hints for the names and characters of his Titans. As the autumn wore on the task of the watcher grew ever more sorrowful and absorbing, he was obliged to desist from poetry for the time. But his correspondence shows no flagging. Towards the middle of October he began, marking it as A, the first of the series of journal-letters to his brother and sister in America, which give us during the next fifteen months a picture of his outward and inward being fuller and richer than we possess from any other poet, and except in one single particular absolutely unreserved. Despatching the packet on his birthday, that is October 29 or 31, he explains why it is not longer (it is over 7,000 words): 'Tom is rather more easy than he has been: but is still so nervous that I cannot speak to him of these Matters — indeed it is the care I have had to keep his mind aloof from feelings too acute that has made this letter so short a one — I did not like to write before him a letter he knew was to reach your hands — I cannot even now ask him for any Message — his heart speaks to you. Be as happy as you can.' Keats had begun by warning George and his wife, in language of beautiful tender moderation and sincerity, to prepare their minds for the worst, and assuring them of the comfort he took in the thoughts of them: — 'I have Fanny and I have you — three people whose Happiness to me is sacred — and it does annul that selfish sorrow which I should otherwise fall into, living as I do with poor Tom who looks upon me as his only comfort — the tears will come into your Eyes — let them — and embrace each other — thank heaven for what happiness you have, and after thinking a moment or two that you suffer in common with all Mankind hold it not a sin to regain your cheerfulness.' Between the opening and the closing note of tenderness, the letter runs through a wide range of subject and feeling; gossip about the Dilkes and other acquaintances; an account of the humours of his sea-passage from Inverness to London; the unruffled allusion to the Tory reviews from which we have already quoted; two long and curious sex-haunted passages, one expressing his admiration of the same East Indian cousin of the Reynoldses, 'not a Cleopatra, but at least a Charmian,' whom we have found mentioned already in a letter to Reynolds, the other telling what promised to be an equivocal adventure, but turned out quite conventionally and politely, with a mysterious lady acquaintance met once before at Hastings; a rambling discussion on the state of home and foreign politics; a rhapsody, or as he would have called it rant, in a mounting strain of verse which rings like a boy's voice singing in alt, prophesying that the child to be born to George and his wife shall be the first American poet; then more babble about friends and acquaintances; then, as if he knew that the invincible thing, the love-god whose spell he had always at once dreaded and longed for, were hovering and about to swoop, he tries to reassure himself by calling up the reasons why marriage and the life domestic are not for him. The Charmian passage and the passage in which he seeks to stave off the approach of love are among the best known in his letters, but nevertheless the most necessary to quote: —

She has a rich eastern look; she has fine eyes and fine manners. When she comes into a room she makes an impression the same as the Beauty of a Leopardess. She is too fine and too conscious of herself to repulse any Man who may address her — from habit she thinks that nothing *particular*. I always find myself more at ease with such a woman; the picture before me always gives me a life and animation which I cannot possibly feel with anything inferior. I am at such times too much occupied in admiring to be awkward or on a tremble. I forget myself entirely because I live in her. You will by this time think I am in love with her; so before I go further I will tell you I am not — she kept me awake one Night as a tune of Mozart's might do. I speak of the thing as a pastime and an amusement than which I can feel none deeper than a conversation with an imperial woman the very 'yes' and 'no' of whose Lips is to me a Banquet. I don't cry to take the Moon home with me in my Pocket nor do I fret to leave her behind me. I like her and her like because one has no *sensations* — what we both are is taken for granted. You will suppose I have by this had much talk with her — no such thing — there are the Miss Reynoldses on the look out. They think I don't admire her because I did not stare at her. They call her a flirt to me. What a want of knowledge! She walks across a room in such a Manner that a Man is drawn towards her with a magnetic Power. This they call flirting! They do not know things.

In the next passage, almost as the young priest Ion in the Greek play clings to his ministration in the temple of Apollo, so we find Keats cleaving exultingly to his high vocation and to the idea of a life dedicated to poetry alone. But a great spiritual flaw in his nature — or was it only a lack of fortunate experience? — betrays itself in his conception of the alternative from which he shrinks. The imagery under which he figures marriage joys gives no hint of their power to discipline and inspire and sustain, and is trivially sensuous and material.

Notwithstanding your Happiness and your recommendation I hope I shall never marry. Though the most beautiful Creature were waiting for me at the end of a Journey or a Walk; though the Carpet were of Silk, the Curtains of the morning Clouds; the chairs and Sofa stuffed with Cygnet's down; the food Manna, the Wine beyond Claret, the Window opening on Windermere, I should not feel — or rather my Happiness would not be so fine, as my Solitude is sublime. Then instead of what I have described there is a sublimity to welcome me home. The roaring of the wind is my wife and the Stars through the windowpane are my Children. The mighty abstract Idea I have of Beauty in all things stifles the more divided and minute domestic happiness — an amiable wife and sweet Children I contemplate as a part of that Beauty, but I must have a thousand of those beautiful particles to fill up my heart. I feel more and more every day, as my imagination strengthens, that I do not live in this world alone but in a thousand worlds. No sooner am I alone than shapes of epic greatness are stationed around me, and serve my Spirit the office which is equivalent to a King's bodyguard — then 'Tragedy with sceptered pall comes sweeping by.' According to my state of mind I am with Achilles shouting in the Trenches, or with Theocritus in the Vales of Sicily. Or I throw my whole being into Troilus, and repeating those lines, 'I wander like a lost Soul upon the Stygian Banks staying for waftage,' I melt into the air with a voluptuousness so delicate that I am content to be alone. These things, combined with the opinion I have of the generality of women — who appear to me as children to whom I would rather give a sugar Plum than my time, form a barrier against Matrimony which I rejoice in.

Throughout November Keats was so fully absorbed in attendance on his dying brother as to be unfit for poetry or correspondence. On the night of December 1 the end came. 'Early the next morning,' writes Brown, 'I was awakened in bed by a pressure on my hand. It was Keats, who came to tell me that his brother was no more. I said nothing, and we both remained silent for a while, my hand fast locked in his. At length, my thoughts returning from the dead to the living, I said, — "Have nothing more to do with those lodgings, — and alone too! Had you not better live with me?" He paused, pressed my hand warmly, and replied, "I think it would be better." From that moment he was my inmate.'

Chapter XI

DECEMBER 1818-JUNE 1819: KEATS AND BROWN HOUSEMATES: FANNY BRAWNE: WORK AND IDLENESS

Dilke and Brown, as has been said already, had built for themselves a joint block of two houses in a garden near the bottom of John Street, Hampstead, and had called the property Wentworth Place, after a name hereditary in the Dilke family. Dilke and his wife occupied the larger of the two houses forming the block, and Brown, who was a bachelor, the smaller house, standing to the west. The accommodation in Brown's quarters included a front and back sitting-room on the ground floor, with a front and back bedroom over them, and a small spare bedroom or 'crib' where a bachelor guest could be put up for the night. The arrangement with Keats was that he should share household expenses, occupying the front sitting-room for the sake of quiet at his work. His move to his new quarters does not seem to have been quite so immediate as Brown represents it. Beginning a new journal-letter to his brother and sister-in-law a week or two after Tom's death, Keats writes, 'With Dilke and Brown I am quite thick — with Brown indeed I am going to domesticate, that is, we shall keep house together. I shall have the front parlour and he the back one, by which I shall be able to avoid the noise of Bentley's Children — and be better able to go on with my studies — which have been greatly interrupted lately, so that I have not a shadow of an idea for books in my head, and my pen seems to have grown gouty for verse.'

This phase of poetical stagnation, which had naturally set in as his cares for his dying brother grew more engrossing towards the end, passed away quickly. By about the middle of December Keats was settled at Wentworth Place, whither his ex-landlord, Bentley the postman, we are told, carried down his little library of some hundred and fifty books in a clothes-basket from Well Walk. In spite of the noisy children Keats parted not without regret from the Bentleys, and speaks feelingly of Mrs Bentley's kindness and attention during his late trouble. As soon, relates Brown, as the consolations of nature and friendship had in some measure softened his grief, he plunged once more into poetry, his special task being *Hyperion*, at which he had already begun to work before his brother died. But he never got into a quite happy or uninterrupted flow of work on it. Once and again we find him moved to lay it aside for a bout of brotherly gossip with George and Georgiana in America. 'Just now I took out my poem to go on with it — but the thought of my writing so little to you came upon me and I could not get on — so I have begun at random and I have not a word to say — and yet my thoughts are so full of you that I can do nothing else.' And again: 'I have no thought pervading me so constantly and frequently as that of you — my Poem cannot frequently drive it away — you will retard it much more than you could by taking up my time if you were in England. I never forget you except after seeing now and then some beautiful woman — but that is a fever — the thought of you both is a passion with me, but for the most part a calm one.'

This letter, covering some three weeks from mid-December to January 4, enables us, like others to the same correspondents, to lay our finger on almost every strand in the 'mingled yarn' of Keats' life and doings. Of one tiresome interruption which befell him about Christmas he tells nothing, doubtless in order to spare his brother anxiety. This was a request for money from the insatiable Haydon. The correspondence on the matter cannot be read without anger against the elder man and admiring affection for the generous lad — yet not foolishly or recklessly generous — on whom he sponged. Haydon's only excuses are a recent eye-trouble which had hindered his work, and his inflated belief, which had so far successfully imposed both upon himself and his friends, in his own huge importance to art and to his country. Keats writes, showing incidentally how last year's critical rebuffs had changed, more or less permanently, his attitude in regard to the public and public recognition: —

Believe me Haydon I have that sort of fire in my heart that would sacrifice everything I have to your service — I speak without any reserve — I know you would do so for me — I open my heart to you in a few words. I will do this sooner than you shall be distressed: but let me be the last stay — Ask the rich lovers of Art first — I'll tell you why — I have a little money which may enable me to study, and to travel for three or four years. I never expect to get anything by my Books: and moreover I wish to avoid publishing — I admire Human Nature but I do not like Men. I should like to compose things honourable to Man — but not fingerable over by Men. So I am anxious to exist without troubling the printer's devil or drawing upon Men's or Women's admiration — in which great solitude I hope God will give me strength to rejoice. Try the long purses — but do not sell your drawings or I shall consider it a breach of friendship.

Haydon answers in a gush of grandiloquent gratitude, promising to try every corner first, but intimating pretty clearly that he knew his wealthier habitual helpers were for the present tired out with him. One of his phrases is a treasure. 'Ah Keats, this is sad work for one of my soul and Ambition. The truest thing you ever said of mortal was that I had a touch of Alexander in me! I have, I know it, and the World shall know it, but this is a purgative drug I must first take.' 'This' means his own perpetual need and habit of living on other people. In the next letter Haydon of course accepts Keats' offer, and in the Christmas weeks, when he should have been wholly engrossed in *Hyperion*, Keats had much and for some time fruitless ado with bankers, lawyers, and guardian in endeavouring to fulfil his promise. To his brother he only says he has been dining with Haydon and otherwise seeing much of him; mentions the painter's eye-trouble; and quotes him as describing vividly at second hand the sufferings of Captain (afterwards Sir John) Ross and his party on their voyage in search of the North-West passage.

From Ross in Baffin's Bay the same letter rambles to Ritchie in the deserts of Morocco, and thence to gossip about the best way of keeping his own and George's brotherly intimacy unbroken across the ocean; about the 'sickening stuff' printed in Hunt's new *Literary Pocket Book* (it was when he was seeing most of Haydon that Keats was always most inclined to harsh criticism of Hunt); about Mrs Dilke's cats, and about Godwin's novels and Hazlitt's opinion of them, and the rare pleasure he has had at Haydon's in looking through a book of engravings after early Italian frescoes in a church at Milan. 'Milan' must be a mistake, for there are no such engravings, and what Keats saw must certainly have been the fine series by Lasinio, published in 1814, after the frescoes of Orcagna, Benozzo Gozzoli, and the rest in the Campo Santo at Pisa. 'I do not think I ever had a greater treat out of Shakespeare. Full of romance and the most tender feeling — magnificence of draperies beyond everything I ever saw, not excepting Raphael's. But Grotesque to a curious pitch — yet still making up a fine whole — even finer to me than more accomplished works — as there was left so much room for Imagination.' It is interesting to find Keats thus vividly awake, as very few yet were either by instinct or fashion, to the charm of the Italian primitives, and to remember how it was a copy of this same book of prints, in the possession of young John Everett Millais thirty years later, which first aroused the Pre-Raphaelite enthusiasm in him and his associates Gabriel Rossetti and Holman Hunt (the last-named is our witness for the fact).

Keats tells moreover how an unknown admirer from the west country had sent him a letter and sonnet of sympathy, with which was enclosed a further tribute in the shape of a £25 note; how he had been both pleased and displeased, — 'if I had refused it I should have behaved in a very braggadocio dunderheaded manner, and yet the present galls me a little'; and again how he has received through Woodhouse a glowing letter of sympathy and encouragement from Miss Jane Porter, the then famous authoress of *Thaddeus of Warsaw* and *The Scottish Chiefs*, who desires his acquaintance on her own behalf and that of her sister Anna Maria, almost equally popular at the hour by her romance of *The Hungarian Brothers*. By all this, says Keats, he feels more obliged than flattered — 'so obliged that I will not at present give you an extravaganza of a Lady Romancer. I will be introduced to them if it be merely for the pleasure of writing to you about it — I shall certainly see a new race of People.' Pity he failed to carry out his purpose: pen-portraits satirical and other are not lacking of these admired sisters, the tall and tragical Jane, the blonde and laughing Anna Maria, 'La Penserosa' and 'L'Allegra,' but a sketch by Keats would have been an interesting addition to them. Still in the same letter, he complains of the sore throat which he finds it hard to shake off, and tells how he has given up or all but given up taking snuff (nearly everybody in that generation snuffed), and how he has been shooting with Dilke on Hampstead Heath and shot a tomtit, — a feat which for a moment calls up this divine poet to our minds in the guise of one of the cockney sportsmen of Seymour's caricatures. Never mind: he can afford it.

From an enquiry about the expected baby in America, — 'will the little bairn have made his entrance before you have this? Kiss it for me, and when it can first know a cheese from a Caterpillar show it my picture twice a week,' — from this he passes to the reassuring statement that the attack upon him in the Quarterly has in some quarters done him actual service. He tells how constrained and out of his element he feels in ordinary society; a common experience of genius, and part of the price it pays for living at a different level and temperature of thought and feeling from the herd. 'I am passing a Quiet day — which I have not done for a long while — and if I do continue so, I feel I must again begin with my poetry — for if I am not in action of mind or Body I am in pain — and from that I suffer greatly by going into parties where from the rules of society and a natural pride I am obliged to smother my Spirit and look like an Idiot — because I feel my impulses given way to would too much amaze them — I live under an everlasting restraint — never relieved except when I am composing — so I will write away.' And resuming apparently on Christmas Day: — 'I think you knew before you left England, that my next subject would be "the fall of Hyperion." I went on a little with it last night, but it will take some time to get into the vein again. I will not give you any extracts, because I wish the whole to make an impression. I have however a few Poems which you will like, and I will copy out on the next sheet.' Nearly a week later he adds, 'I will insert any little pieces I may write — though I will not give any extracts from my large poem which is scarce began.' The phrase about *Hyperion* must be taken as indicating on how great a scale he had conceived the poem rather than how little he had yet written of it. In point of fact all we have of this mighty fragment must have been written either by his brother's bedside in September-October 1818 (but then certainly only a little) or else in these Christmas weeks from mid-December to mid-January 1818-19. The short poems he sends are the spirited sets of heptasyllabics, *Fancy*, and *Lines on the Mermaid Tavern*, the former one of the best things in the second and lighter class of his work: and with them the fragment written for music, 'I had a dove.' In relation to these he says 'It is my intention to wait a few years before I publish any minor poems — and then I hope to have a volume of some worth — and which those people will relish who cannot bear the burthen of a long poem.'

Presently Charles Lamb comes for a moment upon the scene. 'I have seen Lamb lately — Brown and I were taken by Hunt to Novello's — there we were devastated and excruciated with bad and repeated puns — Brown don't want to go again.' Punning, like snuffing, was the all but universal fashion of that age, as those of us can best realize who are old enough to remember grandfathers that belonged to it; and judging by the specimens Brown and Keats have themselves left, puns too bad for them are scarce imaginable. Novello is of course the distinguished organist, composer and music-publisher, Vincent Novello, whose Sunday evening musical parties were frequented by all the Lamb and Hunt circle, and whose eldest daughter, Mary Victoria, was married some ten years later to Cowden Clarke. At this time she was but a child of ten, but writing many years afterwards she has left a vivid reminiscence of Keats at her father's house, 'with his picturesque head, leaning against the instruments, one foot raised on his knee and smoothed beneath his hands' (an attitude said to have been perpetuated in a lost portrait by Severn). Is the above a memory of the one evening only which Keats himself mentions, or of others when his love of music may have drawn him to the Novellos' house in spite of the puns and of company for the moment not much to his taste? For the ways of Hunt and some of his circle, their mutual flatteries, their habit of trivial, chirping ecstasy over the things they liked, their superfluity of glib, complacent comment rubbing the bloom off sacred beauties of art and poetry and nature, were jarring on Keats' nerves just now; and though perfectly aware of Hunt's essential virtues of kind-heartedness and good comradeship, he writes with some irritability of impatience: —

Hunt has asked me to meet Tom Moore some day so you shall hear of him. The night we went to Novello's there was a complete set-to of Mozart and punning. I was so completely tired of it that if I were to follow my own inclinations I should never meet any one of that set again, not even Hunt who is certainly a pleasant fellow in the main when you are with him — but in reality he is vain, egotistical, and disgusting in matters of taste and in morals. He understands many a beautiful thing; but then, instead of giving other minds credit for the same degree of perception as he himself professes — he begins an explanation in such a curious manner that our taste and self-love is offended continually. Hunt does one harm by making fine things petty and beautiful things hateful. Through him I am indifferent to Mozart, I care not for white Busts — and many a glorious thing when associated with him becomes a nothing. This distorts one's mind — makes one's thoughts bizarre — perplexes one in the standard of Beauty.

A little later he improvises a sample, not more than mildly satirical, from a comedy he professes to be planning on the ways and manners of Hunt and his satellites.

In the same letter a new personage makes her momentous entry on the scene. 'Mrs Brawne who took Brown's house for the summer still resides at Hampstead — she is a very nice woman — and her daughter senior is I think beautiful and elegant, graceful, silly, fashionable, and strange — we have a little tiff now and then, and she behaves better, or I must have sheered off.' This Mrs Brawne was a widow lady of West Indian connexions and some little fortune, with a daughter, Fanny, just grown up and two younger children. She had rented Brown's house while he and Keats were away in Scotland, and had naturally become acquainted with the Dilkes living next door and sharing a common garden. After Brown's return Mrs Brawne moved with her family to a house in Downshire Street close by. The acquaintance with the Dilkes was kept up, and it was through them, not long after he came back from Scotland, that Keats first met Fanny Brawne. His next words about her are these: —

Shall I give you Miss Brawne? She is about my height with a fine style of countenance of the lengthened sort — she manages to make her hair look well — her nostrils are fine — though a little painful — her mouth is bad and good — her Profile is better than her full-face which indeed is not full but pale and thin without showing any bone. Her shape is very graceful and so are her movements — her Arms are good, her hands bad-ish her feet tolerable — she is not seventeen — but she is ignorant — monstrous in her behaviour, flying out in all directions, calling people such names that I was forced lately to make use of the term *Minx* — this is I think not from any innate vice but from a penchant she has for acting stylishly. I am however tired of such style and shall decline any more of it.

An attraction which has begun by repulsion is ever the most dangerous of all. The heightened emotional strain of his weeks of tendance on his dying brother had laid Keats open to both influences at their fullest power; he was ripe, as several passages from his letters have made us feel, for the tremendous adventure of love; and the 'new, strange, and threatening sorrow' from which he had with relief declared himself escaped when the momentary lure of the East-Indian Charmian left him fancy-free, was about to fall on him in good earnest now. Before many weeks he was hopelessly enslaved, and passion teaching him a sensitive secretiveness and reserve, he says to brother and sister no word more of his enslaver except by way of the lightest passing allusion. From his first semi-sarcastic account of her above quoted, as well as from Severn's mention of her likeness to the draped figure in Titian's picture of Sacred and Profane Love, and from the full-length silhouette of her that has been preserved, it is possible to realise something of her aspect and presence.

A brisk and blooming young beauty of a little over eighteen (Keats' 'not seventeen' is a mistake) with blonde hair and vivid palish colouring, a somewhat sharply cut aquiline cast of features, a slight, shapely figure rather short than tall, a liveliness of manner bordering on the boisterous, and no doubt some taking air and effluence of youth and vitality and sex, — such was Fanny Brawne externally, but of her character we have scant means of judging. Neither she nor her mother can have been worldly-minded, or they would never have encouraged the attentions of a youth like Keats, whose prospects were problematical or null. It is clear that, though certainly high-spirited, inexperienced, and self-confident, she was kind and in essentials constant to her lover, and patient and unresentful under his occasional wild outbursts of jealousy and suspicion. But it seems equally clear that she did not half realise what manner of man he was, nor how high and privileged was the charge committed to her. She had no objection to the prospect of a long engagement, and despite her lover's remonstrances held herself free in the meantime to enjoy to the full the pleasures of her age and the admiration of other men. One day early in the new year Keats took the devoted Severn to call on his new friends. Severn was much pleased with the mother, who seems to have been in truth a cultivated kind and gentle person; but he did not take to the daughter or even much admire her looks, and though perceiving her attraction for Keats did not then or till long afterwards realise the fatal strength of its hold upon him. 'That poor idle Thing of Womankind to whom he has so unaccountably attached himself' — so she is styled by Reynolds in a letter to Taylor a year and a half later. Brown, who knew her much better, and whose friendship with her sometimes showed itself in gallantries at which Keats writhed in secret, writes of her always in terms of kindness and respect, but never very explicitly. The very few of Keats' friends who came to be in his confidence, including Dilke and his wife, seem to have been agreed, although they bore her no ill will, in regarding the attachment as a misfortune for him.

So it assuredly was: so probably under the circumstances must any passion for a woman have been. Blow on blow had in truth begun to fall on Keats, as though in fulfilment of the constitutional misgivings to which he was so often secretly a prey. First the departure of his brother George had deprived him of his closest friend, to whom alone he had from boyhood been accustomed to confide those obsessions of his darker hours and in confiding to find relief from them. Next the exertions of his Scottish tour had proved too much for his strength, and laid him open to the attacks of his hereditary enemy, consumption. Coming back, he had found his brother Tom almost at his last gasp in the clutch of that enemy, and in nursing him had both lived in spirit through all his pains and breathed for many weeks a close atmosphere of infection. At the same time the gibes of the reviewers, little as they might touch his inner self, came to teach him the harshness and carelessness of the world's judgments, and the precariousness of his practical hopes from literature. Now were to be added the pangs of love, — love requited indeed, but having no near or sure prospect of fruition: and even love disdained might have made him suffer less. The passion took him, as it often takes consumptives, in its fiercest form: Love the limb-loosener, the bitter-sweet torment, the wild beast there is no withstanding, never harried a more helpless victim.

By what stages the coils closed on him we can only guess. His own account of the matter to Fanny Brawne was that he had written himself her vassal within a week of their first meeting: which took place, we know, some time during the period of watching by Tom's sickbed. After he went to live with Brown in December they must have met frequently. Probably it was this new attraction, as well as his chronic throat trouble and his concern over Haydon's affairs, which made him postpone a promised visit to Dilke's relations in Hampshire from Christmas until mid-January. He then carried out his promise, going to join Brown at Bedhampton, the home of Dilke's brother-in-law Mr John Snook. He liked his hosts and received pleasure from his visit, but was unwell and during a stay of a fortnight only once went outside the garden. This was to a gathering of country clergy reinforced by two bishops, at the consecration of a chapel built by a great Jew-convertor, a Mr Way. The ceremony got on his nerves and caused him to write afterwards to his brother an entertaining splenetic diatribe on the clerical character and physiognomy. He spent also a few days with Dilke's father in Chichester, and went out twice to dowager card parties. These social pleasures were naught to him, and his spirits, like his health, were low. But his genius was never more active. We have seen in the midst of what worries and interruptions he had worked before and during Christmas at *Hyperion*, the fragment which in our language stands next in epic quality to *Paradise Lost*. At Bedhampton in January, on some thin sheets of thin paper brought down for the purpose, he wrote the *Eve of St Agnes*, for its author merely 'a little poem,' for us a masterpiece aglow in every line with the vital quintessence of romance.

No word of Keats' own or of his friends prepares us for this new achievement or informs when he began first to think of the subject. It must of course have been ripening in his mind some good while before he thus suddenly and swiftly cast it into shape. When he wrote three months earlier of having to seek relief beside the sickbed of his brother by 'plunging into abstract images,' were they images of primeval Greek gods and Titans only, or were these contrasted figures and colours of mediæval romance beginning to occupy his imagination at the same time? Had the subject perhaps come into his mind as long ago as the preceding March, when Hunt and Reynolds and he were having the talks about Boccaccio which resulted in Keats' *Isabella* and Reynolds's *Garden of Florence* and *Ladye of Provence*? We shall see that Boccaccio counts for something in Keats' treatment of the St Agnes' Eve story, so that the supposition is at least plausible. Or may it even have been of this story and not, as is commonly assumed, of *Hyperion* that he was thinking as far back as September 1817 when he wrote to Haydon from Oxford of the 'new romance' he had in his mind? Woodhouse does not throw much light on such questions when he tells us that 'the subject was suggested by Mrs Jones.' This name, uncongenial to the muse (excepting the muse of Wordsworth) is otherwise unknown in connexion with Keats. Did the same lady also tell him of the tradition concerning St Mark's day (April 25th), and so become the 'only begetter' of that remarkable fragment *The Eve of St Mark*, which he wrote (Woodhouse again is the authority for the dates) between the 13th and 17th of February after his return to Hampstead? In connexion with Keats few stones have been left unturned for further personal or critical research, but here is one.

Keats was back at Hampstead by the end of January and it must have been very soon afterwards that he became the declared and accepted lover of Fanny Brawne, savouring intensely thenceforward all the tantalising sweets and bitters of that estate, though nothing was said to friends about the engagement. From the first he suffered severely from the sense of her freedom to enjoy pleasures and excitements for which neither his health nor his social habits and inclinations fitted him. The tale of the *Eve of St Mark*, begun and broken off just at this time, may possibly, as Rossetti thought, have been designed to turn on the remorse of a young girl for sufferings of a like kind inflicted on her lover and ending in his death. However that may be, we have two direct cries from his heart, one of pure love-yearning, the other of racking jealousy, which were written, if I read the evidences aright, almost immediately after the engagement and can be dated almost to a day. These are the first version, which has only lately become known, of the 'Bright Star' sonnet, and the ode *To Fanny* published posthumously by Lord Houghton. Both carry internal evidence of having been written before the winter was out: the sonnet in the words which invoke the star as watching the moving waters,

> Or gazing at the new soft-fallen mask
> Of snow upon the mountains and the moors;
> the ode in the lines,
> I come, I see thee as thou standest there,
> Beckon me not into the wintry air.

Now it happens that this year there was frost and rough weather late in February, with snowfalls on the afternoon of the 24th and again the following morning. I imagine both sonnet and ode to have been written while the cold spell lasted, the sonnet probably before dawn on the actual morning of the 25th. As slightly changed in form a year and a half later this sonnet has been long endeared to us all as one of the most beautiful in the language: I shall defer its discussion till we come to the date of this recast. The ode has flaws, for to make good or even bearable poetry out of that humiliating and grotesque passion of physical jealousy is a hard matter. It begins poorly, with a sense of discord, in the first stanza, between the choking violence of feeling expressed and the artificial form into which its expression is cast. But if we leave out this stanza, and also the fifth and sixth, which are a little common and unequal, we get an appeal as painful, indeed, as it is passionate, yet lacking neither in courtesy nor dignity, and conveyed in a strain of verse almost without fault: —

> Ah! dearest love, sweet home of all my fears,
> And hopes, and joys, and panting miseries, —
> Tonight, if I may guess, thy beauty wears
> A smile of such delight,
> As brilliant and as bright,
> As when with ravished, aching, vassal eyes,
> Lost in soft amaze,
> I gaze, I gaze!
> Who now, with greedy looks, eats up my feast?
> What stare outfaces now my silver moon?
> Ah! keep that hand unravished at the least;
> Let, let the amorous burn —
> But, pr'ythee, do not turn
> The current of your heart from me so soon.
> O! save, in charity,
> The quickest pulse for me.
> Save it for me, sweet love! though music breathe
> Voluptuous visions into the warm air;
> Though swimming through the dance's dangerous wreath,
> Be like an April day,
> Smiling and cold and gay,
> A temperate lily, temperate as fair;
> Then, Heaven! there will be
> A warmer June for me.
> Ah! if you prize my subdu'd soul above
> The poor, the fading, brief pride of an hour;
> Let none profane my Holy See of Love,
> Or with a rude hand break
> The sacramental cake:
> Let none else touch the just new-budded flower:
> If not — may my eyes close,
> Love! on their last repose.

In both of these poems Keats soothes himself with thoughts of dying, and they are doubtless among the things he had in mind when two or three months later, in the ode *To a Nightingale*, he speaks of having invoked Death by soft names 'in many a musèd rhyme.'

Fearing the intrusion of what in another sonnet of the time he calls 'The dragon-world and all its hundred eyes,' he was intensely jealous in guarding his secret from friends and acquaintances; and in writing even to those dearest to him he lets slip no word that might betray it. To his brother he merely says, 'Miss Brawne and I have now and then a chat and a tiff,' while to his young sister he writes on February 27th that he wishes he could come to her at Walthamstow for a month or so, packing off Mrs Abbey to town, and get her to teach him 'a few common dancing steps,' — for what reason, to us too pathetically evident, he of course gives no hint.

On February 14th, about a fortnight after his return from Hampshire, and on the very day when according to Woodhouse he began *The Eve of St Mark*, Keats had put pen to a new journal-letter for America. A straw showing how the wind was blowing with him is his mention that the Reynolds sisters, whose company used to be among his chief pleasures, are staying at the Dilkes next door and that he finds them 'very dull.' So, we may guess, will they on their parts have found him. His only other correspondents in these weeks are Haydon and his young sister

Fanny. Early in March Haydon returned to the charge about the loan. 'My dear Keats — now I feel the want of your promised assistance.... Before the 20th if you could help me it would be nectar and manna and all the blessings of gratified thirst.' Keats had intended for Haydon's relief some of the money due to him from his brother Tom's share in their grandmother's gift; which he expected his guardian to make over to him at once on his application. But difficulties of all sorts were raised, and for some time after the new year he had the annoyance of finding himself unable to do as he had hoped. When by-and-by Haydon writes, in the true borrower's vein, reproaching him with his promise and his failure to keep it, Keats replies without loss of temper, explaining that he had supposed himself to have the necessary means in his hand, but has been baffled by unforeseen difficulties in getting possession of his money. Moreover he finds that much less remains of his small inheritance than he had supposed, and even if all he had were laid on the table, the intended loan would leave him barely enough to live on for two years. Incidentally he mentions that he has already lent sums to various friends amounting in all to near £200, of which he expects the repayment late if ever. The upshot of the matter was that Keats contrived somehow to lend Haydon thirty pounds which he could very ill spare.

To his young sister Keats' letters during the same period are charming. He lets her perceive nothing of his anxieties, and is full of brotherly tenderness and careful advice; of interest in her preparation for her approaching confirmation; of regrets that she is kept so much from him by the scruples of Mr and Mrs Abbey, with humorous admonitions to patience under that lady's 'unfeeling and ignorant gabble'; and of plans for coming over to see her when the weather and his throat allow or when he is in cash to pay the coach fare. On one day he is serious, begging her to lean on him in all things: — 'We have been very little together: but you have not the less been with me in thought. You have no one else in the world besides me who would sacrifice anything for you — I feel myself the only Protector you have. In all your little troubles think of me with the thought that there is at least one person in England who if he could would help you out of them — I live in hopes of being able to make you happy.' Another day he is all playfulness, thinking of various little presents to please her, a selection of Tassie's gems, flowers from the Tottenham nursery garden, drawing materials — and here follows the passage above quoted (p. 10) against keeping live birds or fishes: —

They are better in the trees and the water, — though I must confess even now a partiality for a handsome globe of gold-fish — then I would have it hold ten pails of water and be fed continually fresh through a cool pipe with another pipe to let through the floor — well ventilated they would preserve all their beautiful silver and crimson. Then I would put it before a handsome painted window and shade it all round with Myrtles and Japonicas. I should like the window to open on to the Lake of Geneva — and there I'd sit and read all day like the picture of somebody reading.

For some time, in these letters to his sister, Keats expresses a constant anxiety at getting no news from their brother George at the distant Kentucky settlement whither he and his bride had at their last advices been bound. Pending such news, he keeps writing up his journal for them, and for nearly four months it grew and grew. Still in February, he promises to send in the next packet his '*Pot of Basil*, *St Agnes' Eve*, and if I should have finished it, a little thing called the *Eve of St Mark*. You see what fine Mother Radcliffe names I have — it is not my fault — I do not search for them. I have not gone on with *Hyperion*, for to tell the truth I have not been in great cue for writing lately — I must wait for the spring to rouse me up a little!'

As it fell out, he never went on either with *Hyperion* or with the *Eve of St Mark*, the romance just so promisingly begun. For fully two months after breaking off the latter fragment (February 17th or 18th) he was quite out of cue for writing, and produced nothing except the ode *To Fanny* (if I am right as to its date) and a few personal sonnets. Many causes, we can feel, were working together to check for the time being the creative impulse within him: the mere disturbing influence of the spring season for one thing; discouragement at the public reception of his work for another, though this was a motive external and relatively secondary; the results of a deliberate mental stock-taking of his own powers and performances for a third; and more deep-seated and compulsive, though unexpressed, than any of these, the love-passion by which three-fourths of his soul and consciousness had come to be absorbed. Here, from a letter to Haydon of March 8, is an example of what I mean by his mental stock-taking. The resolution it expresses is of course more a matter of mood than of fixed purpose: —

I have come to this resolution — never to write for the sake of writing or making a poem, but from running over with any little knowledge or experience which many years of reflection may perhaps give me; otherwise I will be dumb. What imagination I have I shall enjoy, and greatly, for I have experienced the satisfaction of having great conceptions without the trouble of sonnetteering. I will not spoil my love of gloom by writing an Ode to Darkness.

With respect to my livelihood, I will not write for it, — for I will not run with that most vulgar of all crowds, the literary. Such things I ratify by looking upon myself, and trying myself at lifting mental weights, as it were. I am three and twenty, with little knowledge and middling intellect. It is true that in the height of enthusiasm I have been cheated into some fine passages; but that is not the thing.

Some five weeks later, about mid-April, we find that Haydon himself has been a contributing cause to Keats' poetic inactivity by his behaviour in regard to the loan which Keats had hoped but so far been unable to make him. The failure he writes, has not been his fault: —

I am doubly hurt at the slightly reproachful tone of your note and at the occasion of it, — for it must be some other disappointment; you seem'd so sure of some important help when last I saw you — now you have maimed me again; I was whole, I had begun reading again — when your note came I was engaged in a Book. I dread as much as a Plague the idle fever of two months more without any fruit. I will walk over the first fine day: then see what aspect your affairs have taken, and if they should continue gloomy walk into the City to Abbey and get his consent for I am persuaded that to me alone he will not concede a jot.

In the journal-letter of these weeks to his brother and sister-in-law, mentioning how he had been asked to join Woodhouse over a bottle of claret at his coffee-house, he breaks into a rhapsody over the virtues and wholesomeness of that beverage and adds 'this same claret is the only palate-passion I have — I forgot game — I must plead guilty to the breast of a Partridge, the back of a hare, the backbone of a grouse, the wing and side of a Pheasant, and a Woodcock *passim* .' Turning to his own affairs, he says, —

I am in no despair about them — my poem has not at all succeeded; in the course of a year or so I think I shall try the public again — in a selfish point of view I should suffer my pride and my contempt of public opinion to hold me silent — but for yours and Fanny's sake I will pluck up a spirit and try again. I have no doubt of success in a course of years if I persevere — but it must be patience — for the Reviews have enervated and made indolent men's minds — few think for themselves. These Reviews are getting more and more powerful, especially the Quarterly — they are like a superstition which the more it prostrates the Crowd and the longer it continues the more powerful it becomes just in proportion to their increasing weakness. I was in hopes that when people saw, as they must do now, all the trickery and iniquity of these Plagues they would scout them, but no, they are like the spectators at the Westminster cockpit — they like the battle — and do not care who wins or who loses.

Among other matters he has a long story to tell about his friend Bailey's fickleness in love. It appears that Bailey, after a first unfortunate love-affair, had during the past year been paying his addresses to Mariane Reynolds, begging that she would take time to consider her answer, and that while her decision was still uncertain Bailey, to the great indignation of all the Reynolds family and a little to Keats' own, had engaged himself in Scotland to the sister of his friend Gleig, afterwards well known as author of *The Subaltern* and Chaplain General to the Forces. Next Keats begins quoting with a natural zest of admiration, almost in full, that incomparable piece of studied and sustained invective, Hazlitt's *Letter to William Gifford Esqr.* , beside which Gifford's own controversial virulences seem relatively blunt and boorish. Half way through Keats has to say he will copy the rest tomorrow, —

for the candles are burnt down and I am using the wax taper — which has a long snuff on it — the fire is at its last click — I am sitting with my back to it with one foot rather askew upon the rug and the other with the heel a little elevated from the carpet — I am writing this on the Maid's tragedy which I have read since tea with Great pleasure. Beside this volume of Beaumont and Fletcher — there are on the table two volumes of Chaucer and a new work of Tom Moore's called *Tom Cribb's Memorial to Congress*, — nothing in it. These are trifles but I require nothing so much of you but that you will give me a like description of yourselves, however it may be when you are writing to me. Could I see that same thing done of any great Man long since dead it would be a great delight: As to know in what position Shakespeare sat when he began 'To be or not to be' — such things become interesting from distance of time or place. I hope you are both now in that sweet sleep which no two beings deserve more than you do — I must fancy you so — and please myself in the fancy of speaking a prayer and a blessing over you and your lives — God bless you — I whisper good night in your ears and you will dream of me.

This is on the 13th of March. Six days later he gives another picture, this time of his state of body rather than of mind: —

This morning I am in a sort of temper, indolent and supremely careless — I long after a stanza or two of Thomson's *Castle of Indolence* — my passions are all asleep, from my having slumbered till nearly eleven, and weakened the animal fibre all over me, to a delightful sensation, about three degrees on this side of faintness. If I had teeth of pearl and the breath of lilies I should call it languor, but as I am I must call it laziness. In this state of effeminacy the fibres of the brain are relaxed in common with the rest of the body, and to such a happy degree that pleasure has no show of enticement and pain no unbearable power. Neither Poetry, nor Ambition, nor Love have any alertness of countenance as they pass by me; they seem rather like figures on a Greek vase — a Man and two women whom no one but myself could distinguish in their disguisement. This is the only happiness, and is a rare instance of the advantage of the body overpowering the Mind.

The criticism is foolish which sees in this passage the expression of a languid, self-indulgent nature, and especially foolish considering the footnote in which Keats observes that at the moment he has a black eye. The black eye was no doubt the mark of the fight in which he had lately well thrashed a young blackguard of a butcher whom he found tormenting a kitten. That the said fight took place just about this time is clear by the following evidences. Cowden Clarke, in his recollections communicated privately to Lord Houghton, writes, 'The last time I saw Keats was during his residence with Mr Brown. I spent the day with him; and he read to me the poem he had last finished — *The Eve of St Agnes*. Shortly after this I removed many miles from London, and was spared the sorrow of beholding the progress of the disease that was to take him from us. When I last saw him he was in fine health and spirits; and he told me that he had, not long before our meeting, had an encounter with a fellow who was tormenting a kitten, or puppy, and who was big enough to have eaten him; that they fought for nearly an hour; and that his opponent was led home.' The reading of the *Eve of St Agnes* fixes the date of Clarke's visit as after Keats' return from Chichester at the end of January, and a remark of Keats, writing to his brother between February the 14th and 19th, that he has not seen Clarke 'for God knows how long', further fixes it as after mid-February; while the latest limit is set by the fact that by Easter Clarke had gone away to live with his family at Ramsgate, where they had settled after his father had given up the Enfield school. What the 'effeminacy' passage really expresses is of course no more than a passing mood of lassitude, gratefully welcomed as a relief from the strain of feelings habitually more acute than nature could well bear. Ambition he was schooling, or trying to school, himself to cherish in moderation, but it was not often or for long that the stings either of poetry or of love abated for him the least jot of their bitter-sweet intensity, or that anticipations of poverty or the fever of incipient disease relaxed their grip.

Though Keats' letters to his brother and sister-in-law contain no confidence on the subject, some of the verses he encloses betray in abstract form the strain of passion under which he was living; notably the fine weird sonnet on a dream which came to him after reading the Paolo and Francesca passage in Dante, and the other sonnet beginning 'Why did I laugh tonight?' In copying this last, he adds careful and considerate words of reassurance lest his brother should take alarm for his sake:

I am ever afraid that your anxiety for me will lead you to fear for the violence of my temperament continually smothered down: for that reason I did not intend to have sent you the following sonnet — but Look over the two last pages and ask yourselves whether I have not that in me which will bear the buffets of the world. It will be the best comment on my sonnet; it will show you that it was written with no Agony but that of ignorance; with no thirst of anything but Knowledge when pushed to the point though the first steps to it were through my human passions — and perhaps I must confess a little bit of my heart —

> Why did I laugh tonight? No voice will tell:
> No God, no Demon of severe response
> Deigns to reply from Heaven or from Hell. —
> Then to my human heart I turn at once —
> Heart! thou and I are here sad and alone;

Say wherefore did I laugh? O mortal pain!
  O Darkness! Darkness! ever must I moan

> To question Heaven and Hell and Heart in vain!
> Why did I laugh? I know this being's lease;
> My fancy to its utmost blisses spreads:
> Yet could I on this very midnight cease
> And the world's gaudy ensigns see in shreds.
> Verse, fame and Beauty are intense indeed
> But Death intenser — Death is Life's High meed.
> I went to bed and enjoyed uninterrupted sleep. Sane I went to bed and sane I arose.

This is yet another of those invocations to friendly Death to which he himself refers in the *Ode to the Nightingale* written a few weeks later, and in its phrase 'on this very midnight cease' anticipates one of the great lines of the ode itself.

No letter of Keats — or of any one — is richer than this of February to May 1819 in variety of mood and theme and interest. It contains two of the freshest and most luminous of his discursive passages of meditation on life and on the nature of the soul and the meaning of things: passages showing a native power of thought untrained indeed, but also unhampered, by academic knowledge and study, and hardly to be surpassed for their union of steady human commonsense with airy ease and play of imaginative speculation. In one, starting from reflections on the unforeseen way in which circumstances, like clouds, gather and burst, reflections suggested by the expected death of the father of his friend Haslam, he calls up a series of pictures of the instinctiveness with which men, like animals, — the hawk, the robin, the stoat, the deer, — go about their purposes; considers the rarity of the exceptional human beings whose disinterestedness helps on the progress of the world; and then turns his thoughts on himself with the comment, —

Even here, though I myself am pursuing the same instinctive course as the veriest human animal you can think of, I am, however young, writing at random, straining at particles of light in the midst of a great darkness, without knowing the bearing of any one assertion, of any one opinion. Yet may I not in this be free from sin? May there not be superior beings, amused with any graceful, though instinctive, attitude my mind may fall into as I am entertained with the alertness of the Stoat or the anxiety of a Deer?

In the other passage he disposes of all Rousseau-Godwin theories of human perfectibility by a consideration of the physical frame and order of the world we live in, the flaws and violences which mar and jar it, and which its human offspring are likely to derive from and share with it until the end; and, provisionally accepting the doctrine of immortality, he broaches of his own a scheme of the spiritual discipline for the sake of which, as he suggests, the life of men on this so imperfect earth may have been designed.

In marked, not always entirely pleasant contrast with these passages of thought and beauty Keats sends his brother such things as a summary of a satiric fairy story of Brown's and an impromptu comic tale of his own in verse, much in Brown's manner, about a princess, a mule, and a dwarf: both of them apparently to his mind amusing, but to us rather silly and the former a little coarse: also some friendly satiric verses of his own on Brown in the Spenserian stanza. He tells how he has been turning over the love-letters palmed off by way of hoax upon his brother Tom by Charles Wells in the character of a pretended 'Amena', and vows fiercely to make Wells suffer for his heartlessness; gossips further of Dilke and his overstrained parental anxiety about his boy at school; asks a string of playful questions about his sister-in-law and her daily doings; and in another place gives us, in the mention of a casual walk and talk with Coleridge, the liveliest record we have of the astonishing variety of matters and mysteries over which that philosopher was capable, in a short hour's conversation, of ranging without pause or taking breath: —

Last Sunday I took a walk towards Highgate and in the lane that winds by the side of Lord Mansfield's park I met Mr Green our Demonstrator at Guy's in conversation with Coleridge — I joined them, after enquiring by a look whether it would be agreeable — I walked with him at his alderman-after-dinner pace for near two miles I suppose. In those two Miles he broached a thousand things — let me see if I can give you a list — Nightingales, Poetry — on Poetical Sensation — Metaphysics — Different genera and species of Dreams — Nightmare — a dream accompanied with a sense of touch — single and double touch — a dream related — First and second consciousness — the difference explained between will and Volition — so say metaphysicians from a want of smoking the second consciousness — Monsters — the Kraken — Mermaids — Southey believes in them — Southey's belief too much diluted — a Ghost story — Good morning — I heard his voice as he came towards me — I heard it as he moved away — I had heard it all the interval — if it may be called so. He was civil enough to ask me to call on him at Highgate.

It is amusing to note how the time and distance covered by his own encyclopædic volubility shrank afterwards in Coleridge's memory. In his *Table Talk* taken down thirteen years later his account of the meeting is recorded as follows (with the name of his companion left blank: I fill it in from Keats' letter): 'A loose, slack, not well-dressed youth met Mr Green and myself in a lane near Highgate. Green knew him, and spoke. It was Keats. He was introduced to me, and stayed a minute or so. After he had left us a little way, he came back, and said, "Let me carry away the memory, Coleridge, of having pressed your hand!" "There is death in that hand," I said to Green, when Keats was gone; yet this was, I believe, before the consumption showed itself distinctly.' The story of Coleridge's observation after the handshake is no doubt exact: the 'not well-dressed' in his description of Keats may very well be so too: but the 'loose' and 'slack' applied to his appearance must have been drawn from the sage's inward eye, as all accounts are agreed as to Keats' well-knit compactness of person. One cannot but regret that Keats failed to follow up the introduction by going, as invited, to see Coleridge at Highgate: but in all cases save those of Hunt and Haydon, his contact with distinguished seniors seems thus to have stopped short at kindly and respectful acquaintance and not to have been pushed to intimacy.

Another, somewhat divergent, account of the meeting taken down, also from Coleridge's lips, by Mr John Frere three years earlier has only lately been published. Its inaccuracy in details is evident, but there is much sense as well as kindness in Coleridge's remarks on the reviews and their effect: —

C. Poor Keats, I saw him once. Mr Green, whom you have heard me mention, and I were walking out in these parts, and we were overtaken by a young man of a very striking countenance whom Mr Green recognised and shook hands with, mentioning my name; I wish Mr Green had introduced me, for I did not know who it was. He passed on, but in a few moments sprung back and said, 'Mr Coleridge, allow me the honour of shaking your hand.' I was struck by the energy of his manner, and gave him my hand. He passed on and we stood still looking after him, when Mr Green said, 'Do you know who that is? That is Keats, the poet.' 'Heavens!' said I, 'when I shook him by the hand there was death!' This was about two years before he died.

F. But what was it?

C. I cannot describe it. There was a heat and a dampness in the hand. To say that his death was caused by the Review is absurd, but at the same time it is impossible adequately to conceive the effect which it must have had on his mind. It is very well for those who have a place in the world and are independent to talk of these things, they can bear such a blow, so can those who have a strong religious principle; but all men are not born Philosophers, and all men have not those advantages of birth and education. Poor Keats had not, and it is impossible I say to conceive the effect which such a Review must have had upon him, knowing as he did that he had his way to make in the world by his own exertions, and conscious of the genius within him.

In the Leigh Hunt circle it had always been the fashion to regard with contempt, mingled with regret, Wordsworth's more childishly worded poems and ballads of humble life such as *The Idiot Boy* and *Alice Fell*. The announcement of his forthcoming piece, *Peter Bell*, now drew from John Hamilton Reynolds an anonymous skit in the shape of an adroit and rather stinging anticipatory parody, which Taylor and Hessey published in the course of this April despite a strong letter of protest addressed to them by Coleridge when he heard of their intention: a protest greatly to his credit considering his and Wordsworth's recent estrangement. Keats copies for his brother the draft of a notice which at Reynolds's request he has been writing of this skit for the *Examiner*, taking care to turn it compatibly with due reverence for the sublimer works of the master parodied. The thing is quite deftly and tactfully done, and seems to show that Keats might have made himself, could he have bent his mind to it, a skilled hand at newspaper criticism. 'You will call it a little politic,' he says to his brother — 'seeing I keep clear of all parties — I say something for and against both parties — and suit it to the tone of the *Examiner* — I mean to say I do not unsuit it — and I believe I think what I say — I am sure I do — I and my conscience are in luck to-day — which is an excellent thing.'

At intervals throughout these two months Keats asserts and reasserts the strength of the hold which idleness has laid upon him so far as poetry is concerned. Thus on March 13 to his brother and sister-in-law: — 'I know not why poetry and I have been so distant lately; I must make some advances or she will cut me entirely': and again to the same on April 15, 'I am still at a standstill in versifying, I cannot do it yet with any pleasure.' To his young sister Fanny he had written two days earlier that his idleness had been growing upon him of late, 'so that it will require a great shake to get rid of it. I have written nothing and almost read nothing — but I must turn over a new leaf.' Within the next two weeks the dormant impulse began to re-awake in him with power. As we have seen, he had never quite stopped writing personal sonnets. Towards the end of the month we find him trying, not very successfully, to invent a new sonnet form, but soon reverting to his accustomed Shakespearean type of three quatrains closed by a couplet. Here is the better of two sonnets which he wrote on April 30 to express the present abatement of his former hot desire for fame: —

> Fame, like a wayward Girl, will still be coy
> To those who woo her with too slavish knees,
> But makes surrender to some thoughtless Boy,
> And dotes the more upon a heart at ease;
> She is a Gipsy, will not speak to those
> Who have not learnt to be content without her;
> A Jilt, whose ear was never whisper'd close,

> Who thinks they scandal her who talk about her;
> A very Gipsy is she, Nilus-born,
> Sister-in-law to jealous Potiphar;
> Ye lovesick Bards, repay her scorn for scorn,
> Ye Artists lovelorn, madmen that ye are!
> Make your best bow to her and bid adieu,
> Then, if she likes it, she will follow you.

The thought here is curiously anticipated in a passage of Browne's *Britannia's Pastorals*, itself reminiscent of a well known line in Theocritus. Is the coincidence a coincidence merely, or had the lines from Browne been working unconsciously in Keats' mind?

> True Fame is ever liken'd to our shade,
> He sooneth misseth her, that most hath made
> To overtake her; who so takes his wing,
> Regardless of her, she'll be following:
> Her true proprieties she thus discovers,
> 'Loves her contemners and contemns her Lovers.'

Two days earlier Keats had copied out in his letter for America, side by side with the words for a commonplace operatic chorus of the *Fairies of the Four Elements*, and as though it were of no greater value, that masterpiece of romantic and tragic symbolism on the wasting power of Love, *La Belle Dame sans Merci*. This title had already been haunting Keats' imagination when he wrote the *Eve of St Agnes*. He calls by it the air to which Porphyro touches his lute beside the sleeping Madeline. It is the title of a cold allegoric dialogue of the old French court poet Alan Chartier, which Keats knew in the translation traditionally ascribed to Chaucer. But except the title, Keats' new poem has nothing in common with the French or the Chaucerian *Belle Dame*. The form, the poetic mould, he chooses is that of a ballad of the 'Thomas the Rhymer' class, in which a mortal passes for a time into the abode and under the power of a being from the elfin world. Into this mould Keats casts — with suchlike imagery he invests — all the famine and fever of his private passion, fusing and alchemising by his art a remembered echo from William Browne, 'Let no bird sing,' and another from Wordsworth, 'Her eyes are wild,' into twelve stanzas of a new ballad music vitally his own and as weirdly ominous and haunting as the music of words can be. The metrical secret lies in shortening the last line of each stanza from four feet to two, the two to take in reading the full time of four, whereby the movement is made one of awed and bodeful slowness — but let us shrink from the risk of laying an analytic finger upon the methods of a magic that calls to be felt, not dissected. Known as it is by heart to all lovers of poetry, I will print the piece again here, partly for the reason that in some of the most accessible and authoritative recent editions it is unfortunately given with changes which rob it of half its magic: —

> O what can ail thee, knight-at-arms
> Alone and palely loitering?
> The sedge is withered from the lake,
> And no birds sing!
> O what can ail thee, knight-at-arms
> So haggard and so woe-begone?
> The squirrel's granary is full,
> And the harvest's done.
> I see a lily on thy brow,
> With anguish moist and fever dew;
> And on thy cheek a fading rose
> Fast withereth too —

I met a lady in the meads
Full beautiful, a faery's child;
Her hair was long, her foot was light,
And her eyes were wild —
I made a garland for her head,
And bracelets too, and fragrant zone;
She looked at me as she did love,
And made sweet moan —
I set her on my pacing steed,
And nothing else saw all day long;
For sideways would she lean, and sing
A faery's song —
She found me roots of relish sweet,
And honey wild, and manna dew;
And sure in language strange she said,
I love thee true —
She took me to her elfin grot,
And there she gazed and sighed full sore,
And there I shut her wild, wild eyes
With kisses four.
And there she lullèd me asleep,
And there I dreamed, ah woe betide,
The latest dream I ever dreamed
On the cold hill side.
I saw pale kings, and princes too,
Pale warriors, death-pale were they all;

Who cried — 'La Belle Dame sans Merci

Hath thee in thrall.'
I saw their starv'd lips in the gloam
With horrid warning gapèd wide,
And I awoke, and found me here
On the cold hill side.
And this is why I sojourn here
Alone and palely loitering,
Though the sedge is withered from the lake,
And no birds sing.

Keats of course gives his brother no hint of what to us seems so manifest, the application of these verses to his own predicament, and only adds a light and laughing comment on one of the rime-words. Closing his packet a few days later (May 3) he adds, as the last poem he has written, the *Ode to Psyche*. He wrote, as is well known, four other odes this spring, those *On Indolence*, *On a Grecian Urn*, *To a Nightingale* and *To Melancholy*. The *Ode to Psyche* has commonly been taken to be the latest of the five. I take it, on the contrary, to have been the first. Had he been ready with any of the others when he finished his letter, I think he would almost certainly have copied and sent on one or more of them also. Coupled with his reiterated assertion of complete poetic idleness, — 'the idle fever of two months without any fruit,' — lasting from mid-February until well past mid-April, the absence of all the four other odes from this packet must count as evidence that the *Ode to Psyche* represents the first wave of a new tide of inspiration — inspiration this time not narrative and creative but lyric and meditative — and that the rest of the odes followed and were composed in the course of May. Personally I am convinced that this was the case. I make no exception in regard to the ode *On Indolence*, although, seeing that it embodies just such a relaxed mood of mind and body as we have found recorded by Keats in his letter to his brother under date March 19, and embodies it with the selfsame imagery, it is usually assumed to have been written at or very nearly about the same date. But Keats in the ode itself expressly tells us otherwise, calling his mood at the hour of writing one of 'summer indolence' and defining the season as May-time, when the outdoor vines are newly bursting into leaf. Of course, it may be answered, a poet writing in March may perfectly well choose to advance the season to May by a poetic fiction. But would Keats in this case have felt any need or impulse to do so? I doubt it. Moreover a reference to the poem by Keats in a letter of early June shows that phrases of it were still hanging freshly in his memory and seems to imply that it was a thing then lately written. What happened, I take it, was either that Keats let the March vision, with its imagery of symbolic figures following one another as on a Greek sculptured urn, ripen in his mind until he was ready to compose upon it, and then attributed the vision itself to the season when he was actually putting it into verse; or else that, having fallen some time in May into a second mood of drowsiness and relaxation nearly repeating that of March, the same imagery for its expression arose naturally again in his mind.

The ode *On a Grecian Urn* is obviously of kindred, and probably of contemporary, inspiration with that *On Indolence*, and if the one belongs to May so doubtless does the other. That this is true of the Nightingale ode we know. Some time early in May, nightingales heard both in the Wentworth Place garden and in the grove beside the Spaniards inn at the upper end of the heath set Keats brooding on the contrast between the age-long permanence of that bird-song, older than history, and the fleeting lives of the generations of men that have listened to it; and one morning he took his chair out under a plum-tree in the garden and wrote down the immortal verses, in and out and back and forth on a couple of loose sheets which Brown, two hours after seeing him go out, found him folding away carelessly behind some books in his room. This discovery, says Brown, made him search for more such neglected scraps; and Keats acquiesced in the search, and moreover gave Brown leave to make copies of anything he might find. Haydon tells how Keats recited the new ode to him, 'in his low, tremulous undertone,' as they walked together in the Hampstead meadows; and it was no doubt on Haydon's suggestion that Keats let James Elmes, a subservient ally of Haydon's in all his battles with the academic powers, have it for publication in his periodical, the *Annals of the Fine Arts*, during the following July. For the date of the *Ode on Melancholy* the clues are less definite. Burton's *Anatomy* has clearly to do with inspiring it, but of this, and especially of the sections on the cure of Love-Melancholy, Keats' letters and some of his verses furnish evidence that he had been much of a reader all the spring. Particular phrases, however, in letters of May and early June expressing a very similar strain of feeling to that of the ode, besides its general resemblance to the rest of the group both as to form and mood, may be taken as approximately dating it.

Following these so fruitful labours (if I am right as to the dates) of May, came a month of strained indecision and anxiety during which Keats again could do no work. Questions of his own fortune and future were weighing heavily on his mind. For the time being he could not touch such small remainder of his grandmother's legacy as was still unexpended. A lawsuit threatened by the widow of his uncle Captain Jennings against his guardian Mr Abbey, in connexion with the administration of the trust, had had the effect for the time being of stopping his supplies from that quarter altogether. Thereupon he very gently asked Haydon to make an effort to repay his recent loan; who not only made none — 'he did not,' says Keats, 'seem to care much about it, but let me go without my money almost with nonchalance.' This was too much even for Keats' patience, and he declares that he shall never count Haydon a friend again. Nevertheless he by and by let old affection resume its sway, and entered into the other's interests and endured his exhortations as kindly as ever. Apart from Mrs Jennings's bequest, there was a not inconsiderable sum which, as we know, had been left invested by Mr Jennings for the direct benefit of his Keats grandchildren; but this sum could not be divided until Fanny Keats came of age, and there seems to have been no thought of John's anticipating his reversionary share. Indeed it is doubtful if the very existence of these and other funds lying by for them had not at this time been forgotten.

In this predicament Keats began very seriously to entertain the idea, which we have seen broached by him several times already, of seeking the post of surgeon on an East Indiaman as at least a temporary means of livelihood. He mentions the idea not only to George and to his young sister, but he debates it with a new correspondent, one of the Miss Jeffrey's of Teignmouth, whom he suddenly now addresses in terms of confidence which show how warm must have been their temporary friendship the year before: —

Your advice about the Indiaman is a very wise advice, because it just suits me, though you are a little in the wrong concerning its destroying the energies of Mind: on the contrary it would be the finest thing in the world to strengthen them — to be thrown among people who care not for you, with whom you have no sympathies forces the Mind upon its own resources, and leaves it free to make its speculations of the differences of human character and to class them with the calmness of a Botanist. An Indiaman is a little world. One of the great reasons that the English have produced the finest writers in the world is, that the English world has ill-treated them during their lives and foster'd them after their deaths. They have in general been trampled aside into the bye paths of life and seen the festerings of Society. They have not been treated like the Raphaels of Italy. And where is the Englishman and Poet who has given a magnificent Entertainment at the christening of one of his Hero's Horses as Boyardo did? He had a Castle in the Appenine. He was a noble Poet of Romance; not a miserable and mighty Poet of the human heart. The middle age of Shakespeare was all clouded over; his days were not more happy than Hamlet's who is perhaps more like Shakespeare himself in his common every day Life than any other of his Characters — Ben Johnson was a common Soldier and in the Low Countries in the face of two armies, fought a single combat with a French Trooper and slew him — For all this I will not go on board an Indiaman, nor for example's sake run my head into dark alleys: I daresay my discipline is to come, and plenty of it too. I have been very idle lately, very averse to writing; both from the overpowering idea of our dead poets and from abatement of my love of fame. I hope I am a little more of a Philosopher than I was, consequently a little less of a versifying Pet-lamb. I have put no more in Print or you should have had it. You will judge of my 1819 temper when I tell you that the thing I have most enjoyed this year has been writing an ode to Indolence.

The reader will have noticed in the phrase about 'versifying Pet-lamb' a repetition from this very ode *On Indolence*. Here is another confidence imparted to the same correspondent concerning his present mood and disposition: —

I have been always till now almost as careless of the world as a fly — my troubles were all of the Imagination — My brother George always stood between me and any dealings with the world. Now I find I must buffet it — I must take my stand upon some vantage ground and begin to fight — I must choose between despair and Energy — I choose the latter though the world has taken on a quakerish look with me, which I once thought was impossible —

> 'Nothing can bring back the hour
> Of splendour in the grass and glory in the flower.'
> I once thought this a Melancholist's dream.

His immediate object in writing had been to ask, in case he should decide against the Indiaman project and in favour of another attempt at the literary life, for the address of a cheap lodging somewhere in the Teign valley, the beauties of which, seen in glimpses through the rain, he had sung in some doggrel stanzas the year before. Brown, more than ever impressed during these last months with the power and promise of his friend's genius, was dead against the Indiaman scheme and in the end persuaded Keats to accept an advance of money for his present needs and to devote the summer to work in the country. Part of such work was to be upon a tragedy to be written by the two in collaboration and on a basis of half profits. Brown had not less belief in

Keats' future than affection for his person, and it was the two combined that made him ready and eager, as he frankly told Keats, to sail in the same boat with him. In the end the Devonshire idea gave place to a new plan, that of joining the invalid James Rice for a stay at Shanklin. 'I have given up the idea of the Indiaman', Keats writes to his young sister on June 9; 'I cannot resolve to give up my favourite studies: so I propose to retire once more. A friend of Mine who has an ill state of health called on me yesterday and proposed to spend a little time with him at the back of the Isle of Wight where he said we might live cheaply. I agreed to his proposal.'

Chapter XII

JUNE 1819-JANUARY 1820: SHANKLIN, WINCHESTER, HAMPSTEAD: TROUBLE AND HEALTH FAILURE

By the last days of June Keats was settled with Rice in the village of Shanklin, in a lodging above the cliff and a little way back from the sea, and forthwith got to work upon a new poetical romance, *Lamia*, at which he seems to have made some beginning before he left Hampstead. He found the subject, that of the enchantress of Corinth who under her woman's guise was really a serpent, in Burton's *Anatomy of Melancholy*, a book in these days often in his hands, and for the form of his narrative chose rimed heroics, only this time leaning on Dryden as his model instead of the Elizabethans.

Rice's health was at this time worse than ever, and Keats himself was far from well; his throat chronically sore, his nerves unstrung, his heart, in despite of distance, knowing little rest from agitation between the pains and joys of love. As long as Rice and he were alone together at Shanklin, the two ailing and anxious men, fast friends as they were, depressed and did each other harm. Things went better when Brown with his settled good health and good spirits came to join them. Soon afterwards Rice left, and Brown and Keats then got to work diligently at the joint task they had set themselves, that of writing a tragedy suitable for the stage. What struggling man or woman of letters has not at one time or another shared the hope which animated them, that this way lay the road to success and competence? Brown, whose opera *Narensky* had made a hit in its day, and brought him in a sum variously stated at £300 or £500, was supposed to possess the requisite stage experience. To him were assigned the plot and construction of the play, for which he was to receive half profits in the event of success, while Keats undertook to compose the dialogue. The subject was one taken from the history of the Emperor Otho the Great. The two friends sat opposite each other at the same table, and Keats wrote scene after scene as Brown sketched it out to him, in each case without enquiring what was to come next. The collaboration of genius and mediocrity rarely succeeds, and it seems hard to conceive a more unpromising mode of it than this. Besides the work by means of which Keats thus hoped, at least in sanguine hours, to find an escape from material difficulties, he was busily engaged working by himself on *Lamia*. But a cloud of depression continued to hang over him. The climate of Shanklin was against him: the quarter where they lodged lay screened by hills except from the south-east, whence, as he afterwards wrote, 'came the damps of the sea, which having no egress, the air would for days together take on an unhealthy idiosyncrasy altogether enervating and weakening as a city smoke.' After a stay of some six weeks, Keats consequently made up his mind to move with Brown to the more bracing air of Winchester.

From these weeks at Shanklin date the earliest of the preserved series of Keats' love-letters to Fanny Brawne. More than any man, more certainly than any other unripe youth fretting in the high fever of an unhopeful love, Keats has had to pay the penalty of genius in the loss of posthumous privacy for the most sacred and secret of his emotions. He thought his name would be forgotten, but posterity in an excess of remembrance has suffered no corner of his soul to escape the searchlight. Once preserved and printed, these love-letters of his cannot be ignored. Unselfish through and through, and naturally well-conditioned in all thoughts and feelings over which he had control, he strives hard in them to keep to a vein of considerate tenderness, and the earlier letters of the series contain charming passages. But often, more often indeed than not even from the first, they show him a prey, despite his best efforts to master himself and be reasonable, to an uncontrollable intensity and fretfulness of passion. Now that experience of love had come to him, it belied instead of confirming the view he had expressed in *Isabella* that too much pity has been spent on the sorrows of lovers, and that

— for the general award of love
The little sweet doth kill much bitterness.

In his own passion there was from the first, and increasingly as time went on, at least as much of bitterness as of sweet. An enraptured but an untrustful lover, alternately rejoicing and chafing at his bondage and passing through a hundred conflicting extremes of feeling in an hour, he finds in the fever of work and composition his only antidote against the fever of his lovesickness. This is written soon after his arrival at Shanklin: —

I am glad I had not an opportunity of sending off a Letter which I wrote for you on Tuesday night — 'twas too much like one out of Rousseau's *Heloise*. I am more reasonable this morning. The morning is the only proper time for me to write to a beautiful Girl whom I love so much: for at night, when the lonely day has closed, and the lonely, silent, unmusical Chamber is waiting to receive me as into a Sepulchre, then believe me my passion gets entirely the sway, then I would not have you see those Rhapsodies which I once thought it impossible I should ever give way to, and which I have often laughed at in another, for fear you should think me either too unhappy or perhaps a little mad. I am now at a very pleasant Cottage window, looking onto a beautiful hilly country, with a glimpse of the sea; the morning is very fine. I do not know how elastic my spirit might be, what pleasure I might have in living here and breathing and wandering as free as a stag about this beautiful Coast if the remembrance of you did not weigh so upon me. I have never known any unalloy'd Happiness for many days together: the death or sickness of some one has always spoilt my hours — and now when none such troubles oppress me, it is you must confess very hard that another sort of pain should haunt me. Ask yourself my love whether you are not very cruel to have so entrammelled me, so destroyed my freedom.

A fortnight later he manages to write a little more at ease of himself, his moods, and his doings: —

Do not call it folly, when I tell you I took your letter last night to bed with me. In the morning I found your name on the sealing wax obliterated. I was startled at the bad omen till I recollected that it must have happened in my dreams, and they you know fall out by contraries. You must have found out by this time I am a little given to bode ill like the raven; it is my misfortune not my fault; it has proceeded from the general tenor of the circumstances of my life, and rendered every event suspicious. However I will no more trouble either you or myself with sad Prophecies; though so far I am pleased at it as it has given me opportunity to love your disinterestedness towards me. I cannot say when I shall get a volume ready. I have three or four stories half done, but as I cannot write for the mere sake of the press, I am obliged to let them progress or lie still as my fancy chooses. By Christmas perhaps they may appear, but I am not yet sure they ever will. 'Twill be no matter, for Poems are as common as newspapers and I do not see why it is a greater crime in me than in another to let the verses of an half-fledged brain tumble into the reading-rooms and drawing-room windows.... Tomorrow I shall, if my health continues to improve during the night, take a look farther about the country, and spy at the parties about here who come hunting after the picturesque like beagles. It is astonishing how they raven down scenery like children do sweetmeats. The wondrous Chine here is a very great Lion: I wish I had as many guineas as there have been spy-glasses in it.

Yet another fortnight, and we find him uttering aloud the same yearning to attain the double goal of love and death together as he had often uttered to himself in secret since he came under the spell. On another day, letting his imagination comply with the longing for Alpine travel and seclusion which since Rousseau had been one of the romantic fashions of the time, he draws her a picture of an imagined future for herself and him which, judging at least by her choice of pleasures until now, would ill have stood the test of reality: —

You would delight very greatly in the walks about here; the Cliffs, woods, hills, sands, rocks, etc., about here. They are however not so fine but I shall give them a hearty goodbye to exchange them for my Cathedral. — Yet again I am not so tired of Scenery as to hate Switzerland. We might spend a pleasant year at Berne or Zurich — if it should please Venus to hear my 'Beseech thee to hear us O Goddess.' And if she should hear, God forbid we should what people call, *settle* — turn into a pond, a stagnant Lethe — a vile crescent, row or buildings. Better be imprudent moveables than prudent fixtures. Open my Mouth at the Street door like the Lion's head at

Venice to receive hateful cards, letters, messages. Go out and wither at tea parties; freeze at dinners; bake at dances; simmer at routs. No my love, trust yourself to me and I will find you nobler amusements, fortune favouring.

The most sanely self-revealing and pleasant passages in the correspondence occur in a letter written in the second week after Keats and Brown had settled at Winchester: —

I see you through a Mist: as I daresay you do me by this time. Believe me in the first Letters I wrote you: I assure you I felt as I wrote — I could not write so now. The thousand images I have had pass through my brain — my uneasy spirits — my unguess'd fate — all spread as a veil between me and you. Remember I have had no idle leisure to brood over you. — 'tis well perhaps I have not. I could not have endured the throng of jealousies that used to haunt me before I had plunged so deeply into imaginary interests. I would fain, as my sails are set, sail on without an interruption for a Brace of Months longer — I am in complete cue — in the fever; and shall in these four Months do an immense deal. This Page as my eye skims over it I see is excessively unloverlike and ungallant — I cannot help it — I am no officer in yawning quarters; no Parson-romeo.... 'Tis harsh, harsh, I know it. My heart seems now made of iron — I could not write a proper answer to an invitation to Idalia.... This Winchester is a fine place: a beautiful Cathedral and many other ancient buildings in the Environs. The little coffin of a room at Shanklin is changed for a large room, where I can promenade at my pleasure.... One of the pleasantest things I have seen lately was at Cowes. The Regent in his Yatch (I think they spell it) was anchored opposite — a beautiful vessel — and all the Yatchs and boats on the coast were passing and repassing it; and circuiting and tacking about it in every direction — I never beheld anything so silent, light, and graceful. — As we pass'd over to Southampton, there was nearly an accident. There came by a Boat, well mann'd, with two naval officers at the stern. Our Bow-lines took the top of their little mast and snapped it off close by the board. Had the mast been a little stouter they would have been upset. In so trifling an event I could not help admiring our seamen — neither officer nor man in the whole Boat mov'd a muscle — they scarcely notic'd it even with words. Forgive me for this flint-worded Letter, and believe and see that I cannot think of you without some sort of energy — though mal à propos. Even as I leave off it seems to me that a few more moments' thought of you would uncrystallize and dissolve me. I must not give way to it — but turn to my writing again — if I fail I shall die hard. O my love, your lips are growing sweet again to my fancy — I must forget them.

The old cathedral city of Winchester, with its peaceful closes breathing antiquity, its hurrying limpid chalk-streams and beautiful elm-shadowed meadow walks, and the tonic climate of its surrounding downs, 'where the air,' he writes, 'is worth sixpence a pint,' exactly suited Keats, and he quickly improved both in health and spirits. The days he spent here, from the middle of August to the second week of October, were the last good days of his life. Working with a steady intensity of application, he managed, as the last extract shows, to steel himself for the time being against the importunity of his passion, although never without a certain feverishness in the effort, and to keep the thought of money troubles at bay by buoying himself up with the firm hope of a stage success. His work continued to be chiefly on *Lamia*, with the concluding part of *Otho*, and the beginning of a new tragedy on the story of King Stephen. In the last act of *Otho* and the opening scenes (which are all he did) of *King Stephen* he laboured alone, without accepting help from Brown. On the 25th of August he writes to Reynolds, as usual more gravely and openly than to any other correspondent, of his present feelings in regard to life and literature.

The more I know what my diligence may in time probably effect, the more does my heart distend with Pride and Obstinacy — I feel it in my power to become a popular writer — I feel it in my power to refuse the poisonous suffrage of a public. My own being which I know to be becomes of more consequence to me than the crowds of Shadows in the shape of men and women that inhabit a kingdom. The soul is a world of itself, and has enough to do in its own home. Those whom I know already, and who have grown as it were a part of myself, I could not do without: but for the rest of mankind, they are as much a dream to me as Milton's

Hierarchies. I think if I had a free and healthy and lasting organization of heart, and lungs as strong as an ox's, so as to be able to bear unhurt the shock of extreme thought and sensation without weariness, I could pass my life very nearly alone though it should last eighty years. But I feel my body too weak to support me to the height, I am obliged continually to check myself, and be nothing.

A letter to his young sister of three days later is in quite another key, but one of wholesome and unforced high spirits: —

The delightful Weather we have had for two Months is the highest gratification I could receive — no chill'd red noses — no shivering — but fair atmosphere to think in — a clean towel mark'd with the mangle and a basin of clear Water to drench one's face with ten times a day: no need of much exercise — a Mile a day being quite sufficient. My greatest regret is that I have not been well enough to bathe though I have been two Months by the sea side and live now close to delicious bathing — Still I enjoy the Weather — I adore fine Weather as the greatest blessing I can have.... I should like now to promenade round your Gardens — apple-tasting — pear-tasting — plum-judging — apricot nibbling — peach-scrunching — nectarine-sucking and Melon-carving. I have also a great feeling for antiquated cherries full of sugar cracks — and a white currant tree kept for company. I admire lolling on a lawn by a water lillied pond to eat white currants and see gold fish: and go to the Fair in the Evening if I'm good. There is not hope for that — one is sure to get into some mess before evening.

A week later (September 5) he discourses pleasantly to Taylor on the virtues and drawbacks of different kinds of country air and on the effects of field labour on the character; and by way of a specimen of his work sends a passage of thirty lines from *Lamia*. By this time Brown had gone off to visit friends at Bedhampton and elsewhere, and Keats was left alone at Winchester. Presently came a disturbing letter from George, established by this time at the then remote trading settlement of Louisville, Ohio, and in difficulties from a heavy loss incurred through a venture into which he had been led, dishonestly as he believed, by the naturalist Audubon. He asks in consequence that Abbey should be pressed to send him the share due to him from their brother Tom's estate. This could only be done if their aunt Jennings could be persuaded to free Abbey's hands by dropping her threatened Chancery suit. Hurrying to London to try and put this business through, Keats stayed there three days (Septr. 10-13), but dared not break his serenity by sight or touch of his enchantress. In a note to her he writes, 'I love you too much to venture to Hampstead, I feel it is not paying a visit, but venturing into a fire.... I am a Coward, I cannot bear the pain of being happy, 'tis out of the question; I must admit no thought of it.' He found few of his friends in town; dined with the Wylies, the family of his sister-in-law; and had much talk with Mr Abbey, who seemed inclined to dangle before him some prospect of employment in the hatter's business which he combined with his tea-dealing, and read to him with approval a passage from *Don Juan* ('Lord Byron's last flash poem,' says Keats) against literary ambition. He went to see his sister Fanny at Walthamstow, passed some time with Rice, and had a long six hours' talk with Woodhouse: of this Keats' own letters make no mention, but Woodhouse's account of it, written a week later to Taylor, has been preserved and is curiously interesting.

Keats, warm from the composition of *Lamia*, had had an impulse to publish it immediately, together with the *Eve of St Agnes*, but the publishers had thought the time inopportune. Woodhouse asked why not *Isabella* too? and Keats answered that he could not bear that poem now and thought it mawkish. Whereupon Woodhouse makes the judicious comment: 'this certainly cannot be so, the feeling is very likely to come across an author on review of a former work of his own, particularly when the object of his present meditations is of a more sober and unimpassioned character. The feeling of mawkishness seems to me that which comes upon us when anything of great tenderness and simplicity is met with when we are not in a sufficiently tender and simple frame of mind to hear it: when we experience a sort of revulsion or resiliency (if there be such a word) from the sentiment or expression.' Keats, full of *Lamia*, read it out to his friend, who comments: 'I am much pleased with it. I can use no other terms for you know how badly he reads his own poetry.' (Other witnesses on the contrary tell of the thrilling effect of Keats' reading — a reading which was half chanting, 'in a low, tremulous undertone' — of his own work.) 'And you know,' continues Woodhouse, 'how slow I am to catch the effect of poetry read by the best reader for the first time.' Nevertheless he is able to give his correspondent a quite accurate sketch of the plot, and adds, 'you may suppose all these events have given K. scope for some beautiful poetry, which even in this cursory hearing of it, came every now and then upon me and made me "start, as tho' a sea-nymph quired."'

The talk turning to the *Eve of St Agnes*, Keats showed Woodhouse some changes he had just made in recopying it. One of these introduced a slight but disfiguring note of cynical realism or 'pettish disgust' into the concluding lines telling of the deaths of old Angela and the beadsman, and is the first sign we find of that inclination to mix a worldly would-be Don Juanish vein with romance which was soon to appear so disastrously in the *Cap and Bells*. The other change was to make it clear that the melting of Porphyro into Madeline's dream, at the enchanted climax of the poem, implied love's full fruition between them then and there. At this point Woodhouse's prudery took alarm. He pleaded against the change vehemently, and Keats to tease him still more vehemently defended it, vowing that his own and his hero's character for virility required the new reading, and that he did not write for misses. The correct and excellent Woodhouse, scandalized though he somewhat was by what he calls his friend's 'rhodomontade,' declares that they had a delightful time together. He was leaving London the same afternoon for Weymouth, and Keats came to the coach-office to see him off. At parting they each promised to mend their ways in the matter of letter-writing, Keats holding out the hope, which was not fulfilled, of a rimed epistle to follow. Woodhouse tells how, being the only inside passenger in the coach, he 'amused himself by diving into a deep reverie, and recalling all that had passed during the six hours we were *tête à tête*.'

Such touches of over-sensitive prudery set aside, the more light we get on this friend of Keats, Richard Woodhouse, the higher grows our esteem both for his character and judgment. In other extant letters to Taylor of this date, he comments with fine insight on Keats' own confessions of secret pride and obstinacy, and on his vice ('for a vice in a poor man it is') of lending more than he could afford to friends in need. And what can be more sagacious than the following, from a letter of Woodhouse to a lady cousin of his own? —

You were so flattered as to say the other day, you wished I had been in a company where you were, to defend Keats. — In all places, and at all times, and before all persons, I would express and as far as I am able, support, my high opinion of his poetical merits — such a genius, I verily believe, has not appeared since Shakspeare and Milton.... But in our common conversation upon his merits, we should always bear in mind that his fame may be more hurt by indiscriminate praise than by wholesale censure. I would at once admit that he has great faults — enough indeed to sink another writer. But they are more than counterbalanced by his beauties: and this is the proper mode of appreciating an original genius. His faults will wear away — his fire will be chastened — and then eyes will do homage to his brilliancy. But genius is wayward, trembling, easily daunted. And shall we not excuse the errors, the luxuriancy of youth? Are we to expect that poets are to be given to the world, as our first parents were, in a state of maturity? Are they to have no season of childhood? are they to have no room to try their wings before the steadiness and strength of their flight are to be finally judged of?... Now, while Keats is unknown, unheeded, despised of one of our arch-critics, neglected by the rest — in the teeth of the world, and in the face of 'these curious days,' I express my conviction, that Keats, during his life (if it please God to spare him to the usual age of man, and the critics not to drive him from the free air of the Poetic heaven before his Wings are fully fledged) will rank on a level with the best of the last or of the present generation: and after his death will take his place at their head. But, while I think thus, I would make persons respect my judgment by the discrimination of my praise, and by the freedom of my censure where his writings are open to it. These are the Elements of true criticism. It is easy, like Momus, to find fault with the clattering of the slipper worn by the Goddess of beauty; but 'the serious Gods' found better employment in admiration of her unapproachable loveliness. A Poet ought to write for Posterity. But a critic ought to do so too.

By September 14 Keats was back at Winchester, where during the next three weeks he had a chance of testing his capacity for solitude. He seems to have looked at *Hyperion* again, but made up his mind to go no farther with it, having got to feel its style too latinized and Miltonic. A very few weeks before, in August, he had written to two different correspondents that *Paradise Lost* was becoming every day a greater wonder to him. Now, in the third week of September he had come to regard it, 'though so fine itself,' as a 'corruption of our language,' a case of 'a northern dialect accommodating itself to Greek and Latin inversions and intonations;' and had convinced himself, paradoxically, that the purest English was Chatterton's, — which is in truth no right English at all, but the attempt of a brilliant self-taught boy to forge himself a fifteenth-century style by gathering miscellaneous half-understood archaisms out of dictionaries and stringing them in fluent stanzas of Spenserian, or post-Spenserian, rhythm and syntax. But it was probably not of Chatterton's vocabulary that Keats was thinking, but rather of the unartificial, straightforward flow of his verse in contrast with Milton's. The apparent suddenness of Keats' change of mind on this matter is characteristic, like his quite unjust return upon himself in regard to *Isabella* , of what Haydon calls his lack of decisions and fixity of aim: — 'One day he was full of an epic poem; the next day epic poems were splendid impositions on the world. Never for two days did he know his own intentions.' By these words, to be taken with the usual discount, Haydon means the same thing as Keats means himself when he speaks of his 'unsteady and vagarish disposition'; let us rather say his sensitive and receptive openness of mind to contradictory impressions, even on questions of that art of which he had become so fine a master, and withal his habit of complete surrender to whatever was the dominant impression of the moment.

With reference to his other occupations of the hour, — *Lamia* he had finished, and for the present he did no more to *King Stephen* . Realizing the low repute into which critical derision had brought him as a member of the Cockney School, he proposed to withhold his next volume of poems in hope that the production of *Otho the Great* at Drury Lane in the autumn might, if successful, create a more favourable atmosphere for its reception; and was in consequence seriously dashed when he learnt that Kean was on the point of starting for America. One of his chief present pursuits was studying Italian in the pages of Ariosto. The wholesome brightness of an unusually fine season continuing to sustain and soothe him, he wrote the last, most unclouded and serenely accomplished of his meditative odes, that *To Autumn* . A sudden return of the epistolary mood came upon him, and between September 17th and 27th he poured himself out to his brother and sister-in-law in a new long journal-letter, full of confidences on every subject that dwelt in or flitted through his mind except the one master-subject of the passion he was striving to keep subdued by absence. 'I am inclined,' he says, 'to write a good deal; for there can be nothing so remembrancing and enchaining as a good long letter, be it composed of what it may.'

Accordingly he ranges as usual over all manner of miscellaneous themes, discussing his own and his brother's situation and future; telling of Haydon and his inconsiderate behaviour about the loan, and of Dilke's political dogmatism and over-anxiety about his boy; giving accounts of the several members of the Hampstead circle, mixed up with playful messages to his sister-in-law, whom he represents as caring nothing for these tiresome people and interrupting her husband's reading of the letter to insist on prattling about her baby. He adds anecdotes of his visit to her family in London, à propos of babies tells of a thing he had heard Charles Lamb say. 'A child in arms was passing by his chair toward its mother, in the nurse's arms. Lamb took hold of the long clothes, saying: "Where, God bless me, where does it leave off?"' With an unexpressed shaft of inward mockery at his own plight, he describes the ridiculous figure cut by a man in love, the victim in this case being his friend Haslam; relates jokes practical and other which had lately passed between Brown, Dilke, and himself, and after a very sensible excursion into history and current politics, to which he was never at all so indifferent as is commonly said, he dwells with a kindly, humorous enjoyment on the sedate maiden-ladylike ways and aspects of the cathedral town where he found the autumn quietude so comforting. This sets him thinking of his fragment of a poem written seven months earlier and breathing a similar spirit, the *Eve of St Mark*; so he transcribes it for their benefit, and also, in odd contrast, a long passage from Burton's *Anatomy* which had tickled some queer corner of his brain by its cumulative effect of exuberant and grotesque disgustfulness, and which he declares he would love to hear delivered by an actor across the footlights.

During the same days at Winchester Keats also wrote intimately and purposefully to Reynolds, Brown, and Dilke. In all these letters we see the well conditioned, wise and admirable Keats, the sane and healthy partner in his so dual and divided nature, for the time being holding firmly, or at any rate hopeful and confident of being able to hold firmly, the upper hand. He resolves manfully to rally his moral powers, to banish over-passionate and fretful feelings and to put himself on a right footing with the world. Imaginary troubles, he declares, are what prey upon a man: real troubles spur him to exertion, and exert himself and fight against morbid imaginings he will. In reference to George's money troubles, 'Rest in the confidence,' he says, 'that I will not omit any exertion to benefit you by some means or other: if I cannot remit you hundreds, I will tens, and if not that, ones:' a promise which we shall find George taking only too literally later on. Of his brothers and his own immediate prospect he writes with seriousness, nevertheless more encouragingly than the occasion well warranted. He will not let himself seem too much depressed even by the heavy check which his and Brown's hopes about *Otho the Great* had just received from the news of Kean's intended departure for America.

We are certainly in a very low estate — I say we, for I am in such a situation, that were it not for the assistance of Brown and Taylor, I must be as badly off as a man can be. I could not raise any sum by the promise of any poem, no, not by the mortgage of my intellect. We must wait a little while. I really have hopes of success. I have finished a tragedy, which if it succeeds will enable me to sell what I may have in manuscript to a good advantage. I have passed my time in reading, writing, and fretting, the last I intend to give up, and stick to the other two. They are the only chances of benefit to us. Your wants will be a fresh spur to me. I assure you you shall more than share what I can get whilst I am still young. The time may come when age will make me more selfish. I have not been well treated by the world, and yet I have, capitally well. I do not know a person to whom so many purse-strings would fly open as to me, if I could possibly take advantage of them, which I cannot do, for none of the owners of these purses are rich.... Mine, I am sure, is a tolerable tragedy; it would have been a bank to me, if just as I had finished it, I had not heard of Kean's resolution to go to America. That was the worst news I could have had.... But be not cast down any more than I am; I feel I can bear real ills better than imaginary ones. Whenever I find myself growing vapourish, I rouse myself, wash, and put on a clean shirt, brush my hair and clothes, tie my shoestrings neatly, and in fact adonize as if I were going out. Then, all clean and comfortable, I sit down to write. This I find the greatest relief.

And again, in still better heart: —

With my inconstant disposition it is no wonder that this morning, amid all our bad times and misfortunes, I should feel so alert and well-spirited. At this moment you are perhaps in a very different state of mind. It is because my hopes are ever paramount to my despair. I have been reading over a part of a short poem I have composed lately, called *Lamia*, and I am certain there is that sort of fire in it which must take hold of people in some way. Give them either pleasant or unpleasant sensation — what they want is a sensation of some sort. I wish I could pitch the key of your spirits as high as mine is; but your organ-loft is beyond the reach of my voice.

To Dilke and Brown he writes at the same time of his own immediate plans, telling them that he is determined to give up trusting to mere hopes of ultimate success, whether from plays or poems, and to turn to the natural resource of a man fit for nothing but literature and needing to support himself by his pen; the resource, that is, of journalism and reviewing. These are some of his words to Dilke: —

Wait for the issue of this Tragedy? No — there cannot be greater uncertainties east, west, north, and south than concerning dramatic composition. How many months must I wait! Had I not better begin to look about me now? If better events supersede this necessity what harm will be done? I have no trust whatever on Poetry. I don't wonder at it — the marvel is to me how people read so much of it. I think you will see the reasonableness of my plan. To forward it I purpose living in a cheap Lodging in Town, that I may be in the reach of books and information of which there is here a plentiful lack. If I can find any place tolerably comfortable I will settle myself and fag till I can afford to buy Pleasure — which if I never can afford I must go without.

He had been living since May on an advance from Taylor and a loan from Brown to be repaid out of the eventual profits of their play, and was uneasy at putting Brown to a present sacrifice. He writes to him accordingly: —

I have not known yet what it is to be diligent. I purpose living in town in a cheap lodging, and endeavouring, for a beginning, to get the theatricals of some paper. When I can afford to compose deliberate poems, I will.... I had got into a habit of mind of looking towards you as a help in all difficulties. You will see it as a duty I owe myself to break the neck of it. I do nothing for my subsistence — make no exertion. At the end of another year you shall applaud me, not for verses, but for conduct.

Brown, returning to Winchester a few days later, found his friend unshaken in the same healthy resolutions, and however loth to lose him for housemate and doubtful of his power to live the life he proposed, respected his motives too much to contend against them. It was accordingly settled that the two friends, after travelling up to London together, should part company, Brown returning to his home at Hampstead, while Keats went to live by himself and look out for employment on the press. The Dilkes, who were living in Great Smith Street, Westminster, at his desire engaged a lodging for him close by, at the corner of College Street (no. 25), and thither he betook himself, it would seem on the 7th or 8th of October.

College Street, as all Londoners or visitors to London know, is one of sedately picturesque Queen Anne or early Georgian houses overlooking the Abbey gardens. No corner of the town could have been more fitted to soothe him with a sense of cathedral quietude resembling that which he had just left. But the wise and purposeful Keats had reckoned without his other self, the Keats distracted by uncontrollable love-cravings. His blood proved traitor to his will, and the plan of life and literary hackwork in London broke down at once on trial, or even before trial. On the 10th he went up to Hampstead, and in a moment all his strength, to borrow words of his own, was uncrystallized and dissolved. It was the first time he had seen his mistress since June. He found her kind, and from that hour was utterly passion's slave again. In the solitude of his London lodging he found that he could not work nor rest nor fix his thoughts. He writes to her three days later: —

This moment I have set myself to copy some verses out fair. I cannot proceed with any degree of content. I must write you a line or two and see if that will assist in dismissing you from my Mind for ever so short a time. Upon my Soul I can think of nothing else. The time is passed when I had power to advise and warn you against the unpromising morning of my Life. My love has made me selfish. I cannot exist without you. I am forgetful of everything but seeing you again — my Life seems to stop there — I see no further. You have absorb'd me.

He seems to have spent the next week going backwards and forwards between Hampstead and London, staying for three nights as a guest at her mother's house ('my three days' dream,' he calls the visit) and for one or two at the Dilkes' in Westminster, and finally about the 20th settling back into his old quarters with Brown at Wentworth Place next door to her. 'I shall be able to do nothing,' he writes. — and again there comes the cry, 'I should like to cast the die for Love or death.'

It was for death that the die was cast, and three months later came the seizure which made manifest the certainty of the issue. In the meantime he lived outwardly through the autumn and early winter much the same life as before among his own friends and Brown's. Some of them noticed in him at times a loss of natural gaiety and an unaccustomed strain of recklessness and moodiness. Severn, who had spent with him part of one of his days at the College Street lodgings, hearing him read *Lamia* and tell of the change of mind about *Hyperion* (to Severn as an ardent Miltonian a sore disappointment), called there again a few days later only to find him flown; and going to see him the next Sunday at Hampstead was perturbed by the change in him. 'He seemed well neither in mind nor in body, with little of the happy confidence and resolute bearing of a week earlier: while alternating moods of apathetic dejection and spasmodic gaiety rendered him a companion somewhat difficult to humour.' His correspondence at the same time falls off, and from mid-October until past Christmas we get only one letter to Severn, one to Rice, one to Taylor the publisher, and three or four to his sister Fanny. For other evidence we have the recollections, fairly full but somewhat enigmatical withal, of his housemate Brown; some blatancies, little to be trusted, of Haydon; and what is more revealing, the tenor of his own attempts at new poetical work, as well as a few private utterances in verse which the stress of passion forced from him.

For some weeks he was able to ply at Wentworth Place a double daily task: one, that of writing each morning in the same sitting-room with Brown, who copied as he wrote, some stanzas of a comic fairy poem which they had devised together, to be called *The Cap and Bells, or The Jealousies*, and to come out under the pseudonym of 'Lucy Vaughan Lloyd': the other, carried on each evening in the seclusion of his own room, that of remodelling *Hyperion* into the form of a Dream or Vision, in which parts of the poem as begun a year before should be incorporated with certain changes of style and diction. At the former scheme Keats worked with great fluency but little felicity: the mere, almost mechanical act of spinning the verses of *The Cap and Bells* seems to have come all the easier to him in that they sprang from no vital or inward part of his imaginative being, and the result is as nearly worthless as anything written by such a man can be conceived to be. In his solitary work on the recast of *Hyperion* Keats wrote, on the other hand, out of the truest — which had come, alas! also to be the saddest — depths of himself; and the fragment needs to be studied with as much care as the best of his earlier work by those who would understand the ripening thoughts of this great, now stricken, spirit on the destinies of poets and the relation of poetry to human life. To that study we shall come by and by. For the present let it be only noted that these twofold occupations seem to have been kept up by Keats through November, and broken off soon afterwards 'owing to a circumstance which,' says Brown, mysteriously, 'it is needless to mention.' But judging by the rest of Brown's narrative, as well as by some of Keats' own private outpourings, no special or external circumstance can have been needed, — his inward sufferings were quite enough of themselves, — to put a stop to his writing. The wasting of his vital powers by latent disease was turning all his sensations and emotions into pain: at once darkening the shadow of impending poverty, increasing the natural importunity of ill-boding instincts at his heart, and exasperating into agony the unsatisfied cravings of his passion. During his 'three days' dream' under the same roof with his betrothed in October he had been able to write peaceably at nightfall: —

> Faded the flower and all its budded charms,
> Faded the sight of beauty from my eyes,
> Faded the shape of beauty from my arms,
> Faded the voice, warmth, whiteness, paradise —
> Vanish'd unseasonably at shut of eve,
> When the dusk holiday — or holinight
> Of fragrant-curtain'd love begins to weave
> The woof of darkness thick, for hid delight;
> But, as I've read love's missal through to-day,
> He'll let me sleep, seeing I fast and pray.
> But now the hunger is uncontrollable: —
> Yourself — your soul — in pity give me all,
> Withold no atom's atom or I die,
> Or living on perhaps, your wretched thrall.

Forget, in the mist of idle misery,
Life's purposes, — the palate of my mind
Losing its gust, and my ambition blind!
And again he cries, what can he do to recover his old liberty? —
When every fair one that I saw was fair,
Enough to catch me in but half a snare,
Not keep me there:
When, howe'er poor or particolour'd things,
My muse had wings,
And ever ready was to take her course
Whither I bent her force,
Unintellectual, yet divine to me; —
Divine, I say! — What seabird o'er the sea
Is a philosopher the while he goes
Winging along where the great water throes?
How shall I do
To get anew
Those moulted feathers, and so mount once more
Above, above
The reach of fluttering Love,
And make him cower lowly while I soar?
Shall I gulp wine? No, that is vulgarism,
A heresy and schism,
Foisted into the canon law of love; —
No, — wine is only sweet to happy men;
More dismal cares
Seize on me unawares, —
Where shall I learn to get my peace again?
To banish thoughts of that most hateful land,
Dungeoner of my friends, that wicked strand
Where they were wreck'd and live a wrecked life;
That monstrous region, whose dull rivers pour,
Ever from their sordid urns unto the shore,
Unown'd of any weedy-haired gods,
Whose winds, all zephyrless, hold scourging rods,
Ic'd in the great lakes, to afflict mankind;
Whose rank-grown forests, frosted, black, and blind,
Would fright a Dryad; whose harsh herbag'd meads
Make lean and lank the starv'd ox while he feeds;
There bad flowers have no scent, birds no sweet song,
And great unerring Nature once seems wrong.

With that image of the seabird winging untroubled its chosen way over the waves, and as free as they, the poet sheds a real light on his own psychology in happier days, while the later lines figure direfully the obsession that now seems to make him think of even his friendships as wrecked and darkened, and of love as a ghastly error in nature, no joy but a scourge that blights and devastates. That he might win peace by marriage with the object of his passion does not seem to have occurred to Keats as possible at the present ebb-tide of his fortune. 'However selfishly I feel,' he had written to her some months earlier, 'I am sure I could never act selfishly.' The Brawnes on their part were comfortably off, but what his instincts of honour and independence forbade him to ask, hers of tenderness could perhaps hardly be expected to offer. As the autumn wore into winter, he was not able to disguise his plight from his affectionate companion Brown, though he shrank from speaking of its causes. Looking back upon the time after ten years Brown records the impression it left upon him thus: —

It was evident from the letters he had sent me, even in his self-deceived assurance that he was 'as far from being unhappy as possible,' that he was unhappy. I quickly perceived he was more so than I had feared; his abstraction, his occasional lassitude of mind, and, frequently, his assumed tranquillity of countenance gave me great uneasiness. He was unwilling to speak on the subject; and I could do no more than attempt, indirectly, to cheer him with hope, avoiding that word however.

Brown then tells of his morning and evening work on *The Cap and Bells* and the revised *Hyperion* and, in the vague terms I have quoted, of its cessation. And then, seeming to assign to money troubles an even greater part than they really bore in causing Keats' distress of mind, Brown goes on —

He could not resume his employment, and he became dreadfully unhappy. His hopes of fame, and other more tender hopes were blighted. His patrimony, though much consumed in a profession he was compelled to relinquish, might have upheld him through the storm, had he not imprudently lost a part of it in generous loans.... He possessed the noble virtues of friendship and generosity to excess; and they, in this world, may chance to spoil a man of independent feeling, till he is destitute. Even the 'immediate cash,' of which he spoke in the extracts I have given from his letters, was lent, with no hope of its speedy repayment, and he was left worse than pennyless. All that a friend could say, or offer, or urge was not enough to heal his many wounds. He listened, and, in kindness, or soothed by kindness, showed tranquillity, but nothing from a friend could relieve him, except on a matter of inferior trouble. He was too thoughtful, or too unquiet; and he began to be reckless of health. Among other proofs of recklessness, he was secretly taking, at times, a few drops of laudanum to keep up his spirits. It was discovered by accident, and, without delay, revealed to me. He needed not to be warned of the danger of such a habit; but I rejoiced at his promise never to take another drop without my knowledge; for nothing could induce him to break his word, when once given, — which was a difficulty. Still, at the very moment of my being rejoiced, this was an additional proof of his rooted misery.

Where Brown hints of his being 'careless of health,' Haydon, referring apparently to this time of his life in particular, declares roundly and crudely as follows: —

Unable to bear the sneers of ignorance or the attacks of envy, not having strength of mind enough to buckle himself together like a porcupine, and present nothing but his prickles to his enemies, he began to despond, and flew to dissipation as a relief, which after a temporary elevation of spirits plunged him into deeper despondency than ever. For six weeks he was scarcely sober, and — to show what a man does to gratify his appetites, when once they get the better of him — once covered his tongue and throat as far as he could reach with Cayenne pepper, in order to appreciate the 'delicious coldness of claret in all its glory,' — his own expression.

If Keats really told Haydon that silly, and I should suppose impossible, story about the claret and cayenne it was probably only a piece of such 'rhodomontade' as his friends describe, invented on the spur of the moment to scandalize Haydon or under the provocation of one of his preachments. That he may at moments during these unhappy months have sought relief in dissipation of one kind or another, as Brown tells us he did in drug-taking, is likely: that he was now or at any time habitually given to drink is disproved by the explicit testimony of all his friends as well as of Brown, his closest intimate. In his few letters of the time his secret misery is betrayed only by a single phrase. Early in December he writes arranging to go with Severn to see the picture with which Severn was competing for, and eventually won, the annual gold medal of the Academy for historical painting. The subject was 'The Cave of Despair' from Spenser. Keats in making the appointment adds parenthetically from his troubled heart, 'you had best put me into your Cave of Despair.' A little later we hear of him flinging out in a fit of angered loyalty from a company of elder artists, Hilton, De Wint and others, where the deserts of the winner were disparaged and his success put down to favouritism.

It would seem that as late as November 17th he was still, or had quite lately been, going on with *The Cap and Bells*. He writes on that date to Taylor depreciating what he has recently been about and indicating in what direction his thoughts, when he could bend them seriously upon work at all, were inclined to turn: —

As the marvellous is the most enticing and the surest guarantee of harmonious numbers I have been endeavouring to persuade myself to untether Fancy and to let her manage for herself. I and myself cannot agree about this at all. Wonders are no wonders to me. I am more at home amongst Men and women. I would rather read Chaucer than Ariosto. The little dramatic skill I may as yet have however badly it might show in a Drama would I think be sufficient for a Poem. I wish to diffuse the colouring of St Agnes eve throughout a poem in which Character and Sentiment would be the figures to such drapery. Two or three such Poems, if God should spare me, written in the course of the next six years, would be a famous gradus ad Parnassum altissimum. I mean they would nerve me up to the writing of a few fine Plays — my greatest ambition — when I do feel ambitious. I am sorry to say that is very seldom. The subject we have once or twice talked of appears a promising one, The Earl of Leicester's history. I am this morning reading Holingshed's *Elizabeth*.

It does not seem clear whether his idea about Leicester was to use the subject for a narrative poem or for a play. Scott's *Kenilworth*, be it remembered, had not yet been written.

In December he writes to his sister Fanny of the trouble his throat keeps giving him or threatening him with on exertion or cold, and says that he has been ordering a thick great coat and thick shoes on the advice of his doctor. He also mentions that he has begun to prepare a volume of poems to come out in the spring, and that he is touching up his and Brown's tragedy in order to brighten its interest. It had been accepted, he tells her, by Drury Lane, but only with the promise of coming out next season, and as that is not soon enough they intend either to insist on its being brought out this season or else to transfer it to Covent Gardens. He has been anxiously expecting, and has just now received, news of George; and has promised to dine with Mrs Dilke in London on Christmas day. Whether he was able to keep this engagement we do not learn; but Brown at any rate was there, and between him and Dilke there arose a challenge on which Keats among others was called to adjudicate. The conversation, writes Mrs Dilke, 'turned on fairy tales — Brown's forte — Dilke not liking them. Brown said he was sure he could beat Dilke, and to let him try they betted a beefsteak supper, and an allotted time was given. They had been read by the persons fixed on — Keats, Reynolds, Rice, and Taylor — and the wager was decided the night before last in favour of Dilke. Next Saturday night the supper is to be given, — Beefsteaks and punch — the food of the "Cockney School."'

So life went on for the friends, on the surface, pretty much as usual, into the new year (1820). Early in January George Keats came for a short visit to England to try and advance his affairs and get possession of more capital for his business. He seems not to have realized at all fully the true state of his brother's health or heart. He noticed, indeed, a change, and looking back on the time some years afterwards writes, 'he was not the same being; although his reception of me was as warm as heart could wish, he did not speak with former openness and unreserve, he had lost the reviving custom of venting his griefs.' George was probably too full of his own affairs to enquire very closely into John's, or he would never have allowed John, as he did, to strip himself practically bare of future means of subsistence in fulfilment of the brotherly promises of help conveyed, as we have seen, in his letter from Winchester the previous September. 'It was not fair of him, was it?' John is recorded to have said a little later from his sickbed, referring to George's action in so taking him at his word; and Brown from this circumstance conceived of George a bitter bad opinion which nothing afterwards would shake. Nevertheless there is ample evidence of George's honourable and affectionate character, and it seems clear that in striving for commercial success he had his brother's ultimate benefit in view as much as his own, and that in the meantime he believed he had reason to take for granted the willingness and ability of John's many friends to keep him afloat.

On January 13th, a week after George's arrival, John took up his pen to try and write to his sister-in-law a journal letter in the old chatty affectionate style. If he had the means, he says, he would like to come and pay them a visit in America for a few months. 'I should not think much of the time, or my absence from my books; or I have no right to think, for I am very idle. But then I ought to be diligent, or at least to keep myself within reach of the materials for diligence. Diligence, that I do not mean to say; I should say dreaming over my books, or rather over other people's books.' He gossips about friends and acquaintances, less good-naturedly than usual, as he seems to be aware when he says, 'any third person would think I was addressing myself to a lover of scandal. But we know we do not love scandal, but fun; and if scandal happens to be fun, that is no fault of ours.' He tells how George is making copies of his verses, including the ode to the Nightingale; lets his inward embitterment show through for an instant when he says, 'If you should have a boy, do not christen him John, and persuade George not to let his partiality for me come across: 'tis a bad name, and goes against a man;' describes a dance he has been to at the Dilkes, and among a good deal of rather irritable and wry-mouthed social satire, to which he tries to give a colour of pleasantry and playfulness, strikes into sharp definition with the fewest possible words the characters of some of his friends and acquaintances: —

I know three witty people, all distinct in their excellence — Rice, Reynolds, and Richards. Rice is the wisest, Reynolds the playfullest, Richards the out-o'-the-wayest. The first makes you laugh and think, the second makes you laugh and not think, the third puzzles your head. I admire the first, I enjoy the second, I stare at the third.... I know three people of no wit at all, each distinct in his excellence — A, B, and C. A is the foolishest, B the sulkiest, C is a negative. A makes you yawn, B makes you hate, as for C you never see him at all though he were six feet high. — I bear the first, I forbear the second, I am not certain that the third is. The first is gruel, the second ditch-water, the third is spilt — he ought to be wiped up.

This was written on January 17th. Ten days later George started on his return journey, and John, having forgotten to hand him for delivery at home the budget he had been writing, was obliged to send it after him by post. A week later again, on February 3rd, came the crash towards which, as we can now see, Keats' physical constitution had been hastening ever since the over exertion of his Scottish tour twenty months before. The weather had been very variable, almost sultry in mid-January, then bitter cold with frost and sleet, then a thaw, whereby Keats was tempted to leave off his greatcoat. Coming from London to Hampstead outside the stage coach on the night of Thursday February 3rd, the chill of the thaw caught him. Everyone knows the words in which Brown relates the sequel: —

At eleven o'clock, he came into the house in a state that looked like fierce intoxication. Such a state in him, I knew, was impossible; it therefore was the more fearful. I asked hurriedly, 'What is the matter? you are fevered?' 'Yes, yes,' he answered, 'I was on the outside of the stage this bitter day till I was severely chilled, — but now I don't feel it. Fevered! — of course, a little.' He mildly and instantly yielded, a property in his nature towards any friend, to my request that he should go to bed. I entered his chamber as he leapt into bed. On entering the cold sheets, before his head was on the pillow, he slightly coughed, and I heard him say, — 'That is blood from my mouth.' I went towards him; he was examining a single drop of blood upon the sheet. 'Bring me the candle, Brown, and let me see this blood.' After regarding it steadfastly he looked up in my face, with a calmness of countenance that I can never forget, and said, — 'I know the colour of that blood; — it is arterial blood; — I cannot be deceived in that colour; — that drop of blood is my death-warrant; — I must die.' I ran for a surgeon; my friend was bled; and, at five in the morning, I left him after he had been some time in a quiet sleep.

Keats lived for twelve months longer, but it was only, in his own words, a life in death. Before narrating the end, let us pause and consider his work of the two preceding years, 1818 and 1819, on which his fame as a great English poet is chiefly founded.

Chapter XIII

WORK OF 1818, 1819. — I. THE ACHIEVEMENTS

The work of Keats' two mature years (if any poet or man in his twenty-third and twenty-fourth years can be called mature) seems to divide itself naturally into two main groups or classes. One class consists of his finished achievements, things successfully carried through in accordance with his first intention; the other of his fragments and experiments, things begun and broken off either from external causes or because in the execution the poet changed his mind or his inspiration failed to sustain itself. I shall ask the reader to consider the two classes separately, the achievements first: not because there may not be even finer work in some of the fragments, but because a thing incomplete, a torso, however splendid in power and promise, cannot be judged on the same terms or with the same approach to finality as a thing of which the whole is before us. One finished thing only, the play of *Otho the Great*, I shall turn over to the second or experimental class, seeing that an experiment it essentially was, and one tried under conditions which made it impossible for Keats to be his true self.

The class of achievements will include, then, besides a score of sonnets and a few minor pieces of various form, the three completed tales in verse, *Isabella or the Pot of Basil*, *The Eve of St Agnes*, and *Lamia*; with the six odes, *To Psyche*, *On Indolence* (not published in Keats' lifetime), *On a Grecian Urn*, *To a Nightingale*, *To Melancholy*, and *To Autumn*. Beginning with the minor things, — the sonnets, being mostly occasional and autobiographical, have been sufficiently touched on in our narrative chapters, and so have several of the shorter lyrics, *In drear-nighted December*, *Meg Merrilies*, and *La Belle Dame Sans Merci*. There remains chiefly the batch of pieces in the seven-syllable couplet metre printed in the *Lamia* volume between the odes *To Psyche* and *To Autumn*. Two of these, *Lines on the Mermaid Tavern* and *Robin Hood*, were written, as we have seen, at the beginning of 1818, in the months when Keats was living alone in Well Walk and resting after his labour on *Endymion*. Both are easy, spirited, and intensely English in feeling; both, for all their gay lightness of touch, are marked with that vivid imaginative life in single phrases which almost from the first, amidst all the rawnesses of his youth, stamps Keats for a poet of the great lineage. Already two years earlier, in the valentine 'Hadst thou liv'd in days of old,' he had shown a fair command of this metre, and now we can feel that he has an ear well trained in its cadences by familiarity with the finest early models, from Fletcher (in the *Faithful Shepherdess*) and Ben Jonson (in the masque of *The Satyr*, the songs *To Celia*, and the *Charis* lyrics) down to *L'Allegro* and *Il Penseroso*.

The other two pieces in the same form, *Bards of Passion and of Mirth* and *Fancy*, date from nearly a year later, when Keats had settled under Brown's roof after Tom's death, and were copied by him for his brother in a letter dated January 2nd 1819. In the *Mermaid Tavern* lines he had followed in fancy the poet-guests of that hostelry to the Elysian fields and asked them if they found there any finer entertainment than in their old haunt. In *Bards of Passion and of Mirth*, which he wrote on a blank page in Dilke's copy of Beaumont and Fletcher, Keats singles out this particular pair of poet-partners to follow beyond the grave, and in a strain somewhat more serious tells of the double lives they lead, — their souls left here on earth in their writings, and themselves —

> Seated on Elysian lawns
> Brows'd by none but Dian's fawns...
> Where the nightingale doth sing
> Not a senseless, trancèd thing,
> But divine, melodious truth;
> Philosophic numbers smooth;
> Tales and golden histories
> Of heaven and its mysteries.

In the affirmation with which the piece concludes, —
Bards of Passion and of Mirth,
Ye have left your souls on Earth!
Ye have souls in heaven too,
Double-liv'd in regions new! —

in this affirmation it seems, as Mr Buxton Forman has pointed out, as though Keats were gaily countering the view of Wordsworth in the well-known stanzas where, declaring how the power of Burns survives 'deep in the general heart of men,' he goes on to ask what need has the poet for any other kind of Elysian after-life.

Following an eighteenth-century practice, Keats calls this set of heptasyllabics an ode, a form which in strictness it no way resembles. A higher place is taken in his work by the longest poem he sends his brother in the same metre, *Fancy*. He calls it a rondeau, again rather at random; but he had already called the Bacchus lyric in *Endymion* a roundelay, and seems to have thought that the name might apply to any set of verses returning upon itself at the end with a repetition of its beginning. In the present case he both opens and closes his poem with the same idea as has been condensed by a later writer in the two-line refrain —

But every poet, born to stray,
Still feeds upon the far-away.
The opening lines run, —
Ever let the Fancy roam,
Pleasure never is at home:
At a touch sweet Pleasure melteth,
Like to bubbles when rain pelteth;
Then let winged Fancy wander
Through the thought still spread beyond her:
Open wide the mind's cage-door,
She'll dart forth, and cloudward soar.
O sweet Fancy! let her loose;
Summer's joys are spoilt by use,
And the enjoying of the Spring
Fades as does its blossoming;
Autumn's red-lipp'd fruitage too,
Blushing through the mist and dew,
Cloys with tasting: What do then?

The answer is that the thing to do is to sit by the chimney corner while Fancy goes ranging abroad to find and bring home a harvest of incompatible and contradictory delights; and after the evocation of a number of such the poem comes round at the end to a slightly altered repetition of its opening couplet, —

Let the winged Fancy roam
Pleasure never is at home.

I like to think that Keats may have drawn his impulse to writing this poem from the fine passage in Fuller's *Holy State* quoted by Lamb in his brief 'Specimens' of that author: —

Fancy. — It is the most boundless and restless faculty of the soul...it digs without spade, sails without ship, flies without wings, builds without charges, fights without bloodshed; in a moment striding from the centre to the circumference of the world; by a kind of omnipotency creating and annihilating things in an instant; and things divorced in Nature are married in Fancy as in a lawless place.

At any rate Keats' poem, in its best and central part, is a delightful embroidery on the ideas here expressed. The notion, or vision, of a lawless place where all manner of things divorced in nature abide together and happily jostle, was one that often haunted him, as witness his verse-epistle to Reynolds from Teignmouth, the fragment he calls *The Castle Builder*, and again the piece beginning 'Welcome joy and welcome sorrow,' to which there has been posthumously given the title *A Song of Opposites*. The lines evoking such a vision in this poem, *Fancy*, are almost his happiest in his lighter vein, and are written in the true Elizabethan tradition: the predominant influence in the handling of the measure being, to my ear, that of Ben Jonson, who is wont to give it a certain weight and slowness of movement by the free use of long syllables in the unaccented places; even so Keats, in the passage quoted above, puts in such places words like 'sweet,' 'rain,' 'still,' 'cage,' 'dart,' 'lipp'd.'

Passing from the minor to the major achievements of the time, the earliest, and to my mind the finest, of these is *Isabella or the Pot of Basil*. During the writing of *Endymion*, Keats had intended his next effort to be on the lofty classic and symbolic theme of the dethronement of Hyperion and the Titans and the accession of Apollo and the Olympians. But certain reading and talk in the Hunt circle having diverted him from this purpose for a while, and made him take up the idea of a volume of metrical tales from Boccaccio to be written jointly by himself and Reynolds, he chose the tale of the Pot of Basil (the fifth of the fourth day in the *Decameron*), made a sudden beginning at it before he left Hampstead at the end of February, (1819), and finished it at Teignmouth in the course of April. As an appropriate vehicle for an Italian story he took the Italian *ottava rima* or stanza of eight. Several of the earlier English poets had used this metre: Keats' main model for it was doubtless Edward Fairfax, who, following other Elizabethan translators, had in his fine version from Tasso, *Godfrey of Bulloigne*, done much more than any of his predecessors towards suppling and perfecting its treatment in English. Since then it had been little employed in our serious poetry, but had lately been brilliantly revived for flippant and satiric uses, after later Italian models, by Hookham Frere and Byron. Keats goes over the heads of these direct to Fairfax, and in certain points at least, in variety of pause and cadence and subtle adaptation of verbal music to emotional effect, by a good deal outdoes even that excellent master. Of course it is of the essence of his treatment to avoid, in the closing couplet of the stanza, the special effect of witty snap and suddenness which fits it so well for the purpose of satire.

Every one knows the story: how a maiden of Messina (Keats chooses to transfer the scene to Florence), living in the house of her merchant brothers, in secret loves one of their clerks: how her brothers, discovering her secret, take out her lover to the forest and there slay and bury him: how his ghost appearing to her in a dream reveals his fate and burial place: how she hastens thither with her nurse, digs till she finds the corpse and having found it carries home the head and sets it in a pot of basil, or sweet marjoram, which she cherishes and waters with her tears until her brothers take it from her, whereupon she pines away and dies.

Boccaccio tells this story with that admirable combination of straightforward conciseness and finished grace which characterizes his mature prose. Keats in his poem romantically amplifies and embroiders it. In his way of doing so we can trace the influence of Chaucer, with whose *Troilus and Criseyde*, that miracle of detailed, long-drawn, yet ever human and rarely tedious narrative, he was by this time familiar. Keats, while avoiding Chaucer's prolixity, diversifies his tale with invocations to Love and to the Muses, with apostrophes to the reader and ejaculatory comments on the events, entirely in Chaucer's manner: only whereas Chaucer relegates the more part of such matter to the 'proems' of his several books, Keats, having plunged into the thick of the story in his first line, finds room for his apostrophes and invocations in the course of the narrative itself. Most critics have taken the view that this is evidence of weak or immature art. To my mind this is not so: the pauses thus introduced are never long enough to hold up the flow and interest of the narrative, while they afford welcome rests to the attention, pleasant changes from a too sustained narrative construction, with consequent beautiful and happy modulations in the movement of the verse.

One of these invocations — invocation and apology together — is to Boccaccio himself, disowning all idea of improving the tale and defining the poet's attempt as made but to honour him, —

To stead thee as a verse in English tongue,
An echo of thee in the north-wind sung.

The definition is exact. The revived spirit of English romantic poetry breathes in every line of the verse, and as in *Endymion*, so here, the southern setting is conceived as though it were English. 'So the two brothers and their murder'd man' (the force of the anticipatory epithet has been celebrated by every critic since Lamb) —

So the two brothers and their murder'd man
Rode past fair Florence, to where Arno's stream
Gurgles through straiten'd banks, and still doth fan
Itself with dancing bulrush, and the bream
Keep head against the freshets.

Another such criticized 'digression' tells of the toilers yoked in all quarters of the world to the service of these avaricious merchant brothers. In calling up their sufferings Keats for a moment strikes an unexpected verbal echo from the *Annus Mirabilis* of Dryden. Dryden, telling of the monopolies of the Dutch in the East India trade, had written, —

For them alone the Heav'ns had kindly heat,
In eastern quarries ripening precious dew:
For them the Idumean balm did sweat,
And in hot Ceilon spicy forests grew.

Keats writes of Isabella's brothers, —

For them the Ceylon diver held his breath,
And went all naked to the hungry shark,
For them his ears gush'd blood —

with more in the same strain, very vividly and humanly imagined, but somewhat unevenly written. On the other hand the last of the rests or interruptions in this poem is to my thinking one of its most original and admirable beauties: I mean the invocation beginning 'O Melancholy, linger here awhile,' repeated with lovely modulations in stanzas lv, lvi, and lxi; the poet deliberately pausing to heighten his effect as it were by an accompaniment of words chosen purely for their pathetic melody and more musical than music itself.

Keats' way of imagining and telling the story is not less delicate than it is intense. Flaws and false notes there are: phrases, as in *Endymion*, too dulcet and cloying, like that which tells how the lover's lips grew bold, 'And poesied with hers in dewy rhyme:' a flat line where it is most out of place — 'And Isabella did not stamp or rave:' a far-fetched rime, as where 'love' and 'grove' draw in after them the alien idea of Lorenzo not being embalmed in 'Indian clove.' But such flaws, abundant in *Endymion*, are in *Isabella* rare and need to be searched for. If we want an example of the staple tissue of the poem we shall rather find it in a stanza like this: —

Parting they seem'd to tread upon the air,
Twin roses by the zephyr blown apart
Only to meet again more close, and share
The inward fragrance of each other's heart.
She, to her chamber gone, a ditty fair
Sang of delicious love and honey'd dart;
He with light steps went up a western hill,
And bade the sun farewell, and joy'd his fill.

The image of love-happiness in the last couplet is as jocund and uplifting as some radiant symbolic drawing by Blake, and poetry has few things more perfect or easier in their perfection.

In a far more difficult kind, where Keats has to deal with the features of the story that might easily make for the repulsive or the *macabre*, he triumphs not by shirking but by sheer force of passionate imagination. 'The excellence of every art is its intensity, capable of making all disagreeables evaporate from their being in close relationship with beauty and truth.' This dictum of Keats can scarcely be better illustrated than by his own handling of the *Isabella* story. Take the vision of the murdered man appearing to the girl at night: —

> Strange sound it was, when the pale shadow spake;
> For there was striving, in its piteous tongue,
> To speak as when on earth it was awake,
> And Isabella on its music hung:
> Languor there was in it, and tremulous shake,
> As in a palsied Druid's harp unstrung;
> And through it moan'd a ghostly undersong,
> Like hoarse night-gusts sepulchral briars among.
> Its eyes, though wild, were still all dewy bright
> With love, and kept all phantom fear aloof
> From the poor girl by magic of their light.

How wonderfully, in these touches, do we feel love prevailing over horror and purging the apparition of all its charnel ghastliness. When we come to the discovery and digging up of the body, Boccaccio turns the difficulty which must inhere in any realistic treatment of the theme by simply saying that it was uncorrupted; as though some kind of miracle had kept it fresh. Keats on the other hand confronts the difficulty and overcomes it. First he acknowledges how the imagination in dwelling on the dead is prone to call up images of corruptibility: —

> Who hath not loiter'd in a green churchyard,
> And let his spirit, like a demon-mole,
> Work through the clayey soil and gravel hard,
> To see scull, coffin'd bones, and funeral stole;
> Pitying each form that hungry Death hath marr'd,
> And filling it once more with human soul?
> Ah! this is holiday to what was felt
> When Isabella by Lorenzo knelt.

Then he compulsively leads away the mind from such images to think only of the passionate absorption with which Isabella flings herself upon her task: —

> She gaz'd into the fresh-thrown mould, as though
> One glance did fully all its secrets tell;
> Clearly she saw, as other eyes would know
> Pale limbs at bottom of a crystal well;
> Upon the murderous spot she seem'd to grow,
> Like to a native lilly of the dell:
> Then with her knife, all sudden, she began
> To dig more fervently than misers can.
> Soon she turn'd up a soiled glove, whereon
> Her silk had play'd in purple phantasies,
> She kiss'd it with a lip more chill than stone,
> And put it in her bosom, where it dries
> And freezes utterly unto the bone

> Those dainties made to still an infant's cries:
> Then 'gan she work again; nor stay'd her care,
> But to throw back at times her veiling hair.

Is any scene in poetry written with more piercing, more unerring, vision? The swift despairing gaze of the girl, anticipating with too dire a certainty the realization of her dream: the simile in the third and fourth lines, emphasizing the clearness of that certainty, and at the same time relieving its terror by an image of beauty: the new simile of the lily, again striking the note of beauty, while it intensifies the impression of her rooted fixity of posture and purpose: the sudden solution of that fixity, with the final couplet, into vehement action, as she begins (with a fine implied commentary on the relative strength of passions) to dig 'more fervently than misers can': — then the first reward of her toil, in the shape of a relic not ghastly, but beautiful both in itself and for the tenderness of which it is a token: her womanly action in kissing it and putting it in her bosom, while all the woman and mother in her is in the same words revealed to us as blighted by the tragedy of her life: then the resumption and continuance of her labours, with gestures once more of vital dramatic truth as well as grace: — to imagine and to write like this is the privilege of the best poets only, and even the best have not often combined such concentrated force and beauty of conception with such a limpid and flowing ease of narrative. Poetry had always come to Keats as naturally as leaves to a tree. So he considered it ought to come, and now that it came of a quality like this, he had fairly earned the right, which his rash youth had too soon arrogated, to look down on the fine artificers of the school of Pope. In comparison with the illuminating power of true imaginative poetry, the closest rhetorical condensations of that school seem thin, their most glittering points and aphorisms mechanical: nay, those who admire them most justly will know better than to think the two kinds of writing comparable.

The final consignment by Isabella of her treasure to its casket is told with the same genius for turning horror into beauty: note the third and fourth lines of the following, with the magically cooling and soothing effect of their open-vowelled sonority; —

> Then in a silken scarf, — sweet with the dews
> Of precious flowers pluck'd in Araby,
> And divine liquids come with odorous ooze
> Through the cold serpent-pipe refreshfully, —
> She wrapp'd it up; and for its tomb did choose
> A garden-pot, wherein she laid it by,
> And cover'd it with mould, and o'er it set
> Sweet Basil, which her tears kept ever wet.
> And she forgot the stars, the moon, and sun,
> And she forgot the blue above the trees,
> And she forgot the dells where waters run,
> And she forgot the chilly autumn breeze;
> She had no knowledge when the day was done,
> And the new morn she saw not: but in peace
> Hung over her sweet Basil evermore,
> And moisten'd it with tears unto the core.

In passages like these of *Isabella* Keats, for one reader at least, reaches his high-water mark in human feeling, and in felicity both imaginative and executive. The next of his three poetic tales, *The Eve of St Agnes*, does not strike so deep, though it is more nearly faultless and lives as the most complete and enchanting English pure romance-poem of its time. Little or none of the effect is due in this case to elements of magic weirdness or supernatural terror such as counted for so much in the general romantic poetry of the day, and had been of the very essence of achievements so diverse as *The Ancient Mariner*, *Christabel*, *The Lay of the Last Minstrel*, and

Isabella itself. The tale hinges on the popular belief that on St Agnes's Eve (January the 20th) a maiden might win sight of her future husband in a dream by going to bed supperless, silent and without looking behind her, and sleeping on her back with her hands on the pillow above her head. This belief is mentioned by two writers at least with whom Keats was very familiar: by Ben Jonson in his masque *The Satyr* and Robert Burton in the *Anatomy of Melancholy*. An eighteenth century book of reference which he may well have known also, Brand's *Popular Antiquities*, cites the superstition and adds from a current chapbook a fuller account of it, mentioning other and alternative rites. But one feature of the promised vision which in Keats' mind was evidently essential, that the lover should regale his mistress after her fasting dream with exquisite viands and music, is not noted in any of these sources: Keats must either have invented it or drawn it from some other authority which criticism has not yet recognized.

It was an obvious and easy idea for Keats to weave into the St Agnes' Eve motive the motive of a love-passion between the son and daughter of hostile houses, and to bring the youth to a festival in the halls of his enemies in a manner which reminds one both of Romeo and Juliet and of the young Lochinvar in Scott's ballad. A remoter source has lately been pointed out as probable for the subsequent incidents of the lover's concealment by the old nurse in a closet next the maiden's chamber, his coming in to her while she sleeps, the melting of his real self into her dream of him, her momentary disenchantment and alarm on awakening, her reassurance and surrender and their ensuing happy union and flight. All these circumstances, it has been shown, except the immediate flight of the lovers, are closely paralleled in Boccaccio's early novel *Il Filocolo*, and look as though they must have been derived from it. The *Filocolo* is an excessively tedious and occasionally coarse amplification in prose, made by Boccaccio when his style was still unformed, of the old French metrical romance, long popular throughout Europe, of *Floire et Blancheflor*. The question is, how should Keats have come to be acquainted with it? At this time he knew very little Italian. He was accustomed to read his *Decameron* in a translation, and eight months later we find him with difficulty making out Ariosto at the rate of ten or a dozen stanzas a day. A French seventeenth-century version of the *Filocolo* indeed existed, but none in English. Can it be that Hunt had told Keats the story, or at least those parts of it which would serve him, in the course of talk about Boccaccio? One would not have expected even Hunt's love of Italian reading to sustain him through the tedium of this early and little known novel by the master: moreover in criticizing *The Eve of St Agnes* he gives no hint that Keats was indebted to him for any of its incidents. But there the resemblances are, too close to be easily explained as coincidences. The part played by the old nurse Angela in Keats' poem echoes pretty closely the part played by Glorizia in the *Filocolo*; the drama, dreaming and awake, played between Madeline and Porphyro, repeats, though in a far finer strain, that between Biancofiore and Florio; so that Keats' narrative reads truly like a magically refined and enriched quintessence distilled from the corresponding chapter in Boccaccio's tale.

But the question of sources is one for the special student, and its discussion may easily tire the lay reader. Passing to the poem and its qualities, we have to note first that, fresh from treading, in his *Hyperion* attempt, in the path of Milton, Keats in *The Eve of St Agnes* went back, so far as his manner is derivative at all, to the example of his first master, Spenser. He shows as perfect a command of the Spenserian stanza, with its 'sweet-slipping movement,' as Spenser himself, and as subtle a sense as his of the leisurely meditative pace imposed upon the metre by the lingering Alexandrine at the close. Narrating at this pace and in this mood, he is able at any moment with the lightest of touches to launch the imagination to music on a voyage beyond the beyonds, and to charge every line, every word almost, with a richness and fullness of far-away suggestion that yet never clogs the easy harmonious flow of the verse. At the same time he does not, in this new poem, attempt anything like the depth of human passion and pathos which he had touched in Isabella, and his personages appeal to us in the manner strictly defined as 'romantic,' that is to say not so much humanly and in themselves as by the circumstances, scenery, and atmosphere amidst which they move.

In handling these Keats' method is the reverse of that by which some writers vainly endeavour to rival in literature the effects of the painter and sculptor. He never writes for the eye merely, but vivifies everything he touches, telling even of dead and senseless things in terms of life, movement, and feeling. From the opening stanza, which makes us feel the chill of the season to our bones, — telling us first of its effect on the wild and tame creatures of wood and field, and next how the frozen breath of the old beadsman in the chapel aisle 'seem'd taking flight for heaven, without a death,' — from thence to the close, where the lovers disappear into the night, the poetry throbs in every line with the life of imagination and beauty. The monuments in the aisle are brought before us, not by any effort of description, but solely through our sympathy with the shivering fancy of the beadsman: —

> Knights, ladies, praying in dumb orat'ries,
> He passeth by; and his weak spirit fails
> To think how they may ache in icy hoods and mails.

Even into the sculptured heads of the corbels supporting the banquet-hall roof the poet strikes life: —

> The carved angels, ever eager-eyed,
> Stared, where upon their heads the cornice rests,
> With wings blown back, and hands put crosswise on their breasts.

The painted panes in the chamber window, instead of trying to pick out their beauties in detail, he calls —

> Innumerable of stains and splendid dyes
> As are the tiger-moth's deep-damask'd wings, —

a gorgeous phrase which leaves the widest range to the colour-imagination of the reader, giving it at the same time a sufficient clue by the simile drawn from a particular specimen of nature's blazonry. In the last line of the same stanza —

> A shielded scutcheon blush'd with blood of queens and kings,

— the word 'blush' makes the colour seem to come and go, while the mind is at the same time sent travelling from the maiden's chamber on thoughts of her lineage and ancestral fame. Observation, I believe, shows that moonlight has not the power to transmit the separate hues of painted glass as Keats in this celebrated passage represents it, but fuses them into a kind of neutral or indiscriminate opaline shimmer. Let us be grateful for the error, if error it is, which has led him to heighten, by these saintly splendours of colour, the sentiment of a scene wherein a voluptuous glow is so exquisitely attempered with chivalrous chastity and awe. If any reader wishes to realise how the genius of Elizabethan romantic poetry re-awoke in Keats, and how much enriched and enhanced, after two hundred years, let him compare all this scene of Madeline's unrobing with the passage from Brown's *Britannia's Pastorals* which was probably in his memory when he wrote it (see above, p. 98).

When Madeline unclasps her jewels, a weaker poet would have dwelt on their lustre or other visible qualities: Keats puts those aside, and speaks straight to our spirits in an epithet breathing with the very life of the wearer, — 'Her warmèd jewels.' When Porphyro spreads the feast of dainties beside his sleeping mistress, we are made to feel how those ideal and rare sweets of sense surround and minister to her, not only with their own natural richness, but with the associations and the homage of all far countries whence they have been gathered —

> From silken Samarcand to cedar'd Lebanon.

Concerning this sumptuous passage of the spread feast of fruits, not unequally rivalling the famous one in Milton, Leigh Hunt has some interesting things to say in his *Autobiography* : —

I remember Keats reading to me, with great relish and particularity, conscious of what he had set forth, the lines describing the supper and ending with the words,

> And lucent syrups tinct with cinnamon.

Mr Wordsworth would have said the vowels were not varied enough; but Keats knew where his vowels were *not* to be varied. On the occasion above alluded to, Wordsworth found fault with the repetition of the concluding sound of the participles in Shakespeare's line about bees: —

> The *singing* masons *building* roofs of gold.

This, he said, was a line which Milton would never have written. Keats thought, on the other hand, that the repetition was in harmony with the continued note of the singers, and that Shakespeare's negligence, if negligence it was, had instinctively felt the thing in the best manner.

The reader will remember how Bailey records this subject of the musical and emotional effect of vowel sounds, open and close, varied or iterated as the case might be, as one on which Keats' talk had often run at Oxford. Whatever his theories, he was by this time showing himself as fine a master of such effects as any, even the greatest, of our poets. This same passage, or interlude, of the feast of fruits has despite its beauty been sometimes blamed as a 'digression.' A stanza which in Keats' original draft stood near the beginning of the poem shows that in his mind it was no mere ornament and no digression at all, but an essential part of his scheme. In revision he dropped out this stanza, doubtless as being not up to the mark poetically: pity that he did not rather perfect it and let it keep its place: but even as it is the provision of the dainties made beforehand by the old nurse at Porphyro's request (stanza xx) proves the feast essential to the story.

While the unique charm of *The Eve of St Agnes* lies thus in the richness and vitality of the accessory and decorative images, the actions and emotions of the personages are not less happily conceived as far as they go. What can be better touched than the figures of the beadsman and the old nurse Angela? How admirable in particular is the debate held by Angela with Porphyro in her

> little moonlight room
> Pale, lattic'd, chill, and silent as a tomb.

Madeline, a figure necessarily in the main passive, is none the less exquisite, whether in her gentle dealing with the nurse on the staircase, or when closing her chamber door she pants with quenched taper in the moonlight, and most of all when awakening she finds her lover beside her, and contrasts his bodily presence with her dream: —

> 'Ah, Porphyro!' said she, 'but even now
> Thy voice was at sweet tremble in mine ear,
> Made tuneable with every sweetest vow;
> And those sad eyes were spiritual and clear:
> How chang'd thou art! how pallid, chill, and drear!
> Give me that voice again, my Porphyro,
> Those looks immortal, those complainings dear!'

In all the doings and circumstances attending the departure of the lovers for a destination left thrillingly vague in the words, 'For o'er the southern moors I have a home for thee,' — in the elfin storm sent to cover their flight (the only touch of the supernatural in the story), their darkling grope down the stairway, the hush that holds the house and guest-chambers, the wind-shaken arras, the porter sprawling asleep beside his empty flagon, the awakened bloodhound who recognizes his mistress and is quiet — in Keats' telling of all these things a like unflagging richness and felicity of imagination holds us spell-bound: and with the deaths of the old nurse and beadsman, once the house has lost its spirit of life and light in Madeline, the poet brings round the tale, after all its glow of passionate colour and music, of trembling anticipation and love-worship enraptured or in suspense, to a chill and wintry close in subtlest harmony with its beginning: —

> They glide, like phantoms, into the wide hall;
> Like phantoms, to the iron porch, they glide;
> Where lay the Porter, in uneasy sprawl,
> With a huge empty flaggon by his side:
> The wakeful bloodhound rose, and shook his hide,
> But his sagacious eye an inmate owns:
> By one, and one, the bolts full easy slide:
> The chains lie silent on the footworn stones;
> The key turns, and the door upon its hinges groans.
> And they are gone: aye, ages long ago
> These lovers fled away into the storm.
> That night the Baron dreamt of many a woe,
> And all his warrior-guests, with shade and form
> Of witch, and demon, and large coffin-worm,
> Were long be-nightmar'd. Angela the old
> Died palsy-twitch'd, with meagre face deform;
> The Beadsman, after thousand aves told,
> For aye unsought for slept among his ashes cold.

The last of the trio of Keats' tales in verse, *Lamia* , owed its origin, and perhaps part of its temper, to his readings in Burton's *Anatomy of Melancholy* . His own experiences under the stings of love and jealousy had led him, during those spring months of 1819 when he could write nothing, to pore much over the treatise of that prodigiously read, satiric old commentator on the maladies of the human mind and body, and especially over those sections of it which deal with the cause and cure of love-melancholy. Entertainment in abundance, information in cartloads, Keats could draw from the matter accumulated and glossed by Burton, but little or nothing to gladden or soothe or fortify him. One story, however, he found which struck his imagination so much that he was moved to write upon it, and that was the old Greek story, quoted by Burton from Philostratus, of *Lamia* the serpent-lady, at once witch and victim of witchcraft, who loved a youth of Corinth and lived with him in a palace of delights built by her magic, until their happiness was shattered by the scrutiny of intrusive and coldblooded wisdom.

In June 1819, soon after the inspiration which produced the Odes had passed away, and before he left Hampstead for the Isle of Wight, Keats made a beginning on this new task; continued it at intervals, concurrently with his attempts in drama, at Shanklin and Winchester; and finished it by the first week in September. It happened that Thomas Love Peacock had published the year before a tale in verse on a nearly similar theme, — that of the beautiful Thessalian enchantress Rhododaphne: one wonders whether Keats may not have felt in Peacock's attempt a challenge and stimulus to his own. Peacock's work, now unduly neglected, is that of an accomplished scholar and craftsman sitting down to tell an old Greek tale of magic in the form of narrative verse then most fashionable, the mixed four-stressed couplet and ballad measure of Scott and Byron, and telling it, for a poet not of genius, gracefully and well. Whether Keats' *Lamia* is a work of genius there is no need to ask. No one can deny the truth of his own criticism of it when he says, 'I am certain there is that sort of fire in it which must take hold of people in some way — give them either pleasant or unpleasant sensation.' But personally I cannot agree with the opinion of the late Francis Turner Palgrave and other critics — I think they are the majority — who give it the first place among the tales. On the contrary, if an order of merit among them there must be, I should put it third and lowest, for several reasons of detail as well as for one reason affecting the whole design and composition.

As to the technical qualities of the poetry, let it be granted that Keats' handling of the heroic couplet, modelled this time on the example of Dryden and not of the Elizabethans, though retaining pleasant traces of the Elizabethan usages of the overrun or *enjambement* and the varied pause, — let it be granted that his handling of this mode of the metre is masterly. Let it be admitted also that there are passages in the narrative imagined as intensely as any in *Isabella* or *The Eve of St Agnes* and told quite as vividly in a style more rapid and condensed. Such is the passage, in the introductory episode which fills so large a relative place in the poem, where Mercury woos and wins his wood-nymph after Lamia has lifted from her the spell of invisibility. Such is the gorgeous, agonized transformation act of Lamia herself from serpent to woman: such again the scene of her waylaying and ensnaring of the youth on his way to Corinth. And such above all would be the whole final scene of the banquet and its break-up, from 'Soft went the music with soft air along' to the end, but for the perplexing apostrophe, presently to be considered, which interrupts it. Still counting up the things in the poem to be most praised, here is an example where the poetry of Greek mythology is very eloquently woven into the rhetoric of love: —

> Leave thee alone! Look back! Ah! goddess, see
> Whether my eyes can ever turn from thee!
> For pity do not this sad heart belie —
> Even as thou vanishest so I shall die.
> Stay! though a Naiad of the rivers, stay!
> To thy far wishes will thy streams obey:
> Stay! though the greenest woods be thy domain,
> Alone they can drink up the morning rain:
> Though a descended Pleiad, will not one
> Of thine harmonious sisters keep in tune
> Thy spheres, and as thy silver proxy shine?

And here a beautiful instance of power and justness in scenic imagination: —

> As men talk in a dream, so Corinth all,
> Throughout her palaces imperial,
> And all her populous streets and temples lewd,
> Mutter'd, like tempest in the distance brew'd,
> To the wide-spreaded night above her towers.
> Men, women, rich and poor, in the cool hours,
> Shuffled their sandals o'er the pavement white,
> Companion'd or alone; while many a light
> Flar'd here and there, from wealthy festivals,
> And threw their moving shadows on the walls,
> Or found them cluster'd in the cornic'd shade
> Of some arch'd temple door, or dusty colonnade.

Turning now to the other side of the account: for one thing, we find jarring and disappointing notes, such as had disappeared from Keats' works since *Endymion*, of the old tasteless manner of the Hunt-taught days: for instance the unpalatable passage in the first book beginning 'Let the mad poets say whate'er they please,' and worse still, with a new note of idle cynicism added, the lines about love which open the second book. Misplaced archaisms also reappear, such as 'unshent' and the participle 'daft,' from the obsolete verb 'daff,' used as though it meant to puzzle or daze; with bad verbal coinages like 'piazzian,' 'psalterian.' Moreover, though many things in the poem are potently conceived, others are not so. The description of the magical palace-hall is surely a failure, except for the one fine note in the lines, —

> A haunting music, sole perhaps and lone
> Supporters of the faery-roof, made moan
> Throughout, as fearful the whole charm might fade.

The details of the structure, with its pairs of palms and plantains carved in cedar-wood, its walls lined with mirrors, its panels which change magically from plain marble to jasper, its fifty censers and 'Twelve sphered tables, by twelve seats insphered,' — all this seems feebly and even tastelessly invented in comparison with the impressive dream-architecture in some of Keats' other poems: I will even go farther, and say that it scarce holds its own against the not much dissimilar magic hall in the sixth canto of *Rhododaphne*.

But the one fundamental flaw in *Lamia* concerns its moral. The word is crude: what I mean is the bewilderment in which it leaves us as to the effect intended to be made on our imaginative sympathies. Lamia is a serpent-woman, baleful and a witch, whose love for Lycius fills him with momentary happiness but must, we are made aware, be fatal to him. Apollonius is a philosopher who sees through her and by one steadfast look withers up her magic semblance and destroys her, but in doing so fails to save his pupil, who dies the moment his illusion vanishes. Are these things a bitter parable, meaning that all love-joys are but deception, and that at the touch of wisdom and experience they melt away? If so, the tale might have been told either tragically or satirically, in either case leaving the reader impartial as between the sage and his victim. But Keats in this apostrophe, which I wish he had left out, deliberately points a moral and expressly invites us to take sides: —

> What wreath for Lamia? What for Lycius?
> What for the sage, old Apollonius?
> Upon her aching forehead be there hung
> The leaves of willow and of adder's tongue;
> And for the youth, quick, let us strip for him
> The thyrsus, that his watching eyes may swim
> Into forgetfulness; and, for the sage,
> Let spear-grass and the spiteful thistle wage
> War on his temples. Do not all charms fly
> At the mere touch of cold philosophy?
> There was an awful rainbow once in heaven:
> We know her woof, her texture; she is given
> In the dull catalogue of common things.
> Philosophy will clip an Angel's wings,
> Conquer all mysteries by rule and line,
> Empty the haunted air, and gnomed mine —
> Unweave a rainbow, as it erewhile made
> The tender-person'd Lamia melt into a shade.

These lines to my mind have not only the fault of breaking the story at a critical point and anticipating its issue, but challenge the mind to untimely questionings and reflections. The wreaths of ominous growth distributed to each of the three personages may symbolize the general tragedy: but why are we asked to take sides with the enchantress, ignoring everything about her except her charm, and against the sage? If she were indeed a thing of bale under a mask of beauty, was not the friend and tutor bound to unmask her? and if the pupil could not survive the loss of his illusion, — if he could not confront the facts of life and build up for himself a new happiness on a surer foundation, — was it not better that he should be let perish? Is there not in all this a slackening of imaginative and intellectual grasp? And especially as to the last lines, do we not feel that they are but a cheap and unilluminating repetition of a rather superficial idea, the idea phrased shortly in Campbell's *Rainbow* and at length in several well-known passages of Wordsworth's *Excursion*, particularly that in the fifth book beginning —

> Ambitious spirits! —
> Whom earth, at this late season, hath produced
> To regulate the moving spheres, and weigh
> The planets in the hollow of their hand;
> And they who rather dive than soar, whose pains
> Have solved the elements, or analysed
> The thinking principle — shall they in fact
> Prove a degraded Race?

Wordsworth had fifteen years earlier written more wisely, 'Poetry is the impassioned expression in the countenance of all science.' The latter-day Wordsworth, and Keats after him, should have realised that the discoveries of 'philosophy,' meaning science, create new mysteries while they solve the old, and leave the world as full of poetry as they found it: poetry, it may be, with its point of view shifted, poetry of a new kind, but none the less poetical. Leigh Hunt, in his review of *Lamia* published on the appearance of the volume, has some remarks partly justifying and partly impugning Keats' treatment of the story in this respect: —

Mr Keats has departed as much from commonplace in the character and moral of this story, as he has in the poetry of it. He would see fair play to the serpent, and makes the power of the philosopher an ill-natured and disturbing thing. Lamia though liable to be turned into painful shapes had a soul of humanity; and the poet does not see why she should not have her pleasures accordingly, merely because a philosopher saw that she was not a mathematical truth. This is fine and good. It is vindicating the greater philosophy of poetry.

So far, this is a manifest piece of special pleading by Hunt on Lamia's behalf. If she is nothing worse than a being with a soul of humanity liable to be turned into painful shapes, why must Apollonius feel it his duty to wither and destroy her for the safeguarding of his pupil, even at the cost of that pupil's life? Her witchcraft must consist in something much worse than not being a mathematical truth, else why is he her so bitter enemy? Hunt proceeds, more to the purpose, to protest against the poet's implication —

that modern experiment has done a deadly thing to poetry by discovering the nature of the rainbow, the air, etc., that is to say, that the knowledge of natural history and physics, by shewing us the nature of things, does away with the imaginations that once adorned them. This is a condescension to a learned vulgarism, which so excellent a poet as Mr Keats ought not to have made. The world will always have fine poetry, so long as it has events, passions, affections, and a philosophy that sees deeper than this philosophy. There will be a poetry of the heart, so long as there are tears and smiles: there will be a poetry of the imagination, as long as the first causes of things remain a mystery. A man who is no poet, may think he is none, as soon as he finds out the physical cause of the rainbow; but he need not alarm himself: — he was none before. The true poet will go deeper. He will ask himself what is the cause of that physical cause; whether truths to the senses are after all to be taken as truths to the imagination; and whether there is not room and mystery enough in the universe for the creation of infinite things, when the poor matter-of-fact philosopher has come to the end of his own vision.

In *Endymion* Keats had impeded and confused his narrative by working into it much incident and imagery symbolic of the cogitations and aspirations, the upliftings and misgivings, of his own unripe spirit. Three years later, writing to Shelley from his sickbed, he contrasts that former state of his mind with its present state, saying that it was then like a scattered pack of cards but is now sorted to a pip. The three tales just discussed, written in the interval, show how quickly the power of sorting and controlling his imaginations had matured itself in him. In them he is already an artist standing outside of his own conceptions, certain of his own aim in dealing with them (subject perhaps to some reservation in the case of *Lamia*), and scarcely letting his personal self intrude upon his narrative at all to complicate or distract it.

For the expression of his private moods and meditations he had perfected during the same interval a new and beautiful vehicle in the ode. He had been accustomed to try his hand at odes, or what he called such, from his earliest riming days: and odes also, to all intents and purposes, are the two great lyrics in *Endymion*, the choral hymn to Pan and the song of the Indian maiden to Sorrow. But those which he composed in quick succession, as we have seen, in the late spring of 1819 are of a reflective and meditative type, new in his work and highly personal.

That which I have shown reason for believing to be the earliest of the group, the *Ode to Psyche* written in the last days of April, differs somewhat from the rest both in form and spirit. Its strophes are longer and more irregular: its strain less inward and brooding, with more of lyric ardour and exaltation. It tells of the poet's delight in that late, exquisitely and spiritually symbolic product of the mythologic spirit of expiring paganism, the story of Cupid and Psyche. What may have especially turned his attention to this fable at that moment we cannot tell. Possibly the mention of it in Burton's *Anatomy* may have set him on to reading the original source, the *Golden Ass* of Apuleius, in Adlington's translation: there are passages in *Lamia* which suggest such a reading, and the noble, rhythmical English of that Elizabethan version, loose as it may be in point of scholarship, could not fail to charm his ear. Or possibly recent study of the plates in the *Musée Napoléon* (as to which more by and by) may have brought freshly to his memory the sculptured group in which the story is embodied. But that he had always loved the story we know from the passage 'I stood tip-toe' beginning —

> So felt he, who first told how Psyche went
> On the smooth wind to realms of wonderment,

as well as from his confession that in boyhood he used to admire its languid and long-drawn romantic treatment in the poem of Mrs Tighe.

Cloying touches of languor, such as often disfigure his own earlier work, are not wanting in the opening lines in which he tells how he came upon the fabled couple in a dream, but are more than compensated by the charm of the scene where he finds them reposing, 'Mid hush'd, cool-rooted flowers fragrant-eyed.' What other poet has compressed into a single line so much of the essential virtue of flowers, of their power to minister to the spirit of man through all his senses at once? Such felicity in compound epithets is by this time habitual with Keats; and of Spenser with his 'sea-shouldering whales' he is now more than the equal. The 'azure-lidded sleep' of the maiden in *St Agnes' Eve* is matched in this ode by the 'soft-conchèd ear' of Psyche, — though the compound is perhaps a little forced and odd, like the 'cirque-couchant' snake in *Lamia*. The invocation in the third and fourth stanzas expresses, with the fullest reach of Keats' felicity in style and a singular freshness and fire of music in the verse, both his sense of the meaning of Greek nature-religion and his delight in imagining the beauty of its shrines and ritual. For the rest, there seems at first something strained in the turn of thought and expression whereby the poet offers himself and the homage of his own mind to the divinity he addresses, in lieu of the worship of antiquity for which she came too late; and especially in the terms of the metaphor which opens the famous fourth stanza: —

> Yes, I will be thy priest, and build a fane
> In some untrodden region of my mind,
> Where branched thoughts, new-blown with pleasant pain,
> Instead of pines shall murmur in the wind.

But in a moment we are carried beyond criticism by that incomparable distillation of one, or many, of his impressions among the Lakes or in Scotland, —

> Far, far around shall those dark-cluster'd trees
> Fledge the wild-ridged mountains steep by steep.

For such a master-stroke of concentrated imaginative description no praise, much as has been showered on it by Ruskin and lesser critics, can be too great.

Keats declares to his brother that this is the first of his poems with which he has taken even moderate pains. That being so, it is remarkable that he should have let stand in it as many as three unrimed line-endings: and what the poem truly bears in upon the reader is a sense less of special care and finish than of special glow and ardour, till he is left breathless and delighted at the threshold of the sanctuary prepared by the 'gardener Fancy,' his mind enthralled by the imagery and his ear by the verse, with its swift, mounting music and rich, vehemently iterated assonances towards the close: —

> A rosy sanctuary will I dress
> With the wreath'd trellis of a working brain,
> With buds, and bells, and stars without a name,
> With all the gardener Fancy e'er could feign,
> With breeding flowers, will never breed the same;
> And thither will I bring all soft delights
> That shadowy thought can win,
> A bright torch, and a casement ope at nights,
> To let the warm Love in!

The four remaining spring odes are slower-paced, as becomes their more musing tenour, and are all written in a succession of stanzas repeated uniformly or with slight variations. Throughout them all each stanza is of ten lines and five rimes, the first and second rimes arranged in a quatrain, the third, fourth and fifth in a sestet: the order of rimes in the sestet varying in the different odes, and in one, the nightingale ode, the third line from the end being shortened so as to have three stresses instead of five.

Let us take first the two in which the imagery has been suggested to the poet by works of Greek sculpture whether seen or imagined. In the *Ode on Indolence* Keats merely revives his memory of a special type of Greek marble urn where draped figures of women, Seasons, it may be, or priestesses, walk with joined hands behind a solemn Bacchus, or priest in the god's guise (see Plate viii, p. 342), — he merely evokes this memory in order to describe the way in which certain symbolic personages have seemed in a day-dream to pass before him and re-pass and again re-pass, appearing and disappearing as the embossed figures on such an urn may be made to do by turning it round. From the 'man and two women' of the March letter they are changed to three women, whom at first he does not recognize; but seeing presently who they are, namely Love, Ambition, and that 'maiden most unmeek,' his 'demon Poesy,' he for a moment longs for wings to follow and overtake them. The longing passes, and in his relaxed mood he feels that none of the three holds any joy for him —

> so sweet as drowsy noons,
> And evenings steep'd in honey'd indolence.

They come by once more, and again, barely aroused from the sweets of outdoor slumber and the spring afternoon, he will not so much as lift his head from where he lies, but bids them farewell and sees them depart without a tear.

Keats did not print this ode, thinking it perhaps not good enough or else too intimately personal. But writing to Miss Jeffrey a few weeks after it was composed, he tells her it is the thing he has most enjoyed writing this year. It is indeed a pleasant, lovingly meditated revival and casting into verse of the imagery which had come freshly into his mind when he wrote to his brother of his fit of languor in the previous March. It contains some powerful and many exquisite lines, but only one perfect stanza, the fifth: and there are slacknesses — shall we say lazinesses — in the execution, as where the need for rimes to 'noons' and 'indolence' prompts the all-too commonplace prayer —

> That I may never know how change the moons,
> Or hear the voice of busy commonsense;

or where, thinking contemptuously of the old 'intercoronation' days with Leigh Hunt, he declines, in truly Cockney rime, to raise his head from the flowery *grass* in order to be fed with praise and become 'a pet-lamb in a sentimental *farce*.'

In bidding the phantoms of this day-dream adieu, Keats avows that there are others yet haunting him, and while imagery drawn from the sculptures on Greek vases was still floating through his mind, he was able to rouse himself to a stronger effort and produce a true masterpiece in his famous *Ode on a Grecian Urn*. It is no single or actually existing specimen of Attic handicraft that he celebrates in this ode, but a composite conjured up instinctively in his mind out of several such known to him in reality or from engravings. During and after those hour-long silent reveries among the museum marbles of which Severn tells us, the creative spirit within him will have been busy almost unaware combining such images and re-combining them. Cricitism can plausibly analyse this creation into its several elements. In calling the scene a 'leaf-fringed legend' Keats will have remembered that the necks and shoulders of this kind of urn are regularly encircled by bands of leaf-pattern ornament. The idea of a sacrifice and a Bacchic dance being figured together in one frieze, a thing scarcely elsewhere to be found, will have come to him from the well known vase of Sosibios (so called from the name of the sculptor inscribed upon it), from the print of which in the *Musée Napoléon* there actually exists a tracing by his hand. But this is a serene and ceremonial composition: for the tumult and 'wild ecstasy' of his imagined frieze, the 'pipes and timbrels,' the 'mad pursuit,' he will have had store of visions ready in his mind, from the Bacchanal pictures of Poussin, no doubt also from Bacchic vases like that fine one in the Townley collection at the British Museum and the nearly allied Borghese vase: while for the

> — heifer lowing at the skies
> And all her silken flanks in garlands drest,

as well as for the thought of the pious morn and the little town emptied of its folk that old deep impression received from Claude's 'Sacrifice to Apollo' will have been reinforced by others from works of sculpture easy to guess at: most of all, naturally, from the sacrificial processions in the Parthenon frieze.

In the ode we read how the sculptured forms of such an imaginary antique, visualized in full intensity before his mind's eye, have set his thoughts to work, on the one hand asking himself what living, human scenes of ancient custom and worship lay behind them, and on the other hand speculating upon the abstract relations of plastic art to life. The opening invocation is followed by a string of questions which flash their own answer upon us — interrogatories which are at the same time pictures, — 'What men or gods are these, what maidens loth?' *etc.* The second and third stanzas express with full felicity and insight the differences between life, which pays for its unique prerogative of reality by satiety and decay, and art, which in forfeiting reality gains in exchange permanence of beauty, and the power to charm by imagined experiences even richer than the real. The thought thrown by Leonardo da Vinci into a single line — 'Cosa bella mortal passa e non d'arte' — and expanded by Wordsworth in his later days into the sonnet, 'Praised be the art,' etc., finds here its most perfect utterance.

> Ah, happy, happy boughs! that cannot shed
> Your leaves, nor ever bid the Spring adieu;
> And, happy melodist, unwearied,
> For ever piping songs for ever new;
> More happy love! more happy, happy love!
> For ever warm and still to be enjoy'd,
> For ever panting, and for ever young;
> All breathing human passion far above,
> That leaves a heart high-sorrowful and cloy'd,

> A burning forehead, and a parching tongue.
> Then the questioning begins again, and again conjures up a choice of pictures, —
> What little town by river or sea shore,
> Or mountain built with peaceful citadel,
> Is emptied of its folk, this pious morn?
> In the answering lines of the sestet —
> And, little town, thy streets for evermore
> Will silent be; and not a soul to tell
> Why thou art desolate, can e'er return, —

in these lines we find that the poet's imagination has suddenly and lightly shifted its ground, and chooses to view the arrest of life as though it were an infliction in the sphere of reality, and not merely, like the instances of such arrest given farther back, a necessary condition in the sphere of art, having in that sphere its own compensations. Finally, dropping such airy play of the mind backward and forward between the two spheres, he consigns the work of ancient skill to the future, to remain, —

> in midst of other woe
> Than ours, a friend to man, to whom thou say'st,
> Beauty is truth, truth beauty, —

thus reasserting his old doctrine, 'What the imagination seizes as beauty must be truth'; a doctrine which amidst the gropings of reason and the flux of things is to the poet and artist — at least to one of Keats' temper — the one anchorage to which his soul can and needs must cleave.

Let us turn now to the second pair — for as such I regard them — of odes written in May-time, those *To a Nightingale* and *On Melancholy*. Like the *Ode on Indolence*, the nightingale ode begins with the confession of a mood of 'drowsy numbness,' but this time one deeper and nearer to pain and heartache. Then invoking the nightingale, the poet attributes his mood not to envy of her song (perhaps, as Mr Bridges has suggested, there may be here an under-reminiscence from William Browne), but to excess of happiness in it. Just as his Grecian urn was no single specimen of antiquity that he had seen, so it is not the particular nightingale he had heard singing in the Hampstead garden that Keats thus invokes, but a type of the race imagined as singing in some far-off scene of woodland mystery and beauty. Thither he sighs to follow her: first by aid of the spell of some southern vintage — a spell which he makes us realize in lines redolent, as are none others in our language, of the southern richness and joy which he had never known save in dreams. Then follows a contrasted vision of all his own and mankind's tribulations which he will leave behind him. Nay, he needs not the aid of Bacchus, — Poetry alone shall transport him. For a moment he mistrusts her power, but the next moment finds himself where he would be, listening to the imagined song in the imagined woodland, and divining in the darkness all the secrets of the season and the night. While thus rapt he remembers how often the thought of death has seemed welcome to him, and feels that it would be more richly welcome now than ever. The nightingale would not cease to sing — and by this time, though he calls her 'immortal bird,' what he has truly in mind is not the song-bird at all, but the bird-song, thought of as though it were a thing self-existing and apart, imperishable through the ages. So thinking, he contrasts its permanence with the transitoriness of human life, meaning the life of the generations of individual men and women who have listened to it. This last thought leads him off into the ages, whence he brings back those memorable touches of far-off Bible and legendary romance in the stanza closing with the words 'in faery lands forlorn': and then, catching up his own last word, 'forlorn,' with an abrupt change of mood and meaning, he returns to daily consciousness, and with the fading away of his forest dream the poem closes.

Throughout this ode Keats' genius is at its height. Imagination cannot be more rich and satisfying, felicity of phrase and cadence cannot be more absolute, than in the several contrasted stanzas calling for the draft of southern vintage, picturing the frailty and wretchedness of man's estate on earth, and conjecturing in the 'embalmed darkness' the divers odours of spring. To praise the art of a passage like that in the fourth stanza where with a light, lingering pause the mind is carried instantaneously away from the miseries of the world into the heart of the imagined forest, — to praise or comment on a stroke of art like this is to throw doubt on the reader's power to perceive it for himself. Let him be trusted to cherish and know the poem, as every lover of English poetry should, 'to its depths,' and let us go on to the last product, as I take it to be, of this spring month of inspiration, and that is the *Ode on Melancholy*.

The music of the word — its hundred associations derived from the early seventeenth-century poetry in which his soul was steeped — foremost among them no doubt Milton's *L'Allegro* and *Il Penseroso*, with the beautiful song from Fletcher's *Nice Valour* which inspired them — his recent familiarity with Burton's *Anatomy*, including those pithy stanzas of alternate praise and repudiation which preface it — all these things will have worked together with Keats' own haunting and deepest mood throughout these days to set him composing on this theme, Melancholy. He had dallied with an idea of doing so as far back as early in March, when being kept from writing both by physical disinclination and a temporary phase of self-criticism, he had written to Haydon, 'I will not spoil my gloom by writing an ode to Darkness.' Now that in May the springs of inspiration were again unlocked in him, such negative purpose fails to hold, and he adds this ode to the rest, throwing into it some of his most splendid imagery and diction. Its temper is nearly akin on the one hand to some of the gloomier passages in his letters to Miss Jeffrey of May 31 and June 9, and on the other to the tragic third stanza of the nightingale ode. Its main purport is to proclaim the spiritual nearness, the all but inseparableness, of joy and pain in human experience when either is present in its intensity. One of the attributes, it will be remembered, which he assigns to his enchantress *Lamia* is —

> a sciential brain
> To unperplex bliss from its neighbour pain.

In no nature have the sources of the two lain deeper or closer together than in his own, and it is from the fullness of impassioned experience that he writes. The real melancholy, he insists, is not that which belongs to things sad or direful in themselves. Having written two stanzas piling up gruesome images of such things, and discarded on reflection the former and more gruesome of the two, he lets the second stand, and goes on, evoking contrasted images of opulent beauty, to show how the true, the utter melancholy is that which is inextricably coupled with every joy and resides at the heart of every pleasure: ending magnificently —

> Ay, in the very temple of Delight
> Veiled Melancholy has her sovereign shrine,
> Though seen of none save him whose strenuous tongue
> Can burst Joy's grape against his palate fine;
> His soul shall taste the sadness of her might,
> And be among her cloudy trophies hung.

One more ode remains, written in a different key and after a lapse of some four months, during which Keats had been away in the country, quieted by absence from the object of his passion and working diligently at *Otho the Great* and *Lamia*. This is the ode *To Autumn*. He was alone at Winchester, rejoicing in perfect September weather and in a mood more serene and contented than he had known for long or was ever to know again. 'How beautiful the season is now,' he writes to Reynolds, 'how fine the air — a temperate sharpness about it. Really, without joking, chaste weather — Dian skies. I never liked stubble fields so much as now — aye, better than the chilly green of the spring. Somehow, a stubble plain looks warm, in the same way that some pictures look warm. This struck me so much in my Sunday's walk that I composed upon it.' The vein in which he composed is one of simple objectivity, very different from the passionate and complex phases of introspective thought and feeling which inspired the spring odes. The result is the most Greek thing, except the fragment *To Maia*, which Keats ever wrote. It opens up no such far-reaching avenues to the mind and soul of the reader as the odes *To a Grecian Urn*, *To a Nightingale*, or *To Melancholy*, but in execution is more complete and faultless than any of them. In the first stanza the bounty, in the last the pensiveness, of the time are expressed in words so transparent and direct that we almost forget they are words at all, and nature herself and the season seem speaking to us: while in the middle stanza the touches of literary art and Greek personification have an exquisite congruity and ease. Keats himself has hardly anywhere else written with so fine a subtlety of nature-observation. Students of form will notice a slight deviation from that of the spring odes, by which the second member of the stanza is now a septet instead of a sestet, one of its rimes being repeated three times instead of twice.

> Season of mists and mellow fruitfulness,
> Close bosom-friend of the maturing sun;
> Conspiring with him how to load and bless
> With fruit the vines that round the thatch-eaves run;
> To bend with apples the moss'd cottage trees,
>
> And fill all fruit with ripeness to the core;
> To swell the gourd, and plump the hazel shells
> With a sweet kernel; to set budding more,
> And still more, later flowers for the bees,
> Until they think warm days will never cease,
> For Summer has o'er-brimm'd their clammy cells.
> Who hath not seen thee oft amid thy store?
> Sometimes whoever seeks abroad may find
> Thee sitting careless on a granary floor,
> Thy hair soft-lifted by the winnowing wind;
> Or on a half-reap'd furrow sound asleep,
> Drows'd with the fume of poppies, while thy hook
> Spares the next swath and all its twined flowers:
> And sometimes like a gleaner thou dost keep
> Steady thy laden head across a brook;
> Or by a cider-press, with patient look,
> Thou watchest the last oozings hours by hours.
> Where are the songs of Spring? Ay, where are they?
> Think not of them, thou hast thy music too, —
> While barred clouds bloom the soft-dying day,
> And touch the stubble-plains with rosy hue;
> Then in a wailful choir the small gnats mourn
> Among the river sallows, borne aloft
> Or sinking as the light wind lives or dies;
> And full-grown lambs loud bleat from hilly bourn;
> Hedge-crickets sing; and now with treble soft
> The red-breast whistles from a garden-croft;
> And gathering swallows twitter in the skies.

Had Keats been destined to know health and peace of mind, who can guess how much more work in this vein and of this quality the world might have owed to him?

Chapter XIV

WORK OF 1818, 1819. — II. THE FRAGMENTS AND EXPERIMENTS

Much of our clearest insight into Keats' mind and genius is gained from the class of his fragments which do not represent any definite poetical purpose or plan, and were never meant to be more than mere snatches and momentary outpourings. Such, though they only express a passing mood, are the lines in his letter to Reynolds of February 1818, translating the early song of the thrush into a warning not to fret after knowledge. Such is the contrasted passage of shifting, perplexed meditation on the problems of life, and the failure of the imagination to solve them alone, in the rimed epistle to the same friend six weeks later. Such, very especially, is the cry declaring that the true poet is the soul sympathetic with every form and mode of life and ready to merge its identity in that of any and every sentient creature: compare the passage in one of his letters where he tells how his own can enter into that of a sparrow picking about the gravel: —

> Where's the Poet? show him! show him,
> Muses nine! that I may know him.
> 'Tis the man who with a man
> Is an equal, be he King,
> Or poorest of the beggar-clan,
> Or any other wondrous thing
> A man may be'twixt ape and Plato;
> 'Tis the man who with a bird,
> Wren, or Eagle, finds his way to
> All its instincts; he hath heard
> The Lion's roaring, and can tell
> What his horny throat expresseth,
> And to him the Tiger's yell
> Comes articulate and presseth
> On his ear like mother-tongue.

Such again are the several passages in which he expressed a mood that frequently beset him, that of being rapt in spirit too high above earth to breathe, too far above his body not to feel an awful intoxication and fear of coming madness: —

> It is an awful mission,
> A terrible division;
> And leaves a gulph austere
> To be fill'd with worldly fear.
> Aye, when the soul is fled
> Too high above our head,
> Affrighted do we gaze
> After its airy maze,
> As doth a mother wild,
> When her young infant child
> Is in eagle's claws —
> And is not this the cause
> Of madness? — God of Song,
> Thou bearest me along
> Through sights I scarce can bear;
> O let me, let me share

> With the hot lyre and thee,
> The staid Philosophy.
> Temper my lonely hours,
> And let me see thy bowers
> More unalarm'd!

But our main business in this chapter must be not with illuminating snatches such as these, but with things begun of set purpose and not carried through.

When Keats, drawing near the end of his work on *Endymion*, was meditating what he meant to be his second long and arduous poem, *Hyperion*, he still thought and spoke of it as a 'romance.' But a phrase he uses elsewhere shows him conscious that its style would have to be more 'naked and Grecian' than that of *Endymion*. Was he trying an experiment in the naked and Grecian style when on May day 1818 he wrote at Teignmouth the beginning of an ode on Maia? He never went on with it, and the fragment as it stands is of fourteen lines only; but these are in a more truly Greek manner than anything else he wrote, not even excepting, as I have just said, the *Ode to Autumn*. The words figuring what Greek poets were and did for Greek communities, and expressing the aspiration to be even as they, bear the true, the classic, mint-mark of absolute economy and simplicity in absolute rightness. Considering how meagre are the hints antiquity has left us concerning Maia, the eldest of the Pleiades and mother of Hermes, and her late identification with the Roman divinity to whom sacrifice was paid on the first of May, and hence how little material for development the theme seems to offer, — considering these things, perhaps it is as well that Keats, despite his promise to finish it 'all in good time,' should have tantalized posterity by breaking off this beautiful thing where he did.

The next fragment we come to is colossal, — it is *Hyperion* itself. From the poem as far as it was written no reader could guess either that it was taken up as a 'feverous relief' from tendance on his dying brother, or that in continuing it later under Brown's roof he had to put force upon himself against the intrusion of private cares and affections upon his thoughts, as well as against a reaction from his own mode of conceiving and handling the task itself. The impression *Hyperion* makes is one, as Woodhouse on first reading it justly noted, of serene mastery by the poet both over himself and over his art: — 'It has an air of calm grandeur about it which is indicative of true power': and again, — 'the above lines give but a faint idea of the sustained grandeur and quiet power which characterize the poem.' Woodhouse goes on to tell what he knew of the scheme of the work as Keats had first conceived it: —

The poem, if completed, would have treated of the dethronement of Hyperion, the former God of the Sun, by Apollo, — and incidentally of those of Oceanus by Neptune, of Saturn by Jupiter, etc., and of the war of the giants for Saturn's reestablishment — with other events, of which we have but very dark hints in the mythological poets of Greece and Rome. In fact the incidents would have been pure creations of the Poet's brain.

The statement inserted by the publishers at the head of the volume in which the poem appeared in 1820, that *Hyperion* was intended to be as long as *Endymion*, is probably also due to Woodhouse, their right-hand man (Keats, we know, had nothing to do with it), and may represent what he had gathered in conversation to have been the poet's original idea. Mr de Sélincourt has shown grounds for inferring that when Keats came to actual grips with the subject he decided to treat it much more briefly and partially. Clearly the essential meaning of the story was for him symbolical; it meant the dethronement of an older and ruder worship by one more advanced and humane, in which ideas of ethics and of arts held a larger place beside ideas of nature and her brute powers. Into this story the poet plunges, not even in the middle but near the close. When his poem opens, the younger gods, the Olympians, have won their victory, and the Titans, all except Hyperion, are already overthrown. In their debate whether to fight again general despondency prevails, and only one of the fallen, Enceladus, strikes a note of defiance; so that it seems as if there were nothing left to tell except the coming defeat or abdication of Hyperion in favour of Apollo. Hyperion, it is true, has not yet spoken when we are called away from the council, and Keats might have made him side with Enceladus and rouse his brethren to a temporary renewal of the strife. Or leaving the Titans conquered, he might, as Woodhouse suggests, have gone on to narrate the second warfare, that waged against the Olympians not by them but later by the Giants in revolt. In either case we should have seen the poet try his hand, hitherto untested in such themes, on scenes of superhuman battle and violence.

Woodhouse is right at any rate in saying that the hints for handling the theme to be found in the ancient poets are few and uncertain, leaving a modern writer free to invent most of his incidents for himself. Beyond the bald notices in his classical dictionaries, Chapman's *Iliad* would have given Keats a picture of the dethroned Saturn: Chapman's Homer's hymn to Apollo might have filled his imagination, even to overflowing, with visions of the youth of that god in Delos, — 'Chief isle of the embowered Cyclades': Hesiod's *Theogony* (which he had doubtless read in the translation of Pope's butt and enemy, Thomas Cooke) would have taught him more, but very confusedly, about the warfare of Gods, Titans, and Giants in general, besides inspiring his vision of the den where the Titans lie vanquished; while he would have gleaned other stray matters from Sandys's notes on certain passages of Ovid. As far as his beloved English poets are concerned, brief allusions occur in the *Faerie Queene* and in *Paradise Lost*, where Milton includes the fallen Titans among the rebel hosts that flock to the standard of Satan in hell. But I think the source freshest in his mind at the moment when he began to write is one which has not hitherto been suggested, the ode of the famous French Renaissance poet Ronsard to his friend Michel de l'Hôpital. We know by his translation of the sonnet *Nature ornant Cassandre* that Keats had the works of Ronsard in his hands — lent, it would seem, by Mr Taylor — exactly about this time. The ode in question, partly founded on Hesiod, partly on Horace, but largely on Ronsard's own invention, relates the birth of the Muses, their training by their mother Mémoire (= Mnemosyne), their desire as young girls to visit their father Jupiter, their mother's consent, their undersea journey to the palace of Oceanus where Jupiter is present at a high festival, their choral singing before him, first of the strife of Neptune and Pallas for the soil of Attica, and then of the battle of the gods and giants: —

> Après sur la plus grosse corde
> D'un bruit qui tonnait jusqu'aux cieux,
> Le pouce des Muses accorde
> L'assaut des Géants et des Dieux.

Keats, although he writes of the battle of the Gods not against the Giants but against the earlier Titans, yet when he rolls out rebel names like this, —

> Cœus, and Gyges, and Briareus;
> Typhon, and Dolor, and Porphyrion
> Were pent in regions of laborious breath
> Dungeon'd in opaque elements, —

Keats, when he rolls out these rebel names, has surely been haunted by the strophes of Ronsard:
—

> Styx d'un noir halecret rempare
> Ses bras, ses jambes, et son sein,
> Sa fille amenant par la main
> Contre Cotte, Gyge, et Briare.

·······

> Neptune à la fourche estofée
> De trois crampons vint se mesler
> Par la troupe contre Typhée
> Qui rouoit une fonde en l'air:
> Ici Phoebus d'un trait qu'il jette
> Fit Encelade trébucher,
> Là Porphyre lui fit broncher
> Hors des poings l'arc et la sagette.

For such an epic theme Keats felt instinctively, when he set to work, that an epic and not a romance treatment was necessary; and for an English poet the obvious epic model is Milton. Ever since his visit to Bailey at Oxford, and especially during his stay at Teignmouth the next year, Keats had been absorbing Milton and taking him into his being, as formerly he had taken Shakespeare and the Elizabethans, and now he can utter his own thoughts and imaginations almost with Milton's voice. Speaking generally of the blank verse of *Hyperion*, its rhythms are almost as full and sonorous as Milton's own, but simpler; its march more straightforward, with less of what De Quincey calls 'solemn planetary wheelings'; its periods do not sweep through such complex evolutions to so stately and far foreseen a close. The Miltonisms in *Hyperion* are rather matters of diction and construction — construction almost always derived from the Latin — than of rhythm: sometimes also they are matters of direct verbal echo and reminiscence. To take a single instance out of many: —

> For as among us mortals omens drear
> Fright and perplex, so also shuddered he.

It is only in *Hyperion* that Keats habitually thus puts the noun Latin-wise before the adjective: and the omens that 'perplex' are derived from the eclipse which in *Paradise Lost* 'with fear of change Perplexes monarchs.' Throughout the fragment Keats uses frequently and with fine effect the Miltonic figure of the 'turn' or rhetorical iteration of identical words to a fresh purport, as in that noble phrase which seems to have inspired one of the finest passages in Shelley's *Defence of Poesy* :

> How beautiful, if Sorrow had not made
> Sorrow more beautiful than Beauty's self.

It has been said, and justly, that Keats has done nothing greater than the debate of the fallen Titans in their cave of exile, modelled frankly in its main outlines on that of the rebel angels in *Paradise Lost*, but with the personages and utterances nevertheless entirely his own. In creating and animating these colossal figures between the elemental and the human, what masterly imaginative instinct does he show — to take one point only — in the choice of similitudes, drawn from the vast inarticulate sounds of nature, by which he seeks to make us realise their voices. Thus of the murmuring of the assembled gods when Saturn is about to speak: —

> There is a roaring in the bleak-grown pines
> When Winter lifts his voice; there is a noise
> Among immortals when a God gives sign,
> With hushing finger, how he means to load
> His tongue with the full weight of utterless thought,
> With thunder, and with music, and with pomp:
> Such noise is like the roar of bleak-grown pines.

This is not a whit the less Keats for his use of the Miltonic 'turn' in rounding the period by a repetition in the last line of the 'bleak-grown pines' from the first. Again, of Oceanus answering his fallen chief: —

> So ended Saturn; and the God of the Sea,
> Sophist and sage, from no Athenian grove,
> But cogitation in his watery shades,
> Arose, with locks not oozy, and began,
> In murmurs, which his first-endeavouring tongue
> Caught infant-like from the far-foamed sands.

Here the affirmation by negation in the second and fourth lines is a Latin usage already employed by Keats in the *Pot of Basil* : the 'locks not oozy' are a reminiscence from *Lycidas* and the 'first-endeavouring tongue' from *The Vacation Exercise* . But into what a vitally apt and beautiful new music of his own has Keats moulded and converted all such echoes. Once more, of Clymene following Enceladus in debate: —

> So far her voice flow'd on, like timorous brook
> That, lingering along a pebbled coast,
> Doth fear to meet the sea: but sea it met,
> And shudder'd; for the overwhelming voice
> Of huge Enceladus swallow'd it in wrath:
> The ponderous syllables, like sullen waves
> In the half-glutted hollows of reef-rocks,
> Came booming thus.

In this last example the sublimity owes nothing to Milton except in the single case of the repetition in the third line. Even the scoffing Byron recognized after Keats' death the authentic 'large utterance of the early gods' in passages like these, though Keats in his modesty had himself refused to recognize it.

Further to compare Keats with Milton, — the poet of *Hyperion* is naturally no match for Milton in passages where the elder master has been inspired by lifelong impassioned meditation on his readings of history and romance, like that famous one ending with

> What resounds
> In fable or romance of Uther's son.
> Begirt with British and Armoric knights
> Or all who since, baptized or infidel
> Jousted in Aspramont or Montalban,
> Damasco, or Marocco, or Trebizond,
> Or whom Biserta sent from Afric shore
> When Charlemain with all his peerage fell
> By Fontarrabia —

On the other hand Milton, even in the sweetness and the nearness to nature of *Comus* and his other early work, is scarce a match for Keats when it comes to the evocation, even in a mode relatively simple, of nature's secret sources of delight, — as thus:

> throughout all the isle
> There was no covert, no retired cave
> Unhaunted by the murmurous noise of waves
> Though scarcely heard in many a green recess:

while comparison is scarcely possible in the case of the nature images most characteristically Keats' own, for instance: —

> As when, upon a tranced summer night,
> Those green-robed senators of mighty woods,

> Tall oaks, branch-charmed by the earnest stars,
> Dream, and so dream all night without a stir —.

Neither to the Greek nor the Miltonic, but essentially to the modern, the romantic, sentiment of nature does it belong to try and express, by such a concourse of metaphors and epithets, every effect at once, to the most fugitive, which a forest scene by starlight can have upon the mind: the pre-eminence of the oaks among the other trees — their quasi-human venerableness — their verdure, unseen in the darkness — the sense of their preternatural stillness and suspended life in an atmosphere that seems to vibrate with mysterious influences communicated between earth and sky.

All good poems, it has been said, begin well. None begins better than *Hyperion*, with its 'Deep in the shady sadness of a vale,' and its grand mournful dialogue between the discrowned Saturn and the Titaness Thea, his would-be comforter. Then, with a rich contrast from this scene of despondency, comes the scene, dazzling and resplendent for all its ominousness, of the mingled wrath and terror of the threatened sun-god in his flaming palace. The second book, relating the council of the dethroned Titans, has neither the contrasted sublimities of the first nor the intensity, rising almost to fever-point, of the unfinished third, where we leave Apollo undergoing a convulsive change under the afflatus of Mnemosyne, and about to put on the full powers of his godhead. But it has a rightness and controlled power of its own which place it, to my mind, fully on a level with the other two. And it is in this book, in the speech of Oceanus, that Keats sets forth the whole symbolical purport and meaning of the myth as he had conceived it: —

> Now comes the pain of truth, to whom 'tis pain;
> O folly! for to bear all naked truths,
> And to envisage circumstance, all calm,
> That is the top of sovereignty. Mark well!
> As Heaven and Earth are fairer, fairer far
> Than Chaos and blank Darkness, though once chiefs;
> And as we show beyond that Heaven and Earth
> In form and shape compact and beautiful,
> In will, in action free, companionship,
> And thousand other signs of purer life;
> So on our heels a fresh perfection treads,
> A power more strong in beauty, born of us
> And fated to excel us, as we pass
> In glory that old Darkness: nor are we
> Thereby more conquer'd, than by us the rule
> Of shapeless Chaos. Say, doth the dull soil
> Quarrel with the proud forests it hath fed,
> And feedeth still, more comely than itself?
> Can it deny the chiefdom of green groves?
> Or shall the tree be envious of the dove
> Because it cooeth, and hath snowy wings
> To wander wherewithal and find its joys?
> We are such forest-trees, and our fair boughs
> Have bred forth, not pale solitary doves,
> But eagles golden-feather'd, who do tower
> Above us in their beauty, and must reign
> In right thereof; for 'tis the eternal law
> That first in beauty should be first in might:

That difficulty, to which we have referred, of surmising how there could have remained material to fill out a poem on the Titanomachia which had begun with the Titans, all but one, dethroned already, seems to increase when we consider the above speech of Oceanus, setting forth with resigned prophetic wisdom the fated necessity of their fall. It increases still further when Clymene, following on the same side as Oceanus, tells how she has heard the strains of a new and ravishing music from the lyre of Apollo which have made her cast away in despair the instrument of her own formless music, the sea-shell; and still further again when in the next book we witness the meeting of Apollo with the Titaness Mnemosyne, mother of the Muses, who for his sake has 'forsaken old and sacred thrones,' and when we hear him proclaim how in the inspiration of her presence,

> Knowledge enormous makes a God of me.
> Names, deeds, grey legends, dire events, rebellions,
> Majesties, sovran voices, agonies,
> Creations and destroyings, all at once
> Pour into the wide hollows of my brain,
> And deify me, as if some blithe wine
> Or bright elixir peerless I had drunk,
> And so become immortal.

Before the glory of this new-deified Apollo, what could long have delayed the defeat or abdication of the elder sun-god Hyperion? — what could have remained for Keats to invent that should have much enriched or lengthened out his poem? The sense of the difficulty of sustaining the battle of the primeval powers against these new and nobler successors may well have been one of the things (even had he not had Milton's comparative failure with the warfare in heaven to warn him) that hindered his going on with his poem. To the reader there occurs another and even greater difficulty: and that is that Keats had already given to his fallen elder gods or Titans so much not only of majesty but of nobleness and goodness that it is hard to see wherein he could have shown their successors excelling them. He had represented Saturn as wroth, indeed, at his downfall, but chiefly because it leaves him

> — smother'd up,
> And buried from all godlike exercise
> Of influence benign on planets pale,
> Of admonition to the winds and seas,
> Of peaceful sway above man's harvesting,
> And all those acts which Deity supreme
> Doth ease its heart of love in.

Increase of knowledge, of skill in the arts of life and of beauty, the gods of the new dynasty might indeed extend to mankind, but what increase of love and beneficence? Even the relations of Saturn to his father Coelus (the Greek Uranus), which in the ancient cosmogony are of the crudest barbarity, Keats in *Hyperion* makes benignant and sympathetic.

Such inherent difficulties as these might well have made Keats diffident of his power to complete his poem as a rounded or satisfying whole had its intended scope been what we are told. But I am sometimes tempted to conjecture that his root idea had been other than what his friends attributed to him, — that battle, and the victory of the Olympians over the Titans or Giants or both, would not in fact have been his main theme, but that he intended to present to us Apollo, enthroned after the abdication of Hyperion, in the character of a prophet and to have put into his mouth revelations of things to come, a great monitory vision of the world's future. To such a supposition some colour is surely lent by the speech of Apollo above quoted on the 'knowledge enormous' just poured into his brain by Mnemosyne. On the other hand it has to be remembered that Keats himself, in a forecast of his work made ten months before it was written, shows clearly that he then meant his Apollo to be above all things a god of action.

Keats himself, writing some eight months later, when he had finally decided to give up his epic attempt, cites as his chief reason a reaction of his critical judgment against the Miltonic style, at least as a style suitable for him, Keats, to work in: —

I have given up *Hyperion* — there were too many Miltonic inversions in it — Miltonic verse cannot be written but in an artful, or rather, artist's humour. I wish to give myself up to other sensations. English ought to be kept up. It may be interesting to you to pick out some lines from *Hyperion* , and put a mark * to the false beauty proceeding from art, and one to the true voice of feeling. Upon my soul 'twas imagination — I cannot make the distinction — Every now and then there is a Miltonic intonation — But I cannot make the division properly.

And again: 'I have but lately stood on my guard against Milton. Life to him would be death to me. Miltonic verse cannot be written, but is the verse of art. I wish to devote myself to another verse alone.' This reaction was certainly not fully conscious or formulated in Keats' mind by the previous winter. But it would seem none the less to have been working in him instinctively: for the moment he had turned, in *The Eve of St Agnes* , to a romance in the flowing, straightforward, Spenserian-Chattertonian manner of narration, he had been able to carry his task through with felicity and ease.

This was on his excursion to Hampshire in the latter half of January. Within three weeks of his return he was at work again on a kindred theme of popular and traditional belief, *The Eve of St Mark* . The belief was that a person standing in the church porch of any town or village on the evening before St Mark's day (April 24th) might thereby gain a vision of all the inhabitants fated to die or fall grievously sick within the year. Those destined to die would be seen passing in but not returning, those who were to be in peril and recover would go in and after a while come out. The heroine of the poem, to whom this vision would appear, was to be a maiden of Canterbury named Bertha, no doubt after the first Christian queen of Kent, the Frankish wife of Ethelbert; the scene, Canterbury itself, memories of the poet's stay there in 1817 mingling apparently with impressions of his recent visit to Chichester. Keats never got on with this poem after his first three or four days' work (February 14th-17th 1819), and it remains a mere fragment, tantalizing and singular, of a hundred and twenty lines' length. Why? Perhaps merely because it was begun almost at the very hour when he became the accepted lover of Fanny Brawne. We have seen how various causes, but chiefly the obsession of that passion, paralysed his power of work for the next two months, and what were the thoughts and tasks that held him fully occupied afterwards. It has been suggested by the late Dante Gabriel Rossetti that Keats meant to give the story a turn applicable to himself and his mistress, and that the present fragment would have served as the opening of a poem which afterwards, in sickness, he mentioned to her as being in his mind: — 'I would show some one in love, as I am, with a person living in such Liberty as you do.' I can find no sure evidence, internal or external, either to refute the suggestion or confirm it.

The fragment of *The Eve of St Mark* is Keats' only attempt at narrative writing in the eight-syllabled four-stress couplet. Its pace and movement are nearer to Chaucer in *The Romaunt of the Rose* or *The House of Fame* than to Coleridge or Scott or any other model of Keats' own time. That he was writing with Chaucer in his mind is proved by some lines in which he tries in Rowley fashion to reproduce Chaucer's actual style and vocabulary, thus: —

> Gif ye wol stonden hardie wight —
> Amiddes of the blacke night —
> Righte in the churche porch, pardie
> Ye wol behold a companie
> Approchen thee full dolourouse
> For sooth to sain from everich house
> Be it in city or village
> Wol come the Phantom and image

>   Of ilka gent and ilka carle
>   Who coldè Deathè hath in parle
>   And wol some day that very year
>   Touchen with foulè venime spear
>   And sadly do them all to die —
>   Hem all shalt thou see verilie —
>   And everichon shall by thee pass
>   All who must die that year, Alas.

These lines give us a sure key to the main motive of the story which was to follow. With some others in the same style, they are quoted by the poet as composing a gloss written in minute script on the margin of a wonderful illuminated book over which the damsel is found poring and which is to have some mysterious influence on her destiny. More noticeable and interesting than their somewhat random Rowleyism is the way in which some of the descriptive lines in the body of the poem anticipate the very cadences of Chaucer's great latter-day disciple, William Morris. The first eight or ten lines of the following might have come straight from *The Man born to be King* or *The Land East of the Sun*, and provide, as it were, in the history of our poetry a direct stepping-stone between Chaucer and Morris: —

>   The city streets were clean and fair
>   From wholesome drench of April rains;
>   And, on the western window panes,
>   The chilly sunset faintly told
>   Of unmatur'd green vallies cold,
>   Of the green thorny bloomless hedge,
>   Of rivers new with spring-tide sedge,
>   Of primroses by shelter'd rills,
>   And daisies on the aguish hills.
>   Twice holy was the Sabbath-bell:
>   The silent streets were crowded well
>   With staid and pious companies,
>   Warm from their fireside orat'ries;
>   And moving, with demurest air,
>   To evensong, and vesper prayer.
>   Each arched porch, and entry low,
>   Was fill'd with patient folk and slow,
>   With whispers hush, and shuffling feet,
>   While play'd the organ loud and sweet.

The relation of this fragment to the Pre-Raphaelites of the mid nineteenth century and their work is altogether curious and interesting. It was natural that it should appeal to them by the pure and living freshness of English nature-description with which it opens, by the perfectly imagined scene of hushed movement in the twilight streets that follows, perhaps most of all by the insistent delight in vivid colour, and in minuteness of animated and suggestive detail, which marks the final indoor scene of the maiden Bertha over her book by firelight. But what is strange is that Rossetti should not only have coupled the fragment with *La Belle Dame sans Merci* as 'the chastest and choicest example of Keats' maturing manner,' an opinion which may well pass, but that he should have claimed it as showing 'astonishingly real mediævalism for one not bred an artist,' and even as the finest picture of the Middle Age period ever done. The truth is that the description of the Sabbath streets and the maiden's chamber are not mediæval at all and probably not intended to be, while the one thing so intended, the illuminated manuscript from which she reads, is a quite impossible invention jumbling fantastically together things that never could have figured in the same manuscript, things from the Golden Legend, from the book of Exodus, the book of Revelation, with others from no possible manuscript source at all. Keats evidently took some interest in mediæval illuminations, for in speculating on the old skulls of supposed monks at Beauly Abbey he had apostrophized one of them, —

> Poor Skull, thy fingers set ablaze
> With silver saint in golden rays,
> The holy Missal: thou didst craze
> Mid bead and spangle,
> While others pass'd their idle days
> In coil and wrangle.

But he can have seen few and made no study of them, and his imagined mystically illuminated book in *The Eve of St Mark* is invented with no such fine instinctive tact or likelihood as his imagined Grecian urn of the ode.

An elder member of the Rossetti circle, that shrewd and caustic, very originally minded if only half accomplished Scottish poet and painter, William Bell Scott, was much exercised over his friend's misconception in this matter. I will give his comment, certainly in some points just, as written to me in 1885. 'On reading the fragment it seems to me impossible to resist the conclusion that the scene represented is of the present day. The dull and quiet Sunday evening represented is of our time in any cathedral town in England, not the Sunday evening of old when morning Mass was the religious observance, and the evening was spent in long-bow and popinjay games and practice. The weary girl sits at a coal fire with a screen behind her, a Japanese screen apparently,' [Japanese or old English lacquer imitating Oriental the screen certainly is]. 'Every item of the description is modern. But alas! what shall we say to the ancient illuminated MS. she has in hand, with the pictures of early martyrs dying by fire, the Inquisition punishment of heretics, and the writing annotated, the notes referred to modern printers' signs? As he describes a mediæval MS. book so badly, it may be said he intended the scene of the poem to be mediæval, but did the description also so badly. But no, the description of the dreariness of Sunday evening, utterly silent but for the passing of the people going to evening sermon, is admirable.' By 'badly' my old friend meant inexactly. But Keats never was nor tried to be exact in his antiquarianism. If we take *The Eve of St Agnes* as intended to be a faithful picture from the Middle Ages, it simply goes to pieces in the line —

> And the long carpets rose along the gusty floor.

Probably neither *The Eve of St Agnes* nor *St Mark's Eve* were dated with any definiteness in the poet's mind at all. A reference he makes to the last-named piece in a letter from Winchester the following autumn lends no definite support either to the modern or the mediæval interpretation: — 'Some time since I began a poem called *The Eve of St Mark*, quite in the spirit of town quietude. I think it will give you the sensation of walking about an old country town on a coolish evening.' The impression of mediævalism which the two poems convey is not by any evidence of antiquarian knowledge or accuracy but by the intense spirit of romance that is in them, — by that impassioned delight in vivid colour and beautiful, imaginative detail which we have noted.

After his four days' start on this poem in February came the spell of two months' idleness which towards its close yielded *La Belle Dame sans Merci* and came to an end with the *Ode to Psyche*, followed in the course of May by the four other odes. The choral *Song of the Four Fairies*, for some inchoate opera, sent by Keats to his brother together with *La Belle Dame*, is not worth pausing upon, and we may pass to Keats' main work of the ensuing July and August, *Otho the Great*. This is no fragment, having been duly finished to the last scene of the last act; but it is very much of an experiment. The question whether Keats, had he lived, might have become a great dramatic poet and creator is one of the most interesting possible. His intense and growing interest in humankind, together with his recorded and avowed liability to receive ('like putty,' as modern criticism has conjectured of Shakespeare) the impression of any character he might come in contact with, has led many students to believe that he had in him the stuff of a great creative playwright. *Otho the Great* does nothing to solve the question. The plot and construction, as we have said, were entirely Brown's, building with quite arbitrary freedom on certain bald historical facts of the rebellion raised against Otho, in the course of his Hungarian wars, by his son Ludolf and the Red Duke Conrad of Lorraine, whom the emperor subsequently forgave. Creation demands fore-knowledge, premeditation on the characters you desire to create and the situations in which they are to be placed, and Keats, Brown tells us, only foreknew what was coming in any scene after they had sat down at the table to work on it. His business was to supply the words, and what the result shows is only the surprising facility with which he could by this time improvise poetry to order. The speeches in Otho are much more than passably poetical, they are often quite brilliant and touched with Keats' unique genius for felicity in lines and phrases. But they affect us as put into the mouths of puppet speakers, not as coming out of the hearts and passions of men and women.

In rhythm they are vital and varied enough, in style extremely high-pitched, and they resemble much Elizabethan work of the second order in smothering action and passion under a redundance and feverish excess of poetry. There is violence amounting to hysteria alike in the villainy of Conrad and of his sister Auranthe, the remorse of Albert, and the mixture of filial devotion and lover's blindness in Ludolf, with his vengeful frenzy when he finds how he has been gulled. Keats, it is recorded, had in his eye the special gift of Edmund Kean for enacting frantic extremes and long-drawn agonies of passion; and it is possible that as played by him the last act, of which Keats took the conduct as well as the writing into his own hands, might have proved effective on the stage. It shows the maddened Conrad bent on executing vengeance on the traitress Auranthe, and insanely stabbing empty air while he imagines he is stabbing his victim, until curtains drawn aside disclose an inner apartment where she has at the very moment fallen self-slain. But it is doubtful whether any acting could carry off a plot so ultra-romantically extravagant and in places so obscure, or characters so incommensurably more eloquent than they are alive. Nor do lovers of Keats commonly care to read the play twice, for all its bursts and coruscations of fine poetry, feeling that these do not spring from the poet's own inner self and imagination, but are rather as fireworks fitted by a man of genius on to a frame which another man, barely of talent, has put together.

The case is different when we come to *King Stephen*, the brief dramatic fragment on which Keats wrought alone after *Otho the Great* was finished. This teaches us one thing at any rate about Keats, that he could at will call away his imagination from matters luxurious or refreshing to the spirit, from themes broodingly meditative or tragically tender, to deal in a manner of fiery energy with the clash of war. He is still enough a child of the Renaissance to make his twelfth-century knights and princes quote Homer in their taunts and counter-taunts; but in the three-and-a-half scenes which he wrote he makes us feel his Stephen, defiant in defeat, a real elemental force and not a mere mouther of valiant rhetoric, fine and concentrated as the rhetoric sometimes is, as for instance when an enemy taunts him with being disarmed and helpless and he cries back, 'What weapons has the lion but himself?'

In persuading Keats to work with him on a tragedy for the stage, Brown had had the entirely laudable motive of putting his friend in the way of earning money for them both. But what would we not have given that the time and labour thus, as it turned out, thrown away should have yielded us from Keats' self another *Isabella* or *Eve of St Agnes*, or a finished *Eve of St Mark*, or even another *Lamia*? Brown's next piece of suggestion and would-be help was far more unfortunate still. We have seen how in the unhappy weeks after Keats' return from Winchester in October, he spent his mornings in Brown's company spinning the verses of a comic and satiric fairy tale the scheme of which they had concocted together, — *The Cap and Bells* or *The Jealousies*. The idea of the friends in this was no doubt to throw a challenge to Byron, the first cantos of whose *Don Juan* had lately been launched upon a dazzled and scandalized world. Byron's genius, the spirit, that is, of brilliant devilry and worldly mockery which was the sincerest part of his genius, with his rich experiences of life, travel and society, of passion and dissipation and the extremes of fame and obloquy, and his incomparable address and versatility in playing tricks of legerdemain with ideas and language, had here all found their perfect opportunity for display. Attempts at worldly banter and satire by the tender-hearted, intensely loving and imagining Keats, with his narrow and in the main rather second-rate social experience, were never more than wry-mouthed as I have called them, ineffectual, and essentially against the grain.

His collaborator Brown imagined he had a gift for satiric fairy tales, but his recorded efforts in that kind are silly and dull as well as inclining to coarseness. What happier result could be expected from their new joint work than that which posterity deplores in *The Cap and Bells*? The story is of an Indian Faery emperor Elfinan, — a name suggested by Spenser, — enamoured of an English maiden Bertha Pearl, — the very Bertha of *The Eve of St Mark*, resuscitated to our amazement, — but having for political reasons to seek in marriage a Faery princess Bellanaine, who herself is in love with an English youth named Hubert. The eighty-eight stanzas which Keats wrote on those autumn mornings in Brown's room carry the tale no farther than Elfinan's despatching his chancellor Crafticanto on an embassy to fetch Bellanaine on an aerial journey from her home in Imaus, his consultation with his magician Hum as to the means of escaping the marriage and conveying himself secretly to England, his departure, and the arrival of Bellanaine and her escort to find the palace empty and the emperor flown. How the seriously, perhaps tragically, conceived Bertha of *St Mark's Eve*, with the mystic book fated to have influence on her life, could have been worked, as they were evidently meant to be worked, into this new ridiculous narrative, we cannot guess, nor how the relations of Bellanaine with her mortal lover would have been managed.

Before Keats' deepening despondency and recklessness caused him to drop writing altogether, which apparently happened early in December, he was evidently out of conceit with *The Cap and Bells*. One of the most unfortunate things about the attempt is the choice of the Spenserian stanza for its metre. Keats had probably wished to avoid seeming merely to imitate Byron, as he might have seemed to do had he written in the *ottava rima* of Don Juan, the one perfectly fit measure for such a blend of fantasy and satire as he was attempting. But not even Keats' power over the Spenserian stanza could make it a fit vehicle for his purpose. Thomson and Shenstone had used it in work of mild and leisurely playfulness, but to bite in satire or sting in epigram it cannot effectively be bent. To my sense the precedent most in Keats' mind was not these, but the before-mentioned translation of Wieland's *Oberon* by Sotheby. Sotheby had invented a modified form of the Spenserian stanza riming *abbaccddc* instead of *abcbbdbdd* and keeping the final alexandrine. Much of the machinery and spirit of *The Cap and Bells* — the magic journeys through the air — the comic atmosphere and adventures of the courts — are closely akin to the jocular parts of this *Oberon*. Some of the passages of mere fun and playfulness are pleasant enough, like that description of a dilapidated hackney coach (much resembling the four-wheeler of our youth) which Hunt selected to publish in the *Indicator* while Keats was lying sick in his house the next year: but the attempts at social satire are almost always feeble and tiresome, and still more so those at political satire, turning for the most part rather obscurely on the scandals, then at their height, attending the relations of the Prince and Princess of Wales. In the faery narrative itself there break forth momentary flashes from the true genius of the poet, such as might delight the reader if he could lose his sense of irritation at the rubbish from amidst which they gleam. As thus, of the princess's flight through the air (was Keats thinking, in the first line, of the children carried heavenward by angels in Orcagna's *Triumph of Death*?)

> As in old pictures tender cherubim
> A child's soul thro' the sapphir'd canvas bear,
> So, thro' a real heaven, on they swim
> With the sweet princess on her plumag'd lair,
> Speed giving to the winds her lustrous hair.

Or this, telling how Bertha of Canterbury, in Keats' queer new conception of her, was really a changeling born in the jungle: —

> She is a changeling of my management;
> She was born at midnight in an Indian wild;
> Her mother's screams with the striped tiger's blent,
> While the torch-bearing slaves a halloo sent
> Into the jungles.

Or again, some of the stanzas describing the welcome prepared in Elfinan's capital for the faery princess after her flight: note in the last the persistence with which Keats carries into these incongruous climates his passion for the English spring flowers: —

> The morn is full of holiday; loud bells
> With rival clamours ring from every spire;
> Cunningly-station'd music dies and swells
> In echoing places; when the winds respire,
> Light flags stream out like gauzy tongues of fire;
> A metropolitan murmur, lifeful, warm,
> Comes from the northern suburbs; rich attire
> Freckles with red and gold the moving swarm;
> While here and there clear trumpets blow a keen alarm.

And again: —

> As flowers turn their faces to the sun,
> So on our flight with hungry eyes they gaze,
> And, as we shap'd our course, this, that way run,
> With mad-cap pleasure, or hand-clasp'd amaze;
> Sweet in the air a mild-ton'd music plays,
> And progresses through its own labyrinth;
> Buds gather'd from the green spring's middle-days,
> They scatter'd, — daisy, primrose, hyacinth, —
> Or round white columns wreath'd from capital to plinth.

After his mornings spent in Brown's company over the strained frivolities of *The Cap and Bells* , Keats was in the same weeks striving, alone with himself of an evening, to utter the new thoughts on life and poetry which he found taking shape in the depths of his being. He took up again the abandoned *Hyperion* , and began rewriting it no longer as a direct narrative, but as a vision shewn and interpreted by a supernatural monitress acting to him somewhat the same part as Virgil acts to Dante. In altering the form and structure of the poem Keats also takes pains to alter its style, de-Miltonizing and de-latinizing, sometimes terribly to their disadvantage, the passages which he takes over from the earlier version. It is not in these, it is in the two hundred and seventy lines of its wholly new preamble or introduction that the value of the altered poem lies.

The reader remembers how Keats had broken off his work on the original *Hyperion* at the point where Mnemosyne, goddess of Memory and mother of the Muses, is enkindling the brain of Apollo by mysteriously imparting to him her ancient wisdom and all-embracing knowledge. Following a clue which he had found in a Latin book of mythology he had lately bought, he now identifies this Greek Mnemosyne with the Roman Moneta, goddess of warning or admonition; and being possibly also aware that the temple of Juno Moneta on the Capitol at Rome was not far from that of Saturn, makes his Mnemosyne-Moneta the priestess and guardian of Saturn's temple. His vision takes him first into a grove or garden of trees and flowers and fountains, with a feast of summer fruits spread on the moss before an embowered arbour. The events that follow, and the converse held between the poet and the priestess, are in their ethical and allegoric meanings at many points obscure, and capable, like all symbols that are truly symbolic, of various interpretations. But the leading ideas they embody can be recognised clearly enough.

They are primarily the same ideas, developed in a deeper and more sombre spirit, as had been present in Keats' mind almost from the beginning: the idea that in the simple delights of nature and of art as unreflectingly felt in youth there is no abiding place for the poetic spirit, that from the enjoyment of such delights it must rise to thoughts higher and more austere and prompting to more arduous tasks: the further idea that to fit it for such tasks two things above all are necessary, growth in human sympathy through the putting down of self, and growth in knowledge and wisdom through strenuous study and meditation. Such ideas had already been thrown out by Keats in *Sleep and Poetry*; they had been developed with much more fullness, though in a manner made obscure from redundance of imagery, in *Endymion*, especially in the third book: they had been expressed with a difference under the new and clearer symbolism of the Two Chambers of Thought in Keats' letter to Reynolds from Teignmouth. About the same hour, the hour, as I think, of the finest achievement of Keats' genius as well as of its highest promise, — there had appeared in his letters and some of his verses the quite new idea, which would have been inconceivable to him a year earlier, of questioning whether poetry was a worthy pursuit at all in a world full of pain and destruction. Musing beside the sea on a calm evening of April, he anticipates the Tennysonian vision of 'nature, red in tooth and claw With ravine.' In letters written during the next few weeks he insists over and over again alike upon the acuteness of his new sense that the world is 'full of Misery and Heartbreak, Pain, Sickness and Oppression,' and upon the poet's need of knowledge, and again knowledge, and ever more knowledge, to take away the heat and fever and ease 'the Burden of the Mystery.' The first passage that shows the dawn of a desire in his mind to do good to a suffering world by means possibly other than his art is that well-known and deeply significant one: —

I find earlier days are gone by — I find that I can have no enjoyment in the world but continual drinking of knowledge. I find there is no worthy pursuit but the idea of doing some good to the world. Some do it with their society — some with their wit — some with their benevolence — some with a sort of power of conferring pleasure and good humour on all they meet — and in a thousand ways, all dutiful to the command of great Nature — there is but one way for me. The road lies through application, study, and thought. I will pursue it.

The next time he expresses such an idea, it comes struck from him in a darker mood and in phrases of greater poignancy: — 'were it in my choice, I would reject a Petrarcal coronation, — on account of my dying day, and because women have cancers...I am never alone without rejoicing that there is such a thing as death — without placing my ultimate in the glory of dying for a great human purpose.'

The pressure of the sense of human misery, the hunger of the soul for knowledge and vision to lighten it, though they naturally do not colour his impersonal work of the next year and a half, nevertheless set their mark, the former strain in especial, upon his most deeply felt meditative verse, as in the odes to the Nightingale and the Grecian Urn, and reappear occasionally in his private confessions to his friends. Now, after intense experience both of personal sorrow and of poetic toil, and under the strain of incipient disease and consuming passion, it is borne in upon his solitary hours that such poetry as he has written, the irresponsible poetry of beauty and romance, has been mere idle dreaming, a refuge of the spirit from its prime duty of sharing and striving to alleviate the troubles of the world. It seems to him that every ordinary man and woman is worth more to mankind than such a dreamer. If poetry is to be worth anything to the world, it must be a different kind of poetry from this: the true poet is something the very opposite of the mere dreamer: he is one who has prepared himself through self-renunciation and arduous effort and extreme probation of the spirit to receive and impart the highest wisdom, the wisdom that comes from full knowledge of the past and foresight into the future. Of such wisdom *The Fall of Hyperion* in its amended form, as revealed and commented by Mnemosyne-Moneta, the great priestess and prophetess, remembrancer and admonisher in one, was meant to be a sample, — or such an attempt at a sample as Keats at the present stage of his mental growth could supply. But the attempt soon proved beyond his strength and was abandoned.

The preamble, or induction, he had finished; and this, if we leave out the futile eighteen lines with which it begins, contains much lofty thought conveyed in noble imagery and in a style of blank verse quite his own and independent of all models. Take the feast of fruits, symbolic of the poet's early unreflecting joys, and the new thirst for some finer and more inspiring elixir which follows it: —

> On a mound
> Of moss, was spread a feast of summer fruits,
> Which, nearer seen, seem'd refuse of a meal
> By angel tasted or our Mother Eve;
> For empty shells were scattered on the grass,
> And grape-stalks but half bare, and remnants more
> Sweet-smelling, whose pure kinds I could not know.
> Still was more plenty than the fabled horn
> Thrice emptied could pour forth at banqueting,
> For Proserpine return'd to her own fields,
> Where the white heifers low. And appetite,
> More yearning than on earth I ever felt,
> Growing within, I ate deliciously, —
> And, after not long, thirsted; for thereby
> Stood a cool vessel of transparent juice
> Sipp'd by the wander'd bee, the which I took,
> And pledging all the mortals of the world,
> And all the dead whose names are in our lips,
> Drank. That full draught is parent of my theme.

The draught plunges him into a profound sleep, from which he awakens a changed being among utterly changed surroundings. The world in which he finds himself is no longer a delicious garden but an ancient and august temple, — the noblest and most nobly described architectural vision in all Keats' writings: —

> I look'd around upon the curved sides
> Of an old sanctuary, with roof august,
> Builded so high, it seemed that filmed clouds
> Might spread beneath as o'er the stars of heaven.
> So old the place was, I remember'd none
> The like upon the earth: what I had seen
> Of grey cathedrals, buttress'd walls, rent towers,
> The superannuations of sunk realms,
> Or Nature's rocks toil'd hard in waves and winds,
> Seem'd but the faulture of decrepit things
> To that eternal domed monument.

The sights the poet sees and the experiences which befall him within this temple; the black gates closed against the east, — which must symbolize the forgotten past of the world; the stupendous image enthroned aloft in the west, with the altar at its foot, approachable only by an interminable flight of steps; the wreaths of incense veiling the altar and spreading a mysterious sense of happiness; the voice of one ministering at the altar and shrouded in the incense — a voice at once of invitation and menace, bidding the dreamer climb to the summit of the steps by a given moment or he will perish utterly; the sense of icy numbness and death which comes upon him before he can reach even the lowest step; the new life that pours into him as he touches the step; his accosting of the mysterious veiled priestess who stands on the altar platform when he has climbed to it; all these phases of the poet's ordeal are impressively told, but are hard to interpret otherwise than dubiously and vaguely. Matters become more definite a moment afterwards, when in answer to the poet's questions the priestess tells him that none can climb to the altar beside which he stands, — the altar, we must suppose, of historic and prophetic knowledge where alone, after due sacrifice of himself, the poet can find true inspiration, — except those

> to whom the miseries of the world
> Are misery and will not let them rest.

The poet pleads that there are thousands of ordinary men and women who feel the sorrows of the world and do their best to mitigate them, and is answered, —

> 'Those whom thou spakest of are no visionaries'
> Rejoin'd that voice; 'they are no dreamers weak;
> They seek no wonder but the human face,
> No music but a happy-noted voice:
> They come not here, they have no thought to come;
> And thou art here, for thou art less than they.
> What benefit canst thou do, or all thy tribe,
> To the great world? Thou art a dreaming thing,
> A fever of thyself: think of the earth;
> What bliss, even in hope, is there for thee?
> What haven? every creature hath its home,
> Every sole man hath days of joy and pain,
> Whether his labours be sublime or low —
> The pain alone, the joy alone, distinct:
> Only the dreamer venoms all his days,
> Bearing more woe than all his sins deserve.

What a pilgrimage has the soul of Keats gone through, when he utters this heartrending cry, from the day, barely three years before, when he was never tired of singing by anticipation the joys and glories of the poetic life and of the end that awaits it: —

> These are the living pleasures of the bard,
> But richer far posterity's award.
> What shall he murmur with his latest breath,
> When his proud eye looks through the film of death?

The truth is that, in all this, Keats in his depression of mind and body has become fiercely unjust to his own achievements and their value: for if posterity were asked, would it not reply that the things of sheer beauty his youth has left us, draughts drawn from the inmost wells of nature and antiquity and romance, are of greater solace and refreshment to his kind than anything he could have been likely to achieve by deliberate effort in defiance of his natural genius or in premature anticipation of its maturity?

At this point there follows a fretful passage, ill-written or rather only roughly drafted, and therefore not included in the transcripts of the fragments by his friends, in which his monitress affirms contemptuously the gulf that separates the romantic dreamer from the true poet. He accepts the reproof and the threatened punishment, the more willingly if they are to extend to certain 'hectorers in proud bad verse' (he means Byron) who have aroused his spleen. Reverting to a loftier strain, and acknowledging the grace she has so far shown him, the poet asks his monitress to reveal herself. He had probably long before been impressed by engravings of the well-known ancient statue of the seated Mnemosyne sitting forward with her chin resting on her hand, her arm and shoulder heavily swathed in drapery: but his vision of her here seems wholly independent, and is noble and mystically haunting. When she has signified to him in a softened voice that the gigantic image above the altar is that of Saturn, and that the scenes of the world's past she is about to evoke before him are those of the fall of Saturn, the poet relates: —

> As near as an immortal's sphered words
> Could to a mother's soften were these last:
> And yet I had a terror of her robes,
> And chiefly of the veils that from her brow
> Hung pale, and curtain'd her in mysteries,
> That made my heart too small to hold its blood.
> This saw that Goddess, and with sacred hand
> Parted the veils. Then saw I a wan face,
> Not pin'd by human sorrows, but bright-blanch'd
> By an immortal sickness which kills not;
> It works a constant change, which happy death
> Can put no end to; deathwards progressing
> To no death was that visage; it had past
> The lilly and the snow; and beyond these
> I must not think now, though I saw that face.
> But for her eyes I should have fled away;
> They held me back with a benignant light,
> Soft, mitigated by divinest lids
> Half-clos'd, and visionless entire they seem'd
> Of all external things; they saw me not,
> But in blank splendour beam'd, like the mild moon,
> Who comforts those she sees not, who knows not
> What eyes are upward cast.

The aspirant now adoringly entreats her to disclose the tragedy that he perceives to be working in her brain: she consents, and from this point begins the original *Hyperion* re-cast and narrated as a vision within the main vision, with comments put into the mouth of the prophetess. But the scheme, which under no circumstances, one would say, could have been a prosperous one, was soon abandoned, and this, the last of Keats' great fragments, breaks off near the beginning of the second book.

Chapter XV

FEBRUARY-AUGUST 1820: HAMPSTEAD AND KENTISH TOWN: PUBLICATION OF LAMIA VOLUME.

Such and so gloomy, although with no ignoble gloom, had been Keats' deeper thoughts on poetry and life, and such the imagery under which he figured them, during the last weeks when the state of his health enabled his mind to work with anything approaching its natural power. From the night of his seizure on February 3rd 1820, which was three months after his twenty-fourth birthday, he never wrote verse again: unless indeed the lines found on the margin of his manuscript of *The Cap and Bells* were written from his sickbed and in a moment of bitterness addressed in his mind to Fanny Brawne: but from a certain pitch and formality of style in them, I should take them rather to be meant for putting into the mouth of one of the characters in some such historical play as he had been meditating in the weeks before Christmas: —

> This living hand, now warm and capable
> Of earnest grasping, would, if it were cold
> And in the icy silence of the tomb,
> So haunt thy days and chill thy dreaming nights
> That thou would wish thine own heart dry of blood
> So in my veins red life might stream again,
> And thou be conscience-calm'd — see here it is —
> I hold it towards you.

For several days after the hæmorrhage he was kept to his room and his bed, and for nearly two months had to lead a strictly invalid life. At first he could bear no one in the room except the doctor and Brown. 'While I waited on him day and night,' testifies Brown, 'his instinctive generosity, his acceptance of my offices, by a glance of his eye, a motion of his hand, made me regard my mechanical duty as absolutely nothing compared to his silent acknowledgment.' (How often have these words come home to the heart of the present writer in days when he used to be busy about the mute sickbed of another of these shining ones!) Severn, nursing Keats later under conditions even more trying and hopeless, bears similar testimony to his unabated charm and sweetness in suffering. Almost from the first he was able to write little letters to his sister Fanny, and is careful to give them a cheering and reassuring turn. When after some days he is down on a sofa-bed made up for him in the front parlour he tells her what an improvement it is: —

Besides I see all that passes-for instance now, this morning — if I had been in my own room I should not have seen the coals brought in. On Sunday between the hours of twelve and one I descried a Pot boy. I conjectured it might be the one o'clock beer — Old women with bobbins and red cloaks and unpresuming bonnets I see creeping about the heath. Gipseys after hare skins and silver spoons. Then goes by a fellow with a wooden clock under his arm that strikes a hundred and more. Then comes the old French emigrant (who has been very well to do in France) with his hands joined behind on his hips, and his face full of political schemes. Then passes Mr David Lewis, a very good-natured, good-looking old gentleman who has been very kind to Tom and George and me. As for those fellows the Brickmakers they are always passing to and fro. I mustn't forget the two old maiden Ladies in Well Walk who have a Lap dog between them that they are very anxious about. It is a corpulent Little beast whom it is necessary to coax along with an ivory-tipp'd cane. Carlo our Neighbour Mrs Brawne's dog and it meet sometimes. Lappy thinks Carlo a devil of a fellow and so do his Mistresses.

Very soon his betrothed was allowed to pay him little visits from next door, and he was able to take pleasure in these and in a constant interchange of notes with her. He tells her of his thoughts and some of his words (which are not quite the same as Brown puts in his mouth) at the moment of his seizure: —

You must believe — you shall, you will — that I can do nothing, say nothing, think nothing of you but what has its spring in the Love which has so long been my pleasure and torment. On the night I was taken ill — when so violent a rush of blood came to my Lungs that I felt nearly suffocated — I assure you I felt it possible I might not survive, and at that moment thought of nothing but you. When I said to Brown 'this is unfortunate' I thought of you. 'Tis true that since the first two or three days other subjects have entered my head.

On the whole his love-thoughts keep peaceable and contented, and his jealousies are for the moment at rest. But he has to struggle with the sense that considering his health and circumstances he is bound in fairness to release her from her engagement: an idea which to her credit she seems steadily to have refused to entertain.

My greatest torment since I have known you has been the fear of you being a little inclined to the Cressid; but that suspicion I dismiss utterly and remain happy in the surety of your Love, which I assure you is as much a wonder to me as a delight. Send me the words 'Good night' to put under my pillow....

You know our situation — what hope is there if I should be recovered ever so soon — my very health will not suffer me to make any great exertion. I am recommended not even to read poetry, much less write it. I wish I had even a little hope. I cannot say forget me — but I would mention that there are impossibilities in the world. No more of this. I am not strong enough to be weaned — take no notice of it in your good night.

The healthier and more tranquil tenor of his thoughts and feelings for the time is beautifully expressed in the often quoted letter written to James Rice a fortnight after his attack: —

I may say that for six months before I was taken ill I had not passed a tranquil day. Either that gloom overspread me, or I was suffering under some passionate feeling, or if I turned to versify, that acerbated the poison of either sensation. The beauties of nature had lost their power over me. How astonishingly (here I must premise that illness, as far as I can judge in so short a time, has relieved my mind of a load of deceptive thoughts and images, and makes me perceive things in a truer light), — how astonishingly does the chance of leaving the world impress a sense of its natural beauties upon us! Like poor Falstaff, though I do not 'babble', I think of green fields; I muse with the greatest affection on every flower I have known from my infancy — their shapes and colours are as new to me as if I had just created them with a superhuman fancy. It is because they are connected with the most thoughtless and the happiest moments of our lives. I have seen foreign flowers in hothouses, of the most beautiful nature, but I do not care a straw for them. The simple flowers of our Spring are what I want to see again.

Some time in the month he owns to his beloved that the thoughts of what he had hoped to do in poetry mingle with his thoughts of her: —

How illness stands as a barrier betwixt me and you! Even if I was well — I must make myself as good a Philosopher as possible. Now I have had opportunities of passing nights anxious and awake I have found other thoughts intrude upon me. 'If I should die,' said I to myself, 'I have left no immortal work behind me — nothing to make my friends proud of my memory — but I have lov'd the principle of beauty in all things, and if I had had time I would have made myself remember'd.' Thoughts like these came very feebly whilst I was in health and every pulse beat for you — now you divide with this (may I say it?) 'last infirmity of noble minds' all my reflection.

Presently we learn from his letters that Reynolds, Dilke, and one or two other friends have been dropping in to see him. He expresses himself touched by the courtesy of a new poetical acquaintance of much more prosperous worldly connexions than his own, Mr Bryan Waller Procter ('Barry Cornwall') in sending him copies of his volumes lately published. Keats does not mention that one of these contains a version, *The Sicilian Story*, of the same tale from Boccaccio as his own as yet unpublished *Isabella*: but he cannot quite conceal his perception of those qualities in Barry Cornwall's work, its prevailing strain of fluent imitative commonplace, its affectations and exaggerations of Hunt's and his own leanings towards over-lusciousness, which Shelley, as we shall see, found so exasperating. 'However,' he adds, 'that is nothing — I think he likes poetry for its own sake not his.' Before the end of the month we find him taking pleasure, as in earlier Februaries, in the song of the thrush, which portends, he hopes, an end of the north-east wind. The month of March brings signs of gradually returning strength. Brown, he says, declares he is getting stout; and having in the first weeks of his illness avowed that he was so feeble he could be flattered into a hope in which faith had no part, he now begins really to believe in his own recovery and to let his thoughts run again on fame and poetry. He writes to Fanny Brawne the most trustful and least agitated of all his love letters: —

You uttered a half complaint once that I only lov'd your Beauty. Have I nothing else then to love in you but that? Do not I see a heart naturally furnish'd with wings imprison itself with me? No ill prospect has been able to turn your thoughts a moment from me. This perhaps should be as much a subject of sorrow as joy — but I will not talk of that. Even if you did not love me I could not help an entire devotion to you: how much more deeply then must I feel for you knowing you love me. My Mind has been the most discontented and restless one that ever was put into a body too small for it. I never felt my Mind repose upon anything with complete and undistracted enjoyment — upon no person but you. When you are in the room my thoughts never fly out of window: you always concentrate my whole senses. The anxiety shown about our Loves in your last note is an immense pleasure to me: however you must not suffer such speculations to molest you any more: nor will I any more believe you can have the least pique against me.

And again: 'let me have another opportunity of years and I will not die without being remember'd. Take care of yourself dear that we may both be well in the summer.'

He began to get about again, and by the 25th of March was well enough to go into town to the private view of Haydon's huge picture, finished at last, of Christ's Entry into Jerusalem. This was the occasion which Haydon in his autobiography describes in language so vivid and with a self-congratulation so boisterous and contagious that it is impossible in reading not to share his sense of the day's triumph. As in the case of the Elgin marbles three years earlier, he had achieved his object in the face of a thousand difficulties and enmities, living the while on the bounty of friends, some of them rich, others, as we know, the reverse, whom his ardour and importunity had whipped up to his help. At the last moment he had contrived to scrape together money enough to stop the mouths of his creditors and to pay the cost of hiring the Egyptian Hall and hanging up his gigantic canvas there, with the help of three gigantic guardsmen, his models and assistants; and the world of taste and fashion, realising how Haydon had been right and the established dilettanti wrong in regard to the Elgin marbles, were determined to be on the safe side this time in case he should turn out to be right also about the merits of his own work.

Some exalted and many distinguished personages had been to see the picture in his studio, and now, on the opening day, the hall was thronged in answer to his invitations. 'All the ministers and their ladies, all the foreign ambassadors, all the bishops, all the beauties in high life, all the geniuses in town, and everybody of any note, were invited and came.... The room was full. Keats and Hazlitt were up in a corner, really rejoicing.' Hazlitt expressed in the *Edinburgh Review* for the following August a tempered, far from undiscriminating admiration of certain qualities in the painting. Keats himself merely mentions to his sister Fanny, without comment, the fact of his having been there. One wonders whether he witnessed the scene which Haydon goes on in his effective way to narrate.

He had tried to treat the head of Christ unconventionally, had painted and repainted it, and was nervous and dissatisfied over the result. The crowd seemed doubtful too. 'Everybody seemed afraid, when in walked, with all the dignity of her majestic presence, Mrs Siddons, like a Ceres or a Juno. The whole room remained dead silent, and allowed her to think. After a few minutes Sir George Beaumont, who was extremely anxious, said in a very delicate manner, "How do you like the Christ?" Everybody listened for her reply. After a moment, in a deep, loud, tragic tone she said, "It is completely successful." I was then presented with all the ceremonies of a levee, and she invited me to her house in an awful tone.'...I think it is not recorded whether Northcote's acid comment in a different sense, 'Mr Haydon, your ass is the Saviour of your picture', was made on this famous occasion or privately. Certainly the ass, judging by photographs of the picture as it now hangs in a wrecked condition at Cincinnati, is the object that first takes the eye with its black ears and shoulders strongly relieved against the white drapery of Christ, and what looks like the realistic treatment of the creature in contrast with the 'ideal,' that is the vapidly pompous and pretentious, portraiture of geniuses past and present, Newton, Voltaire, Wordsworth, Hazlitt, Keats, introduced among the crowd in the foreground.

In the course of April the improvement in Keats' health failed to maintain itself. We find him complaining much of nervous irritability and general weakness. He is recommended, one would like to know by whom, to avoid the excitement of writing or even reading poetry and turn to the study of geometry — of all things! — as a sedative. He has no strength for the walk to Walthamstow to see his young sister, and even shrinks from the fatigue of going by coach. Brown having arranged to let his house again and go for another tramp through Scotland — not, one would have said under the circumstances, the course of a very considerate or solicitous friend, but he was probably misled by Keats' apparent improvement the month before — Brown having made this arrangement, Keats, also on the recommendation of the doctors, thinks of sailing with him on the packet and returning alone, in hopes of getting strength from the sea-trip to Scotland and back. This plan, when it came to the point, he gave up, and only accompanied his friend down the river as far as Gravesend. Having to turn out of Wentworth Place in favour of Brown's summer tenants, he thought of taking a lodging a few doors from the house where Leigh Hunt was then living in Kentish Town, then still a village on the way between London and Hampstead. Almost at the same time he writes to Dilke in regard to his future course of life, 'My mind has been at work all over the world to find out what to do. I have my choice of three things, or at least two, South America, or surgeon to an Indiaman; which last, I think, will be my fate.' For the present he moved as he had proposed to Kentish Town (2 Wesleyan Place). Here he stayed for six or seven weeks (approximately May 6-June 23), and then, having suffered a set-back in the shape of two slight returns of hæmorrhage from the lung, moved for the sake of better nursing into the household of the ever kind and affectionate, but not less ever feckless and ill-managing, Leigh Hunts at 13 Mortimer Terrace. With them he remained for another period of about seven weeks, ending on August 12th.

Those three months in Kentish Town were to Keats a time of distressing weakness and for the most part of terrible inward fretfulness and despondency. Early in the time he speaks of intending soon to begin (meaning begin again) on *The Cap and Bells*. When we read those vivid stanzas quoted above (p. 446) describing the welcome by the crowd of princess Bellanaine after her aerial journey, we are inevitably reminded of an event — the triumphal approach and entry of Queen Caroline into London from Dover — which happened on the 9th of June this same year. It would be tempting to suppose that Keats may have witnessed the event and been thereby inspired to his description. But he was too ill for such outings, and moreover the earlier of the two stanzas comes well back in the poem (sixty-fourth out of eighty-eight) and it is impossible to suppose that in his then state he could have added so much to the fragment as that would imply. So we must credit the stanzas to imagination only, and take it as certain that his only real occupation with poetry in these days was in passing through the press the new volume of poems (*Lamia*, *Isabella*, etc.,) which his friends had at last persuaded him to put forward. Even on this task his hold must have been loose, seeing that the publishers put in without his knowledge a note which he afterwards sharply disowned, to the effect that his reason for dropping *Hyperion* had been the ill reception of *Endymion* by the critics.

His only outing, so far as we hear, was to an exhibition of English historical portraits at the British Institution, of which he writes to Brown with some interest and vividness. He tells at the same time of an invitation, which he was not well enough to accept, to meet Wordsworth, Southey, Lamb, Haydon, and some others at supper. Leigh Hunt, despite his engrossing literary and editorial occupations and a recent trying illness of his own, did his best, while Keats was his inmate, to keep him interested and amused. Keats in writing to his sister gratefully acknowledges as much. 'Mr Hunt does everything in his power to make the time pass as agreeably with me as possible. I read the greatest part of the day and generally take two half-hour walks a day up and down the terrace which is very much pester'd with cries, ballad singers, and street music.' But the obsession of his passion, its consuming jealousy and hopelessness, gave him little respite. He would keep his eyes fixed all day, as he afterwards avowed, on Hampstead; and once when, at Hunt's suggestion, they took a drive as far as the Heath, he burst into a flood of unwonted tears and declared his heart was breaking.

His letters to his beloved in these same months are too agonizing to read. He is so little himself in them, so merely and utterly, to borrow words of his own, 'a fever of himself,' that many of us could not endure, when they were first published, the thought of this Keats-that-is-no-Keats being exposed before a hastily reading and carelessly judging after-world, and even now cannot but regret it. All the morbid self-torturing elements of his nature, which in health it had been a main part of the battle of his life to subdue, and of which he never suffered those about him to see a sign, now burst from control and flamed out against the girl he loved and the friends he loved next best to her. Once only, at the beginning of the time, he could write contentedly, telling her that he is marking for her the most beautiful passages in Spenser, 'comforting myself in being somewhat occupied to give you however small a pleasure. It has lightened my time very much. God bless you.' His other letters are in a tortured, almost frenzied, strain of jealous suspicion and reproach against her and against those of his intimates who had, as he imagined, disapproved their attachment, or pried into or made light of it, or else had shown her too marked attentions. Among the former were Reynolds and his sisters, from whom for the time being he was tacitly estranged. Among the latter he includes Brown and Dilke, with especial bitterness against Brown. Between them all they had made, he vows, a football of his heart, and again, 'Hamlet's heart was full of such misery as mine is when he cried to Ophelia, "Go to a Nunnery, go, go!".' That these were but the half-delirious promptings of his fevered blood is clear from the fact that a very few weeks both before and after such outbreaks he wrote to Brown as though counting him as much a friend as ever. As for his betrothed, wound as his reproaches might at the time, we know from her own words that they left no lasting impression of unkindness on her memory. Writing in riper years to Medwin, who had asked her whether the accounts current in Rome of Keats' violence of nature were true, she says: —

That his sensibility was most acute, is true, and his passions were very strong, but not violent, if by that term, violence of temper is implied. His was no doubt susceptible, but his anger seemed rather to turn on himself than on others, and in moments of greatest irritation, it was only by a sort of savage despondency that he sometimes grieved and wounded his friends. Violence such as the letter describes, was quite foreign to his nature. For more than a twelvemonth before quitting England, I saw him every day, often witnessed his sufferings, both mental and bodily, and I do not hesitate to say, that he never could have addressed an unkind expression, much less a violent one, to any human being.

These words of Fanny Brawne, then Mrs Lindon, to Medwin are not well known, and it is only fair to quote them as proving that if in youth the lady had not been willing to sacrifice her gaieties and her pleasure in admiration for the sake of her lover's peace of mind, she showed at any rate in after life a true and loyal understanding of his character.

While Keats was staying in Kentish Town Severn went often to see him, and in the second week of July writes to Haslam struggling to keep up his hopes for their friend in spite of appearances and of Keats' own conviction: — 'It will give you pleasure to say I trust he will still recover. His appearance is shocking and now reminds me of poor Tom and I have been inclined to think him in the same way. For himself — he makes sure of it — and seems prepossessed that he cannot recover — now I seem more than ever *not* to think so and I know you will agree with me when you see him — are you aware another volume of Poems was published last week — in which is "Lovely Isabel — poor simple Isabel"? I have been delighted with this volume and think it will even please the million.' During the same period Shelley's friends the Gisbornes twice met him at Leigh Hunt's. The first time was on June 23. Mrs Gisborne writes in her journal that having lately been ill he spoke little and in a low tone: 'the *Endymion* was not mentioned, this person might not be its author; but on observing his countenance and eyes I persuaded myself that he was the very person.' It is always Keats' eyes that strangers thus notice first: the late Mrs Procter, who met him only once, at a lecture of Hazlitt's, remembered them to the end of her long life as like those of one 'who had been looking at some glorious sight.' This first time Keats and Mrs Gisborne had some talk about music and singing, but some three weeks later, on July 12th, the same lady notes, 'drank tea at Mr Hunt's; I was much pained by the sight of poor Keats, under sentence of death from Dr Lamb. He never spoke and looks emaciated.'

Doubtless it was under the impression of this last meeting that Mr Gisborne sent Shelley the account of Keats' state of health which moved Shelley to write in his own and his wife's name urging that Keats should come to Italy to avoid the English winter and take up his quarters with or near them at Pisa. Shelley repeats nearly the same kind and just opinion of *Endymion* as he had previously expressed in writing to the Olliers; saying he has lately read it again, 'and ever with a new sense of the treasures of poetry it contains, though treasures poured forth with indistinct profusion. This people in general will not endure, and that is the cause of the comparatively few copies which have been sold. I feel persuaded that you are capable of the greatest things, so you but will.' At the same time Shelley sends Keats a copy of his *Cenci*. Keats' answer shows him touched and grateful for the kindness offered, but nevertheless, as always where Shelley is in question, in some degree embarrassed and ungracious. He says nothing of the invitation to Pisa, though he was already considering the possibility of going to winter in Italy. As to *Endymion*, he says he would willingly unwrite it did he care so much as once about reputation, and as to *The Cenci*, and *The Prometheus* announced as forthcoming, he makes the well-known, rather obscurely worded criticism of which the main drift is that to his mind Shelley pours out new poems too quickly and does not concentrate enough upon the purely artistic aims and qualities of his work. These, Keats goes on, are 'by many spirits nowadays considered the Mammon. A modern work, it is said, must have a purpose which may be the God. An artist must serve Mammon; he must have 'self-concentration' — selfishness, perhaps. You, I am sure, will forgive me for sincerely remarking that you might curb your magnanimity and be more of an artist, and load every rift of your subject with ore.'

Keats in these admonitions was no doubt remembering views of Shelley's such as are expressed in his words 'I consider poetry very subordinate to moral and political science.' Judging by them, his mind would seem to have veered back from the convictions which inspired the preamble to the revised *Hyperion* the autumn before, insisting, in language which might almost seem borrowed from the preface to *Alastor*, on the doom that awaits poets who play their art in selfishness instead of making it their paramount aim to 'pour balm' upon the miseries of mankind. With reference to the promised *Prometheus* he adds, 'could I have my own wish effected, you would have it still in manuscript, or be but now putting an end to the second act. I remember your advising me not to publish my first blights, on Hampstead Heath. I am returning advice upon your hands.' Finally, mentioning that he is sending out a copy of his lately published *Lamia* volume, he says that most of its contents have been written above two years (a slip of memory, the statement being only true of *Isabella* and of one or two minor pieces) and would never have been published now but for hope of gain.

Shelley's letter was written from Pisa on the 27th of July and received by Keats on the 13th of August. On the previous day he had fled suddenly from under the Leigh Hunts' roof, having been thrown into a fit of uncontrollable nervous agitation by the act of a discharged servant, who kept back a letter to him from Fanny Brawne and on quitting the house left it to be delivered, opened and two days late, by one of the children. His first impulse on leaving the Hunts' was to go back to his old lodging with Bentley the postman, but this Mrs Brawne would not hear of, and took him into her own house, where she and her daughter for the next few weeks nursed him and did all they could for his comfort.

During those unhappy months at Kentish Town Keats' best work was given to the world. First, in Leigh Hunt's *Indicator* for May 20, *La Belle Dame sans Merci*, signed, obviously in bitterness, 'Caviare' (Hamlet's 'caviare to the general'), and unluckily enfeebled by changes for which we find no warrant either in Keats' autograph or in extant copies made by his friends Woodhouse and Brown. Keats' judgment in revising his own work had evidently by this time become unsure. We have seen how in recasting *Hyperion* the previous autumn he changed some of the finest of his original lines for the worse: and it is conceivable that in the case of *La Belle Dame* he may have done so again of his own motion, but much more likely, I should say, that the changes, which are all in the direction of the slipshod and the commonplace, were made on Hunt's suggestion and that Keats acquiesced from fatigue or indifference, or perhaps even from that very sense of lack of sympathy in most readers which made him sign 'Caviare.' Hunt introduced the piece with some commendatory words, showing that he at all events felt nothing amiss with it in its new shape, and added a short account of the old French poem by Alain Chartier from which the title was taken. It is to be deplored that in some recent and what should be standard editions of Keats the poem stands as thus printed in the *Indicator*, instead of in the original form rightly given by Lord Houghton from Brown's transcript, in which it had become a classic of the language.

It is surely a perversion in textual criticism to perpetuate the worse version merely because it happens to be the one printed in Keats' lifetime. No sensitive reader but must feel that 'wretched wight' is a vague and vapid substitute for the clear image of the 'knight-at-arms,' while 'sigh'd full sore' is ill replaced by 'sighed deep,' and 'wild wild eyes' still worse by 'wild sad eyes': that the whimsical particularity of the 'kisses four,' removed in the new version, gives the poem an essential part of its savour (Keats was fond of these fanciful numberings, compare the damsels who stand 'by fives and sevens' in the Induction to Calidore, and the 'four laurell'd spirits' in the Epistle to George Felton Matthew): and again, that the loose broken construction — 'So kissed to sleep' is quite uncharacteristic of the poet: and yet again, that the phrase 'And there we slumbered on the moss,' is what any amateur rimester might write about any pair of afternoon picknickers, while the phrase which was cancelled for it, 'And there she lulled me asleep,' falls with exactly the mystic cadence and hushing weight upon the spirit which was required. The reader may be interested to hear the effect which these changes had upon the late William Morris, than whom no man had a better right to speak. Mr Sydney Cockerell writes me: —

In February 1894 the last sheets of the Kelmscott Press Keats, edited by F. S. Ellis, were being printed. A specimen of each sheet of every book was brought in to Morris as soon as it came off the press. I was with him when he happened to open the sheet on which *La Belle Dame sans Merci* was printed. He began to read it and was suddenly aware of unfamiliar words, 'wretched wight' for 'knight at arms,' verses 4 and 5 transposed, and several changes in verse 7. Great was his indignation. He swiftly altered the words and then read the poem to me, remarking that it was the germ from which all the poetry of his group had sprung — The sheet was reprinted and the earlier and better version restored — I still have the cancelled sheet with his corrections.

Six weeks later, in the first days of July, appeared the volume *Lamia, Isabella, and other Poems* in right of which Keats' name is immortal. *La Belle Dame* was not in it, nor *In drear-nighted December*, nor any sonnets, nor any of the verses composed on the Scotch tour, nor the fragment of *The Eve of St Mark*, nor, happily, *The Cap and Bells*: but it included all the odes except that on Indolence and the fragment *To Maia*, as well as nearly all the other minor pieces of any account written since *Endymion*, such as *Fancy*, the *Mermaid Tavern* and *Robin Hood* lines, with the three finished Tales, *Isabella*, *The Eve of St Agnes*, and *Lamia*, and the great fragment of *Hyperion* in its original, not its recast, form. Keats was too far gone in illness and the hopelessness of passion to be much moved by the success or failure of his new venture. But the story of its first reception is part of his biography, and shall be briefly told in this place.

The first critic in the field was the best: no less a master than Charles Lamb, who within a fortnight of the appearance of the volume contributed to the *New Times* a brief notice, anonymous but marked with all the charm and authority of his genius. He begins by quoting the four famous stanzas picturing Madeline at her prayers in the moonlit chamber, and comments — 'Like the radiance, which comes from those old windows upon the limbs and garments of the damsel, is the almost Chaucer-like painting, with which this poet illumes every subject he touches. We have scarcely anything like it in modern description. It brings us back to ancient days and "Beauty making-beautiful old rhymes."' 'The finest thing,' Lamb continues, 'in the volume is *The Pot of Basil*.' Noting how the anticipation of the assassination is wonderfully conceived in the one epithet of 'the *murder'd* man,' he goes on to quote the stanzas telling the discovery of and digging for the corpse, 'than which,' he says. 'there is nothing more awfully simple in diction, more nakedly grand and moving in sentiment, in Dante, in Chaucer or in Spenser.' It is to be noted that Lamb, who loved things Gothic better than things Grecian, ignores *Hyperion*, which most critics in praising the volume pitched on to the neglect of the rest, and proceeds to tell of *Lamia*, winding up with a return to *The Pot of Basil* : —

More exuberantly rich in imagery and painting is the story of the *Lamia*. It is of as gorgeous stuff as ever romance was composed of. Her first appearance in serpentine form —

— A beauteous wreath with melancholy eyes —

her dialogue with Hermes, the *Star of Lethe*, as he is called by one of these prodigal phrases which Mr Keats abounds in, which are each a poem in a word, and which in this instance lays open to us at once, like a picture, all the dim regions and their inhabitants, and the sudden coming of a celestial among them; the charming of her into woman's shape again by the God; her marriage with the beautiful Lycius; her magic palace, which those who knew the street, and remembered it complete from childhood, never remembered to have seen before; the few Persian mutes, her attendants,

— who that same year
Were seen about the markets: none knew where
They could inhabit; —

the high-wrought splendours of the nuptial bower, with the fading of the whole pageantry, Lamia, and all, away, before the glance of Apollonius, — are all that fairy land can do for us. They are for younger impressibilities. To *us* an ounce of feeling is worth a pound of fancy; and therefore we recur again, with a warmer gratitude, to the story of Isabella and the pot of basil, and those never-cloying stanzas which we have cited, and which we think should disarm criticism, if it be not in its nature cruel; if it would not deny to honey its sweetness, nor to roses redness, nor light to the stars in Heaven; if it would not bay the moon out of the skies, rather than acknowledge she is fair.

Leigh Hunt, who during all this time was in all ways loyally doing his best for Keats' encouragement and comfort, and had just dedicated his translation of Tasso's *Aminta* to him as to one 'equally pestered by the critical and admired by the poetical,' — Leigh Hunt within a month of the appearance of the volume reviewed and quoted from it with full appreciation in two numbers of the *Indicator*. His notice contained those judicious remarks which we have already cited on the philosophical weakness of *Lamia*, praising at the same time the gorgeousness of the snake description, and saying, of the lines on the music being the sole support of the magical palace-roof, 'this is the very quintessence of the romantic.' 'When Mr Keats errs in his poetry,' says Hunt in regard to the *Pot of Basil*, 'it is from the ill-management of a good thing — exuberance of ideas'; and, comparing the contents of this volume with his earlier work, concludes as follows: —

The author's versification is now perfected, the exuberances of his imagination restrained, and a calm power, the surest and loftiest of all power, takes place of the impatient workings of the younger god within him. The character of his genius is that of energy and voluptuousness, each able at will to take leave of the other, and possessing, in their union, a high feeling of humanity not common to the best authors who can less combine them. Mr Keats undoubtedly takes his seat with the oldest and best of our living poets.

But Leigh Hunt's praise of one of his own supposed disciples of the Cockney School would carry little weight outside the circle of special sympathizers. A better index to the way the wind was beginning to blow was the treatment of the volume in Colburn's *New Monthly Magazine*, of which the poet Thomas Campbell had lately been appointed editor, with the excellent Cyrus Redding as acting editor under him: — 'These poems are very far superior', declares the critic, 'to any which the author has previously committed to the press. They have nothing showy, or extravagant, or eccentric about them; but are pieces of calm beauty, or of lone and self-supported grandeur.' In *Lamia*, 'there is a mingling of Greek majesty with fairy luxuriance which we have not elsewhere seen.' *Isabella* is compared with Barry Cornwall's *Sicilian Story*: 'the poem of Mr Keats has not the luxury of description, nor the rich love-scenes, of Mr Cornwall; but he tells the tale with a naked and affecting simplicity which goes irresistibly to the heart. *The Eve of St Agnes* is 'a piece of consecrated fancy', in which 'a soft religious light is shed over the whole story.' In *Hyperion* 'the picture of the vast abode of Cybele and the Titans is 'in the sublimest style of Æschylus': and in conclusion the critic takes leave of Mr Keats 'with wonder at the gigantic stride which he has taken, and with the good hope that if he proceeds in the high and pure style which he has now chosen, he will attain an exalted and a lasting station among English poets.' Of the other chief literary reviews in England, the old-established *Monthly* begins in a strain scarcely less laudatory, but wavers and becomes admonitory before the end, while Keats' dismal monitor of three years before, the sententious *Eclectic Review*, acknowledging in him 'a young man possessed of an elegant fancy, a warm and lively imagination, and something above the average talents of persons who take to writing poetry', proceeds to warn him against regarding imagination as the proper organ of poetry, to lecture him on his choice of subjects, his addiction to the Greek mythology, and to poetry for poetry's sake ('poetry, after all, if pursued as an end, is but child's play'). The *British Critic*, more contemptuous even than Blackwood or the Quarterly in its handling of *Endymion*, this time prints a kind of palinode, admitting that 'Mr Keats is a person of no ordinary genius', and prophesying that if he will take Spenser and Milton for models instead of Leigh Hunt he 'need not despair of attaining to a very high and enviable place in the public esteem'.

Writing to Brown from Hampstead in the latter half of August, Keats seems aware that the critics are being kinder to him than before. 'My book,' he says, 'has had good success among the literary people, and I believe has a moderate sale;' and again, 'the sale of my book has been very slow, but it has been very highly rated.' The great guns of Scottish criticism had not yet spoken. Constable's *Edinburgh* (formerly the *Scots*) *Magazine*, which never either hit or bit hard, and whose managers had preferred the ways of prudence when Bailey urged them two years before boldly to denounce the outrages of the 'Z' gang in Blackwood, in due course praised Keats' new volume, but cautiously, saying that 'it must and ought to attract attention, for it displays the ore of true poetic genius, though mingled with a large portion of dross.... He is continually shocking our ideas of poetical decorum, at the very time when we are acknowledging the hand of genius. In thus boldly running counter to old opinions, however, we cannot conceive that Mr Keats merits bitter contempt or ridicule; the weapons which are too frequently employed when liberal discussion and argument would be unsuccessful.' As to *Blackwood's Magazine* itself, we are fortunate in having an amusing first-hand narrative of an encounter of its owner and manager with Keats' publisher which preceded the appearance of Keats' new volume. The excellent Taylor, staunch to his injured young friend and client even at some risk, as in his last words he shows himself aware, to his own interests, writes from Fleet Street on the last day of August to his partner Hessey: —

I have had this day a call from Mr Blackwood. We shook hands and went into the Back Shop. After asking him what was new at Edinburgh, and talking about Clare, the *Magazine*, Baldwin, Peter Corcoran and a few other subjects, I observed that we had published another Volume of Keats' Poems on which his Editors would have another opportunity of being witty at his expense. He said they were disposed to speak favourably of Mr K. this time — and he expected that the article would have appeared in this month's mag.

'But can they be so inconsistent?' 'There is no inconsistency in praising him if they think he deserves it.' 'After what has been said of his talents I should think it very inconsistent.' 'Certainly they found fault with his former Poems but that was because they thought they deserved it.' 'But why did they attack him personally?' 'They did not do so.'

'No? Did not they speak of him in ridicule as Johnny Keats, describe his appearance while addressing a Sonnet to Ailsa Crag, and compare him as a (?) hen to Shelley as a Bird of Paradise, besides, what can you say to that cold blooded passage when they say they will take care he shall never get £50 again for a vol. of his Poems — what had he done to deserve such attacks as these?'

'Oh, it was all a joke, the writer meant nothing more than to be witty. He certainly thought there was much affectation in his Poetry, and he expressed his opinion only — It was done in the fair spirit of criticism.'

'It was done in the Spirit of the Devil, Mr Blackwood. So if a young man is guilty of affectation while he is walking the streets it is fair in another Person because he dislikes it to come and knock him down.'

'No,' says B., 'but a poet challenges public opinion by printing his book, but I suppose you would have them not criticized at all?'

'I certainly think they are punished enough by neglect and by the failure of their hopes and to me it seems very cruel to abuse a man merely because he cannot give us as much pleasure as he wishes. But you go even beyond his...(?) you strike a man when he is down. He gets a violent blow from the Quarterly — and then you begin.'

'I beg your pardon,' says B., 'we were the first.'

'I think not, but if you were the first, you continued it after, for that truly diabolical thrust about the £50 appeared after the critique in the Quarterly.'

'You mistake that altogether,' said B., 'the writer does not like the Cockney School, so he went on joking Mr K. about it.'

'Why should not the manners of gentlemen continue to regulate their conduct when they are writing of each other as much as when they are in conversation? No man would insult Mr Keats in this manner in his company, and what is the difference between writing and speaking of a person except that the written attack is the more base from being made anonymously and therefore at no personal risk. — I feel regard for Mr Keats as a man of real Genius, a Gentleman, nay more, one of the gentlest of Human Beings. He does not resent these things himself, he merely says of his Opponents "They don't know me." Now this mildness(?) his friends feel the more severely when they see him ill used. But this feeling is not confined to them. I am happy to say that the Public Interest is awakened to the sense of the Injustice which has been done him and the attempts to ruin him will have in the end a contrary effect.' Here I turned the conversation to another subject by asking B. if he read the *Abbot*, and in about 10 minutes more he made his Exit with a formal Bow and a Good Morning.

The above is the Substance and as clearly as possible the words, I made use of. His replies were a little more copious than I have stated but to the same effect. I have written this conversation down on the day it took place because I suspect some allusion may hereafter be made to it in the Mag. and I fully expect that whatever Books we publish will be received with reference to the feeling it is calculated to excite in the bosoms of these freebooting....

In the upshot, the Blackwood critics took no direct notice of the *Lamia* volume at all, but made occasion during the autumn to say their new say about Keats in a review of Shelley's *Prometheus Unbound*. This time the hand is unmistakably that of Wilson. For the last year or more Wilson, following a hint given him by De Quincey, had chosen to take Shelley boisterously under his patronage as a poet of true genius, for whom scarcely any praise would be too high could he only be weaned from his impious opinions. Now, after rebutting a current and really gratuitous charge that the magazine praised Shelley from the knowledge that he was a man of means and family, and denounced Hunt and Keats because they were poor and struggling, the critic blusters characteristically on, in a strain half apologetic in one breath and in the next as odiously insolent as ever: —

As for Mr Keats, we are informed that he is in a very bad state of health, and that his friends attribute a great deal of it to the pain he has suffered from the critical castigation his *Endymion* drew down on him in this magazine. If it be so, we are most heartily sorry for it, and have no hesitation in saying, that had we suspected that young author, of being so delicately nerved, we should have administered our reproof in a much more lenient shape and style. The truth is, we from the beginning saw marks of feeling and power in Mr Keats' verses, which made us think it very likely, he might become a real poet in England, provided he could be persuaded to give up all the tricks of Cockneyism, and forswear for ever the thin potations of Mr Leigh Hunt. We, therefore, rated him as roundly as we decently could do, for the flagrant affectations of those early productions of his. In the last volume he has published we find more beauties than in the former, both of language and of thought, but we are sorry to say, we find abundance of the same absurd affectations also, and superficial conceits, which first displeased us in his writings; — and which we are again very sorry to say, must in our opinion, if persisted in, utterly and entirely prevent Mr Keats from ever taking his place among the pure and classical poets of his mother tongue. It is quite ridiculous to see how the vanity of these Cockneys makes them overrate their own importance, even in the eyes of us, that have always expressed such plain unvarnished contempt for them, and who do feel for them all, a contempt too calm and profound, to admit of any admixture of anything like anger or personal spleen. We should just as soon think of being wroth with vermin, independently of their coming into our apartment, as we should of having any feelings at all about any of these people, other than what are excited by seeing them in the shape of authors. Many of them, considered in any other character than that of authors, are, we have no doubt, entitled to be considered as very worthy people in their own way. Mr Hunt is said to be a very amiable man in his own sphere, and we believe him to be so willingly. Mr Keats we have often heard spoken of in terms of great kindness, and we have no doubt his manners and feelings are calculated to make his friends love him. But what has all this to do with our opinion of their poetry? What, in the name of wonder, does it concern us, whether these men sit among themselves, with mild or with sulky faces, eating their mutton steaks, and drinking their porter at Highgate, Hampstead, or Lisson Green?...Last of all, what should forbid us to announce our opinion, that Mr Shelley, as a man of genius, is not merely superior, either to Mr Hunt, or to Mr Keats, but altogether out of their sphere, and totally incapable of ever being brought into the most distant comparison with either of them.

The critical utterance on Keats' side likely to tell most with general readers was that of Jeffrey in the *Edinburgh Review*. A year earlier Keats had written from Winchester expressing impatience at what he thought the cowardice of the Edinburgh in keeping silence as to *Endymion* in face of the Quarterly attack. 'They do not know what to make of it, and they will not praise it for fear. They are as shy of it as I should be of wearing a Quaker's hat. The fact is they have no real taste. They dare not compromise their judgments on so puzzling a question. If on my next publication they should praise me, and so lug in *Endymion*, I will address them in a manner they will not at all relish. The cowardliness of the Edinburgh is more than the abuse of the Quarterly'. Exactly what Keats had anticipated now took place. Jeffrey's natural taste in poetry was conservative, and favoured the correct, the classical and traditional: but in this case, whether from genuine and personal opinion, or to please influential well-wishers of Keats on his own side in politics and criticism like Sir James Mackintosh, he on the appearance of the new volume took occasion to print, now when Keats was far past caring about it, an article on his work which was mainly in eulogy of *Endymion* : eulogy not unmixed with reasonable criticism, but in a strain, on the whole, gushing almost to excess: —

We had never happened to see either of these volumes till very lately — and have been exceedingly struck with the genius they display, and the spirit of poetry which breathes through all their extravagance. That imitation of our older writers, and especially of our older dramatists, to which we cannot help flattering ourselves that we have somewhat contributed, has brought on, as it were, a second spring in our poetry; — and few of its blossoms are either more profuse of sweetness or richer in promise than this which is now before us. Mr Keats, we understand, is still a very young man; and his whole works, indeed, bear evidence enough of the fact. They are full of extravagance and irregularity, rash attempts at originality, interminable wanderings, and excessive obscurity. They manifestly require, therefore, all the indulgence that can be claimed for a first attempt: but we think it no less plain that they deserve it; for they are flushed all over with the rich lights of fancy, and so coloured and bestrewn with the flowers of poetry, that even while perplexed and bewildered in their labyrinths, it is impossible to resist the intoxication of their sweetness, or to shut our hearts to the enchantments they so lavishly present. The models upon which he has formed himself, in the *Endymion*, the earliest and by much the most considerable of his poems, are obviously the *Faithful Shepherdess* of Fletcher, and the *Sad Shepherd* of Ben Jonson; — the exquisite metres and inspired diction of which he has copied, with great boldness and fidelity — and, like his great originals, has also contrived to impart to the whole piece that true rural and poetical air which breathes only in them and in Theocritus — which is at once homely and majestic, luxurious and rude, and sets before us the genuine sights and sounds and smells of the country, with all the magic and grace of Elysium.

Then, after acknowledgment of the confusedness of the narrative and the fantastic wilfulness of some of the incidents and style, the critic goes on: —

There is no work, accordingly, from which a malicious critic could cull more matter for ridicule, or select more obscure, unnatural, or absurd passages. But we do not take *that* to be our office: — and just beg leave, on the contrary, to say, that any one who, on this account, would represent the whole poem as despicable, must either have no notion of poetry, or no regard to truth. It is, in truth, at least is full of genius as of absurdity; and he who does not find a great deal in it to admire and to give delight, cannot in his heart see much beauty in the two exquisite dramas to which we have already alluded, or find any great pleasure in some of the finest creations of Milton and Shakespeare. There are many such persons, we verily believe, even among the reading and judicious part of the community — correct scholars we have no doubt many of them, and, it may be, very classical composers in prose and in verse — but utterly ignorant of the true genius of English poetry, and incapable of estimating its appropriate and most exquisite beauties. With that spirit we have no hesitation in saying that Mr K. is deeply imbued — and of those beauties he has presented us with many striking examples. We are very much inclined indeed to add, that we do not know any book which we would sooner employ as a test to ascertain whether anyone had in him a native relish for poetry, and a genuine sensibility to its intrinsic charm.

One immediate result of the Edinburgh criticism was to provoke an almost incredible outburst of jealous fury on the part of the personage then most conspicuous on the stage of England's, nay of the world's, poetry, Lord Byron. Byron, with next to no real critical power, could bring dazzling resources of wit and rhetoric to the support of any random opinion, traditional or revolutionary, he might happen by whim or habit to entertain. In these days he was just entering the lists as a self-appointed champion of Pope, the artificial school, and eighteenth century critical tradition in general, against Pope's latest editor and depreciator, the clerical sonneteer William Lisle Bowles. Ever since the Pope-Boileau passage in Keats' *Sleep and Poetry* it had been Byron's pleasure to regard Keats with gratuitous contempt and aversion. When Murray sent him the *Lamia* volume with a parcel of other books to Ravenna, he wrote back, 'Pray send me *no more* poetry but what is rare and decidedly good. There is such a trash of Keats and the like upon my tables that I am ashamed to look at them.... No more Keats, I entreat; — flay him alive; if some of you don't I must skin him myself; there is no bearing the drivelling idiotism of the Mankin.' A month later, evidently not having read a word of Keats' book, he comes across Jeffrey's praise of it in the *Edinburgh Review*, and thereupon falls into a fit of anger so foul-mouthed and outrageous that his latest, far from squeamish editors have had to mask its grossness under a cloud of asterisks. A little later he repeats the same disgusting obscenities in cool blood: his only quotable remark on the subject being as follows: — 'Of the praises of that little dirty blackguard Keates in the Edinburgh, I shall observe as Johnson did when Sheridan the actor got a *pension* : "What, has he got a pension? Then it is time I should give up *mine* ." Nobody could be prouder of the praises of the Edinburgh than I was, or more alive to their censure. At present all the men they have ever praised are degraded by that insane article.' By and by he proceeded to administer his own castigation to 'Mr John Ketch' in a second letter written for the Pope-Bowles controversy: but Keats having died meanwhile he withheld this from publication, and a little later, perhaps at the prompting of his own better mind, but more probably through the good influence of Shelley, took in *Don Juan* the altered tone about Keats which all the world knows, and having been at first thus savagely bent on hunting with the hounds, turned and chose to run part of the way, as far as suited him, with the hare.

Shelley, of course, judged for himself; was incapable of a thought towards a brother poet that was not generous; and had moreover a feeling of true and particular kindness towards Keats. We have seen how wisely and fairly he judged *Endymion* . Were we to take merely his own words written at the time, we might think that he failed to do justice to the new volume as a whole. His first impression of it, coupled with a wildly overdrawn picture which had reached him of Keats' sufferings under the stings of the reviewers, apparently determined him to sit down and draft that indignant letter to Gifford, never completed or delivered, pleading against the repetition of any such treatment of his new volume as *Endymion* had received from the *Quarterly* . In this Shelley speaks of *Hyperion* as though it were the one thing he admired in the book: and writing about the same time to Peacock, he says 'Among modern things which have reached me is a volume of poems by Keats; in other respects insignificant enough, but containing the fragment of a poem called *Hyperion* . I dare say you have not time to read it; but it certainly is an astonishing piece of writing, and gives me a conception of Keats which I confess I had not before.' And again, 'Among your anathemas of modern poetry, do you include Keats' *Hyperion* ? I think it very fine. His other poems are worth little; but if the *Hyperion* be not grand poetry, none has been produced by our contemporaries.' In considering these utterances we should remember that they were addressed to correspondents bound to be unsympathetic. Gifford would be so as a matter of course: while Peacock had from old Marlow days been a disbeliever in Keats and his poetry, and had lately adopted a public attitude of disbelief in modern poetry altogether. We must also remember that Shelley had himself been wrought into a mood of unwonted intolerance of certain fashions in poetry by some of Barry Cornwall's recent performances, which he held to be an out-Hunting of Hunt and out-Byroning of Byron. There is a statement of Medwin's which, if Medwin were ever a witness much to be trusted, we would rather take as representing Shelley's ripened and permanent opinion of the contents of the *Lamia* volume than his own words to Gifford or Peacock. 'He perceived', says Medwin, 'in every one of these productions a marked and continually progressing improvement, and hailed with delight his release from his leading strings, his emancipation from what he called a "perverse and limited school". *The Pot of Basil* and *The Eve of St Agnes* he read and re-read with ever new delight, and looked upon *Hyperion* as almost faultless, grieving that it was but a fragment and that Keats had not been encouraged to complete a work worthy of Milton.' At all events Shelley, apart from the immortal tribute of *Adonais* , has left other words of his own which may content us, addressed to a different correspondent, as to what he felt about Keats and his work and promise on the whole, without reference to one poem rather than another. I mean those in which he expresses to Mrs Leigh Hunt his hope to see and take care of Keats in Italy: — 'I consider his a most valuable life, and I am deeply interested in his safety. I intend to be the physician both of his body and of his soul, to keep the one warm, and to teach the other Greek and Spanish. I am aware, indeed, in part, that I am nourishing a rival who will far surpass me; and this is an additional motive, and will be an added pleasure.'

The opinions of neither of these two famous men, Byron and Shelley, will have had any immediate effect in England. Murray could not possibly disseminate Byron's private obscenities, and Byron's own intended public castigation of Keats in a second letter to Bowles was, as we have seen, withheld. On the other side Shelley made no public use of the draft of his indignant letter to Gifford, and Peacock would not be by way of saying much about his private expressions of enthusiasm for *Hyperion*. But we can gather the impression current in sympathetic circles about Keats' future from a couple of entries in the December diaries of Crabb Robinson. He tells how he has been reading out some of the new volume, first *Hyperion* and then *The Pot of Basil*, to his friends the Aders', and adds, — 'There is a force, wildness, and originality in the works of this young poet which, if his perilous journey to Italy does not destroy him, promise to place him at the head of our next generation of poets. Lamb places him next to Wordsworth — not meaning any comparison, for they are dissimilar'... and again, 'I am greatly mistaken if Keats do not soon take a high place among our poets. Great feeling and a powerful imagination are shown in this little volume.' Had his health held out, such recognition would have been all and more than all Keats asked for or would have thought he had yet earned. But praise and dispraise were all one to him before now, and we must go back and follow the tragedy of his personal history to its close.

Chapter XVI

AUGUST 1820-FEBRUARY 1821: VOYAGE TO ITALY: LAST DAYS AND DEATH AT ROME

In telling of the critical reception of Keats' *Lamia* volume I have anticipated by three or four months the course of time. Returning to his personal condition and doings, we find that by or before the date of his move from Kentish Town to be under the care of the Brawne ladies at Wentworth Place, that is by mid-August, he had accepted the verdict of the doctors that a winter in Italy would be the only thing to give him a chance of recovery. He determined accordingly, not without sore gain-giving and agitation of mind, to make the attempt. In his letter to Shelley acknowledging receipt of *The Cenci* and answering Shelley's invitation to Pisa, he writes: — 'there is no doubt that an English winter would put an end to me, and do so in a lingering, hateful, manner. Therefore, I must either voyage or journey to Italy, as a soldier marches up to a battery'. And again, using the same phrase, he writes to Taylor on August 14th: — 'This journey to Italy wakes me at daylight every morning, and haunts me horribly. I shall endeavour to go, though it will be with the sensation of marching against a battery. The first step towards it is to know the expense of a journey and a year's residence, which if you will ascertain for me, and let me know early, you will greatly serve me.' The next day he sends Taylor a note of his wish that in case of his death his books should be divided among his friends and that any assets arising or to arise from the sale of his poems should be devoted to paying his debts — those to Brown and to Taylor himself ranking first. The good publisher promptly bestirred himself to enquire about sailings and make provision for ways and means. For the latter purpose he bought the copyright of *Endymion* for £100, furnished Keats at starting with a bill on London for £120, and procured promises of eventual help to the extent of £100 more by subscription among persons interested in the poet's fate; James Rice and the painters Hilton and De Wint being among guarantors of £10 each and Lord Fitzwilliam closing the list with a promise of £50.

The vessel chosen for the voyage was a merchant brigantine, the 'Maria Crowther,' having berth accommodation for a few passengers and due to sail from London about the middle of September. The four intervening weeks were spent by the invalid in comparative respite from suffering and distress under the eye and tendance of his beloved. By his desire Haydon came one day to see him, and has told, with a painter's touch, how he found him 'lying in a white bed, with white quilt, and white sheets, the only colour visible was the hectic flush of his cheeks.' Haydon's vehement, self-confident and self-righteous manner of admonition to friends in trouble seems to have had an effect the reverse of consolatory, and elsewhere he amplifies this account of his last sight of Keats, saying, 'He seemed to be going out of life with a contempt for this world and no hopes of the other. I told him to be calm, but he muttered that if he did not soon get better he would destroy himself. I tried to reason against such violence, but it was no use; he grew angry, and I went away deeply affected.' Writing about the same time to his young sister, Keats shows himself, as ever, thoughtful and wise on her behalf and does his best to be reassuring on his own: —

Now you are better, keep so. Do not suffer your Mind to dwell on unpleasant reflexions — that sort of thing has been the destruction of my health. Nothing is so bad as want of health — it makes one envy scavengers and cinder sifters. There are enough real distresses and evils in wait for every one to try the most vigorous health. Not that I would say yours are not real — but they are such as to tempt you to employ your imagination on them, rather than endeavour to dismiss them entirely. Do not diet your mind with grief, it destroys the constitution; but let your chief care be of your health, and with that you will meet your share of Pleasure in the world — do not doubt it. If I return well from Italy I will turn over a new leaf for you. I have been improving lately, and have very good hopes of 'turning a Neuk' and cheating the consumption.

For a companion on his journey, Keats' first thoughts turned to Brown, who was still away on his second tramp through the Highlands. But the letter he wrote asking whether Brown could go with him missed its destination, and he was left with the prospect of having either to give up his journey or venture on it alone, a thing hardly to be thought of in his state of health. At this juncture Haslam, always the most useful of friends in an emergency, betook himself to Severn, whose prospects in London, in spite of the practice he had found as a miniature-painter and of his success in winning the gold medal of the Academy the previous December, seemed far from bright, and urged him to go out with Keats to Rome. Severn at once consented, his immediate impulse of devotion to his friend being strengthened, on reflection, both by the lure of Rome itself and by the idea that he might be able while there to work for, and perhaps win, the travelling studentship of the Royal Academy. He made his arrangements on the shortest possible notice, while Haslam undertook the business of procuring passports and the like. A weird incident marked Severn's departure from his home. His father, passionately attached to him but resenting his resolve to go to Italy now as fiercely as he had before resented his change of profession, on being asked to lend a hand in moving his trunk, in an uncontrollable fit of anger struck and felled him. How and with what rending of the heart Keats took his own farewell from the home of his joy and torment at Hampstead — of this we hear, and may be thankful to hear, nothing. He spent his last days in England with Taylor in Fleet Street, having gone thither on Wednesday September 13th to be at hand for the day and hour when the 'Maria Crowther' might be ready to sail. On the evening of Sunday the 17th of September he and Severn went on board at the London docks. Here the kind Taylor and the serviceable Haslam took leave of them, and their ship weighed anchor and slipped down tide as far as Gravesend, where she came to moorings for the night. Moored close by her was a smack from Dundee, and on board this smack, by one of the minor perversities of fate, who should be a passenger but Charles Brown? He had caught this means of conveyance as the first available when he at last got news of Keats' plans, and had hoped to reach London in time to bid him farewell. But it was all unknowingly that the friends lay that night within earshot of one another.

One lady passenger, a Miss Pidgeon, had come aboard at the docks: a pleasing person, the friends thought at first, but found reason to change their minds later. At Gravesend early the next morning there came another, a pretty and gentle Miss Cotterell, as far gone in consumption as Keats himself. Keats was in lively spirits and exerted himself with Severn to welcome and amuse the new comer. In the course of the day Severn went ashore to buy medicines and other needments for the voyage, and among them, at Keats' special request, a bottle of laudanum. The captain, by name Thomas Walsh, was kind and attentive and did his best, unsuccessfully, to find a goat for the supply of goat's milk to the invalids while on board ship. That evening they put to sea, and Keats' health and spirits seemed to rise with the first excitements of the voyage. The events of the next days are best told in the words of the journal-letter written at the time by Severn to Haslam; vagueness of memory having made much less trustworthy the several accounts of the voyage which he wrote and rewrote in after years. Severn was innocent of all stops save dashes, and I print exactly as he wrote: —

19th Sept. Tuesday, off Dover Castle, *etc.*

I arose at day break to see the glorious eastern gate — Keats slept till 7 — Miss C. was rather ill this morning I prevailed on her to walk the deck with me at half past 6 she recovered much — Keats was still better this morning and Mrs Pidgeon looked and was the picture of health — but poor me! I began to feel a waltzing on my stomach at breakfast when I wrote the note to you I was going it most soundly — Miss Cotterell followed me — then Keats who did it in the most gentlemanly manner — and then the saucy Mrs Pidgeon who had been laughing at us — four faces bequeathing to the mighty deep their breakfasts — here I must change to a minor key Miss C. fainted — we soon recovered her — I was very ill nothing but lying down would do for me. Keats ascended his bed — from which he dictated surgically like Esculapius of old in basso-relievo through him Miss C. was recovered we had a cup of tea each and no

261

more went to bed and slept until it was time to go to bed — we could not get up again — and slept in our clothes all night — Keats the King — not even looking pale.

20th Sept. Wednesday off Brighton. Beautiful morning — we all breakfasted on deck and recovered as we were could enjoy it — about 10 Keats said a storm was hatching — he was right — the rain came on and we retired to our cabin — it abated and once more we came on deck — at 2 storm came on furiously — we retired to our beds. The rolling of the ship was death to us — towards 4 it increased and our situation was alarming — the trunks rolled across the cabin — the water poured in from the sky-light and we were tumbled from one side to the other of our beds — my curiosity was raised to see the storm — and my anxiety to see Keats for I could only speak to him when in bed — I got up and fell down on the floor from my weakness and the rolling of the ship. Keats was very calm — the ladies were much frightened and would scarce speak — when I got up to the deck I was astounded — the waves were in mountains and washed the ship — the watery horizon was like a mountainous country — but the ship's motion was beautifully to the sea falling from one wave to the other in a very lovely manner — the sea each time crossing the deck and one side of the ship being level with the water — this when I understood gave me perfect ease — I communicated below and it did the same — but when the dusk came the sea began to rush in from the side of our cabin from an opening in the planks — this made us rather long faced — for it came by pail-fulls — again I got out and said to Keats 'here's pretty music for you' — with the greatest calmness he answered me only by 'Water parted from the sea.' I staggered up again and the storm was awful — the Captain and Mate soon came down — for our things were squashing about in the dark — they struck a light and I succeeded in getting my desk off the ground — with clothes and books, *etc*. The Captain finding it could not be stopped — tacked about from our voyage — and the sea ceased to dash against the cabin for we were sailing against wind and tide — but the horrible agitation continued in the ship lengthways — here were the pumps working — the sails squalling the confused voices of the sailors — the things rattling about in every direction and us poor devils pinn'd up in our beds like ghosts by daylight — except Keats he was himself all the time — the ladies suffered the most — but I was out of bed a dozen times to wait on them and tell them there was no danger — my sickness made me get into bed very soon each time — but Keats this morning brags of my sailorship — he says could I have kept on my legs in the water cabin I should have been a standing miracle.

20th Sept.

I caught a sight of the moon about 3 o'clock this morning — and ran down to tell the glad tidings — but the surly rolling of the sea was worse than the storm — the ship trembled to it — and the sea was scarcely calmed by daylight — so that we were kept from 2 o'clock yesterday until 6 this morning without anything — well it has done us good, we are like a Quartett of fighting cocks this morning. The morning is serene we are now back again some 20 miles — waiting for a wind — but full of spirits — Keats is without even complaining and Miss Cottrell has a colour in her face — the sea has done his worst upon us. I am better than I have been for years. Farewell my dear fellow.

J. Severn — show this to my family with my love to them.

When you read this you will excuse the manner — I am quite beside myself — and have written the whole this morning Thursday on the deck after a sleepless night and with a head full of care — you shall have a better the next time.

The storm had driven them back from off Brighton more than half way to the Downs, and then abated enough to let them land for a scramble on the shingles at Dungeness, where they excited the suspicions of the coast guard, and to get the above letter posted from Romney. After this calms and contrary airs kept them beating about the channel for many more days yet. At Portsmouth they were held up again, and to pass the time Keats landed and went to call on Dilke's sister Mrs Snook at Bedhampton; again by ill chance barely missing Brown, whom he supposed to be still in Scotland but who was actually only ten miles away, having run down to stay with Dilke's father at Chichester. The next day, while the ship was still hanging in the Solent off Yarmouth, Keats wrote unbosoming himself to Brown of his inward agony more fully than he had ever done in speech: —

I wish to write on subjects that will not agitate me much — there is one I must mention and have done with it. Even if my body would recover of itself, this would prevent it. The very thing which I want to live most for will be a great occasion of my death. I cannot help it. Who can help it? Were I in health it would make me ill, and how can I bear it in my state? I dare say you will be able to guess on what subject I am harping — you know what was my greatest pain during the first part of my illness at your house. I wish for death every day and night to deliver me from these pains, and then I wish death away, for death would destroy even those pains which are better than nothing. Land and sea, weakness and decline, are great separators, but death is the great divorcer for ever. When the pang of this thought has passed through my mind, I may say the bitterness of death is passed. I often wish for you that you might flatter me with the best. I think without my mentioning it for my sake you would be a friend to Miss Brawne when I am dead. You think she has many faults — but, for my sake, think she has not one. If there is anything you can do for her by word or deed I know you will do it. I am in a state at present in which woman merely as woman can have no more power over me than stocks and stones, and yet the difference of my sensations with respect to Miss Brawne and my sister is amazing. The one seems to absorb the other to a degree incredible. I seldom think of my brother and sister in America. The thought of leaving Miss Brawne is beyond everything horrible — the sense of darkness coming over me — I eternally see her figure eternally vanishing. Some of the phrases she was in the habit of using during my last nursing at Wentworth Place ring in my ears. Is there another life? Shall I awake and find all this a dream? There must be, we cannot be created for this sort of suffering.

That night, (September 28) adds Keats, they expected to put into Portland Roads; but calms again held them up, and again they were allowed to land, having made only some few miles' headway down the Dorsetshire coast. The day of this landing was for Keats one of transitory calm and lightening of the spirit. The weather was fine, and 'for a moment,' says Severn, 'he became like his former self. He was in a part that he already knew, and showed me the splendid caverns and grottoes with a poet's pride, as though they had been his birthright.' These are vivid phrases, that about the caverns and grottoes certainly a little over-coloured for the scene, which was Lulworth Cove and the remarkable, but scarcely splendid, rock tunnels and fissures of Stair Hole and Durdle Door. When Severn says that Keats knew the ground, one half wonders whether the Dorsetshire Keatses may really have been kindred of his to whom he had at some time paid an unrecorded visit: or otherwise, whether in travelling to and from Teignmouth in 1818, taking, as we know he did, the southern route from Salisbury by Bridport and Axminster, he may have broken the journey at Dorchester and visited the curiosities of the coast. But in truth, to understand and possess beauties of nature as a birthright, Keats needed not to have seen them before. On board ship the same night Keats borrowed the copy of Shakespeare's Poems which he had given Severn a few days before, and wrote out fair and neatly for him, on the blank page opposite the heading *A Lover's Complaint*, the beautiful sonnet which every lover of English knows so well: —

> Bright star, would I were stedfast as thou art,
> Not in lone splendour hung aloft the night
> And watching, with eternal lids apart,
> Like nature's patient, sleepless Eremite,
> The moving waters at their priestlike task
> Of pure ablution round earth's human shores,
> Or gazing on the new soft-fallen mask
> Of snow upon the mountains and the moors —
> No — yet still stedfast, still unchangeable,

> Pillow'd upon my fair love's ripening breast,
> To feel for ever its soft fall and swell,
> Awake for ever in a sweet unrest,
> Still, still to hear her tender-taken breath,
> And so live ever — or else swoon to death.

Severn in later life clearly cherished the impression that the sonnet had been actually composed for him on the day of the Dorsetshire landing. Lord Houghton in his *Life and Literary Remains* distinctly asserts as much, and it had seemed to us all a beautiful and consolatory circumstance, in the tragedy of Keats' closing days, that his last inspiration in poetry should have come in a strain of such unfevered beauty and tenderness, and with images of such a refreshing and solemn purity. But in point of fact the sonnet was work of an earlier date, and the autograph given to Severn is on the face of it no draught but a fair copy. Its original form had been this —

> Bright star! would I were stedfast as thou art!
> Not in lone splendour hung amid the night;
> Not watching, with eternal lids apart,
> Like Nature's devout sleepless Eremite,
> The morning waters at their priestlike task
> Of pure ablution round earth's human shores;
> Or, gazing on the new soft fallen mask
> Of snow upon the mountains and the moors: —
> No; — yet still steadfast, still unchangeable,
> Cheek-pillow'd on my Love's white ripening breast,
> To touch, for ever, its warm sink and swell,
> Awake, for ever, in a sweet unrest;
> To hear, to feel her tender-taken breath,
> Half passionless, and so swoon on to death.

The sonnet is copied in this form by Charles Brown, under date 1819, in the collection of transcripts from Keats' fugitive verses which from the spring of that year he regularly made as soon after they were written as he could lay hands on them. His dates I have found always trustworthy, and I have shown reason (above, p. 334) for holding the sonnet to have been written in the last week of February, 1819, and the first days of Keats' engagement to Fanny Brawne. All that Keats can actually have done during that evening of tranquillity off Lulworth was to return to it in thought and recopy it for Severn with changes which in the second line heightened the remoteness of the star; in the fourth made an inverted metrical stress normal by substituting 'patient' for 'devout'; in the fifth changed the word 'morning' into 'moving,' in the tenth cancelled one of his defining and arresting compound participles in favour of a simpler phrase; and in the four concluding lines varied a little the mood and temperature of the longing expressed, calling for death not as the sequel to his longing's fulfilment, but as the alternative for it. In Severn's first mention of the subject, which is in a letter written from Rome a few weeks after Keats' death, he shows himself aware that Brown might be in possession already of a version of the sonnet, which of course could only have been the case if it had been composed before Keats left Hampstead. 'Do you know,' he writes, 'the sonnet beginning Bright Star etc., he wrote this down in the ship — it is one of his most beautiful things. I will send it, if you have it not.'

The rest of the voyage, after getting clear of the English Channel, was quick but uncomfortable, the weather variable and often squally. Signs of improvement in Keats' health alternated with alarming returns of hæmorrhage, and the painful symptoms of his fellow-traveller Miss Cotterell preyed sometimes severely on his nerves and spirits. At other times his thoughts ran pleasantly on poems yet to be written, and especially on one he had planned on the story of Sabrina. 'He mentioned to me many times in our voyage', writes Severn within a few weeks of the poet's death, 'his desire to write this story and to connect it with some points in the English history and character. He would sometimes brood over it with immense enthusiasm, and recite the story from Milton's *Comus* in a manner that I will remember to the end of my days.' It is good to think of Keats being thus able to occupy and soothe his fevered spirit with the lovely cadences that tell how Nereus pitied the rescued nymph,

> And gave her to his daughters to imbathe
> In nectar'd lavers strew'd with Asphodel,
> or with those that invoke her in the prayer, —
> Listen where thou art sitting
> Under the glassie, cool, translucent wave,
> In twisted braids of lilies knitting
> The loose train of thy amber-dropping hair, —

it is good to think of this and to try and conceive what Keats while he was in health might have made of this English theme which haunted his imagination now and afterwards at Rome, when the power to shape and almost the power to live and breathe had left him.

Severn took during the voyage an opportunity to make a new drawing of Keats as he lay propped and resting on his berth. Such a drawing would have been an invaluable addition to our memorials of the poet: it remained long in the possession first of one and then of another of Severn's sons, but has of late years unluckily disappeared: stolen, thinks its latest owner, Mr Arthur Severn: let us hope that this mention may perhaps lead to its recognition and recovery. During some rough weather in the Bay of Biscay Keats began to read the shipwreck canto of *Don Juan*, but presently found its reckless and cynic brilliancy intolerable, and flung the volume from him in disgust. Perhaps something of his real feelings, but certainly nothing of his way of expressing them, is preserved in Severn's account of the matter written five-and-twenty years later: —

Keats threw down the book and exclaimed: 'this gives me the most horrid idea of human nature, that a man like Byron should have exhausted all the pleasures of the world so completely that there was nothing left for him but to laugh and gloat over the most solemn and heartrending scenes of human misery, this storm of his is one of the most diabolical attempts ever made upon our sympathies, and I have no doubt it will fascinate thousands into extreme obduracy of heart — the tendency of Bryon's poetry is based on a paltry originality, that of being new by making solemn things gay and gay things solemn.'

In a calm off Cape St Vincent, Keats was delighted with the play of silken colours on the sea, and interested in watching the movement of a whale. The next day there came an alarm: a shot was fired over the bows of the 'Maria Crowther' from one of two Portuguese men of war becalmed close by; but drifting within hail one of the Portuguese captains explained that there were supposed to be privateers in those waters and that he only wanted to learn whether the Englishman had sighted any such.

On October 21, thirty-four days out from London, the 'Maria Crowther' reached Naples harbour and was promptly put in quarantine. In that predicament her passengers sweltered and fumed for ten full days, their number having been increased by the addition of a lieutenant and six seamen, who were despatched from an English man-of-war in the harbour to enquire as to the vessel's name and status, and having thoughtlessly gone on board her were forbidden by the port authorities to go off again. The friends found some alleviation from the tedium of the time through the kindness of Miss Cotterell's brother, a banker in Naples, who kept them supplied with all manner of dainties and luxuries, and especially with abundance of fruit and flowers. 'Keats', says Severn, 'was never tired of admiring (not to speak of eating) the beautiful clusters of grapes and other fruits, and was scarce less enthusiastic over the autumn flowers, though I remember his saying once that he would gladly give them all for a wayside dog-rose bush covered with pink blooms.' The time of detention passed with a good deal of merriment, songs from the man-of-war's men on board, songs, laughter, and gibes from the Neapolitan boatmen swarming round. In all this Keats would join, feverishly enough it is evident, and declared afterwards that he had made more puns in the course of those ten days than in any whole year of his life beside. Once he flashed into a characteristic heat of righteous wrath, when the seamen took to trolling obscene catches in full hearing of the ladies. On the fourth day of their detention he wrote to Mrs Brawne, (to Fanny he dared not write, nor suffer his thoughts to dwell on her at all), saying what he thought of his own state: —

We have to remain in the vessel ten days and are at present shut in a tier of ships. The sea air has been beneficial to me about to as great extent as squally weather and bad accommodations and provisions has done harm. So I am about as I was. Give my love to Fanny and tell her, if I were well there is enough in this Port of Naples to fill a quire of Paper — but it looks like a dream — every man who can row his boat and walk and talk seems a different being from myself. I do not feel in the world.

It is impossible to describe exactly in what state of health I am — at this moment I am suffering from indigestion very much, which makes such stuff of this Letter. I would always wish you to think me a little worse than I really am; not being of a sanguine disposition I am likely to succeed. If I do not recover your regret will be softened — if I do your pleasure will be doubled. I dare not fix my Mind upon Fanny, I have not dared to think of her. The only comfort I have had that way has been in thinking for hours together of having the knife she gave me put in a silver-case — the hair in a Locket — and the Pocket Book in a gold net. Show her this. I dare say no more. Yet you must not believe I am so ill as this Letter may look, for if ever there was a person born without the faculty of hoping I am he. Severn is writing to Haslam, and I have just asked him to request Haslam to send you his account of my health. O what an account I could give you of the Bay of Naples if I could once more feel myself a Citizen of this world — I feel a spirit in my Brain would lay it forth pleasantly — O what a misery it is to have an intellect in splints!

Once released from quarantine and landed at Naples Severn wrote to Haslam fully his impressions of the voyage and of its effects on his friend.

Naples, Nov. 1 1820.

My dear Haslam,

We are just released from the loathsome misery of quarantine — foul weather and foul air for the whole 10 days kept us to the small cabin — surrounded by about 2,000 ships in a wretched hole not sufficient for half the number, yet Keats is still living — may I not have hopes of him? He has passed what I must have thought would kill myself. Now that we are on shore and feel the fresh air, I am horror struck at his sufferings on this voyage, all that could be fatal to him in air and diet — with the want of medicine and conveniences he has weather'd it, if I may call his poor shattered frame and broken heart weathering it. For myself I have stood it firmly until this morning when in a moment my spirits dropt at the sight of his suffering — a plentiful shower of tears (which he did not see) has relieved me somewhat — what he passed still unnerves me. But now we are breathing in a large room with Vesuvius in our view — Keats has become calm and thinks favourably of this place for we are meeting with much kind treatment on every side — more particularly from an English gentleman here (brother to Miss Cottrell one of our lady passengers) who has shown unusually humane treatment to Keats — unasked — these with very good accommodation at our Inn (Villa de Londra) have kept him up through dinner — but on the other hand Dr Milner is at Rome (whither Keats is proposing to go) the weather is now cold wet and foggy, and we find ourselves on the wrong side for his hope for recovery (for the present I will talk to him — he is disposed to it. I will talk him to sleep for he has suffered much fatigue).

Nov. 2.

Keats went to bed much recovered — I took every means to remove from him a heavy grief that may tend more than anything to be fatal — he told me much — very much — and I don't know whether it was more painful for me or himself — but it had the effect of much relieving him — he went very calm to bed.

Poor fellow! he is still sleeping at half past nine, if I can but ease his mind I will bring him back to England *well* — but I fear it never can be done in this world — the grand scenery here affects him a little — but he is too infirm to enjoy it — his gloom deadens his sight to everything — and but for intervals of something like ease he must soon end it —

You will like to know how I have managed in respect to self. I have had a most severe task full of contrarieties what I did one way was undone another. The lady passenger though in the same state as Keats — yet differing in constitution required almost everything the opposite to him — for instance if the cabin windows were not open she would faint and remain entirely insensible 5 or 6 hours together — if the windows were open poor Keats would be taken with a cough (a violent one — caught from this cause) and sometimes spitting of blood, now I had this to manage continually for our other passenger is a most consumate brute — she would see Miss Cottrell stiffened like a corpse — I have sometimes thought her dead — nor ever lend the least aid — full a dozen times I have recovered this lady and put her to bed — sometimes she would faint 4 times in a day yet at intervals would seem quite well — and was full of spirits — she is both young and lively — and but for her we should have had more heaviness — though much less trouble. She has benefited by Keats' advice — I used to act under him — and reduced the fainting each time — she has recovered very much and gratefully ascribes it to us — her brother the same.

The Captain has behaved with great kindness to us all — but more particularly Keats — everything that could be got or done — was at his service without asking — he is a good-natured man to his own injury — strange for a captain I won't say so much for his ship — it's a black hole — 5 sleeping in one cabin — the one you saw — the only one — during the voyage I have been frequently sea-sick — sometimes severely — 2 days together. We have had only one real fright on the seas — not to mention continued squalls — and a storm. 'All's well that ends well,' and these ended well. Our fright was from two Portugese ships of war — they brought us to with a shot — which passed close under our stern — this was not pleasant for us you will allow — nor was it decreased when they came up — for a more infernal set I never could imagine — after some trifling questions they allowed us to go on to our no small delight — our captain was afraid they would plunder the ship — this was in the Bay of Biscay — over which we were carried by a good wind.

Keats has written to Brown — and in quarantine another to Mrs Brawne — he requests you will tell Mrs Brawne what I think of him — for he is too bad to judge of himself — this morning he is still very much better. We are in good spirits and I may say hopeful fellows — at least I may say as much for Keats — he made an Italian pun to-day — the rain is coming down in torrents.

The confession Keats had made to Severn was of course that of the effects of the passion which had so long been racking and wasting him, and the violence of which he had shrunk till now from disclosing to friend or brother. Writing on the same day to Brown, he could not control or disguise the anguish of his heart.

Naples, 1 November 1820.

My dear Brown,

Yesterday we were let out of Quarantine, during which my health suffered more from bad air and the stifled cabin than it had done the whole voyage. The fresh air revived me a little, and I hope I am well enough this morning to write to you a short calm letter; — if that can be called one, in which I am afraid to speak of what I would fainest dwell upon. As I have gone thus far into it, I must go on a little; perhaps it may relieve the load of WRETCHEDNESS which presses upon me. The persuasion that I will see her no more will kill me. My dear Brown, I should have had her when I was in health, and I should have remained well. I can bear to die — I cannot bear to leave her. O, God! God! God! Everything I have in my trunks that reminds me of her goes through me like a spear. The silk lining she put in my travelling cap scalds my head. My imagination is horribly vivid about her — I see her — I hear her. There is nothing in the world of sufficient interest to divert me from her a moment. This was the case when I was in England; I cannot recollect, without shuddering, the time that I was a prisoner at Hunt's, and used to keep my eyes fixed on Hampstead all day. Then there was a good hope of seeing her again — Now! — O that I could be buried near where she lives! I am afraid to write to her — to receive a letter from her — to see her handwriting would break my heart — even to hear of her anyhow, to see her name written, would be more than I can bear. My dear Brown, what am I to do? Where can I look for consolation or ease?

I cannot say a word about Naples; I do not feel at all concerned in the thousand novelties around me. I am afraid to write to her — I should like her to know that I do not forget her. Oh, Brown, I have coals of fire in my breast. It surprises me that the human heart is capable of containing and bearing so much misery. Was I born for this end? God bless her, and her mother, and my sister, and George, and his wife, and you, and all!

During the four days they remained at Naples Keats received a second invitation in the kindest possible terms from Shelley to come and settle near him in Pisa, but determined to carry out his original plan of wintering at Rome, where he was to place Taylor's bill to his credit at Torlonia's and whither he carried a special introduction to Dr (afterwards Sir James) Clark. Severn was also the bearer of one from Sir Thomas Lawrence to Canova. Keats attempted to amuse himself reading *Clarissa Harlowe*, and also seeing some of the sights of Naples. After almost a century there has lately come to light a record, set down at second-hand and probably touched up in the telling, of some things noticed and words spoken by the stricken poet in drives about the city and suburbs in the friendly company of Mr Charles Cotterell, the brother of his invalid fellow-passenger. Keats was driving, says the narrator, Mr Charles Macfarlane, —

— he was driving with Charles Cottrell from the Bourbon Museum, up the beautiful open road which leads up to Capo di Monte and the Ponte Rossi. On the way, in front of a villa or cottage, he was struck and moved by the sight of some rose trees in full bearing. Thinking to gratify the invalid, Cottrell, a ci-devant officer in the British Navy, jumped out of the carriage, spoke to somebody about the house or garden, and was back in a trice with a bouquet of roses. 'How late in the year! What an exquisite climate!' said the Poet; but on putting them to his nose, he threw the flowers down on the opposite seat, and exclaimed: 'Humbugs! they have no scent! What is a rose without its fragrance? I hate and abhor all humbug, whether in a flower or in a man or woman!' And having worked himself strongly up in the anti-humbug humour, he cast the bouquet out on the road. I suppose that the flowers were China roses, which have little odour at any time, and hardly any at the approach of winter.

Returning from that drive, he had intense enjoyment in halting close to the Capuan Gate, and in watching a group of lazzaroni or labouring men, as, at a stall with fire and cauldron by the roadside in the open air, they were disposing of an incredible quantity of macaroni, introducing it in long unbroken strings into their capacious mouths, without the intermediary of anything but their hands. 'I like this,' said he; 'these hearty fellows scorn the humbug of knives and forks. Fingers were invented first. Give them some *carlini* that they may eat more! Glorious sight! How they take it in!'

But the political state and servile temper of the Neapolitan people — though they were living just then under the constitutional forms imposed on the Bourbon monarchy by the revolution of the previous summer — grated on Keats' liberal instincts, and misinterpreting at the theatre the sight of a couple of armed sentries posted (as was the custom of the time and country) on the stage, he broke into a fit of anger and determined suddenly to leave the place. Accordingly on the 4th or 5th of November the friends set out for Rome in a small hired carriage, which jogged so loiteringly on the road that Severn was able to walk beside it almost all the way. Keats suffered seriously at the stopping-places from bad quarters and bad food, and was for the most part listless and dispirited, but would become animated 'when an unusually fine prospect opened before us, or the breeze bore to us exquisite hill fragrances or breaths from the distant blue seas, and particularly when I literally filled the little carriage with flowers. He never tired of these, and they gave him a singular and almost fantastic pleasure which was at times almost akin to a strange joy.' Entering Rome by the Lateran gate they settled at once in lodgings which Dr Clark, to whom Keats had written from Naples, had already secured for them, in the first house on the right going up the steps from the Piazza di Spagna to Sta Trinità dei Monti. Here, according to the manner of those days in Italy, they were left pretty much to shift for themselves. Neither could speak Italian, and at first they were ill served by the trattoria from which they got their meals, until Keats, having bidden Severn see how he would mend matters, one day coolly emptied all the dishes out of the window, and handed them back to the porter: a hint, says Severn, which was quickly taken. For a while the patient seemed better. Dr Clark wished him to avoid the excitement of seeing the famous monuments of the city, so he left Severn to visit these alone, and contented himself with quiet strolls, chiefly on the Pincian close by.

The season was fine, and the freshness and brightness of the air, says Severn, invariably made him pleasant and witty. Clark gave Severn an introduction to Gibson, the then famous American sculptor, and Keats insisted on his delivering it at once and losing no opportunity of making acquaintances in Rome that might be useful to him, and no time in getting to work on his projected competition picture, 'The Death of Alcibiades.' In Severn's absence Keats had a companion he liked in an invalid Lieutenant Elton. In their walks on the Pincian these two often met the famous beauty Pauline Bonaparte, Princess Borghese. Her charms were by this time failing — but not for lack of exercise; and her melting glances at his companion, who was tall and handsome, presently affected Keats' nerves, and made them change the direction of their walks. Sometimes, instead of walking, they would take short invalid rides, on hired mounts suited to their respective statures, about the Pincian or outside the Porta del Popolo, while Severn was working among the ruins.

The mitigation of Keats' sufferings lasted for some five weeks, and filled the anxious heart of Severn with hope. Nevertheless he could not but be aware of the deep-seated dejection in his friend which found expression now and again in word or act, as when he began reading a volume of Alfieri, but dropped it at the lines, too sadly applicable to himself: —

> Misera me! sollievo a me non resta
> Altro che 'l pianto, ed il pianto è delitto.

Notwithstanding signs like this, his mood was on the whole more placid. Severn had hired a piano for their lodgings, and the patient often allowed himself to be soothed with music. His thoughts even turned towards verse, and he again meditated and spoke of his proposed poem on the subject of Sabrina. Severn began to believe he would get well, and on November 30 Keats himself wrote to Brown in a strain far from cheerful, indeed, but much less desperate than before.

I have an habitual feeling of my real life having passed, and that I am leading a posthumous existence. God knows how it would have been — but it appears to me — however, I will not speak of that subject. I must have been at Bedhampton nearly at the time you were writing to me from Chichester — how unfortunate — and to pass on the river too! There was my star predominant! I cannot answer anything in your letter, which followed me from Naples to Rome, because I am afraid to look it over again. I am so weak (in mind) that I cannot bear the sight of any handwriting of a friend I love so much as I do you. Yet I ride the little horse, and, at my worst, even in quarantine, summoned up more puns, in a sort of desperation, in one week than in any year of my life. There is one thought enough to kill me; I have been well, healthy, alert, etc., walking with her, and now the knowledge of contrast, feeling for light and shade, all that information (primitive sense) necessary for a poem, are great enemies to the recovery of the stomach. There, you rogue, I put you to the torture; but you must bring your philosophy to bear, as I do mine, really, or how should I be able to live? Dr Clark is very attentive to me; he says there is very little the matter with my lungs, but my stomach, he says, is very bad. I am well disappointed in hearing good news from George, for it runs in my head we shall all die young. I have not written to Reynolds yet, which he must think neglectful; being anxious to send him a good account of my health, I have delayed it from week to week. If I recover, I will do all in my power to correct the mistakes made during sickness; and if I should not, all my faults will be forgiven. Severn is very well, though he leads so dull a life with me. Remember me to all friends, and tell Haslam I should not have left London without taking leave of him, but from being so low in body and mind. Write to George as soon as you receive this, and tell him how I am, as far as you can guess; and also a note to my sister — who walks about my imagination like a ghost — she is so like Tom. I can scarcely bid you goodbye, even in a letter. I always make an awkward bow.

God bless you!

But on the glimmering hopes of these first weeks at Rome there suddenly followed despair. On Dec. 10, 'when he was going on in good spirits, quite merrily,' says Severn, came a relapse which left no doubt of the issue. Hæmorrhage followed hæmorrhage on successive days, and then came a period of violent fever, with scenes the most piteous and distressing. To put an end to his misery, Keats with agonies of entreaty begged to have the bottle of laudanum which Severn had by his desire bought at Gravesend: and on Severn's refusal, 'his tender appeal turned to despair, with all the power of his ardent imagination and bursting heart.' It was no unmanly fear of pain in Keats, Severn again and again insists, that prompted this appeal, but above all his acute sympathetic sense of the trials which the sequel would bring upon his friend. 'He explained to me the exact procedure of his gradual dissolution, enumerated my deprivations and toils, and dwelt upon the danger to my life and certainly to my fortune of my continued attendance on him.' Severn gently holding firm, Keats for a while fiercely refused his friend's ministrations, until presently the example of that friend's patience and his own better mind made him ashamed.

From these relapses until the end Severn had no respite from his devoted ministrations. Writing to Mrs Brawne a week after the crisis, he says 'Not a moment can I be from him. I sit by his bed and read all day, and at night I humour him in all his wanderings. He has just fallen asleep, the first sleep for eight nights, and now from mere exhaustion.' By degrees the tumult of his soul abated. His sufferings were very great, partly from the nature of the disease itself, partly from the effect of the disastrous lowering and starving treatment at that day employed to combat it. His diet was at one time reduced to one anchovy and a small piece of toast a day, so that he endured cruel pangs of actual hunger. Shunned and neglected as the sick and their companions then were in Italy, the friends had no succour except from the assiduous kindness of Dr and Mrs Clark, with occasional aid from a stranger, Mr Ewing. The devotion and resource of Severn were infinite, and had their reward. Occasionally there came times of delirium or half-delirium, when the dying man would rave wildly of his miseries and his ruined hopes, and of all that he would have done in poetry had life and the fruition of his love been granted him, till his companion was almost exhausted with 'beating about in the tempest of his mind'; and once and again some fresh remembrance of his betrothed, or the sight of her handwriting in a letter, would pierce him with too intolerable a pang. But generally, after the first days of storm, he lay quiet, with his hand clasped on a white cornelian, one of the little tokens she had given him at starting, while his companion soothed him with reading or music. The virulence of the reviewers, which most of his friends supposed to be what was killing him, was a matter, Severn declares, scarcely ever on his lips or in his mind at all. Gradually he seemed to mend and gather a little strength again, till Severn actually began to dream that he might even yet recover, though he himself would admit no such hope. 'He says the continued stretch of his imagination has already killed him. He will not hear of his good friends in England, except for what they have done; and this is another load; but of their high hopes of him, his certain success, his experience, he will not hear a word. Then the want of some kind of hope to feed his voracious imagination' — This is from a letter to Mr Taylor which Severn began on Christmas

Eve and never finished. On the 11th January, in one conveying to Mrs Brawne the reviving hopes he was beginning on the slenderest grounds to cherish, Severn writes: —

Now he has changed to calmness and quietude, as singular as productive of good, for his mind was most certainly killing him. He has now given up all thoughts, hopes, or even wish for recovery. His mind is in a state of peace from the final leave he has taken of this world and all its future hopes; this has been an immense weight for him to rise from. He remains quiet and submissive under his heavy fate. Now, if anything will recover him, it is this absence of himself. I have perceived for the last three days symptoms of recovery. Dr Clark even thinks so. Nature again revives in him — I mean where art was used before; yesterday he permitted me to carry him from his bedroom to our sitting-room — to put clean things on him — and to talk about my painting to him. This is my good news — don't think it otherwise, my dear madam, for I have been in such a state of anxiety and discomfiture in this barbarous place, that the least hope of my friend's recovery is a heaven to me.

For three weeks I have never left him — I have sat up all night — I have read to him nearly all day, and even in the night — I light the fire — make his breakfast, and sometimes am obliged to cook — make his bed, and even sweep the room. I can have these things done, but never at the time when they must and ought to be done — so that you will see my alternative; what enrages me most is making a fire — I blow — blow for an hour — the smoke comes fuming out — my kettle falls over on the burning sticks — no stove — Keats calling me to be with him — the fire catching my hands and the door-bell ringing: all these to one quite unused and not at all capable — with the want of even proper material — come not a little galling. But to my great surprise I am not ill — or even restless — nor have I been all the time; there is nothing but what I will do for him — there is no alternative but what I think and provide myself against — except his death — not the loss of him — I am prepared to bear that — but the inhumanity, the barbarism of these Italians....

O! I would my unfortunate friend had never left your Wentworth Place — for the hopeless advantages of this comfortless Italy. He has many, many times talked over 'the few happy days at your house, the only time when his mind was at ease.' I hope still to see him with you again. Farewell, my dear madam. One more thing I must say — poor Keats cannot see any letters, at least he will not — they affect him so much and increase his danger. The two last I repented giving, he made me put them into his box — unread.

The complaint about the barbarity of Rome and of Italian law was due to a warning Severn had received that on the death of his friend every stick and shred of furniture in the house would have to be burnt. Within a few days the last thread of hope was snapped by fresh returns of hæmorrhage and utter prostration, with renewed feverish agitations of the tortured spirit. Writing to Haslam on January the 15th, Severn shows himself almost broken down by the imminence of money difficulties about to add themselves to his other cares: —

Poor Keats has just fallen asleep — I have watched him and read to him — to his very last wink — he has been saying to me 'Severn I can see under your quiet look — immense twisting and contending — you don't know what you are reading — you are enduring for me more than I'd have you — O that my last hour was come — what is it puzzles you now — what is it happens — 'I tell him that 'nothing happens — nothing worries me beyond his seeing — that it has been the dull day.' Getting from myself to his recovery — and then my painting — and then England — and then — but they are all lies — my heart almost leaps to deny them — for I have the veriest load of care — that ever came upon these shoulders of mine. For Keats is sinking daily — perhaps another three weeks may lose me him for ever — this alone would break down the most gallant spirit — I had made sure of his recovery when I set out. I was selfish and thought of his value to me — and made a point of my future success depend on his candor to me — this is not all — I have prepared myself to bear this now — now that I must and should have seen it before — but Torlonias the bankers have refused any more money — the bill is returned unaccepted — 'no effects' and I tomorrow must — aye must — pay the last solitary crown for this cursed lodging place — yet more should our unfortunate friend die —

all the furniture will be burnt — bed sheets — curtains and even the walls must be scraped — and these devils will come upon me for £100 or £150 — the making good — but above all this noble fellow lying on the bed is dying in horror — no kind hope smoothing down his suffering — no philosophy — no religion to support him — yet with all the most gnawing desire for it — yet without the possibility of receiving it....

Now Haslam what do you think of my situation — for I know not what may come with tomorrow — I am hedg'd in every way that you look at me — if I could leave Keats for a while every day I could soon raise money by my face painting — but he will not let me out of his sight — he cannot bear the face of a stranger — he has made me go out twice and leave him solus. I'd rather cut my tongue out than tell him that money I must get — that would kill him at a word — I will not do anything that may add to his misery — for I have tried on every point to leave for a few hours in the day but he wont unless he is left alone — this won't do — nor shall not for another minute whilst he is John Keats.

Yet will I not bend down under these — I will not give myself a jot of credit unless I stand firm — and will too — you'd be rejoiced to see how I am kept up — not a flinch yet — I read, cook, make the beds — and do all the menial offices — for no soul comes near Keats except the doctor and myself — yet I do all this with a cheerful heart — for I thank God my little but honest religion stays me up all through these trials. I'll pray to God tonight that He may look down with mercy on my poor friend and myself. I feel no dread of what more I am to bear but look to it with confidence.

In religion Keats had been neither a believer nor by any means (except in the earliest days of his enthusiasm for Leigh Hunt) a scoffer; respecting Christianity without calling himself a Christian, and by turns clinging to and drifting from the doctrine of human immortality. Now, on his deathbed, says Severn, among the most haunting and embittering of his distresses was the thought that not for him were those ready consolations of orthodoxy which were within the reach of every knave and fool. After a time, contrasting the steadfast behaviour of the believer Severn with his own, he acknowledged anew the power of the Christian teaching and example, and bidding Severn read to him from Jeremy Taylor's *Holy Dying and Holy Living*, strove to pass the remainder of his days in a temper of more peace and constancy.

The danger of money trouble must have been due to a pure misunderstanding, as the credit at Torlonia's was in fact not exhausted, and a fresh communication from Mr Taylor removed all anxiety on that score. One day Keats was seized with a desire for books and was able for a time to take pleasure in reading those which Severn procured for him. Another and continual pleasure was Severn's playing on the piano, and especially his playing of Haydn's sonatas. 'With all his suffering and consciousness of approaching death,' wrote Severn in after years, 'he never quite lost the play of his cheerful and elastic mind, yet these happier moments were but slight snatches from his misery, like the flickering rays of the sun in a smothering storm. Real rays of sunshine they were, all the same, such as would have done honour to the brightest health and the happiest mind: yet the storm of sickness and death was always going on, and I have often thought that these bursts of wit and cheerfulness were called up of set purpose — were, in fact, a great effort on my account.'

Neither patient nor watcher thought any more of recovery. For a few days Severn had the help of an English nurse. It was doubtless then that Keats made his friend go and see the place chosen for his burial. 'He expressed pleasure at my description of the locality of the Pyramid of Caius Cestius, about the grass and the many flowers, particularly the innumerable violets — also about a flock of goats and sheep and a young shepherd — all these intensely interested him. Violets were his favourite flowers, and he joyed to hear how they overspread the graves. He assured me that he seemed already to feel the flowers growing over him': and it seems to have been gently and without bitterness that he gave for his epitaph the words, partly taken from a phrase in Beaumont and Fletcher's *Philaster*, — 'here lies one whose name was writ in water.' Ever since his first attack at Wentworth Place he had been used to speak of himself as living a posthumous life, and now his habitual question to the doctor when he came in was,

'Doctor, when will this posthumous life of mine come to an end?'. As he turned to ask it neither physician nor friend could bear the pathetic expression of his eyes, at all times of extraordinary power, and now burning with a sad and piercing unearthly brightness in his wasted cheeks. Once or twice he was torn again by too sharp a reminder of vanished joys and hopes. Severn handed him a letter which he supposed to be from Mrs Brawne, but which was really from her daughter. 'The glance of that letter tore him to pieces. The effects were on him for many days — he did not read it — he could not, but requested me to place it in his coffin together with a purse and a letter (unopened) of his sister's — since which time he has requested me not to place *that letter*, but only his sister's purse and letter with some hair.' Loveable and considerate to the last, 'his generous concern for me,' reiterates Severn, 'in my isolated position at Rome was one of his greatest cares.' His response to kindness was irresistibly winning, and the spirit of poetry and pleasantness was with him to the end. Severn tells how in watching Keats he used sometimes to fall asleep, and awakening, find they were in the dark. 'To remedy this one night I tried the experiment of fixing a thread from the bottom of a lighted candle to the wick of an unlighted one, that the flame might be conducted, all which I did without telling Keats. When he awoke and found the first candle nearly out, he was reluctant to wake me and while doubting suddenly cried out, "Severn, Severn, here's a little fairy lamp-lighter actually lit up the other candle."' And again: 'Poor Keats has me ever by him, and shadows out the form of one solitary friend: he opens his eyes in great doubt and horror, but when they fall on me they close gently, open quietly and close again, till he sinks to sleep.'

Life held out for six weeks after the second relapse, but from the first days of February the end was visibly drawing near. On one of his nights of vigil Severn occupied himself in making that infinitely touching deathbed drawing in black and white of his friend with which all readers are familiar. Between the 14th and 22nd of February Severn wrote letters to Brown, to Mrs Brawne, and to Haslam to prepare them for the worst and to tell them of the reconciled and tranquil state into which the dying man had fallen. Death came very peacefully at last. On the 23rd of that month, writes Severn, 'about four, the approaches of death came on. 'Severn — I — lift me up — I am dying — I shall die easy; don't be frightened — be firm, and thank God it has come.' I lifted him up in my arms. The phlegm seemed boiling in his throat, and increased until eleven, when he gradually sank into death, so quiet, that I still thought he slept.' Three days later his body was carried, attended by several of the English in Rome who had heard his story, to its grave in that retired and verdant cemetery which for his sake and Shelley's has become a place of pilgrimage to the English-speaking world for ever.

Chapter XVII

EPILOGUE

The friends of Keats at home had in their love for him tried hard after his departure to nurse some sparks of hope for his recovery. John Hamilton Reynolds, answering from Exmouth a letter in which Taylor told him of the poet's having sailed, wrote, 'I am *very* much pleased at what you tell me. I cannot now but hold a hope of his refreshed health, which I confess his residence in England greatly discouraged.... Keats, then, by this is at sea fairly — with England and one or two sincere friends behind him, — and with a warm clime before his face! If ever I wished well to Man, I wish well to him!' Haslam in a like strain of feeling wrote in December to Severn at Rome: — 'The climate, however, will, I trust, avail him. Keep him quiet, get the winter through; an opening year in Italy will perfect everything. Ere this reaches you, I trust Doctor Clark will have confirmed the most sanguine hopes of his friends in England; and to you, my friend, I hope he will have given what you stand much in need of — a confidence amounting to a faith.... Keats must get himself well again, Severn, if but for us. I, for one, cannot afford to lose him. If I know what it is to love, I truly love John Keats.' The letters written by Severn to this faithful friend during the voyage and from beside the sickbed were handed round and eagerly scanned among the circle. Brown, when they came into his hands, used to read passages from them at his discretion to the Brawne ladies next door, keeping the darkest from the daughter by her mother's wish. Mrs Brawne, evidently believing her child's heart to be deeply engaged, dealt in the same manner with Severn's letters to herself. The girl seems to have divined none the less that her lover's condition was past hope, and her demeanour, according to Brown's account as follows, to have been human and natural. Keats, writes Brown in a broken style, —

Keats is present to me everywhere and at all times — he now seems sitting by my side and looking hard in my face, though I have taken the opportunity of writing this in company — for I scarcely believe I could do it alone. Much as I have loved him, I never knew how closely he was wound about my heart. Mrs Brawne was greatly agitated when I told her of — and her daughter — I don't know how — for I was not present — yet she bears it with great firmness, mournfully but without affectation. I understand she says to her mother, 'I believe he must soon die, and when you hear of his death, tell me immediately. I am not a fool!'

As the news grew worse, it seems to have been more and more kept back from her, injudiciously as Brown thought, and in a mutilated letter he gives glimpses of moods in her, apparently hysterical, of alternate forced gaiety and frozen silence. A letter or two which she had written to her dying lover were withheld from him, as we have seen, by reason of the terrible agitation into which the mere sight of her handwriting threw him. We hear in the meantime of her being in close correspondence with his young sister at Walthamstow. When the news of the end came, Brown writes, — 'I felt at the moment utterly unprepared for it. Then *she* — she was to have it told her, and the worst had been concealed from her knowledge ever since your December letter. It is now five days since she heard it. I shall not speak of the first shock, nor of the following days, — it is enough she is now pretty well, — and thro'out she has shown a firmness of mind which I little expected from one so young, and under such a load of grief.'

Leigh Hunt had written in these days a letter to Severn which did not reach Rome until after Keats' death. I must quote it as showing yet again the strength of the hold which Keats had on the hearts of his friends, and how he, in a second degree only to Shelley, had struck on something much deeper in Hunt's nature than the sunny, kindly, easy-going affectionateness which was all that in most relations he had to bestow: —

Judge how often I thought of Keats, and with what feelings. Mr Brown tells me he is comparatively calm now. If he can bear to hear of us, pray tell him; but he knows it all already, and can put it in better language than any man. I hear he does not like to be told that he may get better, nor is it to be wondered at, considering his firm persuasion that he shall not thrive. But if this persuasion should happen no longer to be so strong upon him, or if he can now put up with such attempts to console him, remind him of what I have said a thousand times, and what I still (upon my honour I swear) think always, that I have seen too many cases of recovery from apparently desperate cases of consumption, not to indulge in hope to the very last. If he still cannot bear this, tell him — tell that great poet and noble-hearted man that we shall all bear his memory in the most precious part of our hearts, and that the world shall bow their heads to it as our loves do. Or if this will trouble his spirit, tell him that we shall never cease to remember and love him, and that Christian or Infidel, the most sceptical of us has faith enough in the high things that nature puts into our heads, to think that all who are of one accord in mind or heart are journeying to one and the same place, and shall meet somehow or other again, face to face, mutually conscious, mutually delighted. Tell him he is only before us on the road, as he was in everything else; or whether you tell him the latter or no, tell him the former, and add, that we shall never forget that he was so, and that we are coming after him. The tears are again in my eyes, and I must not afford to shed them.

During Keats' year of illness and dejection at home, and until the end and after it, the general impression among his friends and acquaintances was that the cause of all his troubles was the agony of mind into which the hostile reviews had thrown him. Severn in the course of his tendance discovered, as we have seen, that this was not so, and learnt the full share which was due to the pangs of unsatisfied, and in a worldly sense hopeless, passion in a consumptive constitution. Brown on his part, although he knew the secret of the heart which Keats so jealously guarded, yet attributed the chief part of his friend's distress to the fear of impending poverty — truly another contributing cause — and conceived a fierce and obstinate indignation against George for having, as he quite falsely imagined, deliberately fleeced his brother, as well as against other friends who had borrowed money from the poet and failed to pay it back. But most of those who knew Keats less intimately, seeing his sudden fall from robustness and high spirits, — having never thought of him as a possible consumptive subject, — and being themselves white-hot with anger against *Blackwood* and the *Quarterly*, — inferred the poet's feelings from their own, and at the same time added fuel to their wrath against the critics, by taking it for granted that it was their cruelty which was killing him.

To no one was this impression conveyed in a more extravagant form than to Shelley, presumably through his friends the Gisbornes. In that letter of remonstrance to Gifford, as editor of the *Quarterly*, which he drafted in the autumn of 1820 but never sent, Shelley writes: —

Poor Keats was thrown into a dreadful state of mind by this review, which I am, persuaded, was not written with any intention of producing the effect, to which it has, at least, greatly contributed, of embittering his existence, and inducing a disease from which there are now but faint hopes of his recovery. The first effects are described to me to have resembled insanity, and it was by assiduous watching that he was restrained from effecting purposes of suicide. The agony of his sufferings at length produced the rupture of a blood-vessel in the lungs, and the usual process of consumption appears to have begun.

In the preface to *Adonais*, composed at San Giuliano, near Pisa, in the June following Keats' death in the next year, Shelley repeats the same delusion in different words, adding the still less justified statement, — probably founded by his informant, Colonel Finch, on expressions used by Brown to Severn about George Keats and other borrowers, — that Keats' misery had been 'exasperated by the bitter sense of unrequited benefits: — the poor fellow seems to have been hooted from the stage of life, no less by those on whom he had wasted the promise of his genius, than those on whom he had lavished his fortune and his care.' Of the critical attacks upon Keats, Shelley seems not to have known the *Blackwood* lampoons, and to have put down all the mischief (as did Byron following him) to the *Quarterly* alone. With his heart and soul full of passionate poetic regret for what the world had lost in the death of the author of *Hyperion*, and of passionate human indignation against the supposed agents of his undoing, Shelley wrote that lament for Keats which is the best of his longer poems and next to *Lycidas* the noblest of its class in the language. Like Milton, Shelley chose to conform to a consecrated convention and link his work to a long tradition by going back to the precedent of the Sicilian pastoral elegies, those beautiful examples of a form even in its own day conventional and literary. He took two masterpieces of that school, the dirge or ritual chant of Bion on the death of Adonis and the elegy of Moschus on the death of Bion, and into strains directly caught and blended from both of these wove inseparably a new strain of imagery and emotion entirely personal and his own.

The human characteristics of the lamented person, the flesh and blood realities of life, are not touched or thought upon. A rushing train of abstractions, such as were at all times to Shelley more inspiring and more intensely realized than persons and things, — a rushing train of beautiful and sorrowful abstractions sweeps by, in *Adonais*, to a strain of music so entrancing that at a first, or even at a twentieth, reading it is perhaps more to the music of the poem than to its imagery that the spiritual sense of the reader attends. Nevertheless he will find at last that the imagery, all unsubstantial as it is, has been floated along the music into his mental being to haunt and live with him: he will be conscious of a possession for ever in that invocation of the celestial Muse to awake and weep for the youngest of her sons, — that pageant of the dead poet's own dreams and imaginations conceived as gathering 'like mist over an autumnal stream' to attend upon his corpse, — the voice of Echo silenced (again a direct adaptation from the Greek) since she has no longer words of his to repeat and awaken the spring withal, — the vision of the coming of Urania to the death chamber, — her lament, with its side-shafts of indignation against the wolves and ravens who have made her youngest-born their prey — the approach and homage of the other 'mountain shepherds,' Byron, Shelley himself, Moore, Leigh Hunt, all figured, especially Shelley, in a guise purely abstract and mythologic and yet after its own fashion passionately true, — the bitter ironic application to the reviewers of the verses from Moschus used as a motto to the poem, —

> Our Adonais has drunk poison — oh!
> What deaf and viperous murderer could crown
> Life's early cup with such a draught of woe? —

the swift change to a consolatory strain exhorting the mourners to cease their grief and recognise that the lost poet is made one with Nature and that it is Death who is dead, not he, — the invitation to the beautiful burial-place at Rome, — the high strain of Platonic meditation on the transcendental permanence of the One while the Many change and pass, — the final vision by the rapt spirit of Shelley of the soul of his brother poet beckoning like a star from the abode of the Eternals.

Looking upon his own work in his modest and unsanguine way, Shelley could not suppress the hope that this time he had written something that should not be utterly neglected. He had the poem printed at Pisa, whence a small number of copies only were sent to England. One immediate effect was to instigate the last and silliest — happily, perhaps, also the least remembered — of the *Blackwood* blackguardries. Not even the tragic experiences of the preceding winter had cured the conductors of that journal of their taste for savage ribaldry. John Scott, the keen-witted and warmhearted editor, formerly of the *Champion* and latterly of Taylor's and Hessey's *London Magazine*, had denounced the 'Z' papers, and demanded a disclosure of Lockhart's share in them and in the management of the magazine, in terms so peremptory and scathing that the threat of a challenge from Lockhart followed as an inevitable consequence. The clumsy, well meant intromission of third parties had only the effect of substituting Lockhart's friend Christie in the broil for Lockhart himself. The duel was fought on January 16, 1821, exactly a week before Keats' death, and Scott was killed. None the less, when late in the summer of the same year copies of *Adonais* reached England, remarks on it outdoing all previous outbreaks in folly and insolence were contributed to *Blackwood* by a comparatively new recruit, the learned and drunken young Dublin scholar William Maginn. Professing absurdly to regard the cockney school as a continuation of the 'Della Cruscan' school laughed out of existence by Gifford some five-and-twenty years earlier, the writer includes Shelley of all men (forgetting former laudations of him) among the cockneys, flings up a heel at the memory of Keats as 'a young man who had left a decent calling for the melancholy trade of cockney-poetry and has lately died of a consumption after having written two or three little books of verse much neglected by the public'; and proceeds to give a comic analysis of *Adonais*, with some specimens of parody upon it, which were afterwards republished without shame under Maginn's name.

Eight years later, as we shall see, it was on the enthusiasm of a band of young Cambridge men for *Adonais* that the fame of Keats began to be spread abroad among our younger generation in England. In the meantime the chief effect of the poem was to confirm in the minds of the few readers whom it reached the sentimental view of Keats as an over-sensitive weakling whom the breath of hostile criticism had withered up. And when two years later Byron printed in the eleventh canto of *Don Juan* his patronizing semi-palinode, part laudatory part contemptuous, on Keats, his closing couplet,

> Strange that the mind, that very fiery particle,
> Should let itself be snuffed out by an article,

stamped that impression for good on the minds of men in far wider circles, until the publication of Monckton Milnes's memoir after five-and-twenty years brought evidence to modify if not to efface it.

None of Keats' friends at home did anything in the days following his death to counteract such impression. Some of them, as we have said, fully shared and helped to propagate it. Haydon, writing to Miss Mitford soon after the news of the death reached England, says 'Keats was a victim of personal abuse and want of nerve to bear it. Ought he to have sunk in that way because a few quizzers told him he was an apothecary's apprentice?... Fiery, impetuous, ungovernable and undecided, he expected the world to bow at once to his talents as his friends had done, and he had not patience to bear the natural irritation of envy at the undoubted proof he gave of strength.' In his private journal Haydon treats the events in the same spirit, not forgetting to imply a contrast between Keats' weakness and his own power of stubbornly presenting his prickles to his enemies. Reynolds, it would seem, had more excuse than others for adopting the same view, inasmuch as Keats had said to him on his sickbed, in one of his extremely rare allusions to the subject, — 'If I die, you must ruin Lockhart.' In the summer following Keats' death, Reynolds published a little volume of verse dedicated to the young bride at whose bidding he was abandoning literature for law, and included in it the two versified tales from Boccaccio which he had originally planned for printing together with Keats' *Isabella* : as to which pieces he says, —

They were to have been associated with tales from the same source, intended to have been written by a friend, but illness on his part, and distracting engagements on mine, prevented us from accomplishing our plan at the time; and Death now, to my deep sorrow, has frustrated it for ever! He, who is gone, was one of the very kindest friends I possessed, and yet he was not kinder perhaps to me, than to others. His intense mind and powerful feeling would, I truly believe, have done the world some service, had his life been spared — but he was of too sensitive a nature — and thus he was destroyed!

Later in the same summer, 1822, befell the tragedy of Shelley's own death, such a tragedy of a poet's death as a poet might have loved to invent with all its circumstances, — the disappearance of the boat in a squall; the recovery of the body with the volume of Keats' poems in the coat-pocket; its consumption on a funeral pyre by the Tuscan shore in the presence of Leigh Hunt, newly come to Italy on Shelley's invitation, of Byron, and of the Cornish sea-rover and social rebel Trelawny, a personage who might well have been a creation of Byron's brain; the snatching of the heart from the flames; the removal of the ashes to Rome, and their deposit in a new Protestant burial-ground adjacent to the old, where the remains of Trelawny were to be laid beside them after the lapse of nearly sixty years.

Two years later again, when Byron had himself died during the struggle for the liberation of Greece, Hazlitt took occasion to criticize Shelley's posthumous poems in the *Edinburgh Review*, and having his own bitter grounds of quarrel with the *Blackwood* gang, strained the bonds of prose in an outburst of half-lyric indignation on behalf of Keats as follows: —

Mr Shelley died, it seems, with a volume of Mr Keats' poetry grasped with one hand in his bosom! These are two out of four poets, patriots and friends, who have visited Italy within a few years, both of whom have been soon hurried to a more distant shore. Keats died young; and 'yet his infelicity had years too many.' A canker had blighted the tender bloom that o'erspread a face in which youth and genius strove with beauty; the shaft was sped — venal, vulgar, venomous, that drove him from his country, with sickness and penury for companions, and followed him to his grave. And yet there are those who could trample on the faded flower — men to whom breaking hearts are a subject of merriment — who laugh loud over the silent urn of Genius, and play out their game of venality and infamy with the crumbling bones of their victims!

Severn, living on at Rome in the halo of sympathy and regard with which the story of his friend's death and his own devotion had justly surrounded him, seems to have done nothing to remove from the minds of the English colony through successive years an impression which he knew to have been only in a very partial measure true. And even Brown, when in the year after Keats' death he came out with his natural son, a child of a few years, to make his home in Italy, in his turn let himself fall in with the view of Keats' sufferings and of their origin which had taken such strong hold on the minds of most persons interested and commended itself so naturally to the tender-hearted and the righteously indignant. Brown did not come to Rome, but established himself first at Pisa and afterwards at Florence. At Pisa he saw something both of Trelawny and of Byron, who took to him kindly; and made several contributions to the *Liberal* during the brief period while Hunt continued to conduct that journal at Pisa after Shelley's death and before his final rupture with Byron and departure from Italy. The Greek adventure having in 1823 carried off Trelawny for a season and Byron never to return, Brown settled at Florence and became for some years a popular member of the lettered English colony in Tuscany, living in intimacy with Seymour Kirkup, the artist and man of fortune who was for many years the centre of that circle, and before long admitted to the regard and hospitality of Walter Savage Landor in his beautiful Fiesolan villa. Landor, as readers will hardly need to be reminded, was an early, firm, and just admirer of Keats' poetry.

It was not until some five years after Byron's death in Greece that Trelawny came back to settle for a while again in Tuscany. Then, in 1829, he and Brown being at the time housemates, Brown helped him in preparing for the press his autobiographical romance, *The Adventures of a Younger Son*, and especially by supplying mottoes in verse for its chapter-headings, chiefly from the unpublished poems of Keats in his possession. One day Trelawny said to him that 'Brown' was no right distinguishing name for a man, or even for a family, but merely the name of a tribe: whereupon and whenceforward, adding to his own Christian name one that had been borne by a deceased brother, he took to styling himself, not always in familiar but regularly in formal signatures, Charles Armitage Brown. It is both anachronism and pedantry to give him these names, as is often done, in writing of him in connexion with Keats, to whom he was never anything but plain Charles Brown.

Of Keats Brown's thoughts had in the meantime remained full. From his first arrival in Italy he had been in close communication with Severn as to the memorial stone and inscription to be placed over the poet's grave at Rome and as to the biography to be written of him. He let the wish expressed by Keats that his epitaph should be 'here lies one whose name was writ in water' stand for him as an absolute command, and studied how to combine those words with others explaining their choice as due to the poet's sense of neglect by his countrymen. In the end the result agreed on between him and Severn was that which, despite much after-regret on Severn's and some on Brown's part and many proposals of change, still stands, having been carefully re-cut and put in order more than half a century after the poet's death: — namely a design of a lyre with only two of its strings strung, and an inscription perpetuating the idea of the poet having been a victim to the malice of his enemies: —

Severn in his correspondence with Brown at Florence, and with Haslam and other friends at home, shows himself always loyally anxious to attribute to his connexion with Keats the social acceptance and artistic success which he found himself enjoying from the first at Rome, and to which in fact his own actively amiable nature, his winning manners and facile, suave pictorial talent, in a great measure contributed. Though the general feeling towards the memory of Keats among English residents and visitors was sympathetic, there were not lacking voices to repeat the stock gibe, —'"his name was writ in water"; yes, and his poetry in milk and water.' Severn eagerly notes any signs of increasing appreciation of his friend's poetry, or of changed opinion on the part of scoffers, that came under his notice. One touching incident he recorded in later life as having happened in the spring of 1832, the eleventh year after Keats' death. Sir Walter Scott, stricken with premature decrepitude from the labour and strain of mind undergone in his six years' colossal effort to clear himself of debt after the Constable crash, had come abroad with his daughter Anne in the hope of regaining some measure of health and strength from rest and southern air. He spent a spring month at Rome, surrounded with attentions and capable of some sight-seeing, but could not shake off his grief for what he had lost in the death there two years earlier of his beloved Lady Northampton, whose beauty and charm and gift for verse and song (her singing portrait by Raeburn is one of the most beautiful in the world) had endeared her to him from childhood in her island home in Mull. Scott's distress in thinking of her was pitiable, and he found some relief in pouring himself out to the sympathetic Severn, who had known her well.

By Scott's desire Severn went every morning to see him, generally bringing some picture or sketch to amuse him. One morning Severn having innocently shown him the portrait of Keats reproduced at page of this book, and said something about his genius and fate, observed Anne Scott turn away flushed and embarrassed, while Scott took Severn's hand to close the interview, and said falteringly, 'yes, yes, the world finds out these things for itself at last.' The story has been commonly, but without reason, scouted as though it implied a guilty conscience in Scott himself as to the *Blackwood* lampoons. It implies nothing of the kind. Scott had indeed had nothing to do with these matters: but one of his nearest and dearest had. The current belief that the death of Keats had been caused or hastened by Lockhart's attack in *Blackwood*, with the tragic circumstances of the Christie-Scott duel, however little he may have said about them, will assuredly have left in a heart so great and tender an abiding regret and pain, and his manner and words on being reminded of them, as recorded by Severn, are perfectly in character.

By degrees the signs of admiration for Keats' work noted by Severn become more frequent. Young Mr Gladstone, coming fresh from Oxford to Rome in this same year 1832, seeks him out because of his friendship for the poet. Another year a group of gentlemen and ladies in the English colony propose to give an amateur performance of the unpublished *Otto the Great*, a proposal never, it would seem, carried out. But despite the loyal enthusiasm of special English circles abroad and the untiring tributes of Leigh Hunt and other friends and admirers at home, his repute among the reading public in general was of extraordinarily slow growth. In the interval of some score of years between the death of Byron and the establishment — itself slow and contested — of Tennyson's position, Byron and Scott held with most even of open-minded judges an uncontested sovereignty among recent English poets; while among a growing minority the fame of Wordsworth steadily grew, and the popular and sentimental suffrage was given to writers of the calibre of Felicia Hemans and Letitia Landon, feminine talents and temperaments truly not to be despised, however ephemeral has proved their fame.

So small was the demand for Keats' poetry that the remaining stock of his original three volumes sufficed throughout nearly this score of years to supply it. The yeast was nevertheless working. We know of one famous instance, so far back as 1825, when a gift of the original volumes of Keats and Shelley inspired the recipient — the lad Robert Browning, then aged fourteen — with a fervent and wholly new conception, as he used afterwards to declare, of the scope and power of poetry. Young John Sterling, writing in 1828 in the *Athenaeum*, of which his friend and senior Frederick Denison Maurice was for the time being editor, showed which way the wind was beginning to blow at Cambridge when he said, 'Keats, whose memory they (the *Blackwood* group) persevered only a few months back in spitting upon, was, as everyone knows who has read him, among the most intense and delightful English poets of our day.' But no reprint of Keats' poems was published until 1829, and then only by the Paris house of Galignani, who printed for the continental market, in a single tall volume with double columns, a collective edition of the poems of Shelley, Coleridge, and Keats. The same year saw the reprint of *Adonais* on the initiative of Arthur Hallam and his group of undergraduate friends at Cambridge, and the visit of three of the group, Hallam himself, Monckton Milnes, and Sunderland, to uphold in debate at Oxford the opinion that Shelley was a greater poet than Byron. Their enthusiasm for *Adonais* implied enthusiasm for its subject, Keats, as a matter of course.

Alfred Tennyson was a close associate of this group; and from the first, among recent influences, it was that of Keats which did most to colour his style in poetry and make him strive to 'load every rift of a subject with ore.' His friend Edward FitzGerald shared the same admiration to the full. But these young pioneer spirits still stood, except for the surviving band of Keats' early friends, almost alone. Wilson, it is true, with whom consistency counted for nothing, had by this time shown signs of wavering, and in his character as Christopher North speaks of Keats' 'genius' being shown to best advantage in *Lamia* and *Isabella*, — but does so, we feel, less for the sake of praising Keats than of getting in a dig at Jeffrey for having praised him tardily and indiscriminately. The *Quarterly* remained quite impenitent, and in a review of Tennyson's second volume of 1832 writes of him with viciously laboured irony as 'a new prodigy of genius — another and brighter star of a galaxy or *milky way* of poetry, of which the lamented Keats was the harbinger'; and then follows a gibing testimony, to be read in the same inverted sense, of the vast popularity which *Endymion* has notoriously attained. So far as popularity was concerned, the *Quarterly* gibe remained justified. It was not until 1840 that there appeared in England the first separate reprint of Keats' collected poems: what is sad to relate is that even this edition found a scanty sale, and that before long 'remainder' copies of it were being bound up by the booksellers with the 'remainders' of another unsuccessful issue of the day, the series of *Bells and Pomegranates* by Robert Browning.

After an interval of thirteen years, John Sterling must still, in 1841, write to Julius Hare as follows: —

Lately I have been reading again some of Alfred Tennyson's second volumes, and with profound admiration of his truly lyric and idyllic genius. There seems to me to have been more epic power in Keats, that fiery beautiful meteor; but they are two most true and great poets. When one thinks of the amount of recognition they have received, one may well bless God that poetry is in itself strength and joy, whether it be crowned by all mankind or left alone in its own magic hermitage.

So late as 1844, Jeffrey, who in spite of the justice he had been induced to do to Keats in his lifetime, had no real belief in the new poetry and was an instinctive partisan of the conventional eighteenth-century style, could write that the 'rich melodies' of Keats and Shelley were passing out of public memory, and that the poets of their age destined to enduring fame were Campbell and Rogers. De Quincey in 1845 could grotesquely insult the memory and belittle the work of Keats in a passage pouring scorn on *Endymion*, treating *Hyperion* as his only achievement that counted, and ending, — 'Upon this mother tongue, upon this English language has Keats trampled as with the hoofs of a buffalo. With its syntax, with its prosody, with its idiom, he has played such fantastic tricks as could only enter the heart of a barbarian, and for which only the anarchy of Chaos could furnish a forgiving audience. Verily it required *Hyperion* to weigh against the deep treason of these unparalleled offences.'

In the meantime none of Keats' friends had succeeded in doing anything to strengthen his reputation or make his true character known by the publication either of a personal memoir or of his poetry that remained in manuscript. Several of them had fully desired and intended to do both these things. But mutual jealousies and dislikes, such as are but too apt to break out among the surviving intimates of a man of genius, had prevented any such purpose taking effect. Taylor and Woodhouse had been first in the field, collecting what material for a memorial volume they could, including the transcripts zealously made by Woodhouse from Keats' papers while he was alive, and others, both verse and correspondence, which they had borrowed from Reynolds. But help both from Brown and from George Keats would have been necessary to give anything like completeness to their work; and Brown, who himself desired to be his friend's biographer, looked askance at them and their project. As for information or material from George Keats, Brown on his part was debarred from seeking it by his obstinate conviction, reiterated in all companies and on all occasions and naturally resented by its subject, that George was a traitor, cheat, and villain. When Fanny Keats came of age in 1824, the duty devolved on Dilke of going into the family accounts and putting pressure on Abbey, who had proved a muddler both of his wards' affairs and of his own, to make over the residue of the estate which he held in trust. In the discharge of this duty Dilke satisfied himself, as a practical man of business, that George's conduct had been strictly upright and his motives honourable. But Brown refused to let his prejudices be shaken; and he and Dilke, though they met both in Italy and later in England, were never again on their old terms of friendship and mutual regard. Brown, criticizing Dilke in his influential position as editor of the *Athenaeum* after 1830 and as a learned and recognized authority on various problems of literary history, declares that he has become dogmatic and arrogant from success. Dilke, writing confidentially of Brown, scouts the notion which had got abroad of his having been a 'generous benefactor' to Keats, and insists that he had always expected to profit by a literary partnership with the poet, and after his death had demanded and received from the estate payment in full, with interest, of all advances made by him.

So much — and the reader may hold it more than enough — in order to explain why no sufficient memoir of Keats or collection of his remains could be published by his surviving friends. Brown, indeed, wrote some ten years after Keats' death the brief memoir of which I have freely made use in these pages, and tried some editors with it, but in vain. Destiny had provided otherwise and better. One of the Cambridge group of Shelley-Keats enthusiasts of 1830, Richard Monckton Milnes, being in Italy with his family not long after his degree, visited Rome and Florence in 1833 and 1834, and with his genius for knowing, liking, and being liked by everybody, made immediate friends with Severn at Rome, and at Florence soon found his way to Landor's home at the Villa Gherardesca, and there met and was quickly on good terms with Brown. Some two or three years later Brown left Tuscany for good and established himself at Laira Green, near Plymouth, where he lived the life of amateur in letters, a busy local lecturer and contributor to local journals, and published his very ingenious interpretation of Shakespeare's sonnets as a cryptic autobiography of the poet, continuing the while to nurse the hope and desire of being Keats' biographer. He had all but concluded an arrangement for the publication of his memoir in the *Monthly Chronicle*, when one day near the end of 1840, having heard a lecture on the prospects of the then young colony of New Zealand, he determined suddenly to emigrate thither with his son, who had been in training as a civil engineer; and before he left designated Monckton Milnes, with whom he had not ceased to keep in touch, as the fit man to do justice to Keats' memory, and handed to him all his own cherished material.

Within a year Brown had died in New Zealand of an apoplectic stroke. Monckton Milnes was faithful to his trust, but not swift or prompt in fulfilling it. That was more than could well have been expected of a man of so many interests and pursuits and so eager in them all, — poet, politician, orator, wit, entertainer, athirst and full of relish for every varied cup of experience and every social or intellectual pleasure or activity, or opportunity for help or kindness, that life had to offer him. It was not until the fifth year after Brown's departure that he buckled to his task. He began by collecting, with some measure of secretarial help from Coventry Patmore, further information and material from all the surviving friends of Keats whom he could hear of. George Keats had died at Louisville, Kentucky, in 1842, leaving an honoured memory among his fellow citizens; and his widow had taken a second husband, a Mr Jeffrey, who on Milnes's request sent him among other material copies, unluckily very imperfect, of Keats' incomparable journal-letters to George and to herself. From Cowden Clarke, the happiest of all Keats' friends in after-life, happy in a perfect marriage, the sunniest of dispositions, and a sustained success in the congenial occupation of a public reader in and lecturer on Shakespeare and other poets, — from Cowden Clarke and from Keats' younger school friend Edward Holmes, Milnes drew the information about Keats' school days which I have quoted above almost in full. Leigh Hunt, the friend whom Keats owed to Clarke and who had had the most decisive influence on his life, had passed with advancing years, not indeed out of his lifelong, lightly borne condition of debt and poverty and embarrassment and household worry, but out of the old atmosphere of obloquy and contention into one of peace, and of affectionate regard all but universal as the most genial and companionable, the most versatile, industrious and sweet-natured of literary veterans, praised and admired, to a pitch almost of generous passion, even by the growler Carlyle, who had nothing but a gibe of contempt to bestow upon the weaknesses of a Lamb or a Keats. In regard to Keats, Hunt had said his say, personal and critical, long ago, in the unwise but in its day grossly over-reviled book *Lord Byron and some of his Contemporaries* (1828), as well as in many incidental notes and observations through thirty years, and especially in that masterpiece in his own vein of criticism, *Imagination and Fancy* (1844). Accordingly he had now little that was fresh to tell the biographer. As for Haydon, the destiny he had in the old days been used to prophesy for Hunt, — even such a destiny, and worse, had in the irony of things befallen himself. That tragic gulf which existed in him between ambition and endowment, between temperament and faculty, had led him through ever fiercer contentions and deeper and more desperate difficulties to the goal of suicide. This had happened in the days when the biographer of Keats was just setting hand to his task; hence such accounts of the poet as I have quoted from Haydon were not at Milnes's disposal, but are drawn from later posthumous publications of the painter's journals and correspondence. By way of farewell to this ill-starred overweening half-genius, I add here the facsimile of a page from a letter he wrote to Elizabeth Barrett in 1834, describing a scene of rather squalid tragi-comedy which he and Keats had witnessed at Hunt's Hampstead cottage seventeen years before, and adding from memory a sketch of Keats' profile, with an answer to his correspondent's conjecture that the poet's expression had been 'too subtle for the brush.'

Among Keats' other intimate friends and associates, Mr Taylor let Monckton Milnes have the loan of the notes and transcripts bequeathed him by Woodhouse, who had died in 1834. Reynolds heard by accident of the intended biography, and never having quite abandoned his own purpose in the matter, wrote at first complainingly, resenting that use should be made of those letters of Keats to himself which he had allowed Woodhouse to copy. But a gracious answer quickly won him over, and he made the new biographer welcome to all his material. His own career had been a rather melancholy failure. He had never quite given up literature in accordance with the purpose he had declared on marriage. Indeed it was not until six years after that declaration, in 1825, that his best piece of work was done, in collaboration with his brother-in-law, Thomas Hood: I mean the anonymous volume of humorous poems, not inferior to *Rejected Addresses*, called *Odes and Addresses to Great People*, which Coleridge confidently declared to be the work of Lamb. In later years Reynolds was a not infrequent contributor to the *Edinburgh Review* and to the *Athenaeum* under the editorship of Dilke. For some unspecified reason he did not prosper in the place which his friend Rice had found for him with the eminent firm of solicitors, the Fladgates; and in later life he was glad to accept a small piece of patronage as deputy clerk of the County Court at Newport in the Isle of Wight. Here, if the latest mention of him is to be trusted, he fell into self-neglecting habits and consequent disrepute. In one of his letters to Milnes he speaks about 'that poor, obscure, baffled thing, myself': in another he declares his entire confidence in his correspondent, and his unfading admiration and affection for his lost friend, as follows: —

All the papers I possess — all the information I can render — whatever I can do to aid your kind and judiciously intended work — are at your service! But a word or two on the great subject of our correspondence. He was hunted in his youth, before he had strength to escape his bandogs. He had the greatest power of poetry in him, of any one since Shakespeare! He was the sincerest friend, the most lovable associate, the deepest listener to the griefs and disappointments of all around him 'that ever lived in the tide of times.' Your expressed intentions as to the Life are so clear and good; that I seem to have the weight of an undone work taken from me.

Haslam in like manner lends all the help he can, and from his office as a solicitor in Copthall Court writes somewhat dispiritedly about himself, and declares that this correspondence 'has been a clean taking me back to a separate state of existence that I had more than thirty years ago, a state that has long appeared to me almost as a dream. The realities of life have intervened, but God be praised they have but been laid upon the surface — have but hidden, not effaced those happy happy days.' He sends a number of letters from Severn, including those written on the voyage to Naples and quoted in full above. But as to letters from Keats himself says he has found none, — 'they probably were so well or intended to be so well taken care of, that every endeavour to lay my hands on them has proved unavailing.' One wonders whether they may not be lurking yet, a forgotten bundle, in the dust of some unexplored corner of a safe in that same office. Severn was at this time living in London, and some correspondence passed between him and Milnes about the biography, Severn's chief point being to insist that not the malice of the critics, but the 'death-stricken' marriage project, was the trouble preying upon Keats in his dying days, and that the outcries of his delirium ran constantly upon his unfulfilled love and unwritten poems together.

As to yet another of Keats' closest friends, Benjamin Bailey, Milnes had somehow been misinformed, and believed and positively stated him to be dead. He had in fact risen to colonial preferment in the Church, and was alive and well as archdeacon of Colombo in Ceylon. Thence on the appearance of Milnes's book he wrote to declare his survival, and forwarded to the biographer, for use in future editions, those memoranda of old days spent in Keats' company upon which I have above (in Chapter V) so fully drawn.

There are a few other points upon which Milnes's information was less accurate than might have been expected. He assumes that the *fiancée* of Keats' tragic passion was identical with the rich-complexioned Charmian described in his autumn letters of 1819, and ignores the existence of Fanny Brawne and of her family. One would have supposed that he must have heard the real story both from Brown and from Dilke, whom Mrs Brawne had appointed trustee for her children, and who had not since lost sight of them. That kind lady herself met an unhappy fate, burned to death upon her own doorstep. Her daughter Fanny, ten years after her poet-lover's death, married a Mr Lindo, who afterwards changed his name to Lindon, and of whom we know little except that he was at one time drawn into the meshes of Spanish politics and was afterwards one of the Commissioners for the Great Exhibition of 1851. Not long before her marriage, Mrs Lindon is recorded to have said of Keats that the kindest thing to his memory would be to let it die. Little wonder, perhaps, that she should have felt thus, when she remembered the tortured, the terrifying vehemence of his passion for herself and when, being probably incapable of independent literary judgment, she saw his name and work still made customary objects of critical derision. It is harder to forgive her when some time later we find her parting with her lover's miniature, under pressure of some momentary money difficulty, to Dilke.

Neither does the biographer seem to have made any attempt to get into touch with Keats' young sister, who had been married long before this to an accomplished Spanish man of letters, Señor Valentine Llanos. He also was at various times involved in the political troubles of his country. Of his and his wife's children, one attained distinction as an artist and assumed the name of Keats y Llanos. Keats had written to his sister once as a child gaily prophesying that they all, her brothers and herself, would live to have 'tripple chins and stubby thumbs.' She in fact fully attained the predicted length of days, and having lived to be well assured of the full and final triumph of her brother's fame died less than thirty years ago at eighty-six. In mature life she had come into touch with one at least of her brother's surviving familiars, that is with Severn at Rome, and with more than one of his admirers in a younger generation. Of these a good friend to her was Mr Buxton Forman, through whose initiative a Civil List pension was awarded her by Lord Beaconsfield. A subtle observer, the poet and humorist, Frederick Locker-Lampson, has left a rather disappointing though not unkindly impression of her as follows: —

Whilst I was in Rome Mr Severn introduced me to M. and *Mme.* Valentine de Llanos, a kindly couple. He was a Spaniard, lean, silent, dusky, and literary, the author of *Don Esteban* and *Sandoval* . She was fat, blonde, and lymphatic, and both were elderly. *She was John Keats' sister!* I had a good deal of talk with her, or rather *at* her, for she was not very responsive. I was disappointed, for I remember that my sprightliness made her yawn; she seemed inert and had nothing to tell me of her wizard brother of whom she spoke as of a mystery — with a vague admiration but a genuine affection. She was simple and natural — I believe she is a very worthy woman.

Gaps and errors there thus were not a few in Monckton Milnes's book when it appeared in two volumes in 1848. But it served its purpose admirably for the time being, and with some measure of revision for long afterwards. Distinguished in style and perfect in temper, the preface and introduction struck with full confidence the right note in challenging for Keats the character of 'the Marcellus of the Empire of English song'; while the body of the book, giving to the world a considerable, though far from complete, series of those familiar letters, to his friends in which his genius shines almost as vividly as in his verse, established on full evidence the essential manliness of his character against the conception of him as a blighted weakling which both his friends and enemies had contrived to let prevail. Among the posthumous poems printed for the first time, the two longest, *Otho* and the *Cap and Bells* were not of his best, but masterpieces like *La Belle Dame* and *The Eve of St Mark* , with many miscellaneous things of high interest, were included. The reception of the book, though not, of course, unmixed, was in all quarters respectful, and the old tone of flippant contempt hardly made itself heard at all. I shall quote only one critical dictum on its appearance, and that is the letter in which the veteran Landor, in his highest style of urbanity and authority, acknowledged a copy sent him by the author: —

Dear Milnes,
On my return to Bath last evening, after six weeks' absence, I find your valuable present of Keatses Works. He better deserves such an editor than I such a mark of your kindness. Of all our poets, excepting Shakespeare and Milton, and perhaps Chaucer, he has most of the poetical character — fire, fancy, and diversity.... There is an effluence of power and light pervading all his works, and a freshness such as we feel in the glorious dawn of Chaucer.

The book appeared just at the right moment, when the mounting enthusiasm of the young generation for the once derided poet was either gradually carrying the elders along with it or leaving them bewildered behind. Do readers remember how the simple soul of Colonel Newcome was perplexed by the talk of his son Clive and of Clive's friends? —

He heard opinions that amazed and bewildered him: he heard that Byron was no great poet, though a very clever man... that his favourite, Doctor Johnson, talked admirably, but did not write English; that young Keats was a genius to be estimated in future days with young Raphael; and that a young gentleman of Cambridge who had lately published two volumes of verses might take rank with the greatest poets of all. Doctor Johnson not write English! Lord Byron not one of the greatest poets of the world! Sir Walter a poet of the second order! Mr Pope attacked for inferiority and want of imagination; Mr Keats and this young Mr. Tennyson of Cambridge, the chief of modern poetic literature! What were these new dicta, which Mr. Warrington delivered with a puff of tobacco smoke; to which Mr. Honeyman blandly assented, and Clive listened with pleasure?

Thackeray's sketch of Clive and his companions scarcely suggests, nor was it meant to suggest, the characteristics of the special group of young artists in whom, almost contemporaneously with the appearance of Milnes's book, the enthusiasm for Keats had begun to burn at its whitest heat. I refer of course to the pre-Raphaelite brotherhood. Of the three leaders of that movement, Holman Hunt, Millais, and Rossetti, it is hard to say which, in the late 'forties and early 'fifties, declared himself first or most ardent in Keats-worship. Of Hunt's exhibited pictures, one of the earliest showed the lovers in the *Eve of St Agnes* stealing past the sprawling porter and the sleeping bloodhound into the night; and of Millais's earliest, one is from *Isabella or the Pot of Basil*, showing the merchant brothers and their sister and her lover at a meal in company (the well-known work, so queerly designed and executed with so much grip and character, now in the Walker Art Gallery at Liverpool). Rossetti had in these early days much less technical skill and training than either of his two associates. But from the first he was poet as well as painter, and instinctively and spiritually stood, we can well discern, much nearer to Keats than they did for all their enthusiasm.

Combining Italian blood and temperament with British upbringing, Rossetti added to his inherited and paternally inculcated knowledge and love of Dante a no less intense love and knowledge of English romance poetry, both that of the old ballads and that of the revival of 1800 and onwards. In boyhood and early youth waves of enthusiasm for different recent poets had swept over him one after another, first Shelley, then Keats, then Browning; but Keats, and next to Keats Coleridge, kept the strongest and deepest hold on him. When his first associates Hunt and Millais had parted from him on their several, widely divergent paths of public success and distinction, Rossetti became, in the comparative seclusion in which he chose to live, a powerful focus of romantic inspiration to younger men who came about him. He is reported to have urged upon William Morris that he should become a painter and not a poet, seeing that Keats had already done all there was to be done in poetry. Of all Keats' poems, it was *La belle dame sans Merci* and *The Eve of St Mark* which most aroused the enthusiasm of Rossetti and his group. We have already seen how the latter fragment stands in our nineteenth-century poetry as a kind of bridge or stepping-stone between Chaucer and Morris. It was the task and destiny of Morris as a writer to give, by his abounding fertility and brooding delight in the telling of Greek and mediæval stories in verse, the most profuse and for the present perhaps the last expression to the pure romantic spirit in English narrative poetry: and to this effort Keats had given him the immediate impulse, though Chaucer was his ultimate great exemplar. Answering a congratulatory letter addressed to him by the veteran Cowden Clarke on the publication of the first volume of the *Earthly Paradise*, Morris speaks of 'Keats for whom I have such a boundless admiration, and whom I venture to call one of my masters.' I have quoted above (page 470) his emphatic later words to a like effect.

While the leaven was thus intensely working among a special group in England, an English poetess of quite other training and associations, Elizabeth Barrett Browning, paid in *Aurora Leigh* (1857) her well-known tribute to Keats in lines that are neither good as poetry nor accurate as fact, but in their chaotic way none the less passionately felt and haunting: —

> By Keats' soul, the man who never stepped
> In gradual progress like another man,
> But, turning grandly on his central self,
> Ensphered himself in twenty perfect years
> And died, not young, (the life of a long life
> Distilled to a mere drop, falling like a tear
> Upon the world's cold cheek to make it burn
> For ever;) by that strong accepted soul,
> I count it strange and hard to understand
> That nearly all young poets should write old.

Thus, between the effects of Monckton Milnes's book and the enthusiasm of various groups of university men and poets and artists, the previously current contempt for Keats was from soon after the mid-century practically silenced and the battle for his fame, at least among the younger generation, won. He has counted for the last sixty years and more, alike in England and in America, as an uncontested great poet, whose works, collected or single, have been in demand in edition after edition. One of the earliest new issues was that edited in 1850 by Monckton Milnes, who continued nearly until the end, under his new style as Lord Houghton, to further by fresh editions and revisions the good work he had begun. Not only every professed critic and historian of our poetry, but nearly all our chief poets themselves, as Aubrey de Vere, James Russell Lowell, Matthew Arnold, Coventry Patmore, Swinburne, and latterly the present poet laureate, have been in various tones public commentators on Keats. All such comments have shed light upon his work in their degree. I can here only touch on a few special points and mention in their order a few of the contributions to the knowledge or appreciation of the poet which I think have helped the most.

One point to be remarked is that very few judges have seemed able to care equally for Keats and Shelley. A special devotion to Shelley, the poet who wedded himself in youth to a set of ready-made beliefs from Godwin, of which the chief was that all the miseries of the world were due to laws and institutions and could be cured by their abolition, who clothed these abstract beliefs in imagery of clouds and winds and ocean-streams, of meteor and rainbow and sunset and all things radiant and evanescent, and sang them to strains of music inimitably swift and passionate, seems incompatible with complete delight in the work of that other young poet who could hold fast no dogma spiritual or social, but found truth wherever his imagination could divine or create living and concrete beauty, and who, as to the sorrows of the world, was convinced that they were inherent in its very fabric and being, and yearned for knowledge and wisdom to assuage them but died before he had attained clearness or found his way. As between these two, Tennyson's final and calm opinion is quoted by his son as follows: — 'Keats would have become one of the very greatest of all poets had he lived. At the time of his death there was apparently no sign of exhaustion or having written himself out; his keen poetical instinct was in full process of development at the time. Each new effort was a steady advance on that which had gone before. With all Shelley's splendid imagery and colour, I find a sort of *tenuity* in his poetry.' FitzGerald was much stronger on the same side, counting Shelley, to use his own words, as not worth Keats' little finger. Matthew Arnold, who has said some memorably fine and just things about Keats, belittles the poetry of Shelley and even paradoxically prefers the prose of his essays and letters to his verse. With ardent Shelley-worshippers on the other hand full appreciation of Keats is rare. Swinburne, for one, has done little for Keats' memory by the torrent of hyperbolical adjectives of alternate praise and blame which he has poured upon it. Mr William Rossetti, for whom Shelley is 'one of the ultimate glories of our race and planet,' has in his monograph on Keats, as I think, been icily unjust to his subject. And I can remember my admirable friend and colleague, Mr Richard Garnett of the British Museum, taking me roundly to task for the opinion, which I still stoutly hold, that the letters of Keats, with all their everyday humanity and fun and gossip, are in their wonderful sudden gleams and intuitions more vitally the letters of a poet than Shelley's. But such preferences between two such contrasted geniuses and creators of beauty are perhaps inevitable, and have at any rate not prevented the equal and brotherly association of the two in the memorial house — the house in which Keats died — lately acquired and consecrated to their joint fame by representative English and Americans at Rome.

One great snare in judging of Keats is his variability of mood and opinion. The critic is apt to seize upon the expression of some one phase or attitude of mind that strikes him, and to theorize and draw conclusions from it as though it were permanent and dominant. The very excellence of what was best both in his poetry and himself is a second snare, tempting us to forget that after all he was but a lad, a genius and character not made but in the making. A third is the obvious and frankly avowed intensity of the sensuous elements in his nature.

But the critic who casts these up against him should remember that it took the same capacity for sense-delights that inspired the rhapsodies on claret-drinking and nectarine-sucking in the letters, to inspire also, being spiritualized into imaginative emotion, the 'blushful Hippocrene' passage in the Nightingale ode or the feast of fruits, in all its pureness, of the revised *Hyperion* ; and also that Keats, with his clear and sane self-consciousness, has rarely any doubt that the master bent within him was not his 'exquisite sense of the luxurious' but his love for the high things and thoughts which he calls 'philosophy.'

It is a pity that the author of the one full and recent history of our poetry, the late Mr W.J. Courthope, should have been debarred from just appreciation of this poet alike by adopted dogma and by natural taste. Both led him to hold that the true power of poetry, the true test by which posterity must judge it, lies in the direct relations which it bears to the social and political activities of its period. That the re-awakening of the Western mind and imagination to nature and romance in the days of the revolutionary and Napoleonic wars was a spiritual phenomenon not less important in human history than the wars themselves would have been a conception that his mind was incapable of entertaining. He supposed that Keats was indifferent to history or politics. But of history he was in fact an assiduous reader, and the secret of his indifference to politics, so far as it existed, was that those of his own time had to men of his years and way of thinking been a disillusion, — that the saving of the world from the grip of one great overshadowing tyranny had but ended in re-instating a number of ancient and minor tyrannies less interesting but not less tyrannical. To that which lies behind and above politics and history, to the general destinies and tribulations of the race, he was, as we have seen, not indifferent but only too acutely and tragically sensitive.

Turning to the chief real contributions to our appreciation and knowledge of Keats, I should give the first place to Matthew Arnold's well-known essay of 1880. With his cunning art in the minting and throwing into circulation of phrases that cannot be forgotten, Arnold balanced the weaknesses against the strength of Keats' work and character, blaming the gushing admirers who injured his memory by their 'pawing and fondness,' insisting on the veins of 'flint and iron' in his nature, insisting on his clear-sightedness, his lucidity, his perception of the vital connexion of beauty with truth and of both with joy, declaring that 'no one else in English poetry, save Shakespeare, has in expression quite the fascinating felicity of Keats, his perfection of loveliness,' and clenching all, with reference to Keats' own saying, 'I think I shall be among the English poets after my death,' by the comment, 'he is, he is with Shakespeare. Almost simultaneously with Matthew Arnold's essay, there appeared the very thoughtful and original study of Mrs F.M. Owen, in which were laid the foundations of a true understanding of *Endymion* as a parable of the experiences of a poet's soul in its quest after Beauty.

The years 1883 and 1884 were great Keats years. In them there appeared the edition of the poems by the late W.T. Arnold, the first which contained a scholar's investigations into the special sources of Keats' poetic style and vocabulary: also the edition for the Golden Treasury Series by Francis Turner Palgrave, with a studiously collated text and a preface of more glowing and scarcely less just critical admiration than Matthew Arnold's, only flawed, as I think, by a revival of that obsolete heresy of the 'deadness' of the Grecian mythology: and thirdly, the first issue of the late Mr Buxton Forman's edition of the poetry and prose works together. All students know the results of this editor's devoted and unremitting industry, maintained through a full quarter of a century, in the textual criticism of his author and in the publication and republication of editions containing every variant reading and every scrap of scattered prose or verse that could be recovered. To the same worker is due the unearthing and giving to the world of two groups of the poet's letters which had been unknown to Monckton Milnes, the wholly admirable and delightful series addressed to his young sister, and the series, in great part distressing and deplorable, to Fanny Brawne. About 1887, I was myself able to put straight two matters that needed it by publishing the true text of the letters to America and by rectifying the current notion that the revised *Hyperion* had been a first draft. Before long came the essay of Mr Robert Bridges, passing the whole of Keats' poetry under review, and dealing out judgments in a terse authoritative style to which, as one poet estimating another, he was fully entitled, and which at all moments commands interest and respect if it sometimes challenges contradiction. On some matters, and especially on the relations of Keats' early poetry to Wordsworth, Mr Bridges has thrown a light too clear and convincing to be questioned.

When in 1892 the late Mr William Sharp compiled his *Life of Joseph Severn* from the vast, almost unmanageable mass of papers in the possession of the artist's family (I had had them previously through my hands and can realize the difficulty of the task), he furnished valuable new material for our knowledge both of the life of Keats and of his after life in the opinions of men. Coming down to more recent years, we have the admirable editorial work of Professor de Sélincourt, as good, I think, as has been bestowed on any English poet, carrying out to the farthest point the researches initiated by W.T. Arnold, and illuminating the text throughout with the comments and illustrations of a keen scholar in classical and English literature. Nor can I leave unmentioned the several lectures by two successive Oxford professors of poetry, that of Mr A.C. Bradley on Keats' letters and that of Mr. J.W. Mackail on his poetry. From these two minds, ripened in daily familiarity with the best literatures of the world, we have, after a hundred years, praise of Keats which almost makes Shelley's seating of him among 'Inheritors of unfulfilled renown' seem like an irony, — praise more splendid than he would have hoped for had he lived to fulfil even the most daring of his ambitions. A special point in Mr Mackail's work is to make clear how strong had been upon Keats the influence of the *Divine Comedy*, his pocket companion on his Scottish tour, and how in *Hyperion*, written in the next months after his return, there appears here and there, amid the general Miltonic strain of the verse, a quality of thought and vision drawn straight from and almost matching Dante. Lastly, there has recently come from America a tribute of quite another kind, showing how for purposes of systematic study Keats has been thought worthy of an apparatus hitherto only bestowed on the great classics of literature: I refer to the elaborate and monumental *Concordance* to his poems lately issued from Cornell University.

And must not, it may be asked, all this labour spent upon Keats' memory and remains, all this load of editing and re-editing and commentary and biography and scholiast-work laid upon a poet who declared that all poems ought to be understood without any comment, — must it not by this time have fairly smothered, or is it not at least in danger of smothering, Keats himself and his poetry? Naturally in the course of my own work I have asked myself this question with qualms, bethinking myself of Tennyson's phrase about swamping the sacred poets with themselves. The answer is, — No, such a poet can carry any weight we may choose to lay upon him, and more: he can never be smothered, inasmuch as he has both given the world something it can nevermore cease to want and suggested the existence within him of a power, quenched before its time, to give it something much more and greater yet. If the result of all our commentaries should be to provoke a reaction among readers, and to make them crave for a naked text both of the poems and letters and insist upon being left alone with that and their own meditations upon it, — well, so much the better. Every reader of the English tongue that has the works of Keats often enough in his hands, with or without comment, will find his life enriched with much of the best that poetry can do for human life, with achievements, very near to perfection, of that faculty which is the essential organ of poetry, — to which all others, spiritual and intellectual, are in poetry subordinate, — the faculty of imagination transfusing the vital beauty and magic and secret rhythm of things into the other magic and beauty and rhythm of words. Over and above this, he will find himself living in the familiarity of a great and lovable spirit, dowered at birth with capacities for joy and misery more intense almost than any of which we have record, and retaining its lovableness to the last in spite of circumstances that gave misery too cruelly the upper hand.

But, again the objector may ask, is it so certain that in the coming time the desire of readers for what Keats has to give them will survive without abatement? Have not the last three years been an utterly unprecedented, overwhelming and transforming experience for mankind? Will not the new world after the war be a new world indeed, on the one hand filled, nay, gorged, with recollections of doing and undergoing, of endurance and adventure, of daring and suffering and horror, of hellishness and heroism, beside which all the dreams of bygone romance must forever seem tame and vapid; and on the other hand straining with a hungry forecast towards a future of peace and justice such as mankind has not known before, which it will be its tremendous task to try and establish? Will not this world of so prodigiously intensified experiences and enlarged hopes and besetting anxieties require and produce new poets and a new poetry of its own that shall deal with the realities it has gone through and those it is striving for, and put away and cease to care for the old dreams and thrills and glamours of romance? Have we not in fact witnessed the first-fruits of this new tremendous stimulus in the cloud of young poets who have appeared — too many of them alas! only to perish — since the war began?

And again the answer is, No. However changed the world, work like that of Keats is not what it will ever let perish. The thrills and glamours which pass away are only those of the second-rate and the second-hand sort that come in and go out with literary fashion; not those which have sprung from and struck deep into the innermost places of the spirit. Doubtless there will arise and is arising a new poetry which will be very different from any phase of poetry produced by the romantic revolution and the generations that followed and nourished themselves on it. The new poetry may not be able fully to share Keats' inspiring conviction of the sovereign, the transcendental truth of whatsoever ideas the imagination seizes as beauty. It may perhaps even abjure the direct search for beauty as its primary aim and impulse. But no matter: provided that its organ be the imagination, working with intensity on whatever themes the genius of the age may dictate, it cannot but achieve some phase, some incarnation, of beauty by the way. But gains like those which were made for the human spirit by the poetry of which Keats was one of the chief masters will never be lost again. Those who care for poetry at all must always care for those refreshing and inspiring draughts, as I have called them, from the innermost wells of antiquity, of nature, and of romance, those meditations of mingled joy and sorrow that search into the soul of things. Moreover they will never cease to interest themselves in the question, — If only this great spirit had survived, what would have been those unwritten poems of which he saw in the sky the cloudy symbols, of which he felt the pressure and prescience forcing the blood into his brain or bringing about his heart an awful warmth 'like a load of immortality,' and the perishing of which unborn within him was one of the two great haunting distresses of his dying days?

In letting speculation wander in this field, we are brought up by many problems as to what kind of manhood could have followed a youth like that of Keats, had he had better fortune and had the conditions and accidents of his life been such as to fortify his bodily constitution instead of sapping it. Youth, especially half-trained youth, is always subject to such storms and strains as those which Keats experienced with a violence proportionate to the fervour of his being. To the sane and sweet, the manly and courageous, elements in his character we have found his friends bear unanimous evidence, amply supported by the self-revelation of his letters. But self-revealed also we see the morbid, the corroding elements which lay beneath these, just as beneath his vigorous frame and gallant bearing there lay the bodily susceptibilities that with ill-luck enabled lung disease to fasten on and kill him. What must under any conditions have made life hard for him was the habitual inner contention and disquiet of his instincts and emotions in regard to that most momentous of human matters, love. When he lets his mind dwell on the opposed extremes of human impulse and experience, from the vilest to the most exalted, which the word-of-all-work, love, is used to cover, he is more savagely perplexed and out of conceit with life than from any other cause or thought whatever. The ruling power in himself, as he declares over and over again, was the abstract passion for beauty, the love of the principle of beauty in all things. But even in the poem specially designed to embody and celebrate that passion, in *Endymion*, we find his conception of realized and sexual human love to be mawkish and unworthy. When the actual experience befalls himself, he falls utterly and almost ignominiously a slave, at once enraptured and desperately resentful, to the jealous cravings which absorb and paralyse all his other faculties. Would ripened manhood or a happier experience have been able to bring health and peace to his spirit on this supremely vital matter and to turn him into a poet of love, love both human and transcendental, such as at the outset he had longed and striven to be?

Again, along with his admirable capacity for loyal devotion and sympathy in friendship, we find in him capacities of quite another kind, capacities for disillusionment and for seeing through and chafing at human and social shams and pretensions and absurdities; and we ask ourselves, would this strain in him, which we find expressed with a degree of pettish and premature cynicism, for instance in the *Cap and Bells* and in some of his later letters, have matured with time into a power either of virile satire or genial, reconciling comedy?

And once more, would that haunting, that irrepressible sense of the miseries of the world which we find breaking through from time to time amid the beauty of the odes, or the playfulness and affectionate confidences of the letters, or dictating that tragical return against himself and his achievements in the revised *Hyperion*, — could it and would it with experience have mellowed into such compassionate wisdom as might have made him one of the rare great healers and sages among the poets of the world?

Such speculations are as vain as they are inevitable. Let us indulge ourselves at any rate by remembering that it is the greatest among his successors who have held the most sanguine view as to the powers that were in him. Here are more words of Tennyson's, — 'Keats, with his high spiritual vision, would have been, if he had lived, the greatest of us. There is something magic and of the innermost soul of poetry in almost everything which he wrote.' Leaving with these words the question of what he might have done, and looking only at what he did, it is enough for any man's glory. The days of the years of his life were few and evil, but above his grave the double aureole of poetry and friendship shines eternally.

Appendix

I. *The Alexander fragment*.

Whenne Alexandre the Conqueroure was wayfayringe in yˆe londe of Inde, there mette hym a damoselle of marveillouse beautie slepynge uponne the herbys and flourys. He colde ne loke uponne her withouten grete plesance, and he was welle nighe loste in wondrement. Her forme was everyche whytte lyke yˆe fayrest carvynge of Quene Cythere, onlie thatte yˆt was swellyd and blushyd wyth warmthe and lyffe wythalle.

Her forhed was as whytte as ys the snowe whyche yˆe talle hed of a Norwegian pyne stelythe from yˆe northerne wynde. One of her fayre hondes was yplaced thereonne, and thus whytte wyth whytte was ymyngld as yˆe gode Arthure saythe, lyke whytest lylys yspredde on whyttest snowe; and her bryght eyne whenne she them oped, sparklyd lyke Hesperus through an evenynge cloude.

Theye were yclosyd yn slepe, save that two slauntynge raies shotte to her mouthe, and were theyre bathyd yn sweetenesse, as whenne by chaunce yˆe moone fyndeth a banke of violettes and droppethe thereonne yˆe silverie dewe.

The authoure was goynge onne withouthen descrybynge yˆe ladye's breste, whenne lo, a genyus appearyd — 'Cuthberte,' sayeth he, 'an thou canst not descrybe yˆe ladye's breste, and fynde a simile thereunto, I forbyde thee to proceede yn thy romaunt.' Thys, I kennd fulle welle, far surpassyd my feble powres, and forthwythe I was fayne to droppe my quille.

This queer youthful passage in a would-be Caxton or Wynkyn de Worde spelling seems scarcely worth taking trouble about, but I thought it worth while to try and trace what reading Keats must have been fresh from when he wrote it, and consulted both Prof. Israel Gollancz and Mr Henry Bradley, with the result stated briefly in the text. At first I had thought Keats must have drawn his idea from some one of the many versions of the great mediæval Alexander romance — especially considering that in all forms of that romance a flight into the skies and a trip under the sea are regular incidents, and might later have suggested the parallel incidents in *Endymion*. But neither in the version which Keats is most likely to have known, the English *Alisaunder* as published in Weber's collection of metrical romances, 1810, nor indeed, I believe, in any other, is there any incident closely parallel to this of the Indian maiden; although love and marriage generally come into the story towards the close. In the English version there is a beautiful Candace who declares her passion for the hero: he puts her off for the time being, but goes disguised as an ambassador to her court, where he is recognized and imprisoned. Among things derived from the main mediæval cycle, the nearest approach to such an idea as Keats was working on is to be found in the *Orlando Innamorato* of Boiardo, book ii, canto i, stanzas 6, 21-29; but here the beauty is a lady of Egypt whom Boiardo calls Elidonia. His description of the great painted hall of the giant Agramante at Biserta, adorned with pictures of the life and deeds of Alexander, closes with the following: —

> In somma, ogni sua guerra ivi è dipinta
> Con gran richezza e bella a riguardare.
> Poscia che fu la terra da lui vinta,
> A due grifon nel ciel si fè portare,
> Col scudo in braccia e con la spada cinta;
> Poi dentro un vetro si cala nel mare,
> E vede le balene e ogni gran pesce
> E campa e ancor quivi di fuor n'esce.
> Da poi che vinto egli ha ben ogni cosa,
> Vedesi lui che vinto è dall' amore,
> Perchè Elidonia, quella graziosa,
> Co' suoi begli occhi gli ha passato il core —

And then ensues the history of their loves and of the hero's death.

But Keats in his hospital days knew no Italian, and could only have heard of such a passage in Boiardo through Leigh Hunt. So I think the derivation of his fragment from any of the regular Alexander romances must be given up, and the source indicated in the text be accepted, namely the popular *fabliau* of the *Lai d'Aristote* (probably in Way's rimed version), where the thing happens exactly as Keats tells it, and whence the idea of the sudden encounter with an Indian maiden probably lingered in his mind till he revived it in *Endymion*. As for the sources of the attempt at voluptuous description, it is a little surprising to find Milton's 'tallest pine hewn on Norwegian hills' remembered in such a connexion: other things are an easily recognizable farrago from *Cymbeline*, —

> 'Cytherea,
> How bravely thou becomest thy bed, fresh lily,
> And whiter than the sheets!'
> from *Venus and Adonis*, —
> 'A lily prison'd in a gaol of snow;'
> 'Teaching the sheets a whiter hue than white;'
> from *Lucrece*, —
> — 'the morning's silver-melting dew;'
> from *Twelfth Night*,
> — 'like the sweet sound
> That breathes upon a bank of violets;'

and so forth. Prof. Gollancz suggests that 'Cuthberte' as the name of the author is a reminiscence from the 'Cuddie' of Spenser's *Shepheard's Calendar*, and that the 'good Arthure' may also be some kind of Spenserian reference: but I suspect 'Arthure' here to be a mis-transcription (we have no autograph) for 'authoure.'

II. *Verses written by Brown and Keats after visiting Beauly Abbey*

On Some Skulls in Beauly Abbey, near Inverness
I shed no tears;
Deep thought or awful vision, I had none
By thousand petty fancies I was crossed.
Wordsworth.

And mocked the dead bones that lay scattered by.

Shakspeare.

In silent barren Synod met

> *Within these roofless walls*, where yet

> The shafted arch and carved fret
> Cling to the Ruin
> The Brethren's Skulls mourn, dewy wet,

Their Creed's undoing.
The mitred ones of Nice and Trent
Were not so tongue-tied, — no, they went
Hot to their Councils, scarce content
With Orthodoxy
But ye, poor tongueless things, were meant
To speak by proxy.

The mitred ones of Nice and Trent
Were not so tongue-tied, — no, they went
Hot to their Councils, scarce content
With Orthodoxy
But ye, poor tongueless things, were meant
To speak by proxy.

Your Chronicles no more exist

Since Knox, the Revolutionist
Destroy'd the work of every fist
That scrawl'd black letter
Well! I'm a Craniologist
And may do better.

This skull-cap won the cowl from sloth
Or discontent, perhaps from both
And yet one day, against his oath
He tried escaping
For men, tho' idle may be loth
To live on gaping.

A Toper this! he plied his glass
More strictly than he said the Mass
And lov'd to see a tempting lass
Come to Confession
Letting her absolution pass
O'er fresh transgression.

This crawl'd thro' life in feebleness
Boasting he never knew excess
Cursing those crimes he scarce could guess
Or feel but faintly
With prayer that Heaven would cease to bless
Men so unsaintly.

Here's a true Churchman! he'd affect
Much charity and ne'r neglect
To pray for Mercy on th' elect
But thought no evil
In sending Heathen, Turk and Scot
All to the Devil!

Poor Skull! Thy fingers set ablaze,
With silver saint in golden rays,
The Holy Missal, thou didst craze
'Mid bead and spangle
While others passed their idle days
In coil and wrangle.

Long time this sconce a helmet wore,
But sickness smites the conscience sore,
He broke his sword and hither bore
His gear and plunder
Took to the cowl — then rav'd and swore
At his damn'd blunder!
This lily-coloured skull with all
The teeth complete, so white and small
Belonged to one whose early pall
A lover shaded.
He died ere Superstition's gall
His heart invaded.
Ha! here is 'undivulged crime!'
Despair forbad his soul to climb
Beyond this world, this mortal time
Of fever'd badness
Until this Monkish Pantomime
Dazzled his madness!
A younger brother this! a man
Aspiring as a Tartar Khan
But, curb'd and baffl'd he began
The trade of frightening
It smack'd of power! and how he ran
To deal Heaven's lightning!
This idiot-skull belonged to one,
A buried miser's only son
Who, penitent ere he'd begun
To taste of pleasure
And hoping Heaven's dread wrath to shun
Gave Hell his treasure.
Here is the forehead of an Ape
A robber's mask — and near the nape
That bone — fie on't, bears just the shape
Of carnal passion
Ah! he was one for theft and rape
In Monkish fashion!
This was the Porter! — he could sing

Or dance, or play — do anything
And what the Friars bade him bring
They ne'er were balked of;
Matters not worth remembering
And seldom talk'd of.
Enough! why need I further pore?
This corner holds at least a score,
And yonder twice as many more
Of Reverend Brothers,
'Tis the same story o'er and o'er
They're like the others!

Ode to a Nightingale

1.

My heart aches, and a drowsy numbness pains
My sense, as though of hemlock I had drunk,
Or emptied some dull opiate to the drains
One minute past, and Lethe-wards had sunk:
'Tis not through envy of thy happy lot,
But being too happy in thine happiness, —
That thou, light-winged Dryad of the trees,
In some melodious plot
Of beechen green, and shadows numberless,
Singest of summer in full-throated ease.

2.

O, for a draught of vintage! that hath been
Cool'd a long age in the deep-delved earth,
Tasting of Flora and the country green,
Dance, and Provençal song, and sunburnt mirth!
O for a beaker full of the warm South,
Full of the true, the blushful Hippocrene,
With beaded bubbles winking at the brim,
And purple-stained mouth;
That I might drink, and leave the world unseen,
And with thee fade away into the forest dim:

3.

Fade far away, dissolve, and quite forget
What thou among the leaves hast never known,
The weariness, the fever, and the fret
Here, where men sit and hear each other groan;
Where palsy shakes a few, sad, last gray hairs,
Where youth grows pale, and spectre-thin, and dies;
Where but to think is to be full of sorrow
And leaden-eyed despairs,
Where Beauty cannot keep her lustrous eyes,
Or new Love pine at them beyond tomorrow.

4.

Away! away! for I will fly to thee,
Not charioted by Bacchus and his pards,
But on the viewless wings of Poesy,
Though the dull brain perplexes and retards:
Already with thee! tender is the night,
And haply the Queen-Moon is on her throne,
Cluster'd around by all her starry Fays;
But here there is no light,
Save what from heaven is with the breezes blown
Through verdurous glooms and winding mossy ways.

5.

I cannot see what flowers are at my feet,
Nor what soft incense hangs upon the boughs,
But, in embalmed darkness, guess each sweet
Wherewith the seasonable month endows
The grass, the thicket, and the fruit-tree wild;
White hawthorn, and the pastoral eglantine;
Fast fading violets cover'd up in leaves;
And mid-May's eldest child,
The coming muskrose, full of dewy wine,
The murmurous haunt of flies on summer eves.

6.

Darkling I listen; and, for many a time
I have been half in love with easeful Death,
Call'd him soft names in many a mused rhyme,
To take into the air my quiet breath;
Now more than ever seems it rich to die,
To cease upon the midnight with no pain,
While thou art pouring forth thy soul abroad
In such an ecstasy!
Still wouldst thou sing, and I have ears in vain —
To thy high requiem become a sod.

7.

Thou wast not born for death, immortal Bird!
No hungry generations tread thee down;
The voice I hear this passing night was heard
In ancient days by emperor and clown:
Perhaps the selfsame song that found a path
Through the sad heart of Ruth, when, sick for home,
She stood in tears amid the alien corn;
The same that ofttimes hath

Charm'd magic casements, opening on the foam
Of perilous seas, in faery lands forlorn.

8.

Forlorn! the very word is like a bell
To toll me back from thee to my sole self!
Adieu! the fancy cannot cheat so well
As she is fam'd to do, deceiving elf.
Adieu! adieu! thy plaintive anthem fades
Past the near meadows, over the still stream,
Up the hillside; and now 'tis buried deep
In the next valley-glades:
Was it a vision, or a waking dream?

Fled is that music: — Do I wake or sleep?

The original manuscript

www.ingramcontent.com/pod-product-compliance
Lightning Source LLC
LaVergne TN
LVHW011929070526
838202LV00054B/4555